I0760181

WARREN H. MANNING

Landscape Architect and Environmental Planner

WARREN H. MANNING

Landscape Architect and Environmental Planner

Edited by Robin Karson, Jane Roy Brown, and Sarah Allaback

LIBRARY OF AMERICAN LANDSCAPE HISTORY AMHERST, MASSACHUSETTS

THE UNIVERSITY OF GEORGIA PRESS ATHENS

A volume in the series
Critical Perspectives in the History of Environmental Design
Edited by Daniel J. Nadenicek

Publication of this book was made possible in part by the
Bruce and Georgia McEver Fund for the Arts and Environment.

Published by the University of Georgia Press
Athens, Georgia 30602
www.ugapress.org

Designed by Jonathan D. Lippincott
Set in Bembo
Printed and bound by Four Colour Print Group

The paper in this book meets the guidelines for permanence and durability of the Committee on Production Guidelines for Book Longevity of the Council on Library Resources.

Printed in China

18 19 20 21 C 5 4 3 2

Library of Congress Cataloging-in-Publication Data
Names: Karson, Robin S., editor. | Brown, Jane Roy, editor. | Allaback, Sarah, 1965– editor. | Library of American Landscape History.
Title: Warren H. Manning, landscape architect and environmental planner / edited by Robin Karson, Jane Roy Brown, and Sarah Allaback.
Description: Athens : University of Georgia Press, [2016] | Series: Critical perspectives in the history of environmental design | "Library of American Landscape History, Amherst, Massachusetts." | Includes bibliographical references and index.
Identifiers: LCCN 2016006358 | ISBN 9780820350660 (hardcover : alk. paper)
Subjects: LCSH: Manning, Warren H. (Warren Henry), 1860–1938. | Landscape architects—United States—Biography. | Landscape design—United States. | Gardens—United States—Design. | Landscape architecture—United States.
Classification: LCC SB470.M25 W37 2016 | DDC 712.092—dc23
LC record available at http://lccn.loc.gov/2016006358

Frontispiece: Warren H. Manning. Undated photograph, courtesy Warren H. Manning Collection, Center for Lowell History, University of Massachusetts Lowell Libraries.

To the first three presidents of the Library of American Landscape History, in recognition of their generous support, wise counsel, and steadfast encouragement:

Nancy R. Turner (1992–2002)
John Franklin Miller (2002–2008)
Michael Jefcoat (2008–2014)

Contents

Series Editor's Preface

DANIEL J. NADENICEK

Several years ago when researching the pioneer landscape architect Horace Cleveland at the Minnesota Historical Society, I came across a sketch by Warren Manning depicting the home of University of Minnesota president William Watts Folwell. The drawing suggested to me that Manning likely had other reasons for his visit to Minneapolis, perhaps related to ongoing work on that city's park system initiated by Cleveland in 1883. I was intrigued by how quickly Manning had moved into the void created by Cleveland's retirement at the end of the nineteenth century. While Cleveland lived in Chicago and later moved to Minneapolis as he oversaw his Twin Cities' projects, Manning managed a national practice. And because his home was in Massachusetts and he practiced coast to coast, he traveled continuously, mostly by train.

Notes in the same file as the Folwell sketch indicated to me that Manning must have been skilled at building personal relationships and networks of clients. Indeed, the relationships he built across the nation did lead to multiple private and public sector commissions. Because they ranged from small gardens to grand planning projects, it was imperative for Manning to develop replicable and highly efficient analysis techniques. He continued and refined the overlay technique first developed by Charles Eliot in the Olmsted office. He also managed to rally large-scale participation and grassroots support, where massive volunteer labor was needed to build new parks at low cost.

These themes—the amazing feat of maintaining a national practice before common air travel, Manning's great skill at relationship building and networking, the development of sophisticated analysis techniques in order to work across a range of scales, and the cultivation of participatory methods that inspired the involvement of large groups of people—come up throughout the text of *Warren H. Manning, Landscape Architect and Environmental Planner*. While I rarely use the term, this book is a tour de force. I am so pleased that it is a volume in the Critical Perspectives in the History of Environmental Design series which the

Library of American Landscape History maintains with the University of Georgia Press.

The full impact of Manning's national practice will become immediately clear to any reader who simply scans the table of contents because the entire book is organized into project essays grouped by state—and there are sixteen in all. These compelling project descriptions were written by a national network of distinguished researchers, beautifully illustrated and designed in keeping with the high standards of the LALH publishing program.

The essential context for those essays is brilliantly presented in Robin Karson's introduction titled "The Career of Warren H. Manning." There, Karson brings Manning to life as a person with great strengths and many shortcomings. He emerges as a dynamic, high-energy person, who also could let his manic nature undermine his effectiveness. Manning was sophisticated in his methods of analysis, such as the overlay technique, but disorganized in managing his own office. He often had great clarity of vision, and he was as well blinded by deep biases and prejudices.

Despite his failings, Manning's achievements were unprecedented, especially given the relatively small size of his firm. In addition to maintaining a national practice, Karson explains how Manning developed a national plan at his own expense, which, while politically impractical, provided visionary environmental planning insights well ahead of their time.

The text details how Manning influenced the future in other ways, too. For example, he trained a number of young landscape architects including Fletcher Steele, A. D. Taylor, and Dan Kiley, who later became nationally significant designers in their own right. He was a major figure in developing and leading professional organizations including the American Park and Outdoor Art Association, which later merged with the American League of Civic Improvement to form the American Civic Association. He was a founding member and president of the American Society of Landscape Architects. Manning also put his ideas into print throughout his career, publishing in *Landscape Architecture* and planning journals, as well as popular magazines and horticultural encyclopedias.

Manning's extraordinary landscape architecture and environmental planning story has long deserved to be told. I am pleased that the Library of American Landscape History assumed the challenge and completed the important work that led to this volume.

Acknowledgments

The origins of this book date back more than a decade, to when Jane Roy Brown and I began to work on an initiative to systematically research Warren Manning's built work. With a client list of more than 1,600 far-flung projects, and most of his office records destroyed in the years after his death, Manning presented a daunting prospect for any single individual historian. We reasoned that a national, collaborative network of research volunteers could accomplish the work far more efficiently. When Reid Bertone-Johnson, a graduate student in the Landscape Architecture and Regional Planning (LARP) program at the University of Massachusetts, joined the LALH staff as an intern in 2005, a collaborative research model began to coalesce.

As a first step, we asked Bertone-Johnson to conduct a pilot study of about twenty-five of Manning's western Massachusetts landscape commissions, creating a Web-based survey to gather detailed information about the physical aspects of each site as well as the quantity and quality of research materials available. To select which projects to survey nationwide, we cross-referenced Manning's client list with other sources of information, such as news articles and information from historians and practitioners in regions where Manning had designed large clusters of projects. We came up with a list of about two hundred survey-worthy projects and located researchers in several states willing to participate to conduct the surveys.

Our next step was to select surveyed projects for inclusion in the projected book, a process aided immeasurably by Mackenzie Greer, also an LARP graduate student, who succeeded Bertone-Johnson as coordinator of what had become the Warren H. Manning Research Project. We based our decisions on criteria that included the project's significance—from information in Manning's unpublished autobiography, for example, or the number of plans Manning designed for it—its condition, and its research potential. About one hundred projects fit the bill. In the end, about two-thirds of these proved substantial enough to include in the projected book. We strove for a balance of private estates, institutional grounds, parks and park systems, residential subdivisions, campus plans, and city plans to present a credibly rich, though far from exhaustive, overview of Manning's career.

As the individual entries were written and historical illustrations compiled, we realized that new photographs of current conditions would provide up-to-date information on the sites and bring the book into the present—making it a valuable resource for today's environmentally oriented designers. We enlisted Carol Betsch, who has photographed for many LALH projects, to take on this task. Over the course of five years, Betsch traveled to twenty-five sites and recorded them in hundreds of images, about one hundred of which are included here.

The final task was to write an overview to provide a broad picture of Manning's career and significance and an introduction to the site essays. In a way, the piece brought us full circle: integrating disparate data about a diverse and far-flung body of work would have been impossible to conceive without the information and illustrations in the essays.

I am grateful to all the researchers who contributed so generously to this volume. Special thanks are due Reid Bertone-Johnson, Mackenzie Greer, and Matthew Medeiros, who as a graduate student in the LARP program wrote several entries and compiled valuable information about Manning's practice from financial records, employee rosters, and office locations. Medeiros also created a comprehensive chronology of Manning's life and practice, which I relied on extensively in developing the overview. I am also grateful to Keith Hannon, another graduate of the LARP program, who collated many different types of data gleaned from various archives and created a database of every image gathered related to the project. Katharine Laliberte, an early intern from LARP, assembled a list of Manning's published articles, a version of which appears in this volume.

Jane Roy Brown, former LALH director of educational outreach, came to serve as the Manning Project coordinator, provided enormous help throughout the long process of collecting surveys, soliciting and editing entries, and locating illustrations. She also interviewed members of the Manning family and contributed several entries to the volume. I am deeply grateful to her for her work at every stage.

Over the course of this twelve-year initiative, we were assisted immeasurably by Martha Mayo, librarian at the University of Massachusetts Lowell, Center for Lowell History, and by the staff of the Special Collections and University Archives at the Parks Library, Iowa State University. Material related to Manning's life and work is held by both repositories. During trips to Iowa State, William J. Grundmann was helpful and encouraging, as was Heidi Hohmann, who also read and commented on portions of the manuscript. Arnold R. Alanen at the University of Wisconsin and the preservation planner Lynn Bjorkman were generous with their knowledge of Manning's planning work, and both contributed important entries to this volume. The landscape historian Phyllis Andersen helped strategize in the early phase. George W. Curry at SUNY College of Environmental Science and Forestry offered insightful commentary on the manuscript. In later stages, David Schuyler and Gregory J. Kaliss of Franklin and Marshall College drew my attention to significant correspondence related to Manning they discovered during their research preparing volume 9 of the Olmsted Papers project.

Joan Randall, formerly of the Ohio Historic Preservation Office in Columbus, helped us locate other researchers and also served as a contributor. I am grateful to her and to Elizabeth Igleheart of the Landscape Institute at the Arnold Arboretum in Boston, who assigned Manning projects in her courses and shared the results with us. Arthur H. Miller, retired archivist and librarian for special collections at Lake Forest College, contributed several key entries and facilitated our research forays north of Chicago. Eleanor Ames helped during the project's early years with information about the Megunticook Country Club, Aldermere Farm, and other Maine projects. Closer to home, the Northampton-based landscape architect Martha H. Lyon assisted with the project from its earliest days and also took on several Manning entries related to his work at Pinehurst. I am also grateful to Ethan Carr at the University of Massachusetts, who helped establish a conceptual framework for the project and offered valuable comments on the manuscript.

The far-reaching illustration program of this volume was enriched by the efforts of many individuals, including the landscape historian Pamela Hartford, who investigated the career of Arthur G. Eldredge, a gifted photographer and landscape architect from whom Manning commissioned dozens of photographs, many of which appear in this book. Further illuminating this volume are several postcards from Manning's own collection and many images from the Manning family archive, generously lent by William C. Manning. The local historian Dan Malloy supplied historic images of Hopedale, an epicenter of early work by Manning. I am also grateful to Richard Candee for bringing to our attention a group of Manning photographs discovered in an antiques store in Maine and to Thyrza Whittemore of Middlebury, Connecticut, who generously provided scans of many historic photographs of Tranquillity Farm.

The multiyear process of photographing the sites would not have been possible without the assistance of many individuals. For their generosity on these shoots, I thank Marjorie Longenecker White of Mountain Brook, Alabama; Christopher Bond, former horticulturalist, and Ana Locci, director, Case Western Reserve University Farm; Gloria Schreiber, horticulturalist and preservationist, Akron, Ohio; Catherine Stone of Great Hill, Marion, Massachusetts; Professor Michael Barton and local historian Dan Deibler of Harrisburg, Pennsylvania; Frederick H. Chatfield Jr. of Aldermere Farm, Rockport, Maine; Mary Randolph Ballinger and Esley Hamilton of St. Louis; C. Michael Jacob and Dr. and Mrs. W. Scott Peterson of Tranquillity Farm, Middlebury, Connecticut. For her hospitality during our early photography at Gwinn, in Cleveland, Ohio, I am grateful to Lucy Ireland Weller.

The Manning project was underwritten by the financial support of many generous organizations and individuals. Prominent among these is the Viburnum-Trilobum Fund at the New York Community Trust, advised by Nancy R. Turner, who has been an ardent and loyal supporter of our Manning research for many years. I am also grateful to the William Gwinn and Elizabeth Ring Mather Fund in Cleveland, Ohio, and their trustees, including Lucy Ireland Weller, for their early and generous support of the Manning project. My deep thanks go as well to Nicholas Thaw, trustee of the International Music and Art Foundation, who saw the value in including contemporary photographs and generously supported Carol Betsch's work through a foundation grant. These photographs not only add immeasurably to the dynamism of the book but contribute significantly to Manning's archive and to the historic record of designed landscapes in the United States.

Special thanks are due the directors of the Hubbard Educational Foundation for their enthusiastic support and generous underwriting of the volume. I am grateful as well to the Stanley Smith Horticultural Trust for its support and extraordinary patience as we completed our work. Thanks are also due Randall Wade, descendent of Manning's Cleveland client, and the Vanderbilt Family Foundation for its support. I am also deeply grateful to Craig Barrow III. A grant from the Bruce and Georgia McEver Fund for the Arts and Environment at the University of Georgia Press aided production of the volume.

Several generous individuals offered invaluable financial underwriting during the course of this project: I thank Ann and Clayton Wilhite; Carolyn Marsh Lindsay; John K. Notz Jr.; Susan L. Klaus; Cynthia Hewitt and Dan Holloway; and Dr. and Mrs. W. Scott Peterson. Each of these individuals has made other LALH projects possible over the years, for which I am also grateful. My gratitude goes to all the directors of the LALH board, especially to Sarah L. Turner, whose support of LALH through the Aurora-Viburnum Fund of the California Community Foundation has been extremely generous. I also extend deepest thanks to Daniel J. Nadenicek, dean of the School of Environment and Design at the University of Georgia and editor of the series Critical Perspectives in the History of Environmental Design, of which *Warren H. Manning* is the second volume.

At LALH, office manager Neil Brigham assisted the project in countless ways; our former digital media manager Jessica Dawson lent her expertise in organizing the illustration program; and managing editor Sarah Allaback brought great incisiveness to our editorial team. Mary Bellino copyedited, fact-checked, and prepared the manuscript for production; Jonathan Lippincott created the superb design; Carol Betsch proofread and made the index. Profound thanks to all of them and to the staff of the University of Georgia Press, especially acquiring editor James Patrick Allen and director Lisa Bayer.

This book is dedicated with profound gratitude to the three past presidents of LALH: Nancy R. Turner, whose unflagging support and generosity has made so much possible; John Franklin Miller, who directed the first preservation initiative of Manning's work at Stan Hywet Hall and Gardens; and Michael Jefcoat, whose generosity, enthusiasm, and appreciation for fine landscapes, fine photographs, and the highest standards in research and writing have been a source of enduring inspiration.

Robin Karson
Executive Director, LALH

Note on Illustration Sources

There are two main repositories of archival material related to Manning's professional life. The Warren H. Manning Collection, Center for Lowell History, University of Massachusetts Lowell (MCL) holds the wider assortment. These documents include Manning's unpublished writings (including his autobiography), firm financial records, photographs, plans, drawings, scrapbooks, and journals relating to Manning's work, as well as many documents and photographs related to Manning family history.

The Warren H. Manning Papers, Special Collections Department, Iowa State University Library (MPI), comprises 138.64 linear feet of material donated by Manning's office in the years after his death. Philip H. Elwood, professor of landscape architecture at Iowa State, selected this material from Manning's professional archive for teaching purposes. His selection includes a broad range of typologies and geographic areas. Fifty-eight projects are represented, along with extensive material relating to Manning's National Plan.

WARREN H. MANNING

Landscape Architect and Environmental Planner

The Career of Warren H. Manning

ROBIN KARSON

Warren Manning (1860–1938) was one of the twentieth century's most influential landscape architects and planners. Building on the social and environmental principles of his mentors at the Olmsted firm, he significantly enlarged the imaginative scope of twentieth-century landscape architecture and city planning. Manning was the first landscape practitioner to envision regional and national planning initiatives to control transportation, utility, and natural resource systems, and he was the first to establish a national practice based on principles of environmental design. He made extensive use of overlay maps—a method of land planning and design that forecast the revolutionary approach Ian McHarg featured in his 1969 book, *Design with Nature*. Each of Manning's sixteen hundred career projects was undertaken with the same objective: to utilize natural resources most efficiently, for the purpose of enriching individual and civic life. He brought to these commissions a sense of urgency, optimism, and extraordinary attention to the physical characteristics of site.

Among the eleven founding members of the American Society of Landscape Architects, Manning was also a key protagonist in its formation in 1899. He served as president in 1914, using this platform to promote legislation for a new National Park Service, a project that resonated with his own strong beliefs in the need for national planning. He published frequently, initially in horticultural magazines such as *Gardening* and *Vick's Illustrated Monthly* and later in *Landscape Architecture, The American City,* and other professional journals, where he argued for comprehensive initiatives to address the effects of rapid urbanization and diminishing natural resources, the topics also of countless lectures he delivered to progressive, reform-minded audiences. Manning employed and guided the development of some of the twentieth century's most influential practitioners, among them Fletcher Steele, Albert Davis Taylor, and Dan Kiley.[1]

The scope and the extent of Manning's practice were, in some measure, a reflection of his driven personality. At once affable and dogmatic, he persuaded many clients to increase both the range and the number of their commissions. Consequently, scores of individuals who initially sought out Manning's services for private estates went on to commission new schools, libraries, parks, hospitals, subdivisions, resorts, and company towns. Captains of industry, in particular, were drawn to Manning's progressive ideas and cost-effective methods, which made the best and most efficient use of existing resources. Manning's eye for scenic potential and regard for the distinctive character of place was unmatched among his peers, as was his capacity to evaluate the lay of the land in areas comprising many thousands of acres—much of this on horseback.

The same expansiveness that compelled Manning to map and reimagine the American landscape in such detail, however, also drove him to acquire more jobs than he could handle, leaving major problems to be worked out by talented but inexperienced assistants. Manning's work was also undermined by his boundless faith in his own design ideas, which focused primarily, often exclusively, on nature-based principles. The most dramatic example of Manning's single-mindedness was his National Plan, an independent project financed at extraordinary personal cost that was also wildly impractical in its visionary recommendations. Having the capacity to imagine a better world—in extensive detail—Manning was convinced that American society would follow his fantastical schemes.

That Manning produced as much compelling work as he did—projects ranging from the Harrisburg, Pennsylvania, parks to the towns of Gwinn, Michigan, and Warren, Arizona, the Finger Lakes State parks outside Ithaca, Goodyear Heights in Akron, and Mountain Brook Estates outside Birmingham—is a reflection of his deeply felt response to place and the incisive force of his imagination. The roster of wealthy and socially powerful clients who engaged Manning's services, many of them repeatedly, bear witness to his ability to sustain deep, personal ties and to utilize these relationships to realize his environmental ideals.

Manning applied a wide, regional (at times, national) perspective to his work, which he also projected well into the future. He imagined, for example, great estates bequeathed as public parks, residential developments giving way to industry as cities grew, and large tracts of land providing recreation for populations that had not yet been established. Manning began most of his commissions by mapping site data, in some instances recording it on gridded, translucent maps that could be overlaid in order to correlate disparate geographical information.[2] His design process also benefited from his unusual capacity to rapidly shift his scale of focus—from the intimate characteristics of lichen or moss, for example, to broad patterns of forest vegetation.

Even at a backyard-garden scale, Manning meticulously recorded resources, from the hydrologic to the vegetative, geologic, and cultural—including historic elements such as wellheads, which he avidly incorporated into new designs. Manning's next step, inspired, he claimed, by Thomas Jefferson, was to remove extraneous plants, revealing the garden that Jefferson believed latent in the American landscape.[3] Paths and roadways were invariably laid out in relation to commanding views, large trees, watercourses, wetlands, and other natural features of interest. Streams were dammed to form ponds, and plants were installed, in great variety. Although he championed the use of hardy, common, and native plants, Manning also introduced imported species, citing their color values in particular.

Manning's estate designs were characterized by a sense of rural informality that contrasted with more geometrically determined layouts of his Beaux-Arts–influenced colleagues. Throughout his articles and client correspondence he points to the superior virtues of meadows, orchards, woods, wild gardens, and ponds, criticizing the stiff artificiality of parterres and formal pools typical of Italian- and French-influenced flower garden schemes. Manning's landscape layouts generally reflect the principles of the Picturesque, the same approach that guided the garden, estate, and park designs of his mentors, Olmsted Sr., Charles Eliot, and John Charles Olmsted. His essential Anglophilia, and that of many of his clients, undoubtedly played a role in this choice too. But the Picturesque may have proved most attractive for the versatility it offered the designer, who found in this approach ample opportunity to integrate wild gardens, the type he preferred above all.

Such features made use of existing scenic resources, amplifying the impression of wildness through massed plantings of mostly hardy and native trees, shrubs, and ground covers. Although Manning frequently argued for this approach by emphasizing savings in construction and maintenance costs, his motives were philosophical as well as pragmatic; he believed that wild gardens rewarded owners with more profoundly restorative experiences than formal gardens could.[4] "The ideal estates of the future," he wrote late in life, ". . . will be large, wild land areas with much variation in surface conditions—hills with far-reaching views—valleys—streams—ponds—the great lakes and the sea—and much forested areas."[5]

Park design was a particular specialty of Manning's practice. Like estates, new parks frequently required new land acquisitions—typically far more than civic leaders initially imagined, and Manning's capacity to evaluate and analyze land on a vast scale proved invaluable. In principle and practice, Manning owed a great debt to his mentors at the Olmsted firm, the first American practitioners to promote the uniquely salutary role of urban nature and to conceptualize parks as vital open space components of systems that also included parkways, cemeteries, and institutional grounds.

In his park work, Manning designed in relation to each site's topography, views, vegetation, and water features, even as he accommodated utilitarian concerns such as recreational needs, circulation, and transportation linkages. To realize smaller parks, Manning pioneered the use of Community Days, events that involved thousands—in some cases, tens of thousands—of volunteers, who planted parks and playgrounds often in a single day. This form of community-based participatory design, still in use today, was first used by Manning in Reading, Massachusetts, in 1889, when participants planted elms along the town's Main Street.[6]

Parks and park systems were integrated into town plans primarily to provide residents with access to nature. These features also functioned in practical ways, to absorb storm water, for example, and as safeguards against fire. Planning projects were complex, and it was in the course of such work that Manning's mapping methods were most intensively applied. These projects were also necessarily collaborative; Manning worked with engineers, sanitation and traffic specialists, civic leaders, and architects in realizing them. His public presentations in support of new parks were unusually persuasive. Manning successfully advocated for the donation of thousands of acres of private lands to realize his expansive schemes.

Manning's subdivisions combined many of

his principles for gardens and parks. His aim in new developments was to use existing resources to create parklike environs that would provide open space for outdoor recreation as well as scenic distinction. The siting of large developments also involved critical assessment of transportation networks in relation to civic centers, libraries, schools, commercial zones, and recreation areas. Manning's plans for new company towns utilized similar methods; transportation systems—rail and, increasingly, automobile routes—and utilities were primary considerations. His exhaustive maps also recorded soil and minerals, hydrology (wetlands, rivers, lakes, and watersheds), settlement patterns, wildlife, vegetation, scenic resources, and more.

In its scope and purpose, no project of Manning's was more ambitious than his National Plan, completed in 1919, at the height of the Progressive era, and published in a condensed version by *Landscape Architecture* in 1923. His singular achievement in this initiative was to develop a system for classifying land according to disparate geographic data, collated and analyzed to guide designs that would most efficiently use and thereby protect natural resources. The study comprised 427 pages of typescript and 320 plans and graphs selected from more than one thousand sketches, studies, and drawings, gathered over five years. Toward the end of his life, in his autobiography, Manning described the National Plan and its motivating idea.

> It seemed to me essential that National Planning studies should be made to prevent waste in such natural economic resources as soil, forests, oil, gas, coal, minerals, and wildlife; and to establish connected reservation systems to include notable land and water scenic values and ample room for all types of travel ways to serve business and the recreational, educational, and inspirational values. A National Plan would aim to conserve values, to make prosperity dominant and to minimize adversity by eliminating waste and securing the best possible use of our material, human, and aesthetic resources.[7]

FORMATIVE YEARS

Warren Henry Manning was born in Reading, Massachusetts, in 1860 and reared in a large home whose landscape also served as the grounds for Reading Nursery (figs. 1, 2). His vocation had its roots in a New England childhood that included plant-hunting expeditions with his father, the renowned nurseryman Jacob Warren Manning (1826–1894), and a close and affectionate relationship with his mother, Lydia Brooks Chandler Manning (1839–1908). Manning later credited his father's skill as a "landscape designer and plantsman and observer of landscape values" as a fundamental part of his training (fig. 3). He remembered his mother encouraging him to "make America a finer place in which to live."[8]

Warren and his four younger brothers helped prepare nursery stock for customers in the United States, England, and Europe, all the while absorbing their father's Victorian fascination with plants of every type, including newly fashionable American natives, such as white pine and yucca. As a young man, Manning spent summers with his maternal grandfather, Abiel Chandler, in Concord, New Hampshire, where he worked in the farm fields and greenhouses, and he accompanied his father on visits to commercial nurseries, including that of Charles Downing (brother of

Figure 1. Warren Manning, age five, 1865. Photograph courtesy William C. Manning.

Figure 3. Jacob W. Manning, age forty-eight. Photograph courtesy William C. Manning.

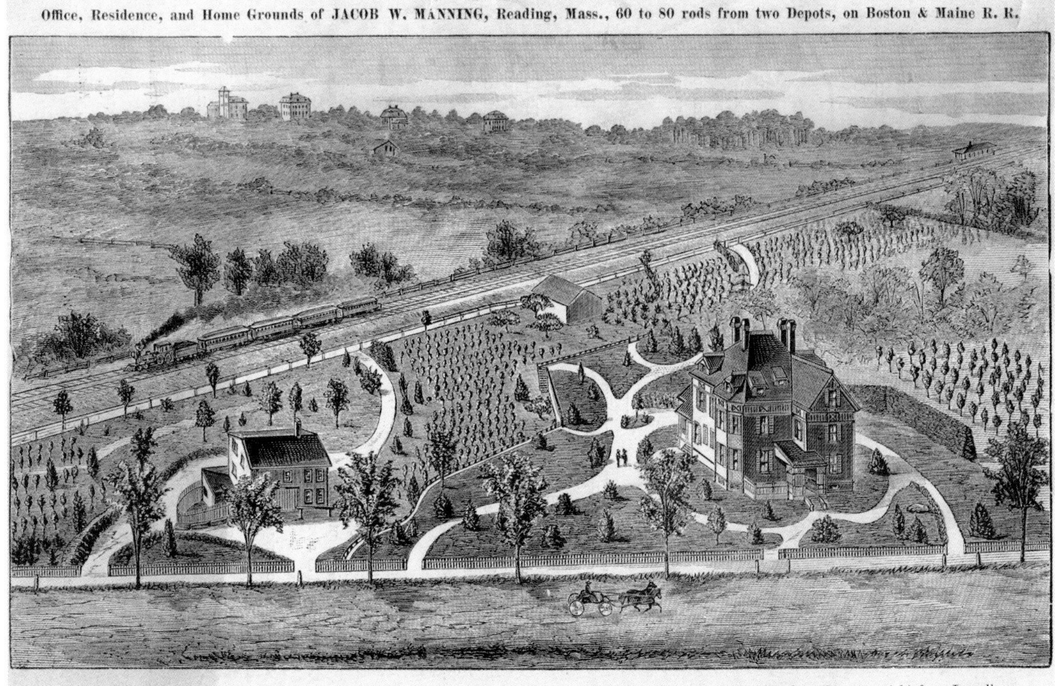

Figure 2. Promotional flyer, Reading Nursery, 1899. Courtesy William C. Manning.

A. J. Downing) in Newburgh, New York. On Saturdays he visited Harvard's Arnold Arboretum to spend time with Jackson Dawson, the arboretum's propagator. During these years Manning developed a deep and spiritual relationship with the workings of nature. Memories of particular thunderstorms, sunsets, and snowstorms—some from his childhood—continued to evoke strong emotion when he wrote about them in his autobiography toward the end of his life.[9]

When Manning was seventeen, his family moved into a fashionable Stick-style home at 142 High Street in Reading. He took one year at General Russell's Military School in New Haven, in 1879 graduated from Reading Public High School, and then attended French's Business School in Boston for one semester (fig. 4). In 1884 a business circular from Reading Nursery advertised his design services to prospective clients; the following year, he recorded two commissions, both for residential landscapes.[10]

Figure 4. Manning at General Russell's Military School, New Haven, Conn. Photograph courtesy William C. Manning.

Loquacious, gregarious, and energetic—in his work life, arguably manic—Manning found early success as a lecturer to various horticultural organizations and as a contributor to new magazines aimed at an expanding number of home gardeners. After his marriage to Henrietta (Nettie) Hamblin Pratt in 1885, he briefly worked as a graphic designer for the publisher Franklin Howard Gilson, of Fort Hill Square, Boston. But Manning's interest in horticulture and conservation proved more enduring. In 1887 he was among the founders of a group advocating for the conservation of the Middlesex Fells outside Boston, an effort that put him in touch with Charles Eliot, Charles Sprague Sargent, Sylvester Baxter, and other luminaries of the horticultural world.[11]

On his twenty-seventh birthday in November of that year, Manning wrote to Frederick Law Olmsted Sr. seeking work with the nation's largest and most highly esteemed landscape architectural office. Manning's letter emphasized his horticultural skills, particularly his success in moving large trees. He wrote of his "knowledge of hardy trees, shrubs, and herbaceous plants & their treatment & the effects produced by them, the common & botanical names & botanical relationships."[12]

Olmsted offered Manning a position as a planting assistant in January 1888 (fig. 5). He reported directly to Olmsted, recording several conversations with his boss, beginning on his first day on the job, February 28, 1888, when he noted in his diary that Olmsted "set me to work at once on a list for a nursery for Mr. Whitelaw Read, Rye, Westchester Co., N.Y." By mid-May, the senior partner was advising Manning on books to consult on architecture and ornament. In June they had an extended discussion of Olmsted's design for Central Park. "Mr. O had gained his ideas of treatment," Manning wrote, "by a study of nature

Figure 5. Fairsted, the Olmsted firm office, Brookline, Mass. Photograph by Jack E. Boucher. Library of Congress, Prints and Photographs Division, Historic American Buildings Survey.

on a broad scale by travelling through large sections of country, [and] he had looked rather for the general effects than for the details that made up these effects[;] . . . he did not think of every detail that went to make up [the effect] but only of producing that appearance in the most effective way."[13] For an obsessive, planted-oriented practitioner, this perspective must have been liberating.

In November, Manning recorded Olmsted's account of a ride through Franklin Park with the park's superintendent, an incident that may have marked another milestone in his professional growth: "The beauty and attractiveness of the place was evidently a revelation to him. . . . As the design of the park gradually was brought to Mr. Whitney's mind he was delighted and remarked 'how well every part fits into another.' Mr. O replied, it is our business. We are planners."[14] And so Manning's practical education continued, as he absorbed the principles that would guide his future professional life. Primary among these was the critical role of planning in the modern profession.

Manning's private notes from his years with the firm also record minutiae from these jobs, including the varieties and quantities of plants ordered and their costs—an example of the compulsive record-keeping that would characterize his professional methods. In addition to Olmsted Sr., he also worked closely with J. C. Olmsted, with whom he shared a particularly warm relationship, and with Charles Eliot.[15] Among the most valuable professional methods Manning acquired during his tenure as superintendent of planting in the Brookline office was the use of overlay maps as a means of recording and analyzing site data.[16] Manning would apply the same method in his own practice, adding layer upon layer of information in the service of resource-based design and planning projects.

Over the course of the eight years, Manning worked with the partners and their assistants on the firm's most important projects. He estimated that there were 125 altogether. Among the most significant were the grounds of the U.S. Capitol; Rock Creek Park and the National Zoo in Washington, D.C.; Stanford University; park systems in Louisville, Rochester, and Buffalo; the park system designed for the Boston Metropolitan District Commission; the Pocantico Hills, New York, estate of John D. Rockefeller; Point d'Acadie, George Washington Vanderbilt's summer home in Bar Harbor, Maine; and the World's Columbian Exposition in Chicago. When the Olmsted associate Henry Sargent Codman died suddenly during construction of the White City in early 1893, Manning took his place, overseeing installation of the vast program of new plants.[17]

Manning acquired still more autonomy in the firm while working at Biltmore, the estate, farm, village, and scientific forest of George Washington Vanderbilt, in Asheville, North Carolina, where he supervised the acquisition of hundreds of thousands of acres and, beginning in 1893, became involved in planning an arboretum. Letters to his wife convey Manning's sense of his rising importance in the firm. "My position here is a much more satisfactory one than at any other time, for I am recognized as Mr. O's representative and get about what I want," he wrote in November of that year.[18]

Olmsted's son and namesake had also been dispatched to Biltmore, in his case to complete an education that had begun with an undergraduate degree from Harvard. At age twenty-three—ten years younger than Manning—Olmsted Jr. was new to the field and though ambivalent about the profession, he was eager to prove his horticultural mettle. Through a series of detailed letters written to the firm partners in 1895, he criticized Manning's purchases for Biltmore's arboretum, making a case that Manning had undermined the purposes of the collection by introducing a large number of horticultural varieties that were "'strikingly abnormal' in foliage or habit." Further, he claimed that Manning had unwittingly purchased the same plants under many different names from different growers, which seems to have been the case. By Olmsted Jr.'s count, about 3,000 of the 4,374 specimens purchased for the arboretum by February 1895 were "valuable neither in landscape nor for economic forestry," the criteria that had been established by Vanderbilt and Olmsted Sr.[19]

Olmsted Jr.'s letters also criticize Manning's lack of education: "We should naturally turn to Mr. Manning to do this work" (drawing up a definitive list of the arboretum's holdings) "but there are several drawbacks to our throwing it upon him. For example, it has been pointed out that much the greater part of the books to be consulted are in Latin, French, and German," none of which Manning read. "Unless I am very much mistaken, neither is Manning a scientific botanist," Olmsted Jr. wrote more pointedly in another

Figure 6. Manning (with beard) and his four younger brothers at the Manning Manse, North Billerica, Mass. Photograph courtesy William C. Manning.

Figure 7. Henrietta (Nettie) Pratt Manning with son, Harold W. Manning, and dog, Rex. Photograph courtesy MCL.

Figure 8. Manning with Rex at the Manse. Photograph courtesy MCL.

letter. "He is an unattached and expanded nurseryman, with a nurseryman's preconceived ideas on many points."[20] The younger practitioner's ire may have been amplified by his own horticultural insecurities, but it also not too subtly illuminated the divide between the well-traveled, Ivy League–educated partners—who had, by 1895, come to include Charles Eliot—and Manning, whose roots were in trade.[21] Manning tendered his resignation from the firm the following year.[22]

As he departed, Manning launched a project that would bolster his pride and connection to his own family roots: the restoration of his seventeenth-century ancestral homestead, the *Manning Manse, in North Billerica, Massachusetts.[23] The country place was to serve as the headquarters of the newly formed Manning Association, of which Manning was founder and president. It would be a museum—a shrine, essentially, to the long history of the Manning family in America. The Manse also functioned as a summer retreat for Warren, Nettie, and their son, Harold, and a site for family reunions (figs. 6, 7, 8). Firm employees would sometimes be invited there to use Manning's extensive professional library, and in later years he required young practitioners to work on the grounds as part of their training.[24]

FIRST DECADE OF PRACTICE

Manning's warmth and horticultural sensitivity appear to have been prime factors in the decision of many Olmsted firm clients to transfer their projects to him, and his former employers graciously accommodated his requests, as was their custom.[25] In the first years of the 125 Tremont Street office, several clients from the Olmsted roster are listed, and together they constituted a strong basis for Manning's budding practice. There were six in particular who would provide rich networks for the new firm's client base: George A. Draper of Hopedale, Massachusetts; John Howard Whittemore of Middlebury, Connecticut; James W. Tufts of Pinehurst, North Carolina; Cyrus H. McCormick II of Lake Forest, Illinois; William Mather of Cleveland; and Frank H. Peavey of Minneapolis.[26] Through multiplying commissions for these individuals, Manning made the acquaintence of other businessmen who were also inspired by Progressive-era goals, and they in turn promoted his services to colleagues, extended families, neighbors, and friends. By the end of 1897, his first full year in business, Manning listed sixty-six new jobs in eighteen states and Canada. About two-thirds of these were small home grounds and estates. He also recorded seven jobs related to parks and parkways.

The year after he left the Olmsted firm, Manning had written to Charles Eliot to ask his help in forming a professional association; Eliot thought that there were too few landscape architects to make such a group effective and suggested instead an organization with a more general membership that would also include foresters, horticulturalists, and gardeners. That year Manning and several colleagues formed the American Park and Outdoor Art Association, of which Manning was secretary.[27] He continued to lobby for the professional association for landscape architects, however, and eventually gained the support of John Charles Olmsted and others. In 1899 that effort coalesced into the American Society of Landscape Architects, a professional network that established standards for the modern profession and laid the groundwork for its rising stature through the Progressive era.

One of Manning's earliest jobs in independent practice was for James W. Tufts, who wanted to build a health resort on some of the eight hundred acres of land he had recently purchased near Southern Pines, North Carolina. The project had begun under the auspices of the Olmsted office in 1895; after the firm transferred it to Manning the following year, it grew rapidly. ⋆Pinehurst soon had a nursery, a farm with herds of Jerseys and Holsteins, and a nine-hole golf course. When James Tufts died in 1902, his son Leonard added several thousand acres to the project. Manning continued to work for Leonard through the 1920s, at Pinehurst and beyond, adding more golf courses, residential developments, hotels, and hundreds of miles of bridle paths through land surrounding the village. Over time, Manning would work on twenty-nine projects for Tufts; he and Leonard would remain friends for life.

Many park commissions came to Manning in these early years, too. He was hired for work in Minneapolis, where an extensive park system had been laid out by Horace Cleveland in the 1880s, and in ⋆Milwaukee, for an expansion of a park system that had originated in the Olmsted office. In 1899 Manning secured a job for ⋆Wilcox Park, a town park in Westerly, Rhode Island, and he created a plan for ⋆The Parklands, a new 187-acre park in Hopedale, Massachusetts, on the millpond of a textile factory (fig. 9). That same year he completed a general plan for the Bronx Zoo, listing four assistants, one of whom was his brother J. Woodward Manning. By 1901, the year Manning began a new park system for Harrisburg, Pennsylvania, he had taken on Woodward as a partner, renaming the business Manning Brothers.

In its scope and national significance, the ⋆Harrisburg commission was the firm's most important project to date; Manning later identified it as one of the most important of his career.[28] The design approach had been inspired by the Olmsted firm's treatment of the Muddy River Improvement in Boston, as well as by the urban park system that Olmsted & Vaux had created for Buffalo—an armature for an expanding metropolis, with separate parks devoted to different purposes linked by parkways (fig. 10).

Figure 9. The Hopedale Parklands, with Draper Corporation factory buildings at the edge of Hopedale Pond. Photograph by Carol Betsch, 2010.

Figure 10. Wildwood Lake, Harrisburg, Pa. Photograph by Carol Betsch, 2012.

Manning's contact in Harrisburg was his friend and colleague J. Horace McFarland, who was among the initiators of a public campaign to clean up the polluted Susquehanna River—the scenic centerpiece of Manning's far-ranging proposal. The two had come to know each other through their involvement with the American Park and Outdoor Art Association and would remain lifelong friends.[29] Manning's success soon led to another planning job in that city, a new 132-acre residential subdivision, *Bellevue Park. He was hired in 1907 by the Union Real Estate Company, almost certainly on the recommendation of McFarland, who was company secretary and one of eight investors in the real estate venture. Manning based his plan on the same principles that were informing his park and other planning work. The curving roads closely follow the lay of the land, and ponds at the heart of the development provide a parklike core (fig. 11).

Figure 11. Bellevue Park subdivision, Harrisburg. Photograph by Carol Betsch, 2012.

Not every aspect of Manning's Harrisburg park system was realized, but much of it was, and the work became well known—largely through McFarland's far-flung lectures about it for civic-minded audiences in search of their own urban "awakening," McFarland's term for the Harrisburg transformation. The noted city planner Charles Mulford Robinson praised Manning's design for its "broad grasp and far-seeing vision." Frank Waugh, a landscape architect and author of several influential books, included the Harrisburg park system on his list of eleven masterpieces of American landscape architecture.[30] Despite this success, Manning would find few urban park commissions on this scale again; Manning Brothers was also short-lived.[31] Following the death of Jacob Manning in 1904, Woodward resigned to direct operations at Reading Nursery.

Manning never took on another partner. Nor did he develop an office organization that incorporated the rigorous separation of professional responsibilities that characterized the highly efficient Olmsted firm. Manning's method was to hire young practitioners and give them far-ranging responsibilities, supervising their work sporadically.[32] Fletcher Steele, who began working for Manning in 1908 after having dropped out of the new graduate program at Harvard, described a practice in which roles and responsibilities shifted frequently in response to the projects under way and to Manning's frenetic travel schedule. Steele regarded the situation as a remarkable opportunity. "The very lack of system from which [Manning] suffers is the virtue of the place for me," he wrote his father. "A tremendous number of problems is constantly coming into the office. On a large number of them I work in some capacity or another. I get an insight into how a big man with his particular tendencies works away the difficulties."[33] There is little question that Manning's office also profited from a talent like Steele's, undeveloped as it was.

While Steele and his coworkers, among them A. D. Taylor, Charles Gillette, John Noyes, and other gifted practitioners, thrived on the immersion in important tasks, Steele's letters also record frustration with his boss's improvisatory methods and his emotional volatility.[34] "How often I have heard him say 'Is everybody here stupid or am I' with a very clear intonation that means he alone is normal."[35] Manning was also highly distractible, except during the rare occasions that he isolated himself so that he could delve deeply into a complicated project. "It is only a few times a year that the relative importance of great matters seems to come to him," Steele wrote, "& at such times he turns out his greatest work, refusing to see anyone or to consider any matter but the one on which he has his mind. But ordinarily it is quite otherwise. He is approachable by anyone in the office who gets there first, & pounces on anything they may have to say, sometimes before their meaning has been one quarter expressed."[36] Still, the firm prospered. Records show an increasing number of jobs, many for new private estates, as well as increasing profits.[37]

Through the decade, Manning continued to work on several projects that had originated with the Olmsted firm. One of the most important of these was *Tranquillity Farm, in Middlebury, Connecticut, the three-hundred-acre estate of J. H. Whittemore, whose plan had been laid out by Manning collaboratively with Charles Eliot in 1893. Miles of dry-laid stone walls trace the undulating land of central Connecticut; meadows, gardens, and classically styled outbuildings were added through the years (fig. 12). The bond of friendship forged with Whittemore led to a cascade of related commissions in the region. Manning eventually designed about twenty-five projects for the Naugatuck businessman and philanthropist. These included schools, hospitals,

Figure 12. Fieldstone walls, Tranquillity Farm, Middlebury, Conn. Photograph by Carol Betsch, 2015.

civic buildings, and churches. He found other clients in the region as well, including the architect Theodate Pope (later, Riddle), who hired him twice for advice about the grounds of her estate, ★Hill-Stead; he also did the plan for Westover School, in Farmington, the buildings for which Pope designed.

Manning found important estate work in other locations too. In 1904 he began a commission for Jeptha Homer Wade II, a three-thousand-acre winter estate in Thomasville, Georgia, known as ★Mill Pond Plantation. The property was to serve as a lavish hunting retreat, with a large Spanish Colonial Revival house by Hubbell & Benes. In 1905 Wade's business colleague William G. Mather commissioned Manning for work on a country estate on a more modest scale. ★Gwinn was located on five acres east of Cleveland, on a bluff overlooking Lake Erie. Mather engaged the architect Charles A. Platt to design the house and plan the grounds, and he commissioned Manning to design the planting program. The combination of Platt's command of line and proportion and Manning's imaginative planting compositions was a dynamic artistic success, widely published within a few years of the collaboration (fig. 13).[38] Manning went on to create a wild garden on additional acreage that Mather purchased for the purpose. These projects were the harbinger of dozens of additional jobs;

Figure 13. View across front lawn to loggia in formal garden, Gwinn. Photograph by Carol Betsch, 1993.

William Mather commissioned more projects from Manning than any other client.

Among them was the industrial town of *Gwinn, built in 1906 on the Marquette Iron Range of Michigan's Upper Peninsula. Mather contributed many ideas in creating the layout, which was to be a stand-alone settlement for his workers in the Cleveland-Cliffs Iron Mining Company; he had visited model towns in England, Germany, and Sweden a decade earlier to gather ideas firsthand. Manning selected a site for the new town, characteristically near scenic resources—in this case, the fork of the Escanaba River and its East Branch—so that workers could live "within ten minutes of extensive wild wood and river reservations."[39]

Other big planning commissions came to Manning in the first decade. One was for the new copper-mining town of *Warren, Arizona, in collaboration with the architect Huger Elliot and engineer F. A. Applegarth (fig. 14). The 1907 job figures among Manning's most elegant and, in some respects, characteristic plans. Here he balanced a response to the stark beauty of the desert mountains with the utilitarian needs of a new settlement, constructed for workers of the Calumet and Arizona Mining Company. The layout of streets and parks brings to mind the weblike tracery of City Beautiful plans. In its organizing spatial function, Vista Park, a dominant feature of the Arizona scheme, for example, recalls the Mall of the McMillan Plan for Washington, D.C. But Manning's design for Warren was laid out in relation to landscape features rather than abstract geometric ideals. Views from the park align directly with mountains in Mexico, some fifty miles to the south.

In 1904 Manning was invited to plan the *Jamestown Exposition in Norfolk, Virginia, a celebration of the three-hundredth anniversary of the founding of the Jamestown Colony. (The exposition's architect, Robert S. Peabody of Peabody & Stearns, had worked on some of the same projects as Manning, and it may have been this

Figure 14. Manning (far right, in derby) near Bisbee, Ariz., c. 1907. Photograph courtesy MPI.

connection that helped him get the job.)[40] The ambitious project ended in near-complete disaster—deemed "the most colossal failure in the history of expositions" by the *New York Times*. The debacle was entirely due to administrative mismanagement far beyond Manning's control. Despite the problems, old photographs record Colonial Revival and Arts and Crafts–influenced landscapes that were strikingly original (fig. 15).

The Norfolk job may have led to others in the commonwealth, including a plan for the *University of Virginia in 1908, undertaken to accommodate expansion of Thomas Jefferson's notable design. The job held emphatic meaning for Manning, who was a great admirer of Jefferson, about whom he later coauthored a book.[41] Manning's relations with the university were eventually severed over a disagreement about the demolition of a Jefferson-era building that he wanted to save—a position supported by Charles Platt and others—but his recommendations regarding new development were insightful and influenced later decisions. Manning found many other jobs in Virginia. One of these was Piedmont Farm, in Rapidan, where Fletcher Steele oversaw the siting of the house, drive, and box-bordered formal gardens of the colonial-era plantation between 1907 and 1910.[42] Another was renewed work on Richmond College, where Manning had offered advice in 1898, which was carried out from 1911 to 1918.

Figure 15. Jamestown Exposition, 1907. Postcard courtesy William C. Manning.

Figure 16. College Avenue, North Carolina State Normal and Industrial College, 1910. Postcard courtesy Martha Blakeney Hodges Special Collections and University Archives, University Libraries, University of North Carolina at Greensboro.

Other campus planning jobs came to Manning around this time. In 1908 he resumed work on ⋆North Carolina State Normal and Industrial College in Greensboro, where he would continue to consult until 1921 (fig. 16). The same year he was commissioned for planning work at ⋆Massachusetts Agricultural College in Amherst, where Frank Waugh had founded a department of landscape architecture. Manning's 1911 plan revived several concepts from Olmsted Sr.'s 1866 recommendations for the campus, particularly its emphasis on a campus pond as the focal landscape feature. Manning also proposed building a scenic road along the Mill River as it wound through the campus toward the Connecticut River and creating a second pond to enlarge the campus's parklike core.

THE 1910s

As Manning's reputation spread, he attracted more and larger jobs. Hundreds of all sizes came to him in quick succession through the next decade. In 1910–11, he prepared plans for rebuilding the commercial district in ⋆Bangor, Maine, following a series of devastating fires. His recommendations for the city ranged well beyond a new site for the library, which was his initial charge. Manning suggested a new entrance to the city, a dam that would provide a basin for recreation and fire protection, and new parks to flank the waterfront. Both A. D. Taylor and Fletcher Steele were involved in the project, and Steele published a comprehensive account of it in *Landscape Architecture* in 1911.[43]

In 1913 Manning prepared an extensive report for a new state park on ⋆Mackinac Island, Michigan, a project that dovetailed with work on his National Plan. (This would be listed as a firm job the following year. The Michigan work may have been a pilot study for the larger project.) In the Mackinac report, Manning recommended modifications to an existing transportation network to allow greater access to historic resources, implementation of forestry management procedures to promote native growth, and opening vistas to enhance scenic distinction. A year later he created plans for nearby ★Michilimackinac State Park, site of a fort dating to the colonial era, which Manning recommended restoring.

In the early 1910s, commissions for several private estates got under way, the profits from which fueled Manning's operation in greater proportion than any other type of job. From 1909 to 1911, the office worked for Galen L. Stone on ★Great Hill, an estate on a peninsula on Buzzards Bay, in Marion, Massachusetts, with a house by the Boston firm of Chapman & Frazer. The most notable elements of the design are two allées of rhododendron and azalea that intersect to connect the enormous house to the woodland (fig. 17). Fletcher Steele supervised much of this work, which was recorded in detailed letters to his parents.[44] Close by was ★The Meadows, a thirty-five-acre estate for Arthur A. and Alanson B. Houghton, begun in 1910 on Apponagansett Bay, also with houses by Chapman & Frazer.[45] Here, as elsewhere in Manning's work, the estate grounds appear almost wild, tucked into the surrounding landscape. But, like most country estates of the period, The Meadows had its formal gardens too.

Like his mentor Olmsted, Manning did not approve of ornamental flower gardens. He considered them stiff and artificial in contrast to wild gardens, which he believed offered "another type of beauty that is infinitely more varied in detail and in interest."[46] But even Manning's most stalwart wild garden clients insisted on including architectonic, flower-filled gardens on their

Figure 17. Rhododendron allée, Great Hill (Galen L. Stone estate), Marion, Mass. Photograph by Carol Betsch, 2011.

grounds. Formal gardens signified taste and stature to clients, and they provided women, in particular, with links to powerful social networks such as the Garden Club of America.

Several of Manning's rather lackluster formal garden plantings were eventually redesigned by Ellen Shipman, a specialist in the genre, and such was the case at The Meadows. Shipman also redesigned the formal garden plantings at *Stan Hywet, one of Manning's largest estates, commissioned by Frank A. Seiberling and his wife, Gertrude, in Akron, Ohio, beginning in 1911.[47] The dominant design motive at Stan Hywet, however, was provided by a large wild garden surrounding a spring-fed lagoon, which Manning created by flooding an abandoned quarry (fig. 18). Through Seiberling, Manning received many other commissions.

In 1912 he began work on *Goodyear Heights, a company subdivision in Akron, conceived from the first to increase in size as Goodyear Tire and Rubber Company expanded. The plan was dominated by a twenty-eight-acre park with a pond, ball fields, and play areas. Within six years, when the number of lots had quadrupled, sixteen small parks had been created along with the large, centrally located Reservoir Park. Manning's plan also provided new transportation linkages. He laid out a seven-mile extension of Akron's Main Street to Goodyear Heights, on which a bus system—the nation's first—carried residents to work each day. A few years later, he would lay out a plan for Fairlawn Heights, an upscale subdivision for Goodyear executives, also in Akron.

While Manning found many new business connections through client networks, he also steadily built his national reputation through lectures and articles that appeared in popular magazines as well as professional journals, including *Landscape Architecture,* where he published "The Field of Landscape Design" in 1912. He also contributed essays to authoritative books, such as Liberty Hyde Bailey's *Standard Cyclopedia of Horticulture,* where he published "The Art of Making Landscape Gardens" a few years later.[48] Over the course of the century's second decade, Manning's horticultural writings intensified in their criticism of variegated plants, which he characterized as "garish" and "peculiar" with "variously blotched, dissected and twisted foliage." His articles continued to emphasize "distinction" as a key ingredient in American landscape design, a quality that, in his words, "comes from a study of the distinctive beauty of the locality."[49]

The widespread notion that American plants were superior to imported species was, in part, a reaction against lingering Victorian tastes for horticultural oddities, but such language was underscored by elements of nativism, too, particularly at the height of the Progressive era, when the Americanization of European immigrants became an obsession for reform-minded civic leaders. Disparagement of foreign imports was a theme in the writings of several of Manning's contemporaries, particularly the author and horticulturalist Wilhelm Miller, who expressed this perspective throughout *The Prairie Spirit in Landscape Gardening* (1915), and the landscape architect Jens Jensen, who used native plants almost exclusively. Manning's views on non-native plants was less emphatic than either of these colleagues', and it softened over time. He came to adopt a notion of what he called "new native plants" on the grounds that Thoreau had experimented with imports at Walden, and he continued to utilize introductions when they served his practical and aesthetic purposes.

At Harriet and Cyrus McCormick's *Walden, north of Chicago, the landscape architect experi-

Figure 18. View over the lagoon, Stan Hywet, Akron, Ohio. Photograph by Carol Betsch, 1996.

mented with a wide range of plant species to create a naturalistic impression. He worked closely with McCormick on the hundred-acre site, which featured deep ravines and vistas to Lake Michigan. Manning's wild garden aesthetic spread to other North Shore clients too. Between 1911 and 1914 he worked on the conjoined estates of Stanley Field and Albert A. Sprague in *Lake Bluff, laying out the two landscapes simultaneously, treating them as a joint commission. Throughout the sixty-seven-acre site, trails provided sequential experiences of the most striking natural features, particularly the dramatic ravine and lake views from the bluff. Altogether, Manning was commissioned for twenty-three jobs north of Chicago, including *Lake Forest University, where his plan also emphasized the beauty of the ravines.

Office records from 1913 show the promotion of A. D. Taylor to associate, a move that may have coincided with Fletcher Steele's resignation. Net income was about $18,000, Manning's most profitable year yet, with seventeen landscape designers listed on the payroll and Taylor's name on the masthead. As Manning's son, Harold, grew into his adolescent years, Manning came to believe that he should someday be brought in as partner and eventually become his successor in the business.[50] But Harold seems to have had neither the requisite talent nor the interest to follow in his father's footsteps. He did come to work for the firm in a business capacity, and he also chauffeured Manning, whose distractibility made him a terrible driver, on site visits in the region.[51]

In addition to new jobs all over the country, Manning listed many projects closer to home, about forty of them in the greater Billerica area. Most of these were planning and park projects. In 1913 Manning collaborated with the planner Arthur C. Comey to lay out a worker housing development in *Billerica, the first suburb in the United States based on the British garden city model promoted by Ebenezer Howard. Billerica was the site of many Community Days organized by Manning, who also launched a magazine, *Billerica,* to address the town's planning issues.[52]

In 1913 Manning began an important estate job in Oyster Bay, New York, for George Bullock, which featured a photogenic water cascade (fig. 19). The connection may have given Manning a professional boost in Birmingham, Alabama, where Bullock had business interests in a local railway concern. In 1914 Manning began a city plan for the booming steel city that would figure among his most innovative planning work.

Manning's visionary recommendations for *Birmingham included flood control by deftly siting air landing strips in low-lying areas and residential and commercial districts in locations that could become industrialized in time. He urged aggressive acquisition of land not suited to cultivation for public reservations, totaling many thousands of acres. The plan sited permanent residential housing in the highlands, where commercial and industrial development was impossible, and separated burgeoning rail lines and auto roads for efficiency and safety. The utilitarian scheme lacked the cohesiveness and monumentality of typical City Beautiful plans being implemented elsewhere; instead it emphasized natural resources.

Gathering data for the Birmingham project coincided with Manning's most intensive work on the National Plan, which, by 1914, was listed as an office project. Profits from his business shrank that year as a result of the time he was devoting to the comprehensive planning initiative. That was also the year that Manning was elected president of the American Society of Landscape Architects (although he does not appear to have devoted much time to the post). A. D. Taylor appeared on the masthead for the last time in 1914; he would leave Manning's office the following year to open his own Cleveland-based firm. Fletcher Steele had resigned in 1913 to open his own practice. Both departures had been extremely collegial. Manning helped subsidize a European grand tour for Steele shortly after his departure in exchange for a comprehensive report on it.

In 1915 Manning opened an office in North Billerica on Chelmsford Road opposite the Manse. The structure, built by members of his staff, fea-

Figure 19. Water cascade, George Bullock estate, Oyster Bay, N.Y., July 1928. Photograph by Arthur G. Eldredge. Courtesy MCL.

tured a central octagonal area and five radiating wings, each dedicated to a separate purpose—drafting, modeling, library, safe, and furnace (figs. 20, 21). The move may have had a positive effect on business. Mid-decade, Manning acquired several new employees, including Violet Harrison and Carl Lutender, both of whom would remain with the firm for several years.[53] In 1916 net income was about $23,000, an all-time high.

The most important job to come to the office that year was a system of state park reservations in and around Ithaca, New York, where Man-

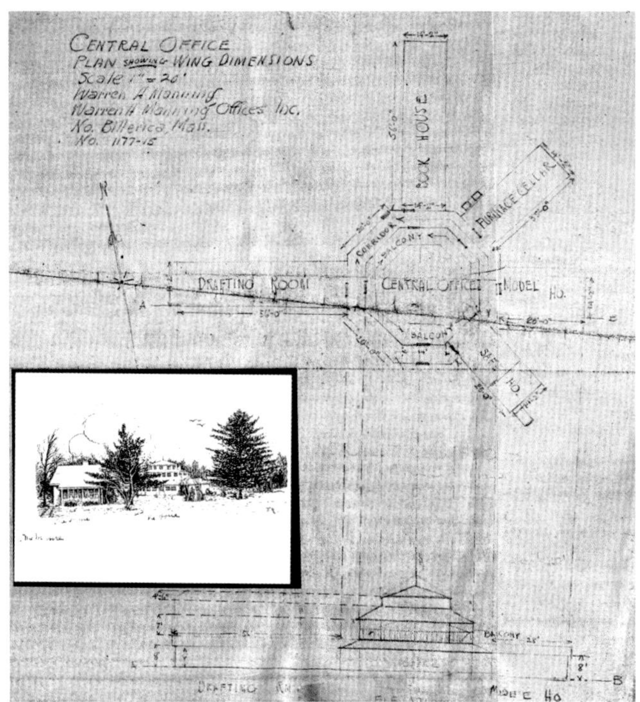

Figure 20. **Manning's octagonal office in North Billerica, Mass., c. 1914.** Blueprint and drawing courtesy MCL.

Figure 21. **Octagonal office under construction, c. 1915.** Photograph courtesy MCL.

Figure 22. **Lucifer Falls.** Undated stereopticon card from The Artistic Series, No. 35, E. & H. T. Anthony & Co. Courtesy William C. Hecht, http://nytompki.org/hecht_index.htm#3.

ning advised Robert H. and Laura Treman on the acquisition of forested parcels laced with gorges and waterfalls. This initiative began with Lucifer Falls, a popular tourist destination southwest of the city and a favorite hiking spot for the Tremans (fig. 22). Dismayed by the increasingly derelict condition of the site, the Ithaca couple purchased forty acres around the falls and turned to Manning to improve access to it. (Treman had known Manning for many years; he had first hired the landscape architect in 1900 for work on an *estate compound he would share with two siblings, Charles Treman and Elizabeth Van Cleef, on Ithaca's East Hill.) Manning convinced his clients of the conservation potential of the gorges and waterfalls in the area, and they eventually acquired close to four hundred acres, which they donated to New York State. Manning's extensive reports on the conditions and potential of individual properties laid the groundwork for a system now known as the *Finger Lakes State Parks.

The acquisition of these parcels occurred over many years, some of it during the tenure of Robert Moses, then secretary of the New York State Association, who admired Manning's vision for the project—though he believed Manning had "overreached himself" in seeking to expand the planning initiative beyond the Finger Lakes region. Ross Kellogg, director of the Finger Lakes State Parks Commission, agreed that Manning's expansive tendencies were "running wild."[54] (It was not the first time that Manning's tendency to enlarge the scope of a project would alarm clients.) Roads, bridges, and trails built during the 1930s by the Civilian Conservation Corps, many suggested by Manning, remain the most conspicuously designed aspects of a network that figures among the most ambitious early state park systems in the nation (fig. 23).

Figure 23. Robert H. Treman State Park, Ithaca, N.Y. Photograph by Carol Betsch, 2009.

WAR AND POSTWAR YEARS

After the United States entered World War I in 1917, Manning's business, like that of other American landscape architects, began a sharp decline. As the war continued, profits plummeted; in 1918 Manning's office netted only $1,665. That year he wrote an article for *The American City,* "Planning the Cantonments," about the urgent effort under way to build barracks for new soldiers. The National Conference on City Planning, held in Kansas City in May 1917, had recommended that the federal government call in planners to assist in locating and selecting the sites for the new cantonments. This was not done, Manning reported, noting a resultant waste of time and money. The Committee on Emergency Construction had prevailed, though, in advising on the configuration of the individual sites, which Manning's article evaluates in some detail. Manning himself had been involved in advising at Camp Sherman in Chillicothe, Ohio, and he visited other sites, including Camp Dix, New Jersey, where Harold was stationed.[55]

During the war years Manning continued efforts on many projects already under way, and he held a number of Community Days to accomplish the work with volunteer labor. The postwar recession continued to undermine his flagging business. He closed his Boston office and cut his employee roster—in 1921 he listed only five. Among them were his brother J. Woodward and Egbert Hans, who would remain one of his most steadfast and trusted workers, as well as Helen Bullard, a planting supervisor who would become a mainstay of his operation.

One of the first design projects in Manning's practice to resume after the war was ⋆Agassiz Park in Calumet, Michigan, where Manning had been engaged to design a twenty-acre park dedicated to the memory of Alexander Agassiz, the renowned scientist and president of the Calumet & Hecla Mining Company. The final plan, completed in 1920, featured a large common, tree-bordered walkways, and a bronze sculpture of the company president. The park was notable because it was built largely by volunteer labor; C & H had its mineworkers prepare the site, and planting was done during two Community Days staged by Manning in 1922 and 1923.

A more significant postwar project for Manning was an expansion of ⋆Mill Creek Park in Youngstown, Ohio, which grew by more than

Figure 24. Mill Creek Park, Youngstown, Ohio. Photograph by Carol Betsch, 2014.

one thousand acres between 1920 and 1932. By damming the creek, Manning created the one-hundred-acre Lake Newport, his most compelling contribution to the composition (fig. 24).

In 1923 Manning left his North Billerica office for smaller quarters in the Brattle Building in Harvard Square, Cambridge, and from there published an abbreviated version of his nine-hundred-page National Plan as a supplement to the July issue of *Landscape Architecture.* Secretary of the Interior Franklin K. Lane contributed a foreword, lauding the study as "fascinating as fiction, yet all very solemn fact." The comprehensive plan had occupied Manning's intellectual, emotional, and financial resources for nearly a decade, predicated on the mistaken belief that its holistic logic would catalyze cooperation among a vast network of national, regional, and local agencies on decisions regarding land use.

The plan's recommendations for national action were visionary but politically naive. Among the most unrealistic was a proposal to redraw state borders according to topography and watersheds.[56] Less laudably, the plan proposed new regional settlement patterns guided by then-rampant notions of geographical determinism. Its recommendations were nativist and, in some instances, blatantly racist. Despite these flaws, however, Manning's plan drew the interest of professional planners, including Charles Eliot II, who later served on the National Resources Planning Board during the Roosevelt administration. Eliot (a nephew of Olmsted's partner) also chaired the ASLA Committee on State Parks and Regional Planning; Manning would serve as a member of that committee too.[57]

Manning's move to Cambridge marked a financial turnaround in his business. That year

Figure 25. Surveyors at Fairyland Estates, Lookout Mountain, Tenn., c. 1923. Photograph courtesy Chattanooga History Center.

he was commissioned to plan an upscale vacation development on the Cumberland Plateau near Lookout Mountain, Tennessee. Named by Frieda Carter, one of the investors in the development, ★Fairyland Estates was a six-hundred-acre neighborhood sited in the mountain wilderness with views of the Tennessee River valley (fig. 25). Manning's plan successfully incorporated the site's rugged topography, and he was hired by several homeowners to design their individual properties as well.

In August 1923 Manning was in Cornelia, Georgia, to deliver a speech to the Georgia State Agricultural and Horticultural Societies. A week later he was invited to Athens to address the chamber of commerce about his experience using natural features in new parks, suggesting that Athens had similar resources. The following year, he was hired by the city to develop a new plan. He stayed in ★Athens for two weeks, surveying the town and using local Boy Scouts to help count trees. Manning's 1925 plan included new parks and trails, streets and intersection realignments, zoning, and a new sewer system. Among its most notable features was a continuous park "reservation" incorporating ravines and floodplains throughout the city. Manning optimistically predicted that private property owners would donate the required land, and the report also suggests that the properties could be cleared with volunteer labor; he held out the example of the help provided by the Boy Scouts two years earlier.

In 1924 Manning found work in Miami, designing Bayfront Park, a project with which he would be associated for several years. He listed another Florida project, "Orange County Beautification," about the same time. Most of the Florida boom projects, however, were going to John Nolen, whose Harvard education and polished stereopticon presentations were more effective than Manning's somewhat rambling speeches, most of which were composed on trains between site visits. By the fall of 1924, Nolen had contracts for twenty new projects in Florida, and he would secure more before the Depression exploded the development bubble.

Manning was confronting other disappointments, too. In 1925 Frank Seiberling, Manning's longtime client, donated about one thousand acres of Stan Hywet to form the Sand Hill Reservation, the first parcel of the new Akron Metropolitan District Commission, and he convinced the city to bring in Olmsted Brothers to plan the new parks. The highly efficient Brookline firm had, by this time, created park systems and subdivisions of great distinction throughout North America. Some measure of their success was due to the delegation of much of this work to trusted associates. Manning, by contrast, had lost his most talented assistants before the war and would rarely again have in his office workers of the caliber of A. D. Taylor or Fletcher Steele. Richard K. Webel (the distinguished founding partner of Innocenti & Webel) appeared on Manning's employee roster in 1924, but he apparently stayed less than a year. On the strength of his own reputation, Manning continued to obtain some important commissions through the mid-1920s, however.

The largest project in the office during the period was *Mountain Brook Estates, a four-

Figure 26. Mountain Brook, Birmingham, Ala. Photograph by Carol Betsch, 2012.

Figure 27. Morton G. Meinhardt estate, Port Chester, N.Y. Photograph by Arthur G. Eldredge, July 1928. Courtesy MCL.

thousand-acre residential subdivision outside Birmingham, commissioned by Robert Jemison beginning in 1926 for a secluded area southeast of the city.[58] Working in collaboration with the engineer J. H. Clanden and the landscape architect W. H. Kessler, Manning laid out a complex road system to provide homeowners with views to the slopes of Shades Mountain. The golf course that dominates the core of the development also provided views from the roads winding through it. Manning sited many of the houses and laid out driveways to be invisible from the street, emphasizing the naturalistic appearance of the subdivision. He strove to make most robust use of two small creeks by bordering them with woods incorporating miles of walking trails. Mountain Brook remains one of the most intact expressions of Manning's approach to suburban planning and an imaginative and sophisticated expansion of his earlier plan for Birmingham (fig. 26).

In 1927 and 1928 Manning commissioned a portfolio of several of his projects from Arthur G. Eldredge, a landscape architect who was also a gifted photographer. Recorded on glass plate negatives, the images capture several of Manning's major projects, most them private estates, at full maturity (fig. 27).[59] Manning's purpose in the investment, which must have been considerable, was likely to attract new clients. But the era of great estates was waning, and, at age sixty-eight, he would not find new private projects on the scale of those that had once filled his office.

The stock market crash of 1929 and ensuing economic depression struck a devastating blow to Manning's business, despite work on several planning projects for former clients. One of these was an "Upper Peninsula Land Use Study" commissioned by William G. Mather, a report that covered eleven million acres (fig. 28).[60] As his business faltered, Manning approached past and prospective clients with suggestions for planning

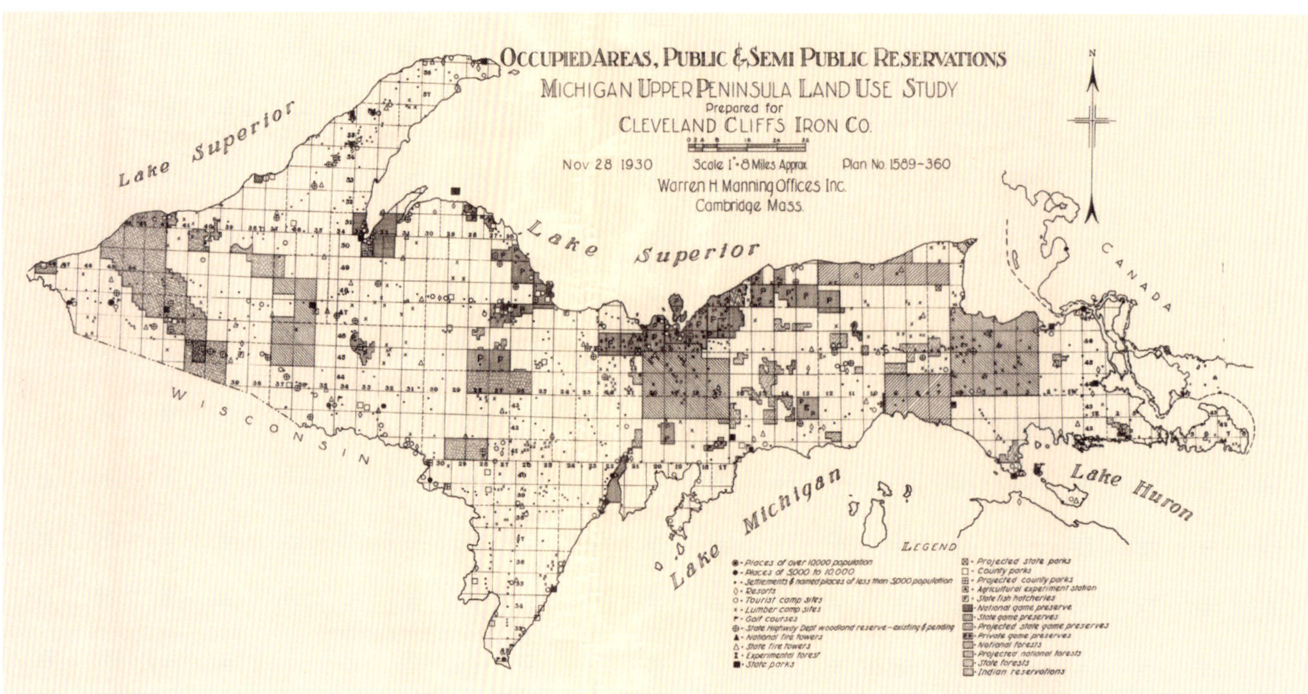

Figure 28. "Occupied Areas, Public & Semi-Public Reservations, Michigan Upper Peninsula Land Use Study, Prepared for Cleveland Cliffs Iron Co.," plan no. 1589-360, November 28, 1930. Courtesy MCL.

and writing projects.[61] He listed Arthur Clayton Sylvester and Dan Kiley as his last employees.

Kiley remembered Manning with fondness and admiration, and in later years he expressed deep appreciation for Manning's planning expertise and plantsmanship and their impact on his own development.[62] One intriguing document to survive from Kiley's association with Manning is "A Snow Storm Tramp Taken on the Wintry Sunday of Jan. 19, 1936," a map drawn by Kiley at 1 in. = 1,250 ft. scale (fig. 29). The charming drawing shows intimate landscape details, such as brooks, swamps, and even individual boulders. Kiley's landscape architectural achievements are frequently praised for their unerring spatial form, but his deep response to the lay of the land—surely nurtured by his formative experiences with Manning—was equally significant to his future artistic success.

Nettie Manning died in 1933, one suspects with many of her dreams unrealized. From the first months of opening his practice, Manning's incessant travel had kept them apart. His wife's letters make it clear that she had anticipated neither these long absences nor her husband's obsession with his National Plan, the expenses of which they bore privately. She found life at the Manse, where they decamped most summers, isolating and dreary. Still, one senses an affectionate bond, enlivened with humor, perspective, and a sense of purpose, between them. After his wife's death, Manning moved in with his son. He worked on minor consultations and he continued his correspondence with clients and colleagues. He also continued his campaign to persuade clients with large land holdings, William Mather among them, to make provisions for donating private lands to form new parks. But none of these efforts

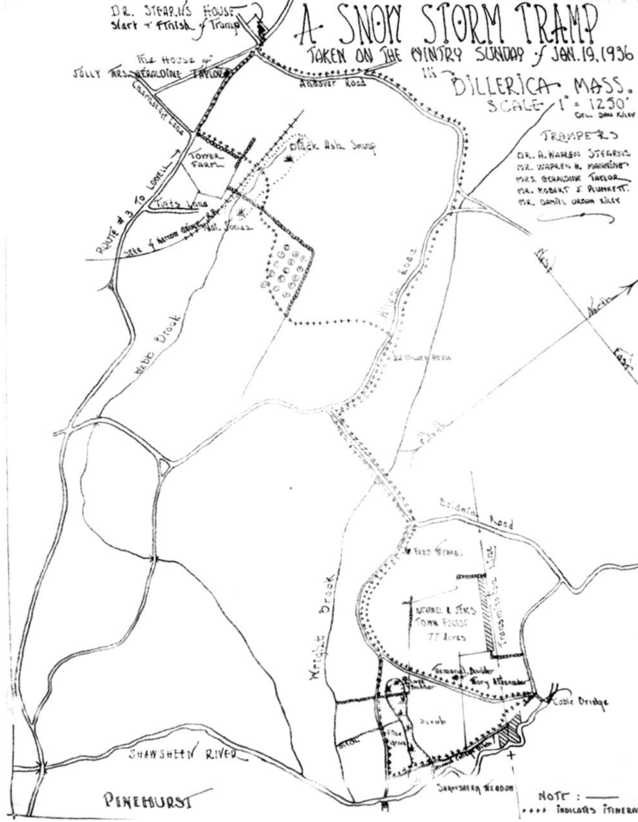

Figure 29. "A Snow Storm Tramp Taken on the Wintry Sunday of Jan. 19, 1936," Billerica, Mass., drawn by Daniel Urban Kiley. Courtesy MCL.

produced much income, and Manning's office records document a series of financial losses ending in 1935, when he closed his practice.

LAST YEARS

Encouraged by friends and former employees to create a narrative of his life's work, Manning turned to writing his autobiography in 1937. It proved a daunting task, far beyond his narrative skill and failing memory. The meandering, discursive account is overwhelmed by minutiae about minor projects, and despite its length—about five hundred typed pages—it fails to bring into focus the monumental achievements of Manning's long career. Egbert Hans, Manning's former associate, attempted to revise the manuscript posthumously (according to suggestions by A. D. Taylor), but the narrative never cohered satisfactorily. Nonetheless, the document remains a valuable source of information about many aspects of Manning's career, and it also offers glimpses into the landscape architect's wide-ranging imagination, which included musings on the implications of futuristic devices such as anti-gravity belts and "glasses attached to our noses and ears, through which we may see what is going on about us in the air in all directions."[63]

In February 1938, at age seventy-eight, Manning died from a heart attack following a strenuous recreational climb. His grandson, George Manning, was with him at the time. In the months afterward, Harold sent letters to the firm's widely dispersed clients, offering the return of plans. Few responded and almost none wanted the documents on offer. Most of Manning's voluminous client files, which included innumerable plans, drawings, and photographs, and sheaves of related correspondence, were subsequently taken to the local landfill. George Manning later estimated that eight truckloads were destroyed.[64] One large group of plans and drawings was saved, however, selected by P. H. Elwood for teaching purposes in the landscape architecture program at Iowa State University.[65] Iowa State also received Manning's collection of glass lantern slides. Other papers relating to Manning's business and many family papers were donated to Lowell University, now the University of Massachusetts Lowell.

Despite a laudatory obituary in *Landscape Architecture,* praising Manning's "vivid Americanism," a near-complete eclipse of his reputation began almost immediately (fig. 30).[66] The loss of many of his client records certainly

Figure 30. From "Warren H. Manning, Landscape Designer: A Tribute to a Pioneer in a New Profession" (obituary), *Landscape Architecture* 28 (April 1938): 148.

contributed to this erasure, but Manning's was not an isolated case. Bauhaus-influenced principles emerged full force at Harvard in the late 1930s, overshadowing the achievements of the previous generation of landscape practitioners. But personal memories of Warren Manning and his impact on the profession are vividly transmitted in the letters of those who had worked closely with him.

"I well remember one incident which occurred nearly forty years ago," J. Horace McFarland wrote about Manning in Harrisburg. "I took him by horse-and-buggy, before the days of automobiles, to see what we then called 'Wetzel's Swamp,' and I stopped under some beautiful pin oaks, not far from a swamp full of flowers, to show it all to Mr. Manning. He got out of the buggy and said, 'Oh, I don't want to talk parks; I want to roll in the grass,' and he did just that."[67]

"He was a bundle of driving, nervous energy during the hours of office work," wrote A. D. Taylor to Manning's son, "and yet had the ability, in the midst of his family surroundings and outside of office hours, to become completely and thoroughly relaxed. No greater contrast of ordered living between the man at work and the man at play ever existed. . . . We shall seldom see in our profession a man of his mental stature and professional accomplishment."[68]

The most heartfelt letter came from Fletcher Steele. "No one ever had a stronger or better influence on my life than he," Steele wrote. "His method of studying landscape problems has been for me a permanent model. And while it would be impossible to overestimate the value of his work, yet to me, it will never approach in my dearest memories the value of his nobility of vision, his simple yet sensitive approach to all that was good and beautiful, and his faith in mankind."[69]

Through fifty years of practice Manning applied the principles of "best possible use of material, human, and aesthetic resources" to each of his design and planning projects, from the smallest backyard garden to the parks, company towns, and city plans that filled his client roster.[70] His understanding of these principles was limited by the science of the day; in the case of his National Plan, it was tragically flawed by genetic misinformation and racism. In spite of Manning's distorted understanding of matters ranging from plant ecology to race and climate, he was one of the most significant landscape architects of the twentieth century, as well as the nation's first environmental planner. His extant projects constitute the most tangible legacy of a visionary practice inspired by nature and enlivened by a sense of urgent purpose to preserve and enhance its resources.

PROJECTS

Manning's octagonal office, c. 1915. Manning seated at left. Manning's son, Harold W. Manning (center), managed the office. Photograph courtesy MCL.

Birmingham District Plan

BIRMINGHAM, ALABAMA

MARJORIE LONGENECKER WHITE

Warren Manning's work in Birmingham began in 1914 with an amusement park and beautification projects along the extensive street railway lines linking the industrial centers of the larger area known as the Birmingham District. George Bullock of Oyster Bay, New York, whose Long Island estate Manning had designed in 1913–14, provided Manning's entrée to the region. His business, the Birmingham Railway, Light & Power Company, was a subsidiary of the New York–based American Cities Company, which also owned railway and power companies in New Orleans, Little Rock, Memphis, Knoxville, and Houston. George Ward, the visionary chair of Birmingham's board of city commissioners, championed Manning's work in an effort to launch a City Beautiful campaign, which would attract local press coverage as well as citizens, large corporations, and industrial plants willing to give "their time and money toward making the city beautiful." This success led to Manning's commission for a plan for the entire district, completed in December 1916. The original typescript report to the city commission was edited, embellished, and published in 1919 by private subscription as *Warren H. Manning's City Plan of Birmingham*.[1]

The 1916 Birmingham District plan proposes a "Great City of the Future" achievable within the next thirty years. The city of Birmingham, founded in 1871, is located in the foothills of the Appalachian Mountains at the center of an industrial "district" rich in minerals for making iron and steel. During the previous decade, Birmingham had annexed surrounding industrial communities, almost tripling its population. Its coal and ore mines, furnaces, mills, and railroads also grew substantially during this period. Manning envisioned further expansion of the city limits and of the space given to industrial use. He also proposed ways to increase the industrial water supply to cool furnaces and mills.

Manning's vision for the region was comprehensive. He planned the future city to extend sixteen miles to the Warrior River on the west, across the hilly Warrior coalfields and through the wide Jones and Opossum valleys, where industrial

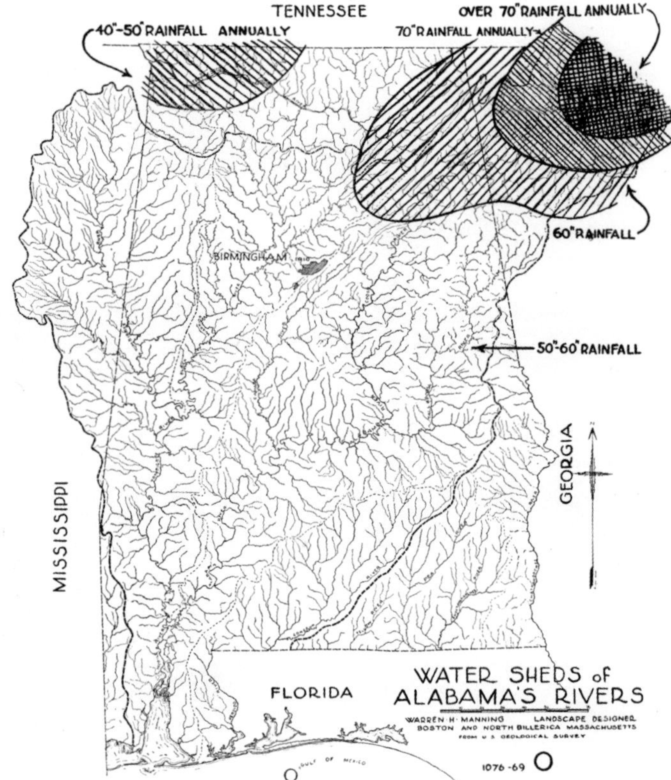

Watershed mapping was critical to Manning's planning efforts on the state, regional, and national levels. "Water Sheds of Alabama's Rivers," plan no. 1076-69. *Warren H. Manning's City Plan of Birmingham* (Birmingham, Ala.: Published by subscription, 1919), 24.

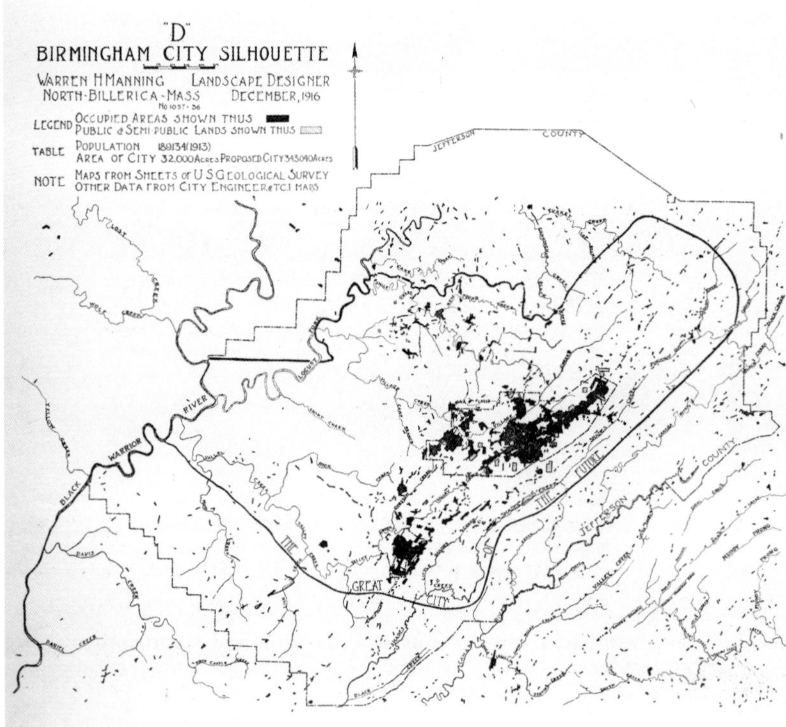

Manning's maps often delineated developed versus public lands, as well as projected growth. He labeled the expanded city perimeter "The Great City of the Future." "Birmingham City Silhouette," plan no. 1057-36. *Warren H. Manning's City Plan of Birmingham*, 3.

plants and the cities of Birmingham, Bessemer, and Fairfield are located, and eastward along the Pinson and Trussville valleys. As proposed, the city would include approximately five hundred square miles. In these great industrial valleys, all residential and commercial development was to be temporary, so that industries had room to expand. To ameliorate flooding, area creeks were to be channeled and roads built along their banks to facilitate transportation. Manning envisioned creekside reservations to provide recreation for industrial workers; such reservations, occupy-

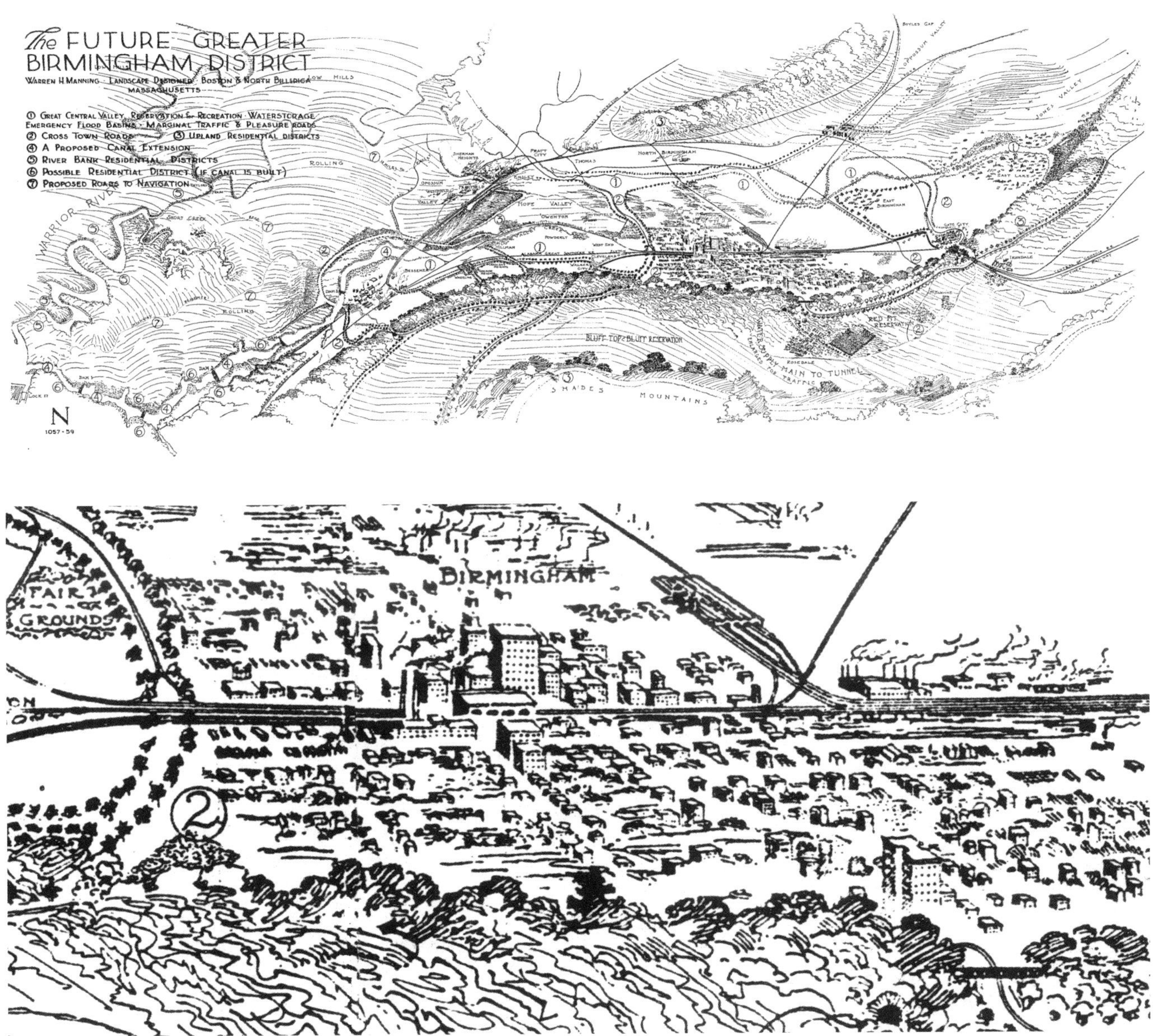

TOP: Transportation routes, waterways, business centers, and residential districts, as well as proposed improvements, are recorded in detail in this bird's-eye view. BOTTOM: (detail) The railway system is depicted in relation to the business and industrial centers of the city. "The Future Greater Birmingham District," plan no. 1057-59, from "The Birmingham District Plan: Report of Warren H. Manning to the City Commission," December 1916. Courtesy Birmingham Historical Society.

ing approximately one-eighth of the future city's land, would also include "aeroplane landings."

Manning delineated routes for 120-foot-wide valley thoroughfares, along with cross-valley and ridge roads. He mapped circuit drives throughout the "mountains, hills, valleys, streams, remarkable springs, [and] high bluffs along the Warrior River," in an area characterized by a "great variety of attractive plant growth and many villages." For people who could choose to live outside the city, residential districts with "estates of the country-loving and well-to-do" were recommended for nearby mountain ridges, close to wooded bluffs and other land unsuitable for cultivation that might be acquired for public reservations.[2] Roads were also to be extended along creeks to the Warrior River, where Manning recommended building port facilities as well as residences and recreational areas. The plan noted with concern more than one hundred grade-level railroad crossings that were increasingly dangerous to both pedestrian and automobile traffic.

Manning's plan documented the region's liberal supply of rail transportation facilities (nine trunk and two local lines), power rates lower than those of almost any U.S. city, a superb location for future national automobile routes, the ability to supply low-cost pig iron to a third of the U.S. market, and an "attractive all-the-year climate." He also noted his preference for multiple "civic centers" rather than the City Beautiful groups of public buildings around a single park space, those "very large and very expensive civic centers such as that at Cleveland, Ohio."[3]

As Manning noted in his autobiography, however, "no action was taken by the city in executing these plans."[4] Indeed, the City of Birmingham took no immediate action to extend its boundary or to buy lands then owned by the industrial corporations for roads and reservations.

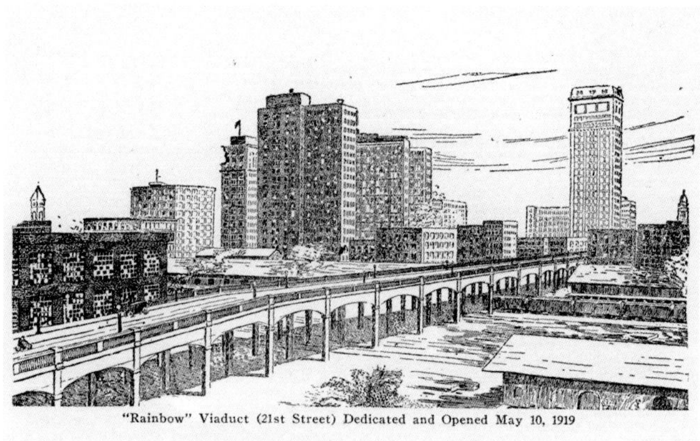
"Rainbow" Viaduct (21st Street) Dedicated and Opened May 10, 1919

The first of many viaducts built to increase the city's water supply. Several were constructed during the 1930s. "'Rainbow' Viaduct (21st Street)." *Warren H. Manning's City Plan of Birmingham*, 39.

In 1916 the city had perhaps the lowest tax rate in the nation and was burdened by debt after annexing several of the surrounding suburbs, a political reality that also led to the loss of the enlightened leadership of George Ward in the 1917 election.

But "no action" does not mean that nothing came of the Manning plan. By 1919, when local civic leaders published the plan, they included images of the proposed Warrior River port facility, still operating today at Port Birmingham, and a completed concrete viaduct, the first of many viaducts and underpasses that would be built in the Birmingham city center in the 1930s to eliminate grade-level crossings. When federal highways were built, they followed routes projected by Manning. City engineers were still trying to build his proposed Red Mountain tunnel to link the Birmingham city center with its southern suburbs in the late 1950s. The proposed Warrior River residential districts are being developed today.

Curiously, in view of Manning's denigration of large civic centers, the published plan also envisions a civic center with classically styled municipal and cultural facilities grouped around a park. City bond issues and federal funds made

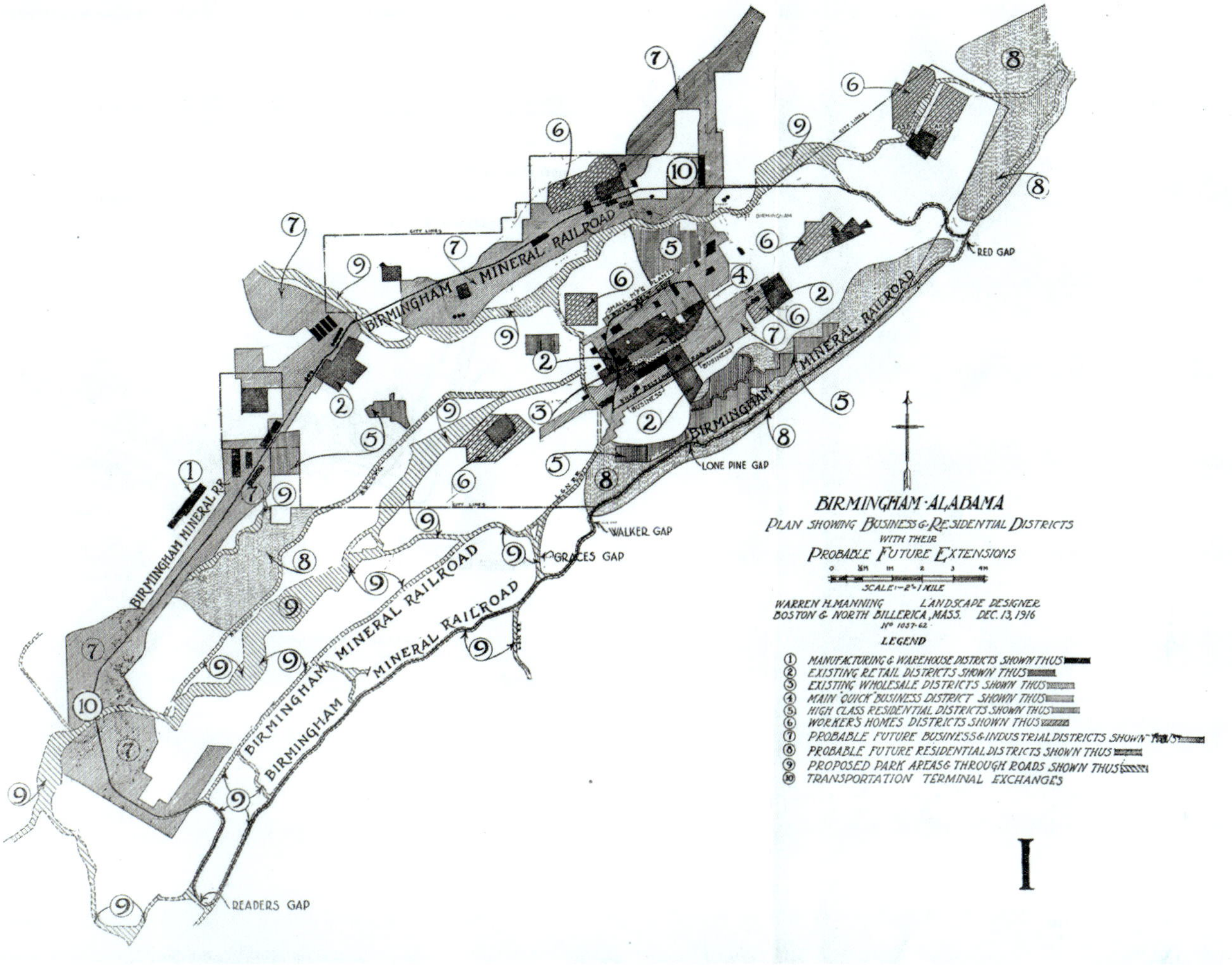

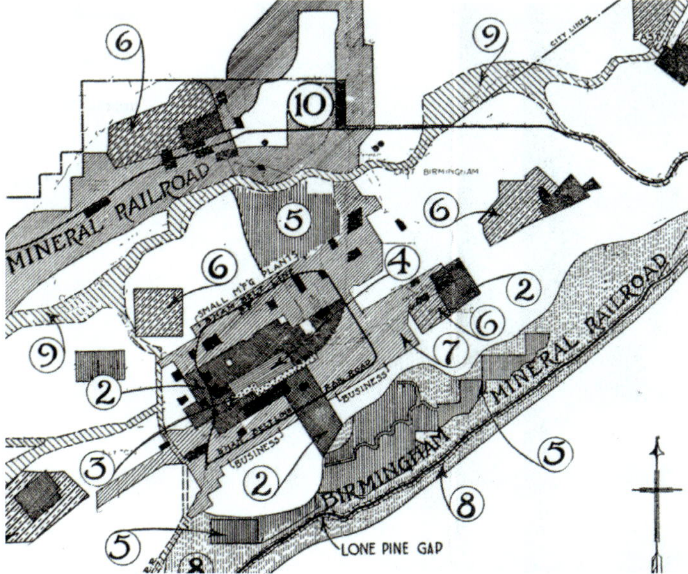

ABOVE: Proposed expansion of the city included a sprawling park and parkway system (areas labeled "9" on the plan). LEFT: (detail) Note the winding course of the proposed park system and its relationship to the various natural gaps. "Plan showing Business & Residential Districts," plan no. 1057-62 from "The Birmingham District Plan." Courtesy Birmingham Historical Society.

available during the late 1920s and the Great Depression supported major improvements not only to grade-level crossings and roads, but also to schools, parks, and playgrounds, and the building of the monumental civic center around today's Linn Park in the downtown area.

In 1924 and 1925, the city retained the Olmsted Brothers firm to plan a park system for Birmingham. The Olmsted plan also recommended vast reservations of public lands along area creeks and mountain ridges. Together with the Manning plan, it continues to provide vision for the acquisition of land and development of parks in the region, where industrial corporations have only recently relinquished ownership of mineral lands.

From 1925 to 1929, Manning returned often to Birmingham to plan the residential development of more than four thousand acres of mountain ridges and valleys lying to the south of the city, an area identified as Red Mountain Reservation in the 1916 plan. His client for the development of Mountain Brook Estates was Robert Jemison Jr., an enlightened and effective developer. Jemison's father had consolidated Birmingham's street railway system and power interests and sold them to the company that became American Cities, the initial client that fostered Manning's Birmingham legacy.[5]

Mountain Brook Estates

MOUNTAIN BROOK, ALABAMA

MARJORIE LONGENECKER WHITE

Reverence for place was central in Warren Manning's approach to developing the residential subdivision of Mountain Brook Estates, south of Birmingham. Identified as "Red Mountain Reservation" in Manning's 1916 district plan, this geographically isolated stretch of ridge and valley lands extends southwest from Red Mountain to Shades Valley and Shades Mountain. His final plan for Mountain Brook, completed in 1929, was designed to showcase the distinctive features of the natural environment—its streams, cliffs, bluffs, hogback ridges, ancient trees, ravines, ridge ponds, springs, rock formations, and views—and to create a subdivision in harmony with these surroundings, a parklike setting for suburban living. Strategies to protect the natural beauty of the landscape included aligning roads and lots with topographic features, reserving floodplains along creeks for scenic value, setting aside areas for recreational use and stormwater management, and using native plants and local materials where possible.

Manning began planning the subdivision in September 1926. Over three years, and through many revisions, he worked out the siting and grading of the roads, open space, and house lots by tramping about in the woods. Among those with him on the planning team were his on-site landscape architect, Carl Lutender, and William Kessler, a Birmingham landscape architect and horticulturalist. By March 1929, Manning had completed a plan that included roads and bridges, residential lots, open-space reservations and deed restrictions, and other community facilities and amenities—a village center, school, riding academy and bridle trails, and a country club as a focal point for the subdivision.[1] Manning associate Egbert Hans, although he apparently never visited the site, drew illustrations and wrote articles, including "The Naturalistic Development of Mountain Brook Estates," published in *American Landscape Architect* in January 1930.

To set the architectural tone for the new residential community, Manning suggested a model country house—a replica of George Washington's Mount Vernon estate, complete with an "Old

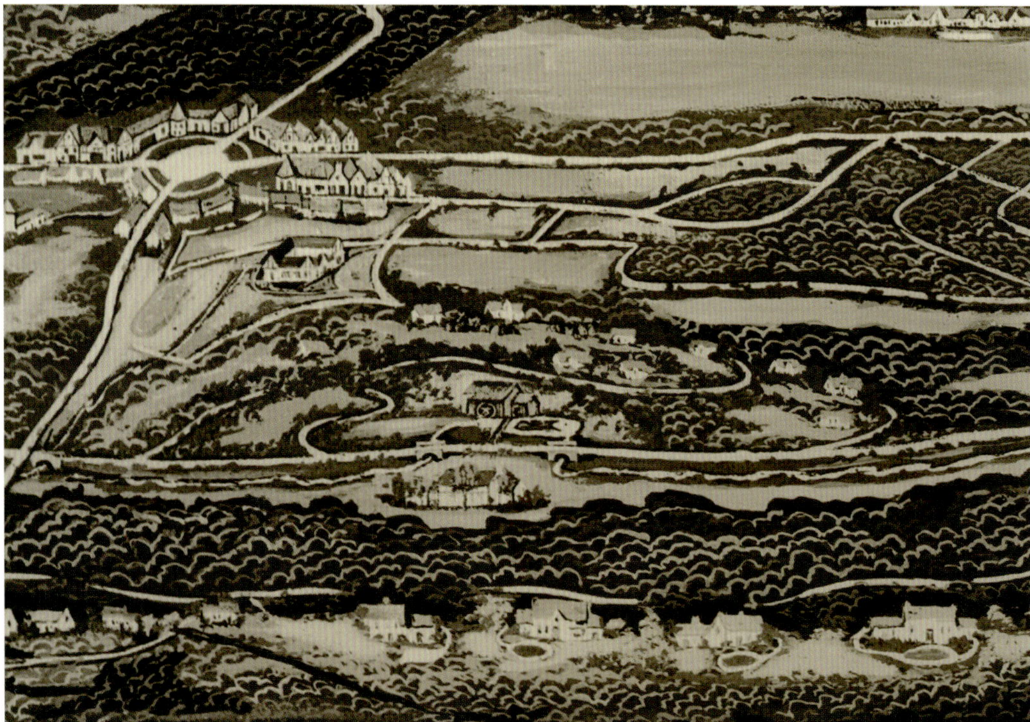

TOP: In this bird's-eye view, Mountain Brook Estates lies in the foreground with the city of Birmingham in the distance. BOTTOM: Several features of the development are recognizable in this detail: the cluster of village shops (upper left) and the replica of Mount Vernon and the Old Mill (center). "Properties of Mountain Brook Land Company & Associates," photographic print of a drawing by Egbert Hans, January 1929. Courtesy Birmingham Public Library.

Mill," which was soon opened to the public as a tea room. Manning designed the setting, gardens, and planting plans, while Kessler drew plans for the Old Mill, which followed in the tradition of the Rock Creek Mill in Rock Creek Park, Washington, D.C., and also took cues from Manning's seventeenth-century family manse near Reading, Massachusetts. The architect Aymar Embury II designed the clubhouse at the Mountain Brook Country Club, and the renowned golf-course architect Donald Ross laid out the eighteen-hole course.[2] Leading local architectural firms drew plans for the subdivision's Tudor Village, riding academy, and school, as well as for model houses in a variety of architectural styles.[3]

The road layout followed the contours of the site, favoring curves and keeping straightaways to a minimum in order to reveal the landscape gradually, in a series of striking views. The banks were planted and graded to slope back from the road edge to ensure visibility. Wooden street signs and stone entrance gates and bridges, both using local materials, continued the naturalistic aesthetic. William Kessler designed the bridges and planting plans for the parkway and entrance gates, and he also sited drives to the house lots.

The development, which comprised about four thousand acres, was twenty times larger than other developments in the area and on its way to becoming a regional showplace when the stock market crashed in 1929. Soon home sales fell and construction in Mountain Brook halted. Although the infrastructure, amenities, and several houses had been built by then, and the subdivision was incorporated as the City of Mountain

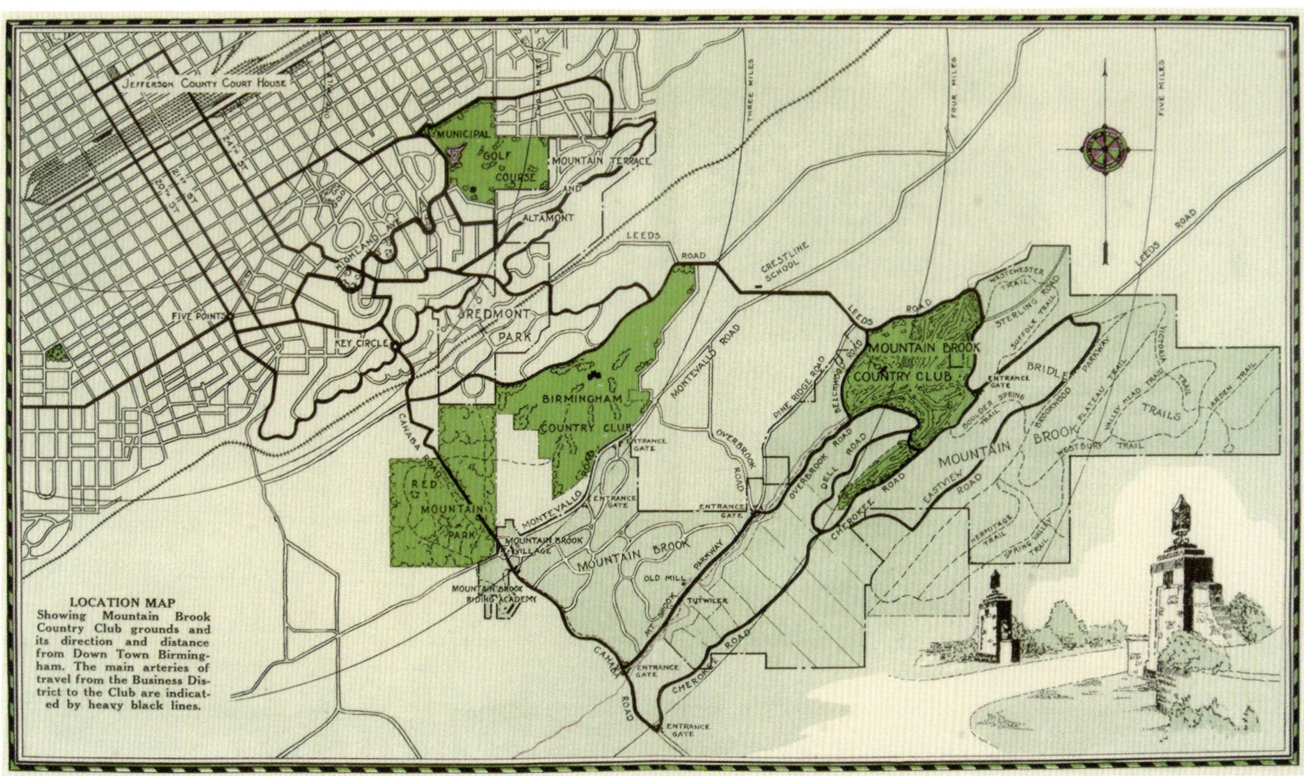

Manning's layout for Mountain Brook Country Club responded to the variable terrain, providing views for residents and car passengers. "Location Map," 1927. Courtesy Birmingham Public Library Archives.

The first house constructed in the suburb was a replica of George Washington's Mount Vernon, a reflection of the patriotic fervor of the 1920s. Photograph by Carol Betsch, 2012.

The Old Mill was inspired by the Manning Manse, Manning's ancestral homestead in North Billerica, Mass. Photograph by Carol Betsch, 2012.

The sinuous course of the entry drive to Mountain Brook Country Club winds across rolling lawns, which also emphasize variations in the lay of the land. Photograph by Carol Betsch, 2012.

Many of the residential driveways in the development were set below grade so they would not interrupt the lawns that coalesce into a unified, parklike landscape. Photograph by Carol Betsch, 2012.

Houses such as this Tudor-inspired residence achieve a quiet grandeur by virtue of the scale of the larger setting. Photograph by Carol Betsch, 2012.

Streams and walking trails wind through Mountain Brook Estates. Photograph by Carol Betsch, 2012.

The setting sun catches the slope of Shades Mountain. Photograph by Carol Betsch, 2012.

Brook in 1942, construction did not resume until the 1950s.

Mountain Brook has grown beyond Mountain Brook Estates, but the original subdivision retains a high level of historical integrity, and the National Park Service has included the community in its Historic American Landscapes Survey. The road system Manning designed is still intact. As it approaches the residential areas, Mountain Brook Parkway appears to wind through a sequence of historical scenes—from the Tudor Village and Mount Vernon estate to the Old Mill—before reaching the Mountain Brook Club and golf course and ending at Irondale Furnace Park. The route follows a creek, and viewsheds gradually widen along the major floodplain, in which Manning laid out a linear park (since extended and named Jemison Park). On the surrounding ridges and knolls, roads meander throughout the residential community, where the heavily wooded landscape suggests an idyllic retreat. The original green corridor now enjoys a wider woodland buffer as an indirect result of the 1929 crash. Deed restrictions had been placed on the adjoining estate-sized lots (thirty-five to sixty acres), which extend from the creek up the face of Shades Mountain. Manning envisioned these as homesites for Jemison's investors in the Mountain Brook venture, but the market collapsed before anything was built. The original deed restrictions, however, still protect the land around Jemison Park from development, creating a green open space at the community's core.

Warren Town Plan

WARREN, ARIZONA

TERRI ROCHON

Copper mining in the southern mountains of Arizona began in the 1880s, and the state soon became a national leader in the industry. By 1905 the Calumet & Arizona Mining Company of Calumet, Michigan, and Bisbee, Arizona, employed a thousand men in its Warren District mines.[1] Seeking to improve living conditions and foster a permanent work force, the company elected to build a town for its employees and created the Warren Realty and Development Company to oversee its development. In the spirit of the City Beautiful movement, the new company town was to provide modern facilities, recreation and entertainment, convenient transportation, affordable housing, and an attractive setting.[2] The company engaged Warren Manning to design the town plan in 1906. Manning, the architect Huger Elliott, and engineer R. A. Applegarth were retained to develop a comprehensive scheme that included the streetscape, architecture, and infrastructure.

Manning had become involved in planning company towns in Michigan's Upper Peninsula—Munising and Ishpeming—and developing the existing community of Marquette. He would soon begin others in that region: Gwinn, Negaunee, and North Lake. These Michigan projects were commissioned by Cleveland-Cliffs Iron Company, owned by William G. Mather of Cleveland.

The new townsite in Arizona was three miles southeast of Bisbee, in a shallow valley with views south to the mountains of nearby Mexico. The El Paso & Southwestern Railroad passed through the valley, and the surrounding hills were free of mining tunnels. Manning's design, while incorporating the geometric layout typical of City Beautiful planning, used the site's natural topography to make the most of views, drainage, interior circulation, and connection to the outer landscape. The town centered on a park Manning called "The Vista" (now Vista Park), a 160-foot-wide linear tract that extended from the northern edge of the valley to an opening in the hills to the south, which was the lowest-lying part of town. Two major

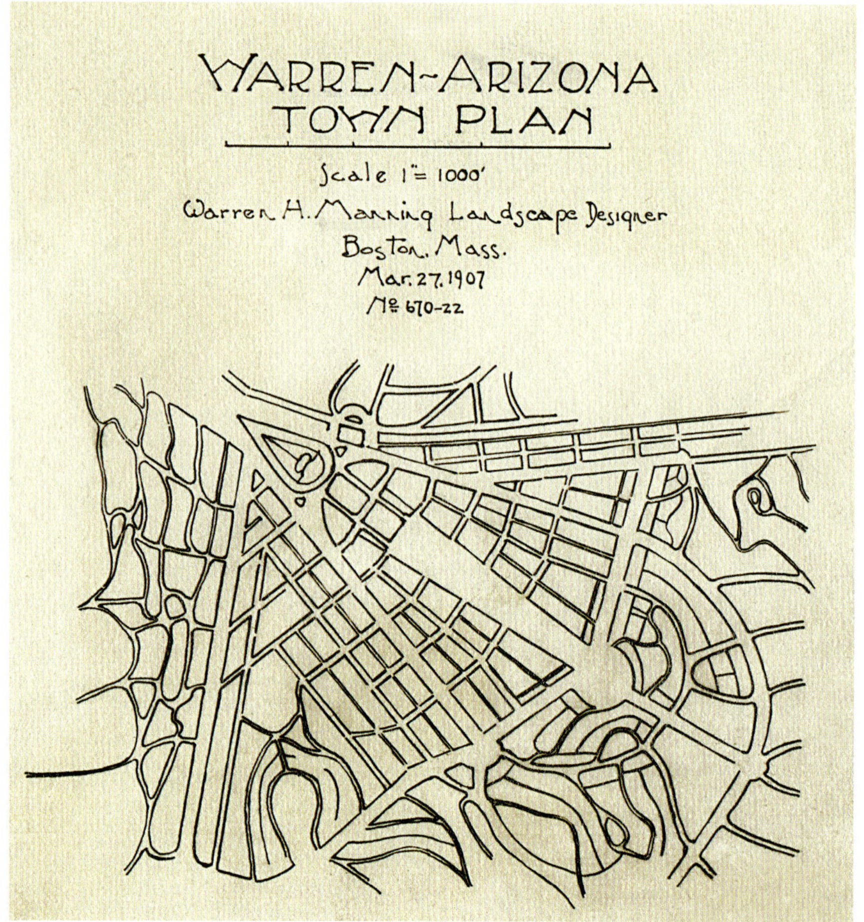

Manning's plan integrated a Beaux-Arts system of streets and parks with his own response to the varied topography of the site and the mountain views from it. "Warren – Arizona, Town Plan," plan no. 670-22, March 1907. Courtesy MPI.

avenues, Arizona and Douglas, extended from the southern terminus of the park and aligned with the natural drainage channels of the valley. A grid of residential streets connected the main avenues. At the upper end of the development the axial streets ended at a winding perimeter road that defined the town and set it apart from the desert landscape beyond. A civic plaza dominated the southern end of the park, and an aqueduct spanned the gap in the hills.[3]

The main business and parkside streets were planned as boulevards with planting strips and deep setbacks. The design addressed water runoff, a crucial issue in a desert lowland prone to flash floods, with cement channels bordering the streets and in alleys between the houses. Arizona Street, to the east of Vista Park, was designated the shopping and entertainment district. The road from Bisbee entered the town on Douglas Street, and Manning located the commercial district there. The new trolley line was to run from the town of Bisbee down Douglas Street, along the southern edge of the park, and up Arizona Street. The clients had specified Spanish Colonial and Pueblo style architecture, and Elliott designed public buildings and residences with stucco-and-tile towers, arcades, and courtyards. The residential areas were to be developed in stages, with the houses of the company officials clustered at the upper end of the park and the miners' cottages below. The realty company representatives requested a palette of local plants that included tree and globe cactus, agave, and yucca, and Manning planned to arrange these for color-gradation effects and to create hedging, ground cover, and shade. Through a system of pipes and flumes, water from the Bisbee mines was gravity-fed to the citizens of Warren. This "copper water" provided free irrigation for gardens and trees. In Elliott's words, the idea was to create a city that would give "miner and mine-owner alike a chance to live in decent surroundings . . . , where the excellence of the sanitary conditions and utilitarian requirements would be equaled by the artistic arrangement of vistas, streets, and public buildings."[4]

The park, main streets, commercial districts, utilities, and trolley line were built and located as designed. Main public buildings were constructed in Spanish Colonial, Pueblo, or Italianate style. Residential development began with the streets east of Vista Park, and the majority of houses in this area were built in the California Bungalow style. The plaza and aqueduct were never realized, and in 1909 the Warren Baseball Park was built on the proposed plaza site. In 1911 Manning was consulted for a planting plan for the southern end of Vista Park, his final official work for Warren.[5] Soon afterward a dance pavilion and swimming pool were built in the park. The Warren Realty Company, now under the management of the Phelps Dodge Mining Company, developed the remaining residential areas, called the Second and Third Additions, in 1916 and 1918. Phelps Dodge employed a company architect, J. A. Holden, to supervise construction in the Third Addition.[6]

Declining copper prices in the 1930s stalled the development of the townsite, and little new construction has taken place since then. By the early 1950s bus service had replaced the trolley line from Bisbee, and Warren roads were extended to neighboring communities. Mine Dump No. 7, located north of town, became the repository for waste from Bisbee's Lavender Pit Mine.

Warren continues to function as a support community for Bisbee, now a haven for retirees

In this aerial view, transportation corridors and Vista Park are clearly visible. Photograph, n.d. Courtesy Bisbee Mining and Historical Museum.

None of the buildings featured in this idealized rendering of the future town of Warren were built at the time it was published; many were never realized. Rendering by Huger Elliott. *Architectural Review* 15 (September 1908).

and artists and a tourist destination for its western and mining history. Other towns have grown around Bisbee, but only Warren exhibits the characteristics of a planned community. The townsite retains the main elements of its original design: Vista Park, the radiating avenues and grid of residential streets, the perimeter road and neighborhoods, and the drainage channels. Many of the buildings have been adapted for reuse, and Arizona and Douglas Streets see a small amount of business activity. The main road to Bisbee now leaves Warren from the Third Addition neighborhood, west of the original connecting road. The presence of Mine Dump No. 7 serves as a backdrop for the grand houses at the head of the park and has prevented further development beyond the perimeter road. Vista Park contains areas of open natural landscape as well as tennis courts and playgrounds. The original streetside planting strips are now used for parking space. The ball park, used by the local high school team, is the oldest in Arizona.[7] The view south to the mountains of Mexico, some fifty miles distant, remains intact.

Alfred A. Pope Estate (Hill-Stead)

FARMINGTON, CONNECTICUT

MARGARET CARPENTER

In 1898 the Ohio industrialist Alfred Atmore Pope and his wife, Ada Brooks Pope, purchased 250 acres of contiguous farmland in Farmington, Connecticut, for an estate where they planned to retire.[1] The Popes undertook the project with the keen involvement of their daughter and only child, Theodate, who would go on to have a successful career as an architect, joining the American Institute of Architects in 1918 under her married name, Theodate Pope Riddle.[2]

From the beginning, Hill-Stead, "a great new house on a hilltop," as the Popes' occasional guest Henry James described it in *The American Scene,* communicated grandeur and permanence.[3] Completed in 1901, the estate lay on a hillside skirting the Farmington River floodplain. The land comprised rolling pastures and meadows, woods, a stream, and wetlands. Theodate Pope designed the rambling, 33,000-square-foot Colonial Revival house—her second architectural project—with Egerton Swartwout, an associate architect at McKim, Mead & White.[4] Although no plans for the Hill-Stead landscape have been found, Warren Manning offered on-site consultation to Theodate in 1896 and 1898, and possibly on other occasions. In a letter to Theodate dated September 1898, her father urged her to "go ahead with road making—wall building and tree planting this autumn taking the advice of Mr. Manning in so doing, if he is the best one to consult."[5]

Hallmarks of Manning's design appear in the landscape's organization, as well as in some of its details. The house is located at the property's highest point, taking in views of Metacomet Ridge. The curving drive, flanked by prominent rustic fieldstone walls and an allée of maples that emphasize the land's hilly contours, ascends a gradual slope and creates a dramatic sense of arrival. Mature elms planted in front establish the domestic landscape. Beyond the house, the plan made graceful provisions for a productive dairy farm, a sheep meadow, an orchard, a pond, a tennis court, a six-hole golf course for Theodate's father, a formal perennial garden with summerhouse, a kitchen and

View toward north end of the large house and barn. The pond was created in consultation with Manning to provide a water view. Theodate Pope was likely inspired to add the feature by developments at nearby Tranquillity Farm, which overlooked Lake Quassapaug. Photograph, n.d. Courtesy Hill-Stead Museum.

cutting garden, greenhouses, and a wild garden (also called the Walking Garden).[6] The arrangement of these functional areas, as well as the layout of roads and drives, is straightforward and harmonious.

Hill-Stead's wild garden—a quarter-acre of naturalistic plantings bordering the entry drive and surrounded by stone walls—is one feature in particular that suggests Manning's influence. Such gardens were not unique to Manning, but he used them often, in part to create a transition from the intensively cultivated areas near the house to more expansive and distant spaces. Archival photographs of Hill-Stead's wild garden show paths winding through patches of dense shade and sunny expanses of lush grass. To create a wild appearance, ground cover and other garden plants—including ferns, artemesia, vinca, phlox, day lilies, and hosta—were allowed to spread. Shrubs, such as rhododendron, azalea, spice bush, and leucothoe, were selected for texture and multiseasonal interest, and the canopy of hardwood trees, bolstered by spruce and white pine, provided shade.[7] Manning's influence is also discernable in the pond that was created by damming the small stream in the late 1890s. Theodate's close relationship with the Whittemore family, who summered in nearby Middlebury, may have played a role in this feature. The new pond provided the same sort of viewshed as Lake Quassapaug did for the Whittemore mansion, albeit on a much smaller scale.

When Theodate died in 1946, the house and property were converted into a museum, as directed in her will. During the next four decades, the museum's board of governors concentrated on keeping the house open for visi-

View toward barn, with self-sown plantings at the pond edge. Photograph by Carol Betsch, 2015.

View toward pond, now obscured by trees and shrubbery at its edge. Photograph by Carol Betsch, 2015.

Hill-Stead's Sunken Garden, with its cobblestone walls, may also have been inspired by landscape developments at Tranquillity Farm, whose plan was begun in 1893, five years before Theodate Pope began her design for Hill-Stead. Photograph by Carol Betsch, 2015.

tors, and owing to a lack of funds, did minimal maintenance on the landscape. In the mid-1980s, two local garden clubs funded the reconstruction of the Sunken Garden, and during the process an undated planting plan for the garden by Beatrix Farrand came to light to guide the project.[8] Members of the Garden Club of Hartford and the Connecticut Valley Garden Club commissioned the landscape architect Shavaun Towers, of Rolland/Towers in New Haven, to reconstruct the Sunken Garden. Hill-Stead was named a National Historic Landmark in 1991.

John H. Whittemore Estate (Tranquillity Farm)

MIDDLEBURY, CONNECTICUT

ROBIN KARSON

Born in Southbury, Connecticut, John Howard Whittemore grew up in the lush countryside west of Hartford, where he spent much of his childhood exploring the shores of Lake Quassapaug.[1] After working briefly for a brokerage firm in New York City, Whittemore returned to settle in nearby Naugatuck and there founded a malleable iron company. In time, the robust boom in railroads, coupled with Whittemore's prescient real estate investments, made him one of the state's wealthiest citizens. He would use his wealth to underwrite a large number of civic projects in Naugatuck and Middlebury, approximately twenty of which involved Warren Manning.[2] In Middlebury he would also build a country estate, Tranquillity Farm.

The project began in July 1893, when Whittemore wrote to Charles Eliot, then a partner in the firm of Olmsted, Olmsted & Eliot, about a "model farm" he proposed to develop on about three hundred acres of recently purchased farmland.[3] Eliot set up a meeting a few weeks later, and by August 29 a rough sketch of the estate layout was in hand. Eliot had heeded Whittemore's request to avoid the expense of a large lawn and to create a scheme in which the farm would dominate. Within a month the firm had prepared a list of trees and shrubs, and by November Whittemore had received several shipments of plants. Simultaneously, Whittemore was commissioning a house for the new estate from McKim, Mead & White, who had designed the family's Naugatuck home in 1888, along with several schools and libraries for the town.[4]

The large Shingle style structure was sited opposite the juncture of what are now Whittemore and Tranquillity Roads. These converging roads divided the property roughly in two; the house, farm, and its environs are on the west side and a wooded hill sits to the east. This was an unusual location for a large house, which was typically sited far from the public way, revealed at the end of a long, curving approach. But this placement did provide the best view of Lake Quassapaug, the scenic centerpiece of the arrangement.

Whittemore proved a meticulous adminis-

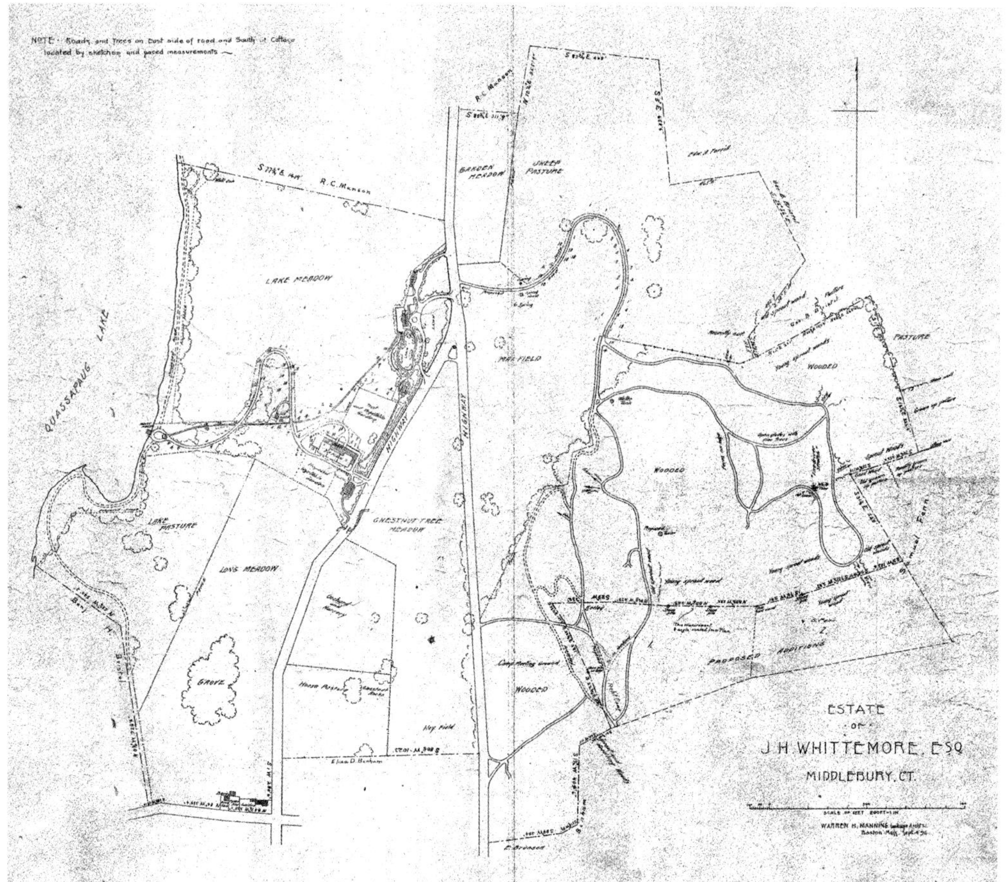

Created one year after Manning took over the project from the Olmsted firm, the 1896 plan shows the house in relation to Lake Quassapaug and the woodlands across the road (now Whittemore Road). "Estate of J. H. Whittmore, Esq.," September 1896. Whittemore family papers.

trator who daily checked invoices from nurseries and contractors and wrote in detail about every aspect of his new initiative. His concise letters to the Olmsted firm reflect growing impatience with both the progress and the budget of the project. References to meetings with John Charles Olmsted and, by 1895, Warren Manning as well as Eliot, indicate that all three men were involved in aspects of the model farm design.[5]

A particularly irate letter from Whittemore to the Olmsted firm on January 1, 1896, lists several complaints regarding charges for visits, grading plans, and planting supervision. After one last, brief note from Whittemore in May of that year, correspondence with the Olmsted firm ceases, and a new stream of letters begins, addressed solely to Manning, who had in the meantime set up an independent business in Boston. With this switch, the tenor of Whittemore's correspondence softens and includes many congenial references to meetings on the site and matters not directly related to Whittemore's projects—such as Manning's recent visit to Hill-Stead, the home of Theodate Pope, in nearby Farmington.[6]

The letters also record an expansion of Manning's role beyond planting and an expansion of the project itself, as the landscape architect urged Whittemore to acquire more property—to protect views and enlarge his woods—and to create new roads and paths.[7] Initially, Whittemore resisted these suggestions, but over time, many of them were implemented.[8] A comprehensive plan created by Manning in September 1896, accompanied by a lengthy memo, marked the new phase of the project.[9] In the 1896 plan, many of the meadows and pastures are named (Chestnut Tree Meadow, Lake Meadow, Sheep Pasture, etc.), as was Manning's custom. From the house, broad meadows defined by hedgerows and stands of trees sloped down to the lake, providing panoramic views of the water and the wooded hills beyond.

According to Manning's recollections, the formal garden, sited below the cobblestone retaining wall not visible in the lake view, was completed in 1897. About the same time, a long flight of steps to the lake surrounded by an idealized woodland was created. A year later, new roads were constructed to take visitors through the wooded parcel to the east. In 1903 a new rose garden was created on the south end of the formal garden. A perennial garden, known as the "long

The level of Lake Quassapaug was raised in the late 1890s, reportedly to increase its prominence in the view from Tranquillity Farm. A variety of crops were raised in the fields in the middle view. Photograph courtesy Thyrza Whittemore.

Prospect from the house terrace. The young boy is Robert Whittemore, J. H. Whittemore's grandson. The gardens were redesigned by Ellen Shipman in 1923. Photograph by Arthur G. Eldredge, 1928. Courtesy MCL.

The women of the Whittemore family (Julia, far right, Gertrude, center) are seen on the stone steps that led from the house. Photograph courtesy Thyrza Whittemore.

garden" and used primarily for cutting flowers for house arrangements, was sited parallel to and near the main road, south of the house. In 1904 a large outdoor fireplace of local stone was constructed in the woods, near the hilltop. A road bordered with fruit-bearing shrubs and trees was built leading from the farm buildings to a boat landing on the lake shore.[10] During these early years, several miles of stone walls were built to line the roadsides, tracing the rise and fall of the rolling land, and a small classically styled boathouse was added to the lake shore. Old photographs record a landscape of varied, subtle beauty.

The trellis frames a view to the sundial in the center of the rose garden. Photograph by Arthur G. Eldredge, 1928. Courtesy MCL.

Many of the landscape improvements were made under the direction of William Martin Shepardson, the property superintendent, but Manning continued to send detailed instructions to thicken existing plantings and to create new ones, one of which was an arboretum of native trees and shrubs for the woods. Whittemore's wife, Julia Spencer Whittemore, was consulted on plantings for the formal gardens, and she also worked with Manning to select plantings for the schools and the library the family was commissioning.[11]

Beginning in 1890 and guided largely by the couple's son, Harris Whittemore, the family

View to the lake over the original birdbath, with 2014 plantings by Thyrza Whittemore, J. H. Whittemore's great-great-granddaughter. Photograph by Carol Betsch, 2015.

View south along the garden wall. Photograph by Carol Betsch, 2009.

View southwest, with 2014 plantings by Thyrza Whittemore. Photograph by Carol Betsch, 2015.

Manning's plantings for the steps to the lake were characteristic of his wild gardens, combining native trees, shrubs, and ferns with imported plants. Photograph by Arthur G. Eldredge, 1928. Courtesy MCL.

amassed one of the largest and most important private collections of Impressionist paintings in America. (In this respect, the Whittemores resembled the Popes of Hill-Stead, in nearby Farmington, who were also avidly collecting such works.) Splendid canvases by Monet, Degas, Whistler, and others were displayed throughout the house.[12] At a time when many wealthy Americans looked to their architects for guidance in furnishings, the unusually sophisticated taste of the Whittemores was evident throughout Tranquillity Farm, indoors as well as out.

After Harris's death in 1927, the estate was subdivided into several large parcels according to a plan commissioned from Manning. Several family members built new homes on the property to the east.[13] In 1985 family descendants made the unusual but effective decision to sell and disassemble the large main house, parts of which were then moved to a site in Westchester County, a resolution that essentially privileged the landscape design over the architecture.[14]

Tranquillity Farm, which was named to the National Register of Historic Places in 1982, remains a remarkably intact example of a late nineteenth–early twentieth-century landscape. The stone walls and brick paths survive, and many of the original trees have grown to great size. The pastures and meadows recorded on Manning's 1896 plan have been maintained according to their original layout. The carriage house is intact, as are the farm cottage, barn, creamery, boathouse, and several small outbuildings. The plantings in the formal garden, designed by Ellen Shipman in 1923, have been restored by Thyrza Whittemore, the great-great-granddaughter of J. H. Whittemore. Remarkably, visitors to Tranquillity Farm today are greeted by the same sense of country expanse that inspired Charles Eliot and Warren Manning when they first visited the place more than a century ago.[15]

Front entry gate, with stone walls constructed atop a ha-ha, which obscures the main road. Photograph by Carol Betsch, 2009.

The stone walls that demarcate the meadows, lawns, and roads of Tranquillity Farm have survived. The property was subdivided in the late 1920s and is now owned by several different individuals. Photograph by Carol Betsch, 2009.

In the 1960s the original McKim, Mead & White house was disassembled and moved to a site in Westchester County. The current owners of Tranquillity Farm reside in the restored carriage house and continue to maintain the core of the historic property. Photograph by Carol Betsch, 2015.

Athens City Plan

ATHENS, GEORGIA

KEVAN WILLIAMS

Warren Manning visited northeast Georgia a year before he developed his plan for the city of Athens. In August 1923 he traveled to Cornelia, forty miles north of Athens, to speak at the annual meeting of the Georgia State Agricultural and Horticultural Societies, where many Athenians were in attendance. A week later Manning arrived in Athens as "the guest of friends," and he spoke at the Chamber of Commerce about "parks, playgrounds, and beautifying a city." He described his experience converting stream valleys and steep ravines to parks in other cities and suggested that Athens offered similar opportunities. His priorities in park design, he said, included creating areas for recreation and enhancing civic beauty, as well as developing a "city transportation system that would relieve much of the growing traffic problem."[1]

A newspaper article reported that Manning was not in Athens "for any commercial purpose," but either Manning was very persuasive or efforts were already under way to bring him to the city in a professional capacity.[2] A year later, in June 1924, Dr. J. M. Reade, a professor of botany at the University of Georgia, who had introduced Manning's talk in Cornelia, gave a speech to the Athens Woman's Club. He spoke of the need for a botanical park and explained that the purpose of Manning's invitation to Athens was to "look the situation over." The discussion continued in Athens, and the Athens Planning and Zoning Committee was formed, raising the money necessary for Manning to develop a city plan. Manning returned to the city later that summer to begin work.[3]

In August Manning visited Athens for two weeks to perform an initial site inventory, inconspicuously surveying the land and counting trees with the assistance of local Boy Scouts while acquainting himself with the city and its residents.[4] In 1926 the plans were displayed in the chamber of commerce. There was interest, at least from the chamber, in starting "a movement to have the city plans adopted and made a part of the law."[5]

Manning himself noted the difficulties of

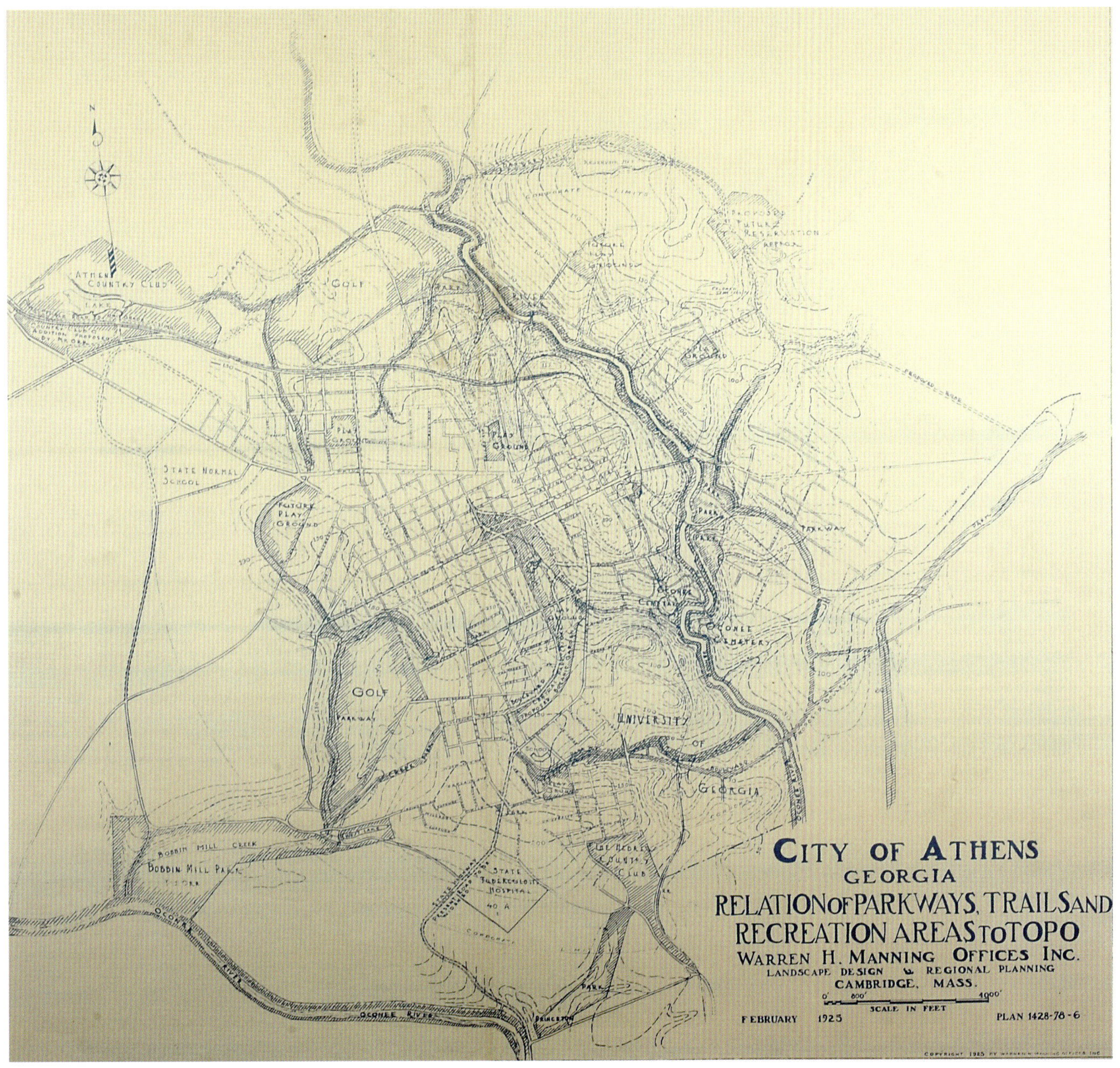

Manning's approach to city planning provided large expanses of park and recreation areas accessible throughout the city. Topography, settlement patterns, and transportation linkages were the dominant factors in locating parks. "Relation of Parkways, Trails and Recreation Areas to Topo," plan no. 1428-78-6, February 1925. Courtesy MPI.

implementing the plan, saying in his report: "I am informed by the City Treasurer that the city is near its bonding limit. Even if this were not so, I believe it is best not to put the city heavily in debt for a park system, especially as I have received sincere assurances from citizens that they are ready to give portions of their lands for this use."[6] This may have been an optimistic sentiment, or perhaps the city, in failing to implement the plan, never solicited land donations.

The recommendations Manning made in his first presentation took form in his final city plan. His comprehensive vision for Athens included parks, playgrounds, and trails; new streets and intersection realignments; zoning; and sewers. He lists several components as comprising the "purpose" of the plan, among them "to designate practicable opportunities for extending and connecting up main, radial, and circuit thoroughfares . . . , to provide large and small public reservations for the healthful recreation of all people, and especially to give children safe walks and playgrounds near their homes, along the running water of constant springs." Echoing Professor

Coordination of transportation byways and park and recreation areas was critical to public access. "Study for Trafficways, Parkways and Recreation Areas," plan no. 1428-77, May 1925. Courtesy MPI.

Reade's desire for a botanic park, he also hoped "to preserve and develop scenic beauty and attractive wild life, in such ways as to make Athens' reservations a laboratory for instructive study as well as for pleasure." Manning then presents his "general principles": traffic needs, public reservations, business centers, industrial regions and workers' homes, and private estates and institutions.[7]

Reade's requested botanic garden appears to be the centerpiece of the plan. Manning calls the long space, which wraps through the north and south branches of Tanyard Creek, a "Central

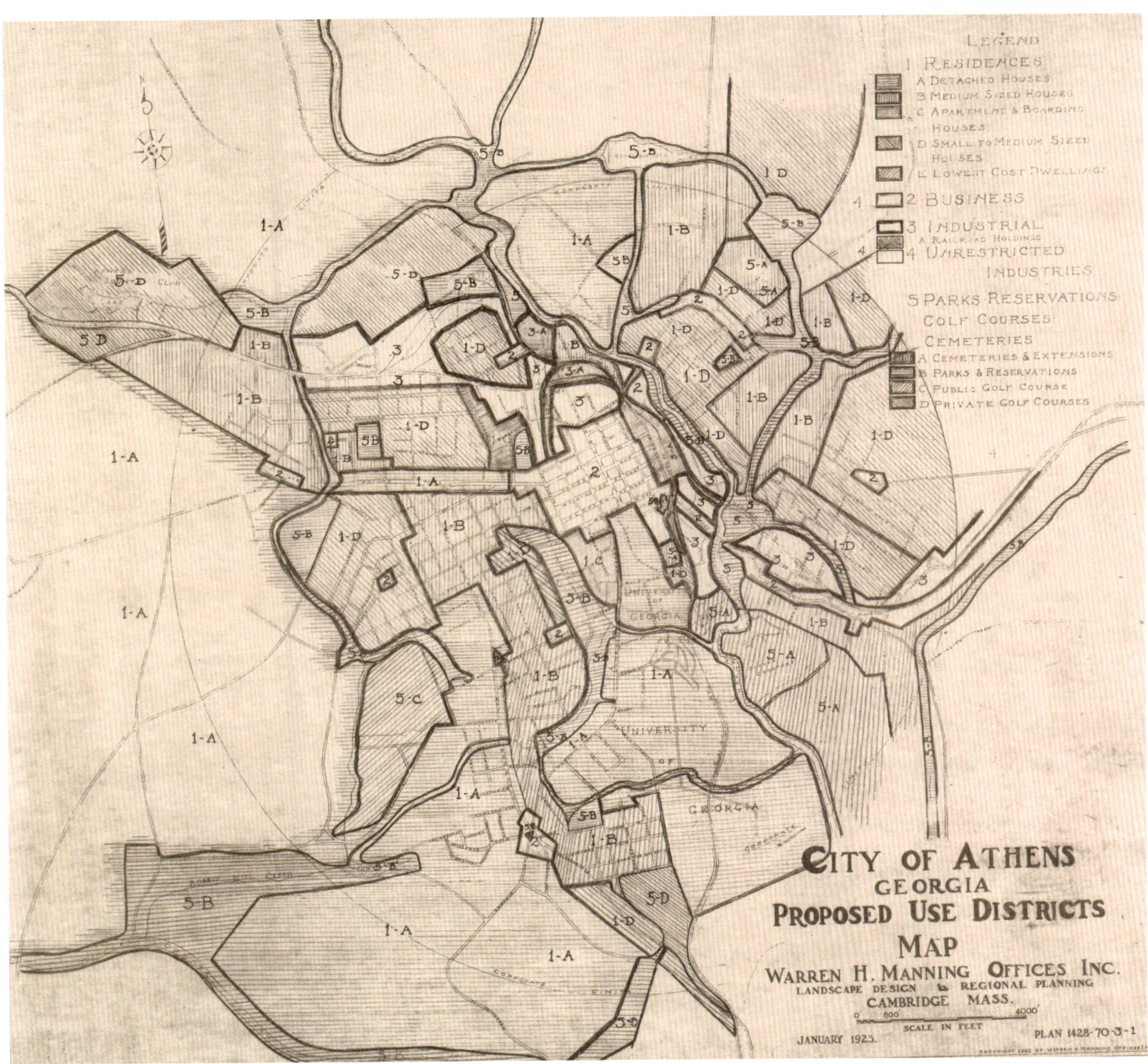

The depiction of a city plan according to zones of use resulted in a jigsaw puzzle–like arrangement of forms, here keyed to a legend that separated residential, business, industry, and park areas. "Proposed Use Districts Map," plan no. 1428-70-3-1, January 1925. Courtesy MCL.

Park." In addition to the garden, the Central Park also includes a playground. Numerous walkways radiate out and connect this space to parks along the North Oconee River and several creeks, and to other playgrounds Manning scattered throughout the city.

Another prominent element of the plan is a parkway-like "special traffic roadway" connecting manufacturing areas on the northern and southern ends of the city and wrapping along the eastern edge of the downtown along the river to dip under existing trestles, bridges, and underpasses. Many specific recommendations support this concept, which Manning illustrates with numerous photographs showing how certain intersections might be realigned to better accommodate the trafficway. He also proposes adjusting a number of streets surrounding the downtown to better interact with railroads in the area. In plan, these adjustments and the new curvilinear parkways are a stark contrast to the city's rectilinear grid.

Manning optimistically suggests that rights-of-way for the roadways be donated, with the assumption that rising land prices would offset the value of the land lost. His "continuous reservation" of parks and trails occurs primarily within ravines and floodplains that he likewise assumes will be donated and ultimately boost nearby property values.[8] He considers the clearing of these properties and the development of trails to be an easy step in the implementation of the larger plan. He also recommends asking volunteers to help with the studies necessary to carry out the plan, referring to the assistance provided by local Boy Scouts a year before.

Although little of Manning's plan appears to have been realized, the ideas it contained were remarkably prescient, and perhaps influential. A broad ring road roughly predicts the alignment

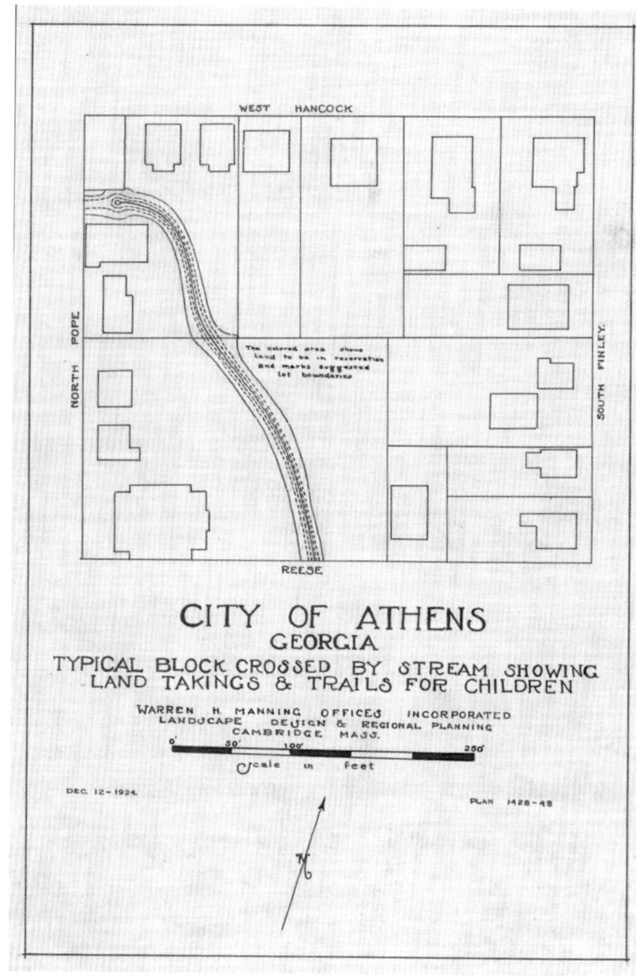

Manning often recommended laying out hiking trails along streams, which were to be reserved for public use even when they cut through private property. "Typical Block Crossed by Stream Showing Land Takings & Trails for Children," plan no. 1428-48, December 1924. Courtesy MPI.

of a divided highway bypass built half a century later, and one of the city's present wastewater treatment plants is sited near where Manning recommended "Sewage Purification Fields." Dudley Park, at the confluence of Trail Creek and the North Oconee River, occupies a site Manning recommended for a park.

Manning's trafficway "without grade railroad crossings from the southerly part of the city to connect with the business centers and with all its freightyards, to pass by the river front manufacturing plants, and on to the northerly manufacturing districts" has largely been realized, though it emerged incrementally, rather than in direct response to his plan.[9] Several reconfigurations of intersections over many decades produced a corridor that largely follows Manning's originally proposed alignment, although the industrial areas his trafficway would have linked no longer exist. The North Oconee River Greenway, the first phase of a larger network of multiuse paths resembling Manning's, runs adjacent to much of this corridor. Another of his proposed corridors is now a foot trail along Sandy Creek. Multiuse paths for Trail Creek, Brickyard Creek, and several other watercourses that Manning identified are in various stages of planning or development. These projects owe their establishment to the work of Charles Aguar, a professor of landscape architecture at the University of Georgia. Aguar, who began advocating for a linear park along the river in the 1970s, drew inspiration from Manning's 1925 city plan and is credited as the "father of the Greenway." A plaza dedicated to his memory occupies the spot that Manning proposed for "The Bluff Park."[10]

The large (30 x 38") plan, drawn to 1' = 300" scale, shows the road system Manning laid out for Mill Pond Plantation. The core of the 3,000-acre estate is visible at left. "Plan of Road System," plan no. 602-61, June 1905. Courtesy MPI.

Jeptha H. Wade Estate (Mill Pond Plantation)

THOMASVILLE, GEORGIA

STACI L. CATRON

In the winter of 1903, Jeptha Homer Wade II and his wife, Ellen Garretson Wade, purchased three thousand acres two miles south of Thomasville to serve as a hunting plantation.[1] The property was in the Red Hills region, which stretches from Thomasville to Tallahassee, Florida, and is home to approximately seventy hunting plantations, most established between 1890 and 1930. Wade, a successful financier, businessman, and philanthropist based in Cleveland, was enticed by the region's climate and abundant wildlife.

Wade commissioned Hubbell & Benes, a prominent Cleveland architectural firm, to design a Spanish Colonial Revival mansion and a complex of hunting lodges.[2] It is likely that Wade became acquainted with Warren Manning through Hubbell & Benes and may have known of his work at George Vanderbilt's Biltmore estate in Asheville, North Carolina, where Manning had been a planting assistant. Wade was also a business colleague of William G. Mather and served as vice president of Mather's Cleveland-Cliffs Iron Company, for which Mather had engaged Manning for work. Before Manning began designing the grounds, Wade was actively involved in preparing the site. He ordered the leveling of a hill to provide a clear view of an existing pond from the main house and requested that Manning create a series of gardens filled with roses, palms, poppies, dogwoods, crabapples, lilies, and tropical ferns and shrubs.[3]

Wade also charged Manning with analyzing and designing the land at large. In keeping with his resource-based design philosophy, in the fall of 1904 Manning developed a detailed survey of the area's topography, vegetation, woodlands, open fields, roads, streams, pond, and plantation-era cemetery.[4] He then drafted a plan for a road system that would respect the site. Manning particularly admired the longleaf pine woodlands and advised that they be left alone.[5] As a reminder of the region's history, Manning incorporated the two existing tree-lined dirt roads that meandered for almost a mile from the main road through longleaf pine forests and open fields. This arrival experience was enhanced by an entrance drive

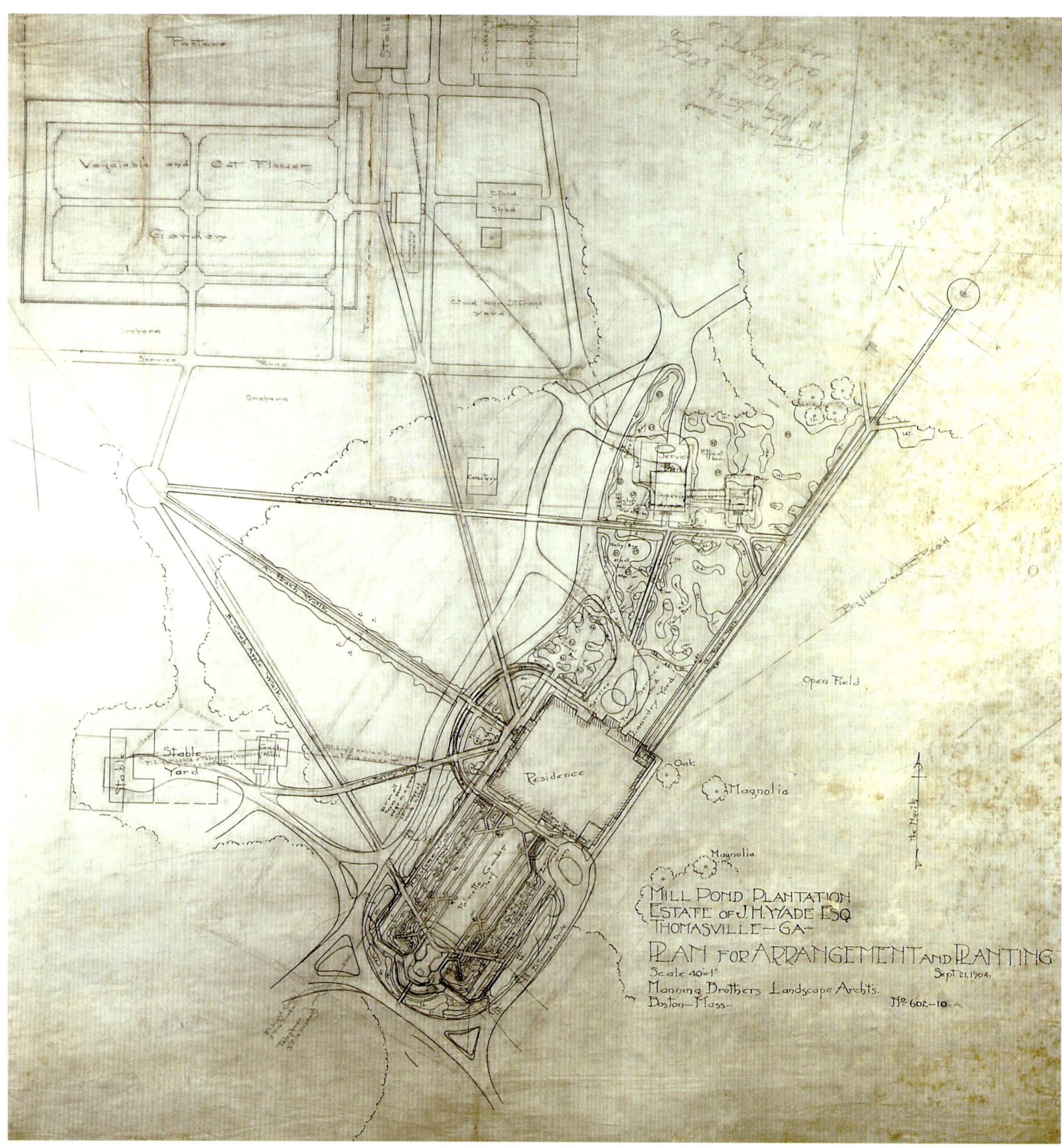

The landscape plan is structured by allées that fan out from the west (front) facade of the house. Plan no. 602-10, September 21, 1904. Courtesy MPI.

that brought visitors to the front of the main entrance on the mansion's south side.

Manning's design for indoor and outdoor spaces at Mill Pond estate created a cohesive composition of architecture and landscape. Inside the mansion, Manning designed the plantings for a 100-by-100-foot courtyard, onto which all of the first floor rooms opened. Roofed in steel and glass, the courtyard was divided into four quadrants, with a brick herringbone-patterned floor and a center pool and fountain beneath a large pergola covered in bougainvillea. Surrounded by arches adorned with creeping fig, the courtyard was filled with sago palms, banana shrubs, tea olives, cast iron plants, numerous varieties of camellia, English ivy, liriope, and many types of tropical flora.[6]

Outside, Manning covered the mansion in creeping fig, shaded it with live oaks, and surrounded it with elaborate gardens and walks. Just off the main entrance, a Spanish Colonial Revival style arbor covered in Chinese wisteria led to the Palm Garden. The center of this geometric, boxwood-lined garden, a long rectangle of turf, terminated in a large water basin surrounded by a variety of palms. Along both sides of the rectangle, a series of three boxwood-lined linear pathways terminated in diagonal paths leading to the outer edges of the Palm Garden. Manning filled the larger outermost beds, also edged in boxwood, with a variety of fragrant shrubs, camellias, and palms, identifying the outer pathways adjacent to these beds "perfume walks" for their fragrance.[7]

To the west of the mansion, Manning placed the Court Garden, a semicircular garden pierced with three diagonal pathways, each punctuated by a Spanish Colonial Revival style arbor covered in Chinese wisteria. He lined the four pie-shaped sections created by the pathways with boxwood, making for a striking view from the west patio. The axial path running next to the west side of the mansion led to a Spanish Colonial Revival pergola with yellow Lady Banks roses and a pink climbing rose. A garden of camellias was located next to the pergola.[8]

Manning also created a five-hundred-foot Rose Walk that extended from the porch on the mansion's north side to the woodlands. Garland posts covered with climbing roses bordered this long avenue. Diagonal paths led from the Palm Garden, the Court Garden, and the Rose Walk to a circular concrete pergola, also in the Spanish Colonial Revival style, called the Tea House. Pleached allées, each bordered with a different variety of fruit tree, defined these pathways. A tree-lined dirt road ran past the formal gardens to a complex of service buildings, where Manning planned a one-acre vegetable and cut flower garden.[9]

After 1903 Wade increased his holdings to almost ten thousand acres, enjoying the unique flora of the Red Hills region and hunting wild quail, turkey, dove, and deer with his family and friends. Since Wade's death in 1926, the property has remained in the hands of descendants. Photographs published in 1933 show the Palm Garden and Rose Walk thriving and the mansion draped in creeping fig and Chinese wisteria.[10] Mill Pond Plantation was added to the National Register of Historic Places in 1976, and in 1979 a portion of the land, a two-hundred-acre old-growth longleaf pine forest, known today as the Wade Tract Preserve, was placed in a conservation easement, the first of its kind in Georgia. Under the stewardship of the Wade descendants, the Sedgwick family, a conservation easement for Mill Pond Plantation is held by the New England Forestry Foundation to allow for consolidated oversight in caring for the land. Mill Pond is now under active

A rose walk extended five hundred feet from the porch on the mansion's north side to the woodland. Postcard, c. 1910. Courtesy Cherokee Garden Library, Kenan Research Center at the Atlanta History Center.

Guests arrived via a long entry drive leading to a wisteria-covered porch at the corner of the Spanish Colonial Revival style house. Postcard, c. 1910. Courtesy Cherokee Garden Library, Kenan Research Center at the Atlanta History Center.

The first floor rooms in the house open onto a glass-roofed courtyard, one hundred feet square. Photograph by Staci Catron, 2014.

The estate's largest garden, the Palm Garden, was bordered by "perfume walks" edged with fragrant shrubs, camellias, and palms. Photograph by Staci Catron, 2014.

management to encourage the growth and continued health of the longleaf pine forest.

Much of Manning's design remains today, including the Courtyard Garden, Palm Garden, and Court Garden, although some of the plants have changed. The Chinese wisteria that adorned the mansion was removed in the 1980s because it put strain on the tile roof. The allées of fruit trees were lost to the native forest, but the pathways to the tea house pergola remain. In the mid-1980s, the Rose Walk was removed, although the long pathway to the woodlands remains. Mill Pond Plantation continues to function as a private hunting plantation.

Stanley Field and Albert A. Sprague II Estates

LAKE BLUFF, ILLINOIS

JANE ROY BROWN

Warren Manning designed the adjacent estates of Stanley Field and Albert A. Sprague II on the shore of Lake Michigan between 1911 and 1914, when he was also working on two other estates nearby.[1] Between 1896 and 1928 Manning designed at least twenty-three country places for wealthy Chicagoans in the neighboring communities of Lake Forest and Lake Bluff, as well as redesigning the campus for Lake Forest College.

Field and Sprague were related by marriage, and both belonged to prominent Chicago mercantile families. Field was the nephew and business successor of the department store magnate Marshall Field and an executive at Marshall Field & Company, while Sprague served as president of his family's wholesale grocery business, Sprague, Warner & Company.[2] Field bought the original parcel of approximately sixty-seven acres on a bluff above Lake Michigan and sold the southern half to Sprague shortly thereafter. Although each chose a different Chicago architect—Field engaged D. H. Burnham & Company, and Sprague hired Harrie T. Lindeberg of Albro & Lindeberg—Manning laid out the landscapes for both clients simultaneously, treating them as a joint commission.[3] Manning created more than six hundred drawings and plans for the two estates, dated April 1911 through November 1913.[4]

The Fields called their estate Lakelandwood.[5] A wooded ravine running east into Lake Michigan formed the property's northern boundary. South of the ravine, the site extended west–east between the main road (Moffett) and the lake bluff, with its panorama of water and sky. The southern boundary, which divided the two estates, cut straight from the main road toward the lake and angled slightly northeast before reaching the bluff.

Burnham's Colonial Revival house stood a few hundred feet from the bluff, its long (east and west) sides aligned with it.[6] The east facade afforded expansive water views. A short servants' wing extended north from the main building, overlapping its northwest corner. The overlap created two L-shaped corners, one bracketing an entry court on the building's west facade, the

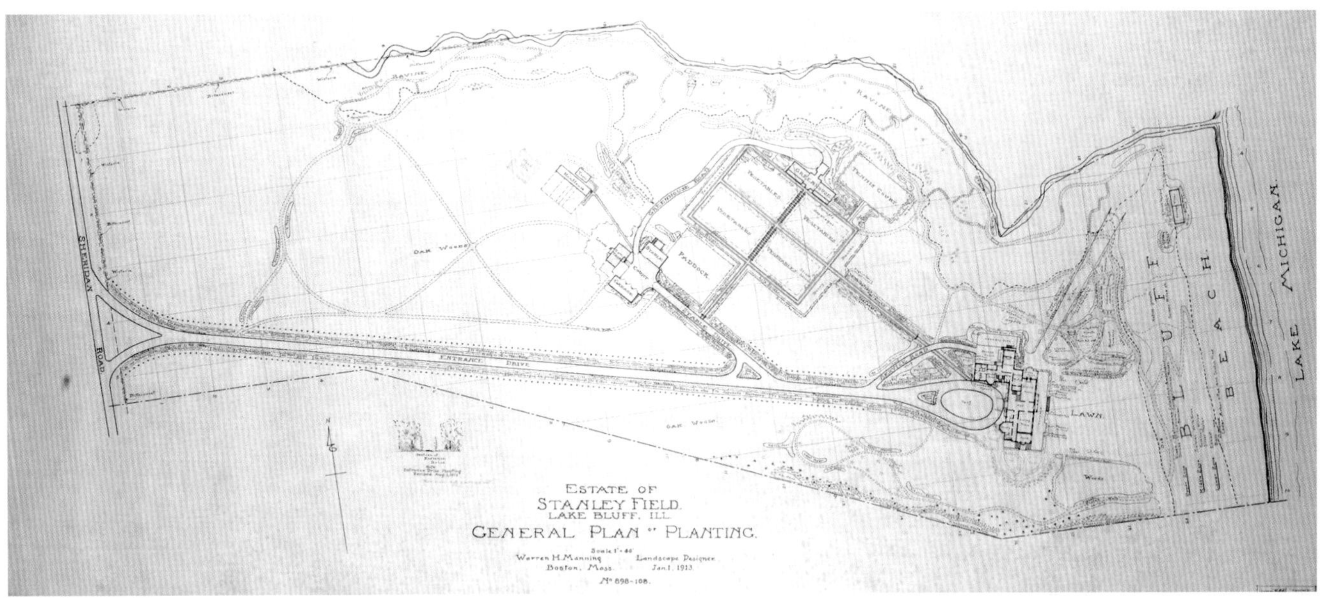

The straight entry drive of the Field estate responded to the unusually narrow lot. By designing the Field and Sprague estates as a single, conjoined property, Manning maximized the impression of expansive woodland for both owners. "General Plan of Planting," plan no. 898-108, January 1913. Courtesy MPI.

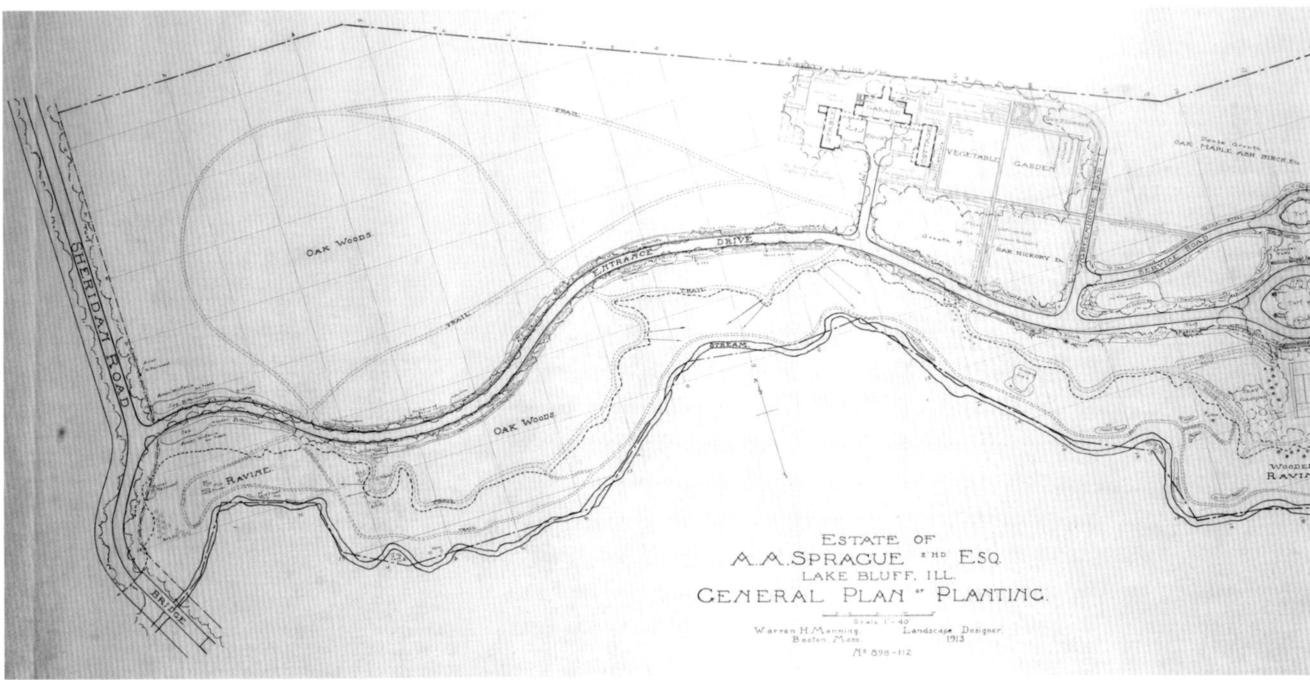

The Sprague drive followed the gentle curve of the stream that demarcated the south boundary of the property. "General Plan of Planting," plan no. 898-112, 1913 (detail). Courtesy MPI.

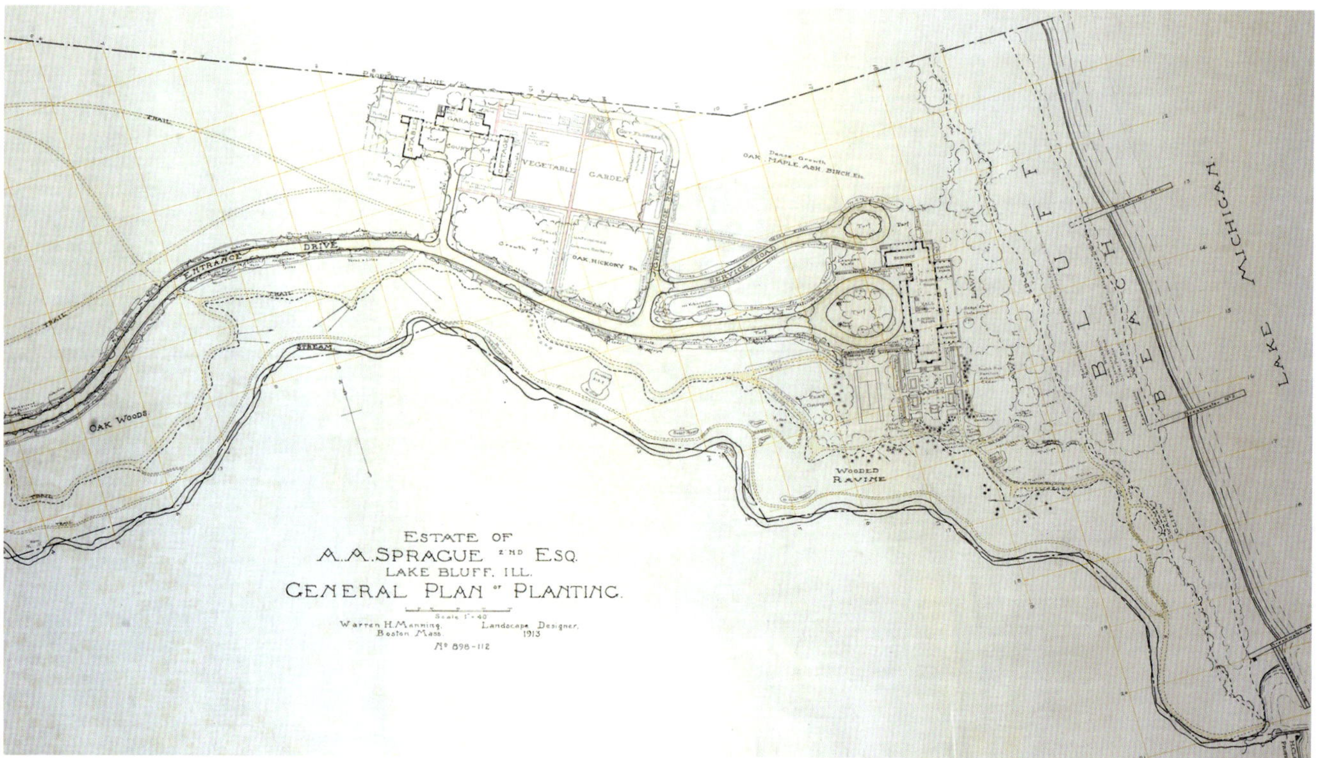

The Sprague formal garden was located, characteristically, at one end of the house, where it would not interrupt views to Lake Michigan. "General Plan of Planting," plan no. 898-112, 1913 (detail).

other opening to the northeast, facing the wooded shoreline and the water beyond.

Most of Lakelandwood's developed landscape lay north of the approach drive, which ran straight east from the main road through an allée of poplars and hemlocks. Manning interplanted the fast-growing poplars with hemlocks that would replace the poplars over time.[7] Service roads branched north to the stable, tennis court, and vegetable gardens and northeast to the servants' wing before the main drive culminated in a turnaround, an irregular ellipse planted in turf, at the house entrance on the west facade. Northeast and southeast of the house, winding paths traced the ravine and linked groups of informal gardens and wooded spaces. Northwest of the vegetable garden complex, an expanse of oak woods stretched to Moffett Road.

As in most of Manning's estate designs, the circulation system did more than connect the estate's buildings and outdoor features. Trails offered an unfolding experience of the site's most striking natural elements, notably the ravine and the bluff. Lushly planted walks became linear gardens that enhanced utilitarian spaces such as the greenhouse and tennis court. Intersecting paths divided the rectangular vegetable garden into four equal sections, each nearly as large as the footprint of the main house, and a long pergola shaded the north–south walk.

Other than the direct view of the lake from the east facade, the most spectacular feature of the designed landscape was a path cut several hundred feet through the woods at a 45-degree angle from the northeast corner of the house, opening a vista to the bluff. Shade-tolerant perennials lined this

Lawns overlooked the lake, and a gate provided entry to the Sprague walled garden. Photograph by Arthur G. Eldredge, c. 1928. Courtesy MCL.

Manning created a forecourt island planted with elms to soften the view of the Sprague mansion from the entry drive. Photograph by Arthur G. Eldredge, c. 1928. Courtesy MCL.

Intimate garden settings throughout the Field property offered a counterpoint to the expansive lake views. Photograph by Arthur G. Eldredge, c. 1928. Courtesy MCL.

broad turf path, which widened as it approached the bluff. Between this woodland vista and the bluff, a looping network of paths defined planted spaces.

The landscape design included at least one formal garden, slightly sunken below grade, as Manning's formal gardens often were, off the south end of the house. Flanked by two brick walls, this semicircular garden featured a fountain and intersecting paths (one turf, one brick) with deep floral borders. The cross-axial brick path continued west beyond the garden, terminating in a hexagonal pavilion.[8]

In 1915 Field built an Arts and Crafts style duplex called the Gardener's Cottage on Ravine Avenue. He also added houses for two of his children on the northwestern corner of the original property, designed by the architect Stanley Anderson, around 1938. The main house and its outbuildings and gardens were razed in 1967. With the exception of a wooded parcel called Moffett Woods purchased by the Village of Lake Bluff, the estate was subdivided into lots for single-family houses. The Anderson-designed houses remain, now on separate lots, as does the duplex on Ravine Avenue. Remnants of the estate's gardens include the minor grade change for the sunken garden and sections of the brick wall at the edge of the bluff. Mature hemlocks still form a legible allée along the entrance drive, although the western half of the drive is now a public road, Lakeland Drive.[9]

Immediately south of the Field estate, the Spragues' original parcel also spanned Moffett Road and the bluff overlooking Lake Michigan. Another curving ravine bounded the property on the south, similar to the Field estate's northern boundary. The two estates also shared similarities in their designed features and spatial organization; each house was aligned parallel to the lake bluff, and a utilitarian complex (garage, stable, vegetable gardens, greenhouse, and so forth) lay

Vista to lake, from the northeast corner of the Field house. Photograph by Arthur G. Eldredge, c. 1928. Courtesy MCL.

Remnants of Manning's bluff plantings remain, although both houses are now gone. Photograph by Carol Betsch, 2009.

north of the entrance drive and west of a service road leading to the north wing of the house. The houses were about the same size and had formal gardens adjacent to the south wings.

Lindeberg's Georgian Revival house for the Spragues was built of red brick, as was the garage, and brick also paved walks close to the house. The winding entrance drive from Moffett Road led to a rectangular courtyard in front of the house, with a planted, elliptical turnaround. Brick walls enclosed the courtyard on three sides, with a tennis court on the other side of the south wall.

The Sprague estate was the more wooded of the two, with an expanse of hardwoods (oak, hickory, maple, ash, and birch) running the length of the property on both sides of the main drive, surrounding the vegetable garden and house complexes. Trails threaded the woods on both sides, though more extensively along the ravine to the south, where Manning created openings to take in views along the wooded path. Even on the east (lake) side of house, Manning either left in place or planted clumps of conifers (hemlock, arborvitae, Scotch pine) throughout the lawn on top of the bluff. The lawn started southeast of the house and tapered to an irregular strand tracing the bluff northeast of the service wing all the way to the Fields' east lawn, forming the only path between the two estates.

Other differences lay in details that presumably reflected individual preferences. The Spragues' formal garden occupied an area significantly larger than the Fields', but their vegetable garden was only about half the size. With the exception of the axial scheme of the formal garden and the vegetable garden complex, the drives and paths of the Sprague estate echo the meandering line of the ravine bounding the property on the south. Although the Spragues' landscape lacked a spectacular axial vista, it included a wide path planted with tulips and other spring garden flowers that wound through the woods between the formal garden and the edge of the bluff.

The Sprague family owned the estate until 1930. In 1939 the owner hired local architect Jerome Cerny to make drastic alterations to the house. Subsequently, the property was subdivided and the house razed. The western two-thirds of the main drive became Forest Cove Road, and single-family houses line both sides.[10]

Finley Barrell Estate

LAKE FOREST, ILLINOIS

ARTHUR H. MILLER

Finley Barrell, a wealthy Chicago commodities and stock broker, likely knew Lake Forest as a child in the early 1870s. The property he and his wife, Grace Witbeck Barrell, chose for their estate four decades later occupied a plateau overlooking one of the great ravines about half a mile from Lake Michigan. The Barrells' large parcel originally straddled Sheridan Road, a major north–south thoroughfare in Lake Forest, and extended from Rosemary Road on the north to Maplewood Road on the south. The wooded ravine, which meanders roughly north–south, formed the parcel's eastern boundary.

Warren Manning and the prominent Chicago architect Howard Van Doren Shaw collaborated on the design for the estate, which was built between 1909 and 1911.[1] The red-brick house, an imposing example of English Revival architecture, fronts Rosemary Road, to the north. With Sheridan Road on the west, the primary landscape views were to the east and south. The east-facing porch afforded the Barrells a long view through a formal garden and a meadow of wildflowers and tall grasses, terminating at the ravine. North of the formal garden lay a grass tennis court and a viewing pavilion. The woods at the edge of the ravine included ground cover and dirt or gravel-surfaced paths. A terraced garden adjoined the south-facing living room. Echoing the proportions and alignment of the interior rooms, this living-room garden literally extended the house into the outdoors. The parcel west of Sheridan Road held a cluster of service buildings including a coach house, two large greenhouses, and quarters for the estate employees. This area also featured gardens with wide dirt paths.

The formal garden east of the house, with its long rectangular pool at the center, loosely resembles a Moorish-inspired garden at the House of the Four Winds (1909), just two miles away, where Shaw collaborated with the Boston landscape designer Rose Standish Nichols.[2] The Barrell garden is also characterized by eclectic architectural details, from an Italianate limestone balustrade bordering the narrow pool to ironwork, masonry, and wooden pergolas that recall

Arts and Crafts designs.[3] The garden descends in two stages from the east porch of the house to the main garden level containing the pool. Beds were framed with clipped boxwood and punctuated by columnar evergreens. The view from the porch takes in the garden and extends to the tall pines at the ravine edge, blending the designed environment into the natural setting.[4] Even when bound to the architectural form of this garden, Manning drew attention to the most dramatic features of

The house, by Howard Van Doren Shaw, seen across a tree-studded meadow. Photograph by William T. Barnum, n.d. Album #2202.2.13, "Summer residence of F. G. Angall [formerly Barrel], Lake Forest, Illinois." Courtesy Lake Forest–Lake Bluff Historical Society, Lake Forest, Ill.

The architecturally determined formal garden stretches east of the house. Photograph by William T. Barnum, n.d. Courtesy Lake Forest–Lake Bluff Historical Society.

the local terrain. One contemporary reviewer also pointed out the contrasts among the greens of the forest and the carefully chosen lilies and roses, the red bricks of the paths and the white pergolas and stonework framing the pools.[5]

A stepping-stone path from the terrace south of the house led to an overlook into the ravine. (This structure of poured concrete, reminiscent of the Ravello at Cyrus McCormick's Walden estate, was demolished in the early twenty-first century.) Another path continued south from the terrace on the fringe of the meadow, where a rustic covered bench provided an opportunity to watch the sun set beyond the framed greensward.[6]

Today the house and adjacent formal gardens occupy less than a quarter of the original lot. Although the ravine still forms the house lot's eastern boundary, the parcel west of Sheridan Road now belongs to Lake Forest College. The main house remains in its original state, and the hardscape of the formal garden is intact, but the plantings are recent. Only a vestige of the meadow has survived. In the 1920s the south half of the property was subdivided, and several small parcels were carved from the property in the 1950s. During this time a new driveway was built along the western edge of the ravine, adjacent to the old overlook, connecting Rosemary Road to a house on this southern portion. The existing midcentury houses on the west side, along Sheridan Road, provide privacy from the roadway and have little impact on the integrity of the estate.

A path stretching south from the house terrace borders the meadow, where a rustic covered bench provided a place to watch the sunset. Photograph by William T. Barnum, n.d. Courtesy Lake Forest–Lake Bluff Historical Society.

As at other Lake Forest estates, Manning's design emphasized the dramatic topography of the ravines. Note the water cascade at right. Photograph by William T. Barnum, n.d. Courtesy Lake Forest–Lake Bluff Historical Society.

Lake Forest University (Lake Forest College)

LAKE FOREST, ILLINOIS

ARTHUR H. MILLER

Warren Manning's redesign of the Lake Forest University campus, on the shore of Lake Michigan about thirty miles north of Chicago, played a central role in the institution's redefinition of itself, both physically and programmatically. Between 1897 and 1908 Manning planned the spatial reorganization of what was then an overcommitted graduate institution in concert with its conversion into a liberal arts college with preparatory-school affiliates. His campus plan of 1897, which likely served as the basis for a subsequent plan in 1906, focused on the network of dramatic ravines that shaped the central spaces, melding the college so seamlessly with these natural features that they came to define the institution's identity. The roadways and natural areas that Manning created and preserved continue to delineate the North and Middle Campuses of what is now Lake Forest College.

The Lake Forest campus dates from the innovative curvilinear street plan for the surrounding community that was laid out in 1857 by Almerin Hotchkiss for the founders, a group of affluent Chicago Presbyterians.[1] The parcel comprised thirteen hundred acres of forested glacial moraines, carved into tablelands by streams flowing east, to the lake, through ravines fifty to eighty feet deep. The forest was originally dominated by oak, maple, and beech, with patches of conifers. These species gradually gave way to black locust and honeysuckle as settlement progressed. As construction created openings in the canopy, understory plants that had grown on the steep, shady banks of the ravines were replaced by more light-tolerant species, including buckthorn.

Most of the streets on the Hotchkiss plan wound sinuously through this landscape in English Picturesque fashion, traversing the gaping chasms between tablelands and offering views of the ravines. In the center, Hotchkiss designated a university campus, or "park," with two smaller satellite campuses for the preparatory schools. Each institution sat on a separate plateau bounded on three sides by ravines and on the fourth by a road. The thirty-acre university campus (today known as Middle Campus) faced west to University Avenue (later Sheridan Road), a major thoroughfare that meanders north–south.[2] Lake Forest Academy for boys occupied ten adjacent acres to the north. The girls' preparatory school, Ferry Hall, lay east of the university campus, near the lake. In 1879 the academy burned; it was rebuilt in 1880, on the university campus one block south, and the university took over the original academy site (now called North Campus).

From 1892 to 1893, the eloquent and cosmopolitan pastor of the community's Presbyterian church, the Reverend James G. K. McClure, served as interim university president. During McClure's tenure, O. C. Simonds was commissioned to create an informal plan for five structures on the new Lake Forest Academy site (now called South Campus). The Simonds plan was carried out, with four of the five projected buildings, including three by the Chicago firm of Pond & Pond, constructed by 1894. They were set within a landscape of young trees (predominantly ash and pine), shrubs, and vines. The plan also suggested locations for future university buildings and bridged the ravine separating the north and central campuses.

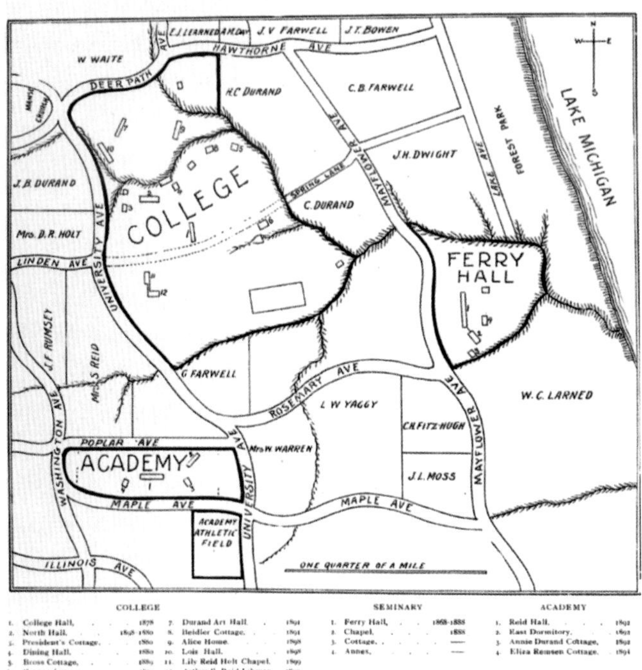

The dominant presence of the ravines is clearly visible in this 1899 map of the campus. Courtesy Archives and Special Collections, Lake Forest College.

During this same period the University of Chicago opened, on Chicago's south side, and invited Lake Forest to join it, essentially as a feeder campus. But the new urban university had Baptist ties, and Lake Forest declined to become a part of it, as it did when approached again in 1896. The second overture prompted Lake Forest's trustees to scale down Lake Forest to a four-year liberal-arts college that would not be in competition with the University of Chicago, and to play up their institution's distinctive bucolic character. McClure again served as president during the transition and began planning a major building program for the two original campuses.[3]

Before construction started, trustee Cyrus H. McCormick II, a son and the business successor of the late "Reaper King," intervened. Warren Manning had designed McCormick's Lake Forest country estate, Walden, and in 1897, when Manning returned to Walden for an annual visit, McCormick engaged him to develop a new campus plan for the scaled-down college. Although this plan has not been located, the accompanying report to the university's leaders has survived. In it, Manning called attention to the unique ravines: "They are of vital importance, they are the key to the whole situation so far as the plan of the grounds is concerned, and they are the one feature that will set these grounds apart from other like institutions." Manning's report proposed four significant changes to emphasize these dramatic features: eliminating a straight east–west road that bisected the main campus and adding a footbridge

The woodland surrounding the ravines that run through the campus influenced the evolving plan. "General Plan of Lake Forest University," June 1906. Courtesy Archives and Special Collections, Lake Forest College.

across the dramatic ravine on the southern edge; replacing that road with a looping carriage drive that traced the edges of the central campus plateau, providing dramatic views into the ravines; converting the large undeveloped southeastern portion of the main campus into a botanical garden of native prairie plants; and planting foundation shrubs and vines to blend buildings into the scenic landscape, as he had done at Walden.[4]

Although the four campus buildings were constructed between 1897 and 1900, it is unclear which of Manning's proposed changes were carried out at that time. This is partly because in 1906 the college commissioned a classically trained New York architect, Benjamin Wistar Morris, to create a plan for four more new buildings.[5] Morris's plan, which credits Manning as "consulting landscape architect," incorporated most of the elements described in Manning's 1897 report. (Manning's office did not record the 1906 project, and it is likely that the college sent Manning's 1897 plan to Morris.) The Morris–Manning plan aimed to strengthen axial ties among the three institutions—the girls' preparatory school, the college, and the boys' academy—across the great chasmlike ravines, while also locating the addi-

Manning's recommendations included adding trees, shrubs, and vines on new buildings to establish a bucolic tone for the campus. Photograph, n.d. Courtesy Archives and Special Collections, Lake Forest College.

tional new buildings. The 1906 plan did, however, preserve Manning's original call for a carriage drive skirting the ravines and circling the institutional complex, offering views into and across the central campus ravines on three sides. Within this picturesque loop, a Beaux-Arts layout connected the three campuses by means of axial routes and sightlines. The plan located the four new college buildings on the north and south sides of a proposed axial allée through the main campus, with a striking Tudor Revival gateway—one of the plan's few elements to be built, and still present—facing southwest, across the south entrance to Manning's loop drive, to the ravine and the boys' academy site. The tree species on the plan remain unknown, although then, as now, slow-growing white oaks were dominant on the campus. Elms, employed elsewhere in town for similar functions, would have been another likely choice.

Photographs of the campus, including aerial views taken during the early twentieth century, document that the proposed buildings and a few landscape elements on the 1906 plan were built. A glass lantern slide from 1911 shows a rustic "Gym Pond Bridge" leading to a tree-skirted meadow, described in a caption as the botanical garden. This restored prairie was lost to campus development as early as 1916. Only a short section of Morris's principal axial allée was planted, and it was near the academy campus, not on the college grounds. It vanished in the late 1940s. The nearly straight road bisecting the campus, which Manning had proposed eliminating in 1897, remained until the early 1940s; it did not become the allée path shown in the 1906 plan. By midcentury parking lots were scattered along the ravine-edge loop drive on the Middle Campus. As Manning had originally recommended, the new buildings were screened with shrubs and ivy; the ivy survived into the mid-1970s, when it was removed in the interest of building preservation.

In 1938, the year of Manning's death, the

Chicago architectural firm of Puckey & Jenkins elaborated on the 1906 plan, but their layout also was not built.[6] The boys' academy, which had been independent since 1925, moved in 1948 to the former J. Ogden Armour estate, Mellody Farm, west of Lake Forest, and the college absorbed the academy campus. As the institution expanded after World War II, it reused the former academy buildings and required little new construction. With the structures added by Morris in 1906, this allowed the two campuses to remain relatively open, as Manning had envisioned, until the early 1960s. In 1974 the girls' school at Ferry Hall, which had occupied the same campus near the lake since 1869, merged with Lake Forest Academy at Mellody Farm. The Ferry Hall campus became a residential development.

At Manning's direction, the large undeveloped southeast portion of the main campus became a botanical garden of native plants. Hand-colored lantern slide, c. 1911. Courtesy Archives and Special Collections, Lake Forest College.

The botanical garden was re-created on the north ravine edge of Middle Campus in the late twentieth century. Still thriving with native prairie plants, this two-and-a-half-acre parcel is known as Shooting Star Savannah. After controlled burns began in 1994, native plants characteristic of an Illinois tallgrass prairie were replanted from commercial stock, including what now is a large stand of yellow pimpernel. Other plants include five varieties of aster, three species of sunflowers, and uncommon specimens that thrive locally. Also, after a decade, several rare natives have reemerged: Michigan lily (*Lilium michiganensis*), smooth yellow false foxglove (*Aureolaria flava*), and woodland dog violet (*Viola conspersa*), a state endangered species. It is likely these would have been found in the similar conditions of the Manning-era botanical garden.[7]

Throughout the twentieth century, the classical formality of the prior architects' plans for the college campus gradually yielded to Manning's naturalistic vision based on the unique features of the site. Perhaps Manning sensed that the powerful topography would foil any concepts to beautify or circumvent the ravines, and indeed the ravines have continued to prevail. A mid-1990s plan executed in the early twenty-first century strengthened an informal pathway extending from North Campus across Middle Campus to South Campus, via two filled-in ravine pathways. It affirmed the original informal, Picturesque approach championed by Manning in 1897.

The perimeter road and its plantings retain the spirit of Manning's design. Photograph by Carol Betsch, 2009.

A prairie planting, inspired by the original botanical garden, offers students an opportunity to study native species. Photograph by Carol Betsch, 2009.

Cyrus H. McCormick II Estate (Walden)

LAKE FOREST, ILLINOIS

ARTHUR H. MILLER

Warren Manning's association with Walden, the estate of Cyrus H. McCormick II and his wife, Harriet Hammond McCormick, began in 1894 and developed into a forty-year relationship with their property.[1] Early records suggest that the McCormicks instructed the Chicago architect Jarvis Hunt to design a Shingle style house that would relate directly to the surrounding natural features. Hunt's work included sketches for the "Ravello," a terrace and shelter at the edge of the bluff overlooking the lake. In many ways, Walden became a collaboration between the clients, the architect, and the landscape architect, as Cyrus McCormick took an active role in selecting and cutting vistas, and Harriet became involved in choosing plantings, orchestrating views, and laying out paths.

The site for the future estate lay at the southern edge of the city of Lake Forest, overlooking Lake Michigan. The McCormicks' choice of location for their new home was influenced by the two years they had lived in Highland Park, another lakeshore community just south of Lake Forest, where Cyrus enjoyed "chopping" in the woods, and their summers at Blair Lodge, a fifteen-acre lakeshore estate they had rented in years past.[2] A great ravine intruded into the Walden property from the lake, splitting into three forks that carved the land into distinct plateaus. These prominent uplands formed ninety-foot bluffs at the water's edge.

Manning first visited the site in the fall of 1894, as a member of the Olmsted firm, and by February 1895 a plan was taking shape under John C. Olmsted. Over the next few months, however, the McCormicks asked Manning to consider a house location farther back from the bluff. According to Cyrus McCormick, Blair Lodge "was about the same distance from the bluff top as the Walden home . . . [and] it was this that determined the setback of the Walden house from the bluff edge." Although the Olmsted office sent a general plan of the building's location, roads, and plantings in September 1896, McCormick arranged for Manning to continue the work at his chosen site. Manning's independent commission

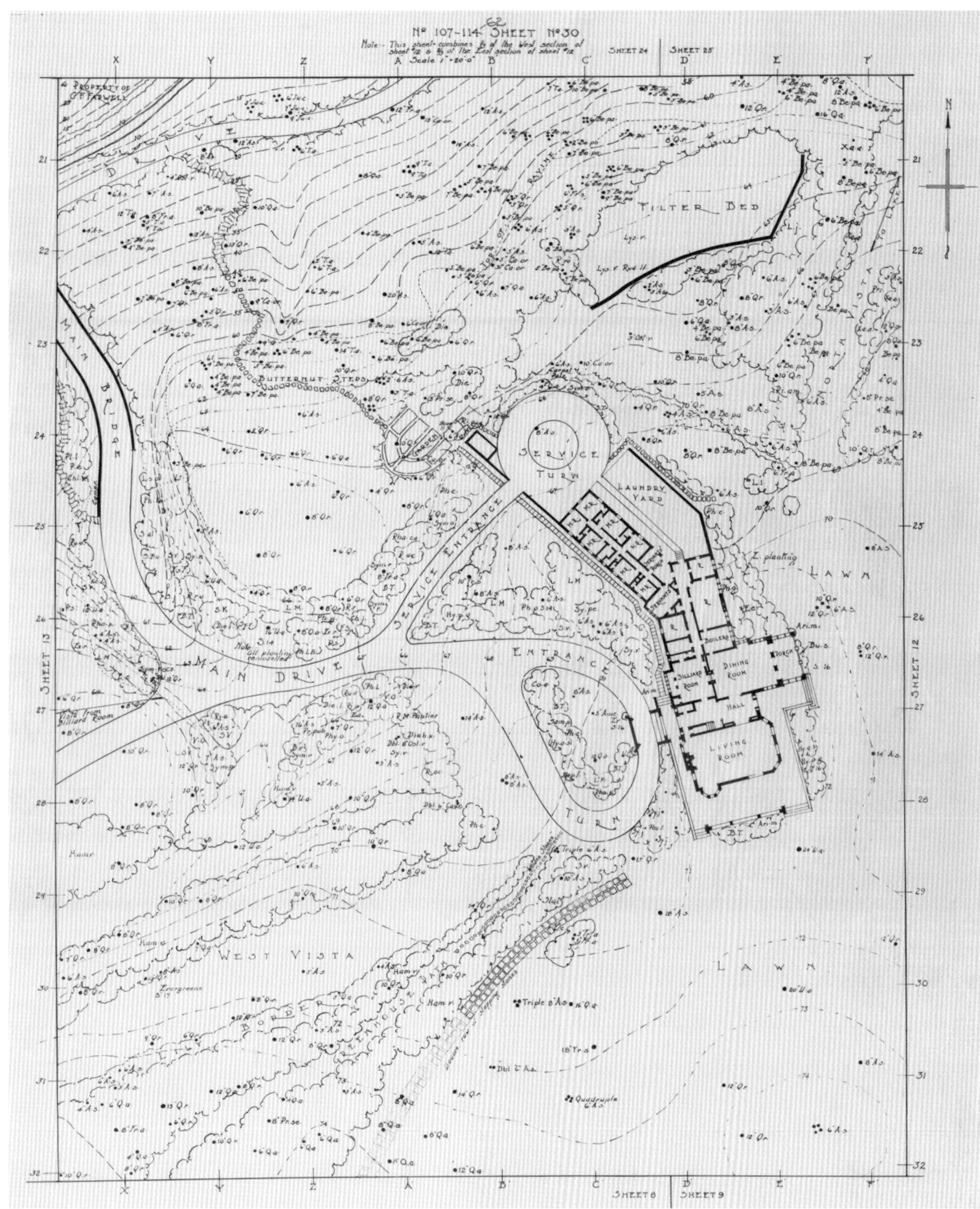

Plans recording the design of Walden were among the most comprehensive in Manning's practice. On oversize sheets, he noted individual tree species, views, trails, bridges, changes in elevation, and hundreds of other details. Plan no. 107-114-62, sheet no. 30, n.d. Courtesy MCL.

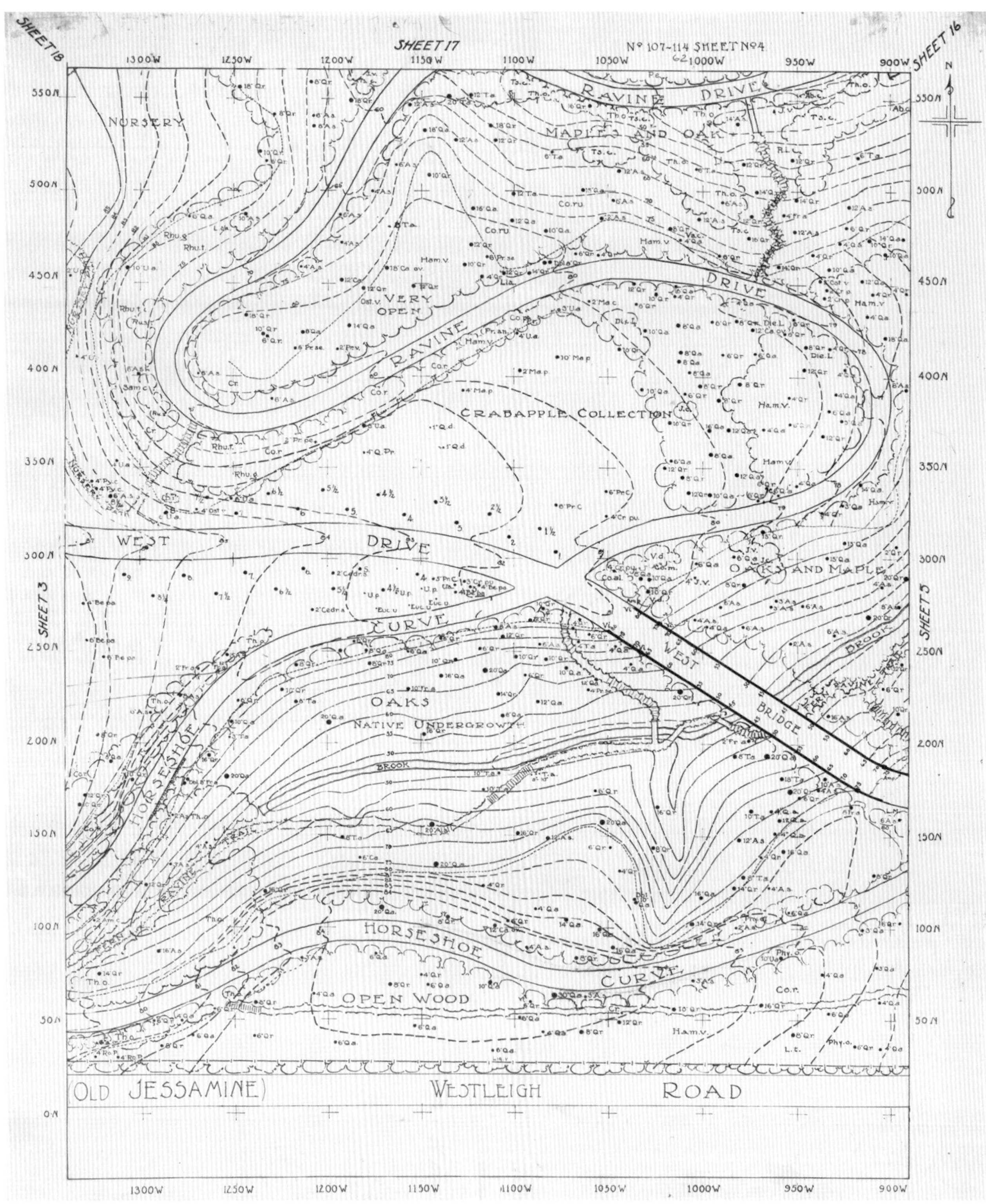

The site's sharp sloping terrain, with its many ravines, is reflected in the grade markings. Plan no. 107-114-62, sheet no. 4, n.d. Courtesy MCL.

was launched with the Olmsted firm's consent. Between 1892 and 1913 the McCormicks bought up surrounding parcels of land, finally accumulating about 103 acres. Walden would become the catalyst for a lifetime friendship between Manning and the McCormicks, as the landscape architect returned each spring until Cyrus's death in 1936. On these visits Manning continued to develop Walden and to undertake other projects for McCormick's many relatives, commissions that extended his practice across the nation.[3]

Walden's site posed several physical challenges, but the instability of the bluffs at the lakefront and within the ravines was the most serious threat to developing the estate. McCormick expanded and improved two existing jetties, built drains, and reduced the angle of the lake bluff to allow for the planting of grasses and shrubs to anchor the sandy incline. Manning's "History of Walden," written for McCormick in 1933, includes seventy-seven typewritten pages of tables documenting experiments with native and exotic plants in various locations.[4]

The region's dramatic topography provided an ideal opportunity for Manning to educate the McCormicks about how to achieve a landscape that balanced a regard for nature with design. The organizing elements of the estate design included the lake bluff and shore, the ravine, and the wooded plateaus. The deep canyon and its three branches provided settings for several bridges (all designed by Cyrus McCormick), the main one crossing the principle chasm just northeast of the house. From its site farther back from the bluff, the house provided dramatic vistas: two tree-framed views east to the lake, a view

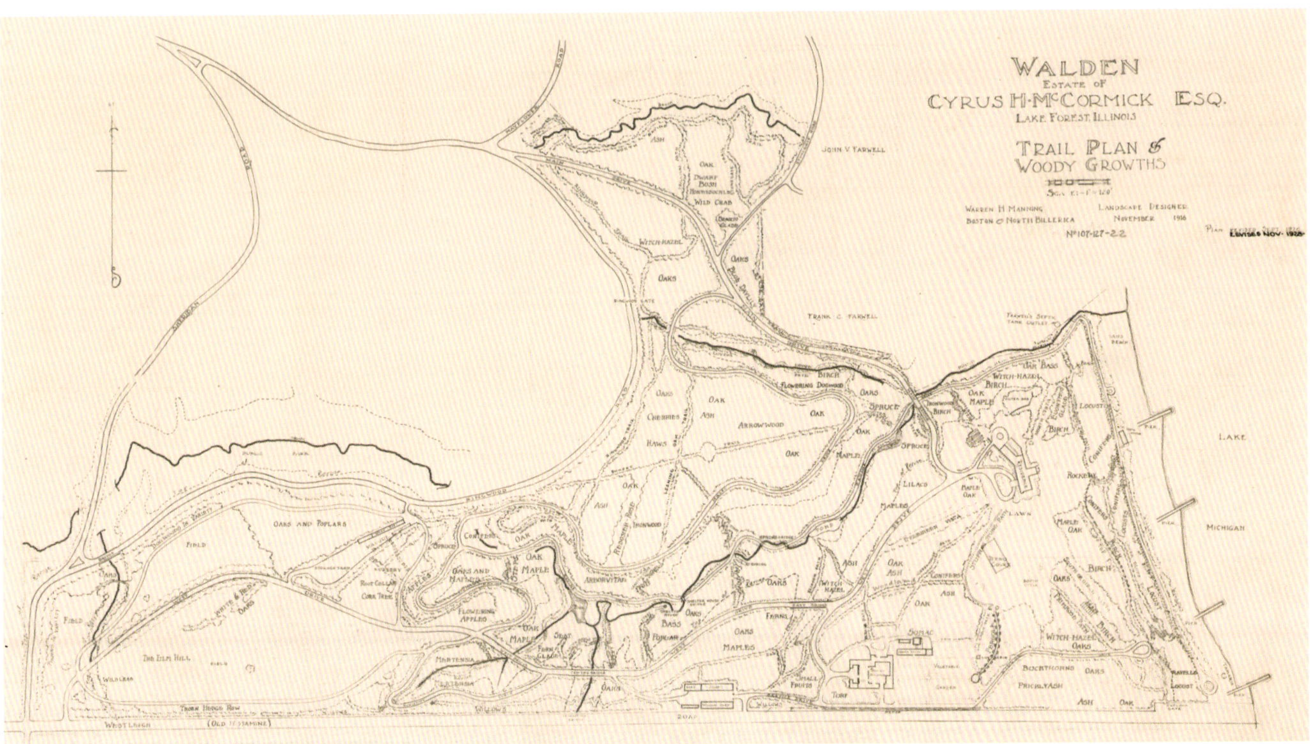

Three vistas radiating from the house are marked on this plan (labeled North, South, and Evergreen). Birches were used extensively near the house, which was surrounded by informal areas of lawn. "Trail Plan & Woody Growths," plan no. 107-127-22, November 1916; revised September and November 1928. Courtesy MCL.

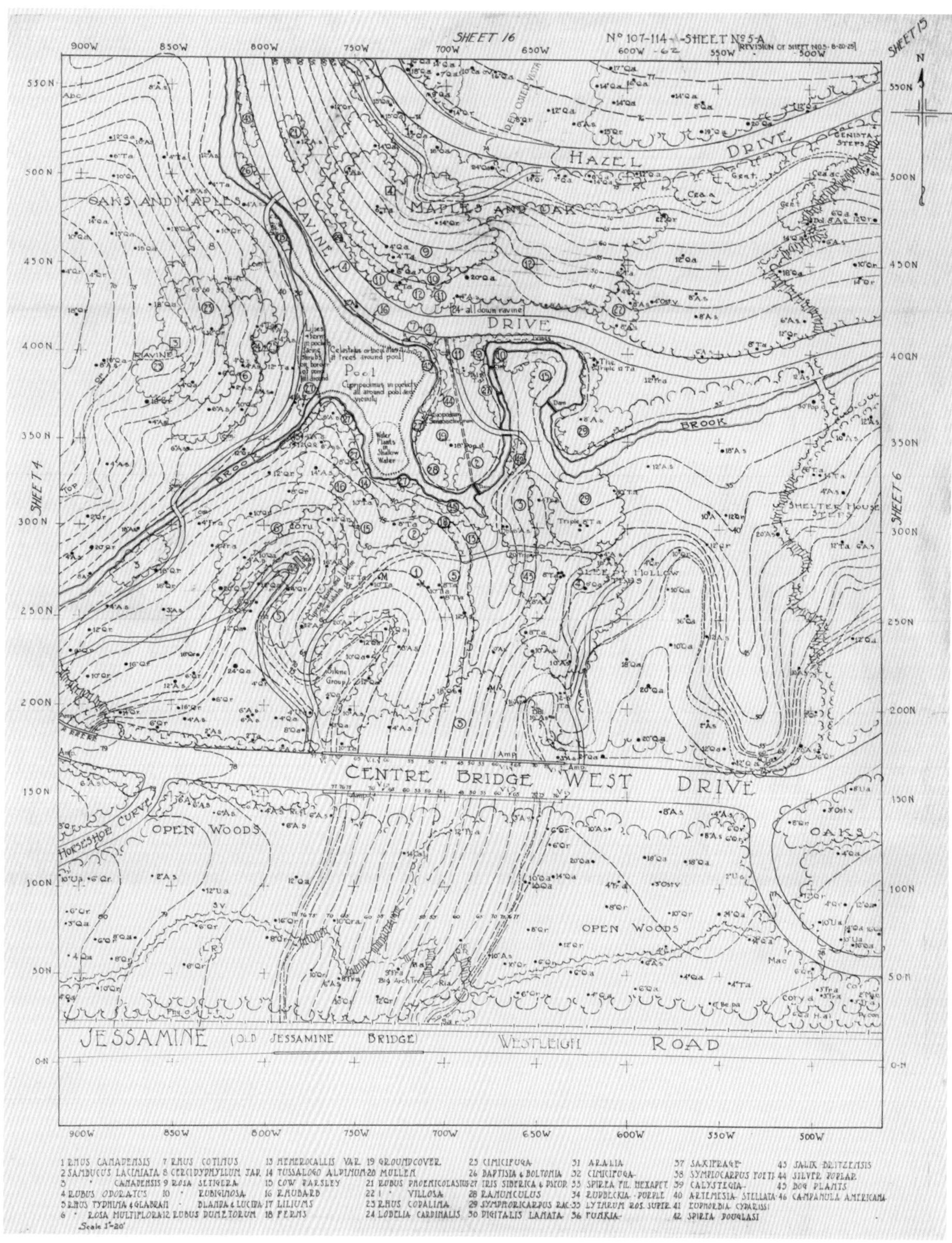

The Ravine Drive was bordered by a pool fed by a small brook. The plan details plantings for its edges and shallows. Plan no. 107-114-62, sheet no. 5A. Courtesy MCL.

The Ravello set up striking views to the lake and was itself an architectural point of interest in the landscape. From Harriet Hammond McCormick, *Landscape Art, Past and Present,* 1923.

Manning and the McCormicks opened vistas throughout the property to provide views for visitors. From McCormick, *Landscape Art, Past and Present.*

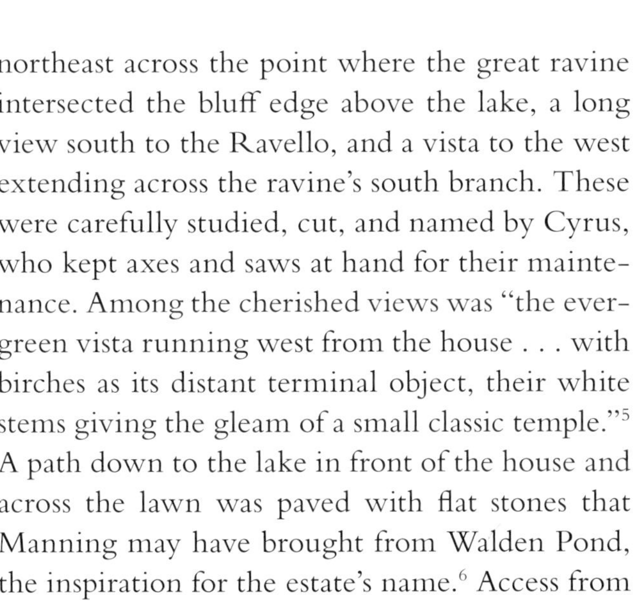

northeast across the point where the great ravine intersected the bluff edge above the lake, a long view south to the Ravello, and a vista to the west extending across the ravine's south branch. These were carefully studied, cut, and named by Cyrus, who kept axes and saws at hand for their maintenance. Among the cherished views was "the evergreen vista running west from the house . . . with birches as its distant terminal object, their white stems giving the gleam of a small classic temple."[5] A path down to the lake in front of the house and across the lawn was paved with flat stones that Manning may have brought from Walden Pond, the inspiration for the estate's name.[6] Access from the house to Lake Forest and its train station was to the northwest by the main bridge leading to Ringwood and Sheridan Roads. At the west end of the property was a small farm devoted to the estate's needs, with its own entrance drive near Sheridan Road (now Westleigh Road). Staff and service buildings were also clustered on this lane, Walden's south boundary. A curving carriage drive led from the service area to the Ravello. In 1908 Manning redesigned the west border of Walden to accommodate the construction of Villa Turicum (1908–1918), an estate for McCormick's brother Harold and his wife, Edith Rockefeller McCormick, featuring a home by Charles Platt.[7]

Hunt's Ravello is still extant, owing in some measure to the longevity of Manning's bluff plantings, which stabilized the wind-buffeted slope. Photograph by Carol Betsch, 2009.

In a 1936 letter Manning describes Cyrus McCormick's request for "souvenirs" from Walden Pond in Concord, Massachusetts, related to Thoreau's life there. These included willows from Minot Pratt's nursery in Concord that were planted on the McCormicks' beach to help retain the sand. During a walk with Pratt, Manning listened to the old man describe helping "Mr. Thoreau put out plants in the wild that were new to the region, with the belief that they would add to the interests of the woods and fields and continue to grow for many years."[8] According to Manning, Thoreau's experiments inspired McCormick to embark on his own tests of non-native species in 1910. Six years later, under Manning's supervision, McCormick launched the "Walden Arboretum study" to record plant data, and Charles Sargent and E. W. Wilson of the Arnold Arboretum in Jamaica Plain, Massachusetts, visited Walden to recommend plants. Over the next several decades, introducing new species and anticipating the pattern of their growth facilitated the transformation of Walden from a private resort into a public arboretum.[9]

Manning's "History" describes over one hundred sources of plants at Walden between 1896 and 1932. Trees and plants came from Manning's friends and clients throughout the nation; from foreign countries, including France and China; from nurseries such as the one owned by Manning's brother J. Woodward Manning, in Duxbury, Massachusetts, and Douglas Nursery in Waukegan, Illinois; and from parks as distant as Golden Gate in San Francisco. Manning also collected plants in Michigan's Upper Peninsula and central Wisconsin, and some of Walden's gardeners, such as Emil Bollinger of Waukegan, Illinois, and W. Tiplady of Lake Geneva, Wisconsin, contributed others. A "Generic Study of Woody Plants" that Manning compiled from 1925 to 1928 illustrates the extraordinary range of plant species at Walden.[10]

Perhaps the most significant record of the Lake Forest Walden was *Landscape Art, Past and*

Lake views are framed by the architecture of the Ravello. Photograph by Carol Betsch, 2009.

Present, published in 1923, two years after Harriet McCormick's death. The book is a reprinting of an 1899 paper by Harriet McCormick and an appraisal of Walden by the noted garden writer Louisa Yeomans King. *Landscape Art* includes valuable descriptions and photographs of the Manning garden. King quotes Harriet McCormick's description of the ravine as "a living picture gallery," with scenes of sylvan beauty along the carriage road and views "constantly enhanced by planting and cutting."[11] Another picture in the gallery was the kitchen garden south and west of the house, near Westleigh Road.[12] A long flower border lined one side of the garden path, and a more informally planted border edged the kitchen garden. Although the border plantings appeared casual, the effect required daily maintenance by estate employees, many of whom lived on the property. Others lived in cottages McCormick built in a nearby neighborhood.

As Manning's practice expanded to include other projects throughout greater Chicago, Walden became widely known. Harriet McCormick, a founder of the Garden Club of America and a leader in establishing the Garden Club of Illinois, opened the place to interested groups. The Garden Club of America, for example, explored Walden as part of its 1919 annual meeting in Chicago. By 1933 Walden was attracting an average of two thousand visitors annually. The estate's picturesque beauty and high visibility, along with the prestige of its owners, may have helped Manning find new clients, in the region and beyond.

In a period when Italianate formal gardens signified social status, Walden was a powerful endorsement of naturalistic design and development, especially in the rugged terrain near Lake Michigan. During the Great Depression, when Manning's practice dwindled, he took solace in the belief that "it is likely that the next special interest in the development of the smaller house grounds, estates, parks, club holdings, and hunting preserves as well as the larger forest holdings will be more and more along the wild garden naturalistic lines." He predicted that this trend would overtake big lawns, expensive formal gardens, and rockeries, all of which "require much upkeep cost" and "show lack of attention very conspicuously."[13]

After Cyrus's death, his second wife, Alice Hoyt McCormick, began to subdivide the estate, a process that continued over the next two decades and culminated in the demolition of the house in 1955. Preserving the famous ravine arboretum became a local concern; the Lake Forest Garden Club acquired it in the 1960s, and by the 1980s it was turned over to the city. Today it is overgrown, with volunteer trees preventing most understory development. The main drive (now Walden Lane) from Ringwood Road toward the house survives, and the main bridge was restored as a pedestrian crossing by the Lake Forest Foundation for Historic Preservation in the 1990s. The Ravello, though privately owned, continues to draw visitors, who approach on the original carriage road. Looking down the steep bluff from the terrace, the bank is solid; the honeysuckle shrubs, locust trees, and other woody plants have secured the slope against erosion for over a century. After wandering through the ravine on the remaining paths, one understands Manning's faith that "the wild garden will not appear to be neglected if let alone."[14]

Bangor City Plan: The Burned District

BANGOR, MAINE

JANE ROY BROWN

In September 1910, the trustees of the Bangor Public Library invited Warren Manning to consult on a site for a new library building. The Penobscot River port of Bangor, then a city of 25,000, was thriving after more than a century of lumbering and related enterprises. The wealth flowed, literally, from the Penobscot's extensive tributary system, which carried logs into Bangor's mills from Maine's vast, forested interior. At the time, Manning found it convenient to travel to Bangor, which lies about thirty-five miles inland from the center of the coast. He was already working on a residential project in the city, as well as several summer estates on Penobscot Bay and the campus of the National Soldiers Home in the state capital of Augusta.[1]

During Manning's visit to the library site, he and the trustees discussed the idea that the building would anchor a new civic center, by which they meant a district of public buildings. With this in mind, Manning toured the city and observed its defining natural and built features. His observations and recommendations for these projects, captured in a draft report, also formed the basis for both his formal report to the library trustees in 1910, before a fire swept the proposed civic center site, and his "Bangor City Plan: The Burned District" the following year.[2]

The Penobscot River runs roughly north to south through the city center, where it is met by Kenduskeag Stream entering from the northwest between steep hills and bluffs. Manning observed that the stream's narrow valley contained the city's oldest and densest settlement, including the site of the library and civic center and a downtown commercial district. Over time, the growing city spilled over the stream bluffs in all directions. Much of Bangor's industry, as well as the busy rail yards, bordered the Penobscot's west shore. Industrial development also flanked Kenduskeag Stream. Yet the steepness of the roads in and out of the Kenduskeag Valley, most of which approached or exceeded a 10 percent grade, effectively separated the old residential and commercial district from the newer parts of the city. Further impeding access to industrial areas and important newer public facilities, such as the railroad station, was the lack of conveniently sited bridges across the Kenduskeag. In short, the topography of the library site, especially in relationship to a civic center, created what Manning viewed as the project's biggest challenge.[3]

Manning recommended that the library be built into a slope, with a new service road approaching the rear entrance. He suggested orienting the building to face an existing road that could be extended to the stream. The extended road would open a view to City Hall on the Kenduskeag's opposite shore, each building becoming a terminus of a diagonal axis, repeating a pattern he had observed on his tour of Bangor. This line of sight also would knit the principal parts of the city together, if only visually. Manning approved of the proximity of the the library to a school and suggested relocating all the city schools closer to the library, in accord with the educational trends of the day.

This cluster of schools near the library and the visual axis figured in Manning's design for the civic center. For these purposes he advised the city to acquire the land "covered with old buildings" between the school grounds and Franklin Street, the northern boundary of the civic center, and an adjacent strip to allow for growth. As Manning envisioned it, the center would include a new road on each side of the stream, a dam to form a recreational basin, and a pedestrian mall, park, and market square.[4]

After his mid-September visit in 1910, Manning's draft report emphasized the importance of the civic center over the library. "Few cities pay as heavy a tribute to a plan that does not fit the land as does Bangor," he wrote, alluding to the steep hills bounding the valley of Kenduskeag Stream. He translated the "tribute" into lost revenue, noting that a pair of horses can draw only two

A fire in Bangor, Maine, presented Manning with the opportunity for a revised city plan that would include new civic and business districts. Lantern slide, n.d. Courtesy Warren H. Manning Digital Collection, Iowa State University.

cords of wood on a 10 percent grade, but they can double the load on a grade of 5 percent.[5] At the same time, he called attention to the stream and its wooded bluffs as the distinguishing natural features of the site. In both his draft and his final report, he advised the city to acquire the forested bluffs that created pleasing views from the bridge entering the civic center, "for if they were cut or burned they could not be replaced in fifty years, whereas burned buildings could be reproduced in . . . a few years." Bangor had experienced four serious fires that year before Manning's September visit, which may have prompted this observation.[6] For the proposed new civic center in particular, the statement proved uncannily prescient.

On the advice of a colleague, Manning's final report, the version he presented to the trustees, reversed its emphasis, giving priority to the library site; but he provided blueprints for both the library and the civic center, all but ensuring that he could present his vision for the latter.[7] In early November, Manning learned that the trustees had responded favorably to his recommendations for both the library and the civic center. But before the planning was complete, a fire on April 30, 1911,

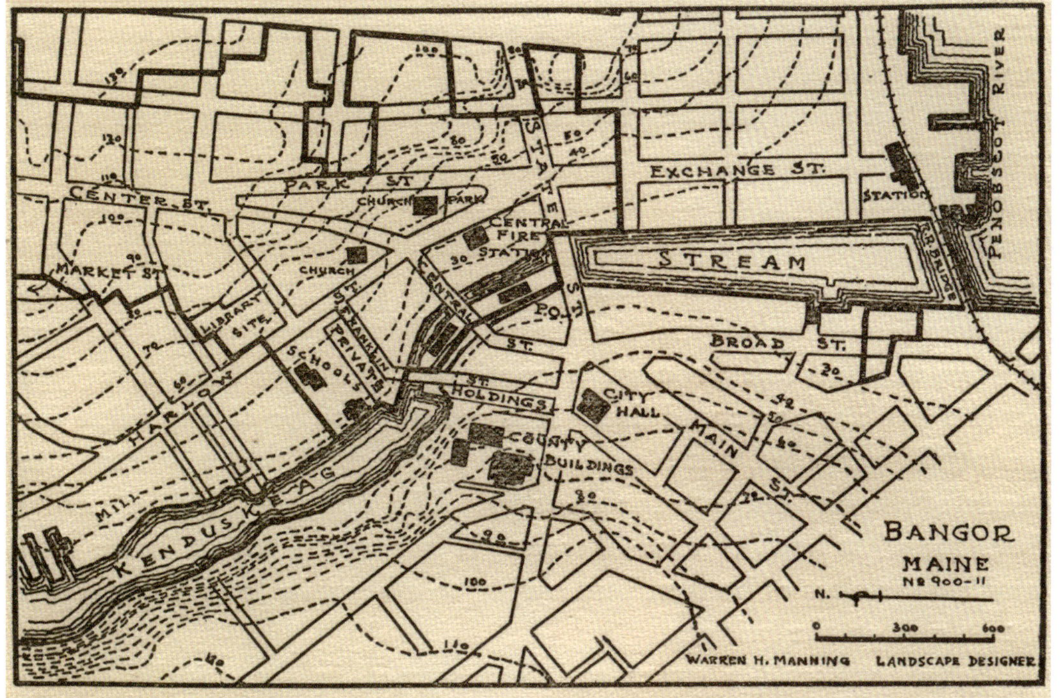

Plan Showing Conditions Before April 30, 1911. Burned District Heavily Outlined

Dominating Manning's sketch of existing conditions downtown is Kenduskeag Stream, which divided the south end of the city in two. "Plan Showing Conditions before April 30, 1911," *Landscape Architecture* 2 (October 1911): 4.

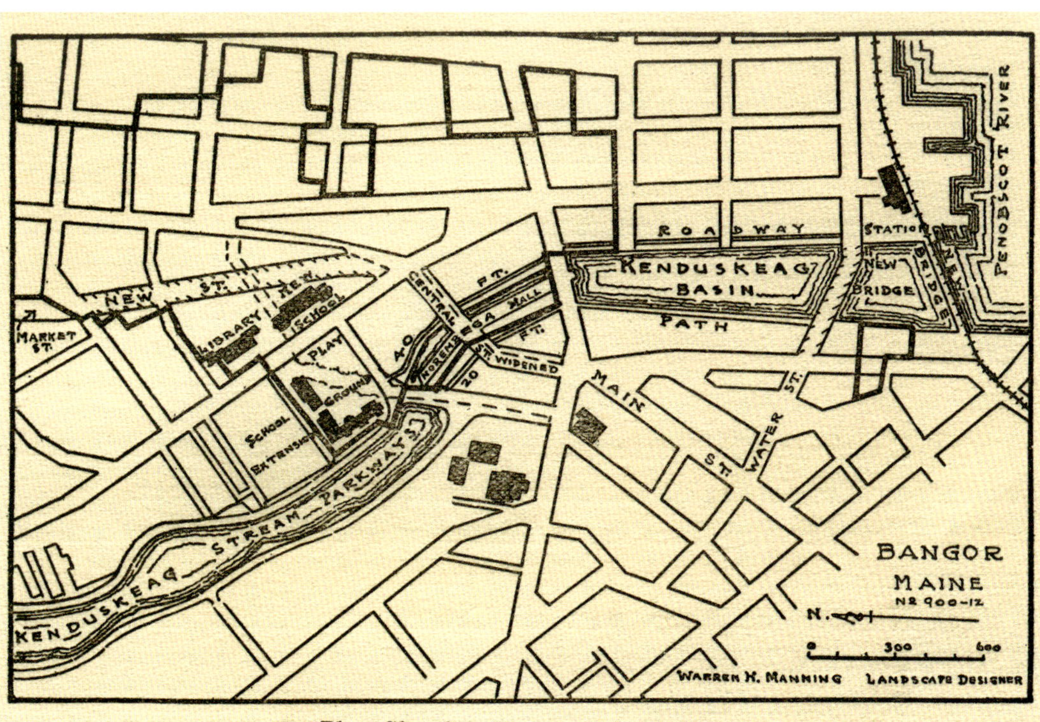

Plan Showing Proposed Conditions

The proposed plan included a new bridge over the stream (here labeled "basin") and parkways bordering the stream to the north. "Plan Showing Proposed Conditions," *Landscape Architecture* 2 (October 1911): 7.

destroyed fifty-five acres encompassing the civic center site.[8]

The fire presented Manning with several opportunities, not the least of which was to repackage his earlier proposals in "an emergency report" for the burned district. (The earlier plan was probably tabled when the fire occurred.)[9] The firm, with associate Fletcher Steele now involved in the project, turned the emergency planning process to its advantage by taking its recommendations directly to the citizens of Bangor.

Immediately after the fire, the mayor, who supported Manning's plan, appointed a civic commission to study the burned district and to make recommendations. The commission retained Manning as its adviser, and within three weeks the firm submitted a report and sketches for improvements that were more specific but in concept nearly identical to those previously accepted by the library trustees. As Steele noted in an article about the project, the report, titled "Bangor City Plan: The Burned District," was cheaply printed for wide distribution, because its success "depended on the strong immediate support of the public at large." The mayor called a mass meeting of Bangor citizens and presented the commission's (that is, Manning's) recommendations directly to them. Surmising that without strenuous intervention, citizens would be inclined to take the expedient route of rebuilding on the existing layout, the commission launched a strategic campaign that laid out the benefits of the more far-reaching plan, circumvented any political obstruction, and countered the influence of an opposing local newspaper.[10] The plan's advocates contacted churches, women's clubs, and other associations, which carried the message to their members.

The report fleshed out the vision that Manning had only sketched in his earlier version. Broadly, the plan focused on solutions to the traffic congestion caused largely by the steep, narrow

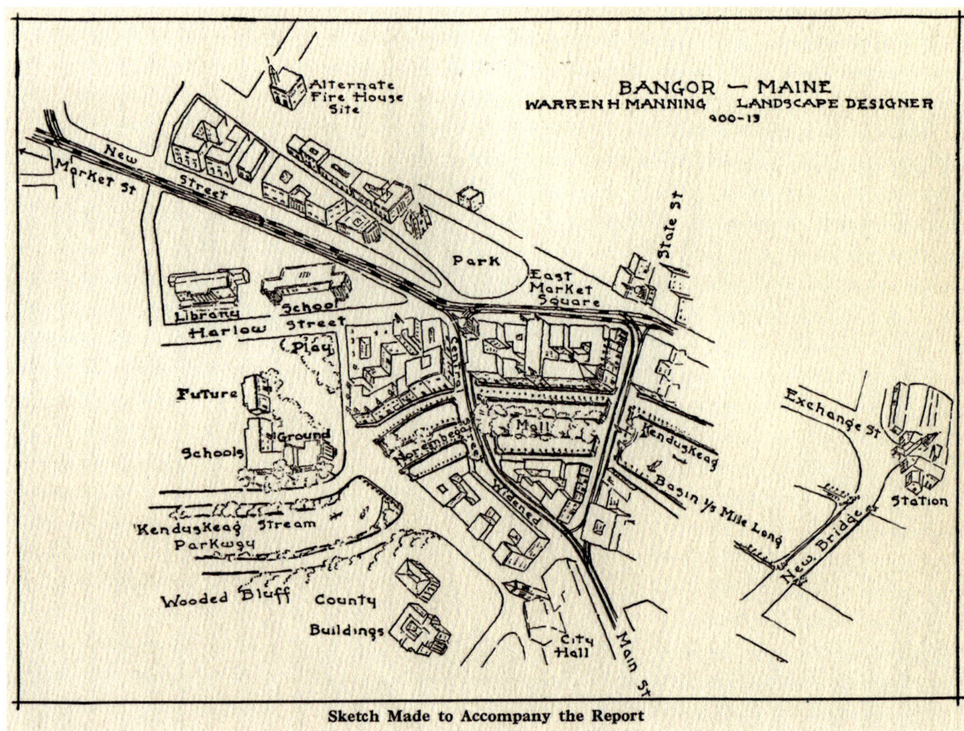

Detailed sketch showing the location of new school buildings, a new fire station, and a pedestrian mall, shown here in axonometric view. "Sketch Made to Accompany the Report," *Landscape Architecture* 2 (October 1911): 7.

Well-executed presentation drawings, such as this view of Kenduskeag Basin, often proved persuasive to clients. Lantern slide. "View of Suggested Improvements of Kenduskeag Basin as seen from Norumbega Mall," plan no. 900-16, November 1913. Courtesy Warren H. Manning Digital Collection, Iowa State University.

streets, with the report stressing that this problem would only worsen in the automobile-dominated city of the future. The plan also envisioned public amenities along a predominantly industrial waterfront. A new bridge across the Kenduskeag near its confluence with the Penobscot would speak to both needs, relieving congestion and serving as the "monumental entrance . . . to this great passage through the city," as Steele put it. Below the bridge, a new dam would form Kenduskeag Basin to hold water for recreation and fire protection, and to retain open space in the midst of the city for better air circulation. Behind the basin, where the stream entered the city center, Manning envisioned linear parks flanking the water to form a pedestrian mall. A parkway extended from the mall along the shores of the stream, conveying traffic to and from the new civic district. The report also recommended conserving waterfront land through a trust, allowing landowners to retain title while turning over property management to a board of trustees for public use.[11]

At the meeting, citizens overwhelmingly endorsed Manning's plan, resulting in its subsequent approval by the city council, which authorized bonds to fund the work. Regrading the streets, rerouting streetcar lines, acquiring adjacent property, and building new schools in the library block could now go forward.[12] The city carried out these and other immediately practical elements of his plan, as well as acquiring some land on riverfront bluffs for conservation; however, despite Steele's optimistic observation in 1911 that "the people at large have given their enthusiastic endorsement" to the plan, Bangor ultimately failed to implement the most visionary components, including the new bridge, river basin, and pedestrian mall.

Ira M. Cobe Estate

NORTHPORT, MAINE

JANE ROY BROWN

In 1892 Ira M. Cobe, a young lawyer from Boston, married Annie Elizabeth Watts of Belfast, Maine. The couple moved to Chicago, where Ira Cobe started a career in finance that rapidly placed the Cobes within the city's circles of wealth and power. In 1899 they commissioned a Shingle style summer cottage, Bohemia Villa, in Bayside, Maine, a vacation community within the town of Northport, just south of Belfast. A decade later the Cobes built anew on Hillside Farm, one hundred acres of boulder-strewn pastures, wetlands, and spruce woods behind their existing oceanfront cottage. Although not directly on the water, the location on a glacial hill two hundred feet above sea level provided panoramic views of Penobscot Bay.[1]

Warren Manning was designing several private estates in nearby Camden at the time, and it may have been through one of these connections that he secured the Cobe job. Manning's firm logged Cobe as a client in 1911, and his earliest known plan is dated December 16 of that year. Construction began on the entrance drive and the house the following spring.[2] The Chicago architectural firm Marshall & Fox built the imposing red-brick Colonial Revival mansion that still stands.[3] Situated about two-thirds of the way up the hillside, the house has a pitched roof and gable ends, with the main entrance on the southwest facade and a colonnade on the northeast facade, where a marble terrace commands the site's principal view of the bay and its backdrop of blue hills.

Manning wrapped the hill in a winding drive, which integrates the building and the landscape, highlights their contrasting forms, and provides a grand arrival experience. Lined with a boulder wall, the drive begins at a 45-degree angle to the slope and then follows the contours for a few hundred feet. The ascending vantage point exaggerates the height of the mansion's columns and its commanding location above a sweep of lawn. The drive then loops around a spruce grove and cuts toward the house, where it branches to outline a teardrop-shaped island opposite the main entrance and a service turn off the west wing.

IRA. M. COBE ESQ.
EAST-NORTHPORT-ME.

PLANTING PLAN FOR HOME GROUNDS.

SCALE 1"=40'

WARREN H. MANNING — BOSTON, MASS.
LANDSCAPE DESIGNER — JULY 23, 1914
NO. 913-85

PLANTING LIST

No	Scientific Name	Common Name
1	Berberis Thunbergii	Japanese Barberry
2	Berberis Vulgaris	Common Barberry
3	Celastrus Articulatus	Bitter Sweet
4	Celastrus Scandens	Bitter Sweet
5	Crataegus Coccinea	American White Thorn
6	Crataegus Cordata	Washington Thorn
7	Forsythia Fortunei	Golden Bell
8	Lonicera Japonica	Hall's Honeysuckle
9	Lonicera Morrowii	Morrow's Honeysuckle
10	Lonicera Tatarica	Tartarian Honeysuckle
11	Rhamnus Frangula	Buckthorn
12	Rhododendron Catawbiense	Rose Bay
13	Rhododendron Maximum	Great Bay
14	Rhodotypus Kerrioides	White Kerria
15	Rosa Rugosa Rubra	Ramanas Rose
31	Hemerocallis Fulva	Tawny Day Lily
16	Spiraea Anthony Waterer	Anthony Waterer's Spirea
17	Spiraea Bumalda	Dwarf Japanese Meadow Sweet
18	Spiraea Callosa	Japanese Meadow Sweet
19	Spiraea Callosa var. Alba	Japanese Meadow Sweet
20	Spiraea Thunbergii	Snow Garland
21	Spiraea Tomentosa	Hard Hack
22	Spiraea Van Houttei	Van Houtte's Spirea
23	Syringa Persica	Persian Lilac
24	Syringa Vulgaris	Common Lilac
25	Symphoricarpus Racemosus	Snowberry
26	Symphoricarpus Vulgaris	Indian Currant
27	Viburnum Dentatum	Arrow Wood
28	Viburnum Opulus	High-bush Cranberry
29	Weigelia Rosea	Rose-colored Weigela
30	Iris Orientalis	Siberian Iris
32	Achillea The Pearl	Achillea The Pearl

N
SERVICE DRIVE
SCATTERED SPRUCE
ENTRANCE TURN
LAWN
SERVICE TURN
RESIDENCE
PLANTING SHOWN ON PLAN NO. 913-84
SPRUCE
NATURAL GROWTH
ENTRANCE DRIVE
WHITE PINE
OLD STAGE ROAD

Manning's layout brought visitors to the front of the house on an entry drive that wound through a naturalistic landscape. The ocean view was revealed on the opposite (north) side of the house. "Planting Plan for Home Grounds," plan no. 913-85, July 1914. Courtesy MCL.

As was often the case in Manning's layouts, the formal garden was located at one end of the house, where it would not interrupt the grander view. Photograph, n.d. Courtesy Bayside Historical Preservation Society, Bayside, Maine.

Manning's design honors the site's glacial topography and its native spruce-fir forest. In 1913, when the landscape was under construction, a local newspaper reported that "many of the surface rock[s] are to be kept in their natural positions, including an immense boulder near the road in the front," and noted that "the plan of the grounds calls for the retention of the natural beauties so far as practical."[4] This naturalistic design for an estate landscape appears to have been unusual enough to merit similar comments in nearly every extant news article describing the property when it was new. Manning incorporated other glacial rubble in a rock garden at the base of the boulder wall that supported a formal garden on a flat site originally built for the tennis court. The wall formed a "rustic parapet" at the top. Boulder steps descended from the formal garden to a stepping-stone path that meandered east through the spruce grove next to the drive.

The formal garden was a rectangular space (140 by 30 feet) off the mansion's east wing. A grass panel, sometimes called "the sunken garden," filled the center of the space, enclosed on three sides by a series of three shallow planting terraces. The east end of this formal garden opened to face a rectangular reflecting pool (about 8 by 16 feet) extending from the east wing, its corners anchored by planters with small conifers that resembled the spires of the surrounding spruce. Slightly elevated above the sunken garden, the pool echoed a distant view of the bay.[5] Plant lists for 1916 and 1917, prepared by Stephen Hamblin of Manning's office, specify a colorful assortment of annuals for an "old-fashioned garden." For the descending terraces he noted shrubs, including barberry, weigela, althea, buddleia, clethra, deutzia, and vitex, flowering in pink, white, purple, and pale lilac.[6] Low arborvitae hedges, lined with straight paved walks, enclosed the entire formal garden. Two parallel paths began on either side of the reflecting pool and continued through the sunken garden, visually attenuating the space.

Elsewhere, plantings, rather than architectural elements, defined the main spaces. A 1914 planting plan shows sinuous borders of perennials (including yarrow and iris) and masses of ornamental shrubs (snowberry, lilac, rhododendron, weigela, viburnum, honeysuckle, spiraea) outlining the roughly elliptical lawn on the northeast slope. Near the service drive, oval beds softened the corner of the west solarium and the house. On the lawn below, spruce, flowering shrubs, and perennials were massed around outcrops of granite. The island near the house entrance was a flat lawn, in which the Cobes created oval flowerbeds. Screening the service drive, woodland plantings of honeysuckle, viburnum, and other native shrubs filled in among scattered spruce. Uphill to the south, old tote roads and trails wound through the woods, where the Cobes erected a water and observation tower.

Since Ira Cobe's death in 1931, the property has had four owners, starting with the George and Gertrude Pingree family (1936–1978).[7] Photos taken in 1936 show the reflecting pool filled in and the sunken garden devoid of plantings, but the walks and spatial layout remained intact. Images from the ensuing decades depict simple flowerbeds flanking the stepping-stone walks and mature trees and flowering shrubs near the house entrance and edging the lower lawn. The Pingrees replaced the sunken garden with a swimming pool in the 1940s or 1950s, but kept the outer borders of shrubs and perennials.[8]

The third owners, John K. and Jean Evans (1978–2001), tore down the stone wall near the property entrance and created an Asian-style garden in the island opposite the house entrance. In 2001, when the fourth and cur-

Plantings in the formal garden underwent many changes through the years, but the architectural structure was essentially unchanged. Photograph, n.d. Courtesy Bayside Historical Preservation Society.

The scale of the house, designed by the Chicago firm Marshall & Fox, dwarfs residents gathered on the portico of its ocean side. Photograph, n.d. Courtesy Bayside Historical Preservation Society.

rent owners, Gerald and Dorothy Reid, bought the estate, the property had decreased from one hundred to fifty acres. The flowering shrubs and perennials were gone, but the old oaks, and the bones of Manning's design, remained. The Reids filled in the swimming pool, leaving the flanking arborvitae hedges beside the sunken garden. Their trunks genuflect four feet above the ground, the point at which they had been clipped for the greater part of a century. Like a genie of the place, the "immense boulder" remains at the base of the hill.

Albert H. Chatfield Estate

ROCKPORT, MAINE

JANE ROY BROWN

In 1899 Albert H. Chatfield, a wealthy Cincinnati businessman, and his wife, Helen Huntington Chatfield, bought a 120-acre sheep farm with shore frontage in the budding resort town of Rockport, Maine.[1] Located on Penobscot Bay, a popular sailing destination, Rockport had recently separated from Camden, an established summer resort community.[2] The Chatfields' parcel overlapped the Rockport and Camden Turnpike, now Russell Avenue, which runs roughly north–south. A small lake called the Lily Pond lay on the west side. Opposite, fields sloped to the ocean.

The Chatfields hired Warren Manning to design a summer estate that would encompass five house sites, with gardens, game courts, a stable, service yards, trails, and drives.[3] Although Albert Chatfield retained ownership of the whole property during his lifetime, four of the house sites formed, in effect, individual estates. These included the Chatfields' central parcel, Aldermere Farm, on which stood an existing wood-frame farmhouse, built around 1860; Kentmoor, a Colonial Revival house with four front gables on an oceanside slope, built in 1901 for Chatfield's sister and brother-in-law, Mary and Frederick Gilbert; a spot near the original course of the Megunticook Golf Club; and The Willows, a nineteenth-century wood-frame farmhouse. A staff cottage, called Hibernia, was built on the fifth site.[4]

During the two periods in which Manning's firm worked on the commission, 1900–1901 and 1911–1913, Manning or his associates oversaw all aspects of the estate's development, from the layout of roads and house sites to the design of formal flower gardens.[5] In October 1900 he visited the property with Willard P. Adden of the Boston architectural firm Brigham & Adden. Based on opportunities presented by existing landforms and plants, Manning suggested locations for building sites, drives, gardens, and utilitarian features of the estate, delving into the Chatfield and Gilbert landscapes in more detail than the other developed areas of the property.[6] Possibly at his suggestion, the Chatfields moved their farmhouse

An aerial view of the rear of the house and the meadows that form the middle ground of the ocean view. Photograph, n.d. Courtesy Frederick H. Chatfield Jr.

from its original location near the road to a spot farther back to provide better views of the bay. The architects eventually designed additions to the house that included dormers, a porch, and a wing on each end, all of which expanded views of the landscape from inside the house.[7]

Manning's proposed landscape plan for Aldermere Farm specified a lawn surrounding the house. In front, a picket fence set off by masses of flowering shrubs and perennials enclosed the yard on both sides of the central driveway, which led to a carriage turn. Behind the house, the lawn extended to a stone retaining wall above the sloping mown field that ended at the ocean. From a rear terrace the Chatfields could look out over a low fence to a hedged, rectangular flower garden on their left and the field straight ahead below the wall.[8] Beyond lay a wild garden: a meadow of native grasses and wildflowers and an existing thicket of alder, arborvitae, and other shrubs and trees growing around a spring. At what point on the slope this garden ended is not clear, but the field stretching from the wild garden to the ocean retained its rustic character, with two looping roads defining space within the open expanse. Manning wrote to his clients more extensively about this wild garden than about any other portion of their property.[9]

Manning located Kentmoor northeast and downhill from the Chatfields', near a clump of existing spruce trees. Two drives, lined with rustic stone walls, enclosed an existing field in which juniper, bayberry, wild rose, winterberry, and other native plants grew around a cluster of boulders, another naturally scenic area for a wild garden.[10] A mown "ramble" meandered through the field between the house and the game courts. A stone wall outlined a separate pasture, where

Plantings designed by Manning included two large American elms. Photograph, n.d. Courtesy Frederick H. Chatfield Jr.

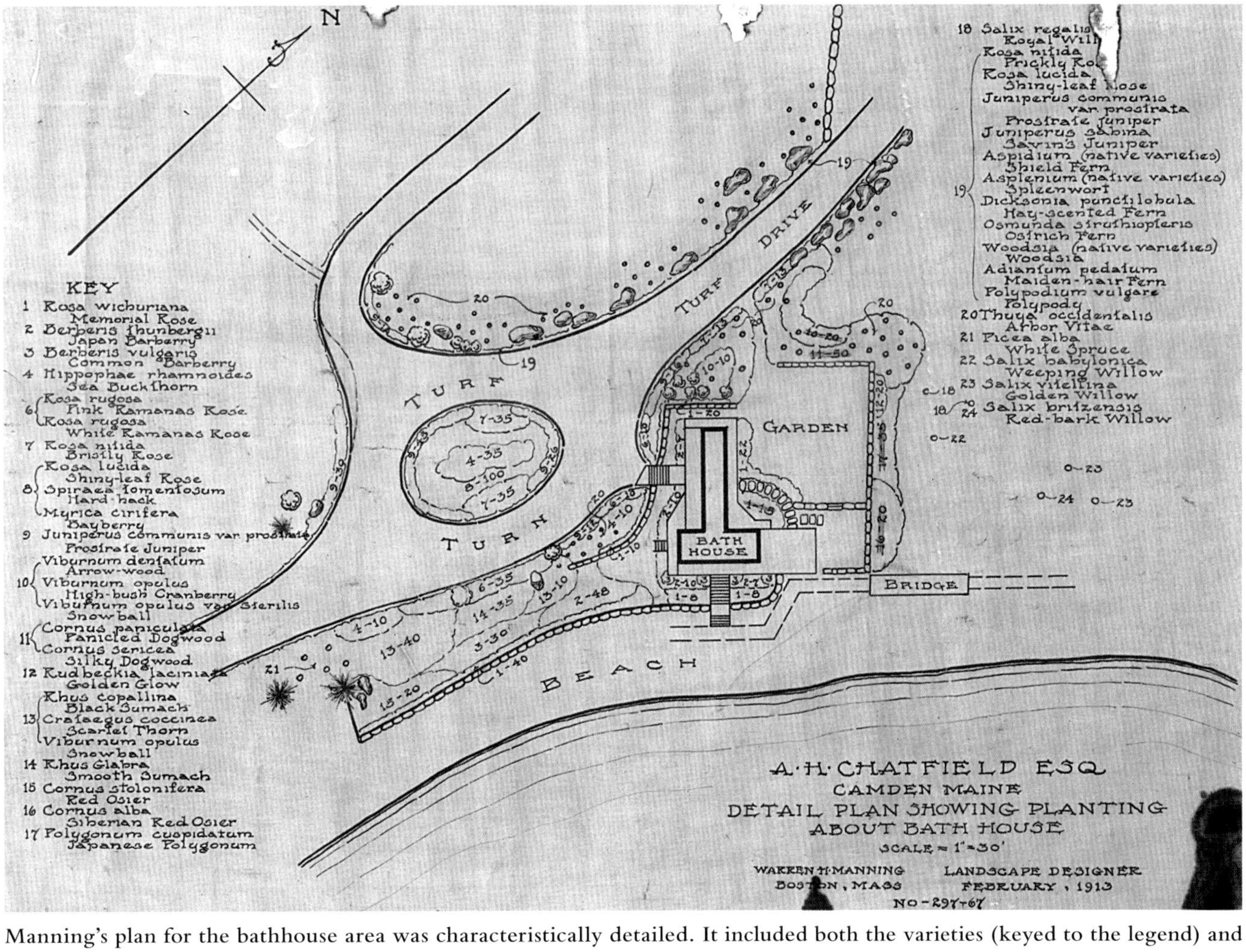

Manning's plan for the bathhouse area was characteristically detailed. It included both the varieties (keyed to the legend) and the quantities of plants to be installed (the number following the hyphen). "Detail Plan Showing Planting about Bath House," plan no. 297-67, February 1913. Courtesy Frederick Chatfield Jr.

Manning suggested keeping sheep or goats. At the bottom of the slope between the Gilbert and Chatfield parcels, a north–south road meandered through woods along an oceanside bluff. Along the route, Manning cut openings in the trees to provide views to the water.[11]

In late November 1900, Manning's former associate Arthur Harrison conducted a survey of the plant species on the property, compiling a twelve-page list that Manning mailed to the Chatfields. In a cover letter, Manning remarked on the richness of the native flora and its value in making the wild garden.[12] Early in 1902, he sent his clients an extensive set of plant lists, plans, and instructions for planting the roadsides, gardens, and environs of the Chatfield and Gilbert houses, explaining his choice of native species that would provide flowers or fruit when the families visited. The longest section of his memo is devoted to the wild garden and illuminates how he developed a design from plants already growing on the land. "This whole wild garden section should be developed with the view of opening or taking advantage of existing compartments in which all sorts of conditions will exist," Manning writes. He explains that such "compartments," or pockets, are created by specific conditions—dry, wet, rocky, and so on—of the soil and terrain, which in turn support particular native plants. He instructs his clients to observe the dominant species that thrive naturally in each spot and "introduce great masses" of them there. Presumably he intends to amplify the horticultural effects of individual pockets as well as the contrast and variety of effects throughout the landscape. In some places, he notes, it may be necessary to improve the soil or even strip out the grass and create beds for the additional quantity of plants, so that they can "spread to cover all bare earth."[13]

In 1911, after an unexplained eight-year hiatus, Manning sent another extensive plant list, this time keyed to an accompanying plan for "Plant-

The house in more recent times, with simplified plantings. Photograph by Carol Betsch, 2010.

View to the putting green, with old stone wall. Photograph by Carol Betsch, 2010.

ing in the Wild." This plan, which apparently responds to the clients' desire for more ornamental plantings, expanded the wild garden to encompass the entire slope around Aldermere Farm and Kentmoor (about forty-eight acres), from the main road to the ocean. Manning explained that this approach allowed the Chatfields to embellish existing attractive plants at a lower cost than buying nursery-grown specimens, maintain the pleasing spatial proportions of the estate, and keep the water views open. As he had proposed years earlier, Manning again suggested mowing a meandering "ramble" through the embellished meadow. "I believe you will get greater pleasure from such a wild garden than you will from any considerable extension of your present flower gardens or lawn plantations," he wrote.[14] The clients apparently agreed, and went on to hire Manning to design a road and a landscape for a bathhouse near the ocean. His plan included white cedars and other native plants consistent with the wild garden concept.[15] Manning's associate A. D. Taylor took over the project from September 1912 through February 1913, overseeing construction of the bathhouse landscape design and making small adjustments elsewhere, as requested by the clients. Taylor's work for the Chatfields extended to the neighboring Megunticook Golf Club, for which A. H. Chatfield donated land to expand the course and paid for a landscape survey in 1914.[16]

Ocean view, across meadow. Photograph by Carol Betsch, 2010.

That year, when Taylor left Manning's firm to start his own practice in Cleveland, Manning assured his client that he should "feel perfectly free" to commission Taylor for ongoing work at either place.[17]

Family photographs and letters suggest that Aldermere's landscape was constructed largely according to extant plans. The house, though reduced in size (subsequent owners tore down portions of it), still stands on about twenty-four acres. The bathhouse near the shore was destroyed in a storm in the early 1940s. The former stable and The Willows are extant, owned and managed as active farmland by Maine Coast Heritage Trust. Kentmoor remains in family hands. An intact expanse of Manning's wild garden still spans most of the slope below the house at Aldermere. The "wild" now dominates the "garden," but the beauty Manning glimpsed in the ocean-side meadow remains.

Meguntícook Golf Course

ROCKPORT, MAINE

JANE ROY BROWN

Warren Manning's associate A. D. Taylor contributed to the design of Megunticook Golf Club from 1912 to 1913 and worked on the course again between 1914 and 1916 as the principal of his own practice in Cleveland, Ohio.[1] The nine-hole course, which remains much the same as it did after Taylor's independent commission, covers sixty-six acres of rolling terrain, much of it enclosed by woods of native white pine and mixed hardwood trees.[2] Stands of pine and white birch, species emblematic of coastal Maine, define the narrow fairways, giving the course a distinctive sense of place. Outcrops of glacier-scoured stone add to the rugged, naturalistic character. The east end abuts Penobscot Bay, which presents a natural water hazard for golfers at the second hole and ocean views from the fairway. Elsewhere, the enclosing trees limit exterior views, save for glimpses of the Camden Hills to the north. Members prize the course for its challenging topography, which reflects the more rustic style of its historical period.

Manning apparently delegated this project to Taylor, but other than a topographical survey and a drainage plan, it is not clear what design elements Taylor contributed to it. At least three of Manning's thirteen clients in the Camden–Rockport area, however, spurred the club's development. One was Lawrence Abbott, a summer resident from New York who brought golf to Rockport in 1898 and, with friends, organized the club the following year. Two other clients, Albert H. Chatfield and Cyrus H. K. Curtis, later served as club officers.[3]

Chatfield had the golf club in mind as early as 1900, when Manning described a site for "a club house . . . in connection with the golf field" on the neighboring property Chatfield had bought for his summer estate the year before. This prospective clubhouse was never built, but the location Manning described was probably the site of the original six-hole course laid out on Chatfield's land (off what is now Chestnut Street in Camden).[4] In 1901 construction began on the present course, laid out by groundskeeper Thomas Grant, and the hip-roofed, one-story clubhouse, designed by

A. D. Taylor, a Manning employee, advised on the expansion of the golf course to the north, as reflected in the 1913 plan.
"General Map of Property," plan no. 980-5, March 1913. Courtesy MPI.

The new section of the course reflected the rustic character of the original 1901 layout.
Photograph by Carol Betsch, 2010.

the architect Charles Brigham of the Boston firm Brigham & Adden. The club officially opened in 1902. This is now Maine's oldest extant golf club building, and both the building and the course are listed on the National Register of Historic Places.[5] In 1903 Chatfield bought and donated two parcels of land, totaling about twelve and a half acres, on the western border of the course, but the club did not develop this area for more than a decade.[6]

After Taylor left the Manning office to open his own firm, Manning wrote to Chatfield to say that he did not mind if his former client hired Taylor to continue working on the estate or the golf club.[7] After acquiring additional land and developing the acres donated by Chatfield, the club added three more holes in 1915 and 1916 and commissioned Taylor to plan the expansion, which encompassed the fifth, sixth, and seventh holes, and to improve the existing eighth and ninth holes. A framed 1916 plan signed by Taylor, crediting both his and Manning's firms in the title block, still hangs in the clubhouse.[8]

The extension provided unusually fine views of the surrounding hills. Photograph by Carol Betsch, 2010.

Massachusetts Agricultural College (University of Massachusetts)

AMHERST, MASSACHUSETTS

MATTHEW MEDEIROS

In June 1911 Warren Manning submitted a campus master plan to the building and grounds commission of Massachusetts Agricultural College. His report was the result of three years of working with the members of the commission and a team of architects who had been hired to design several new buildings.[1] In 1896 Manning had developed designs for Mount Holyoke College in nearby South Hadley, Massachusetts, and in 1908 he had created a campus plan for the University of Minnesota in Minneapolis. While working on the Amherst project, he also drafted plans for the North Carolina State Normal and Industrial College (now UNC Greensboro) and the University of Virginia.[2] A report on campus planning at Massachusetts Agricultural College by the landscape architect Frank A. Waugh, the founder of the institution's department of landscape gardening, notes that the commissioners may have known of Manning because at that time his firm employed an alumnus of the college, "a person of special ability," as Manning later described him, A. D. Taylor.[3]

In 1911 Massachusetts Agricultural College was nearly fifty years old; it had been created in 1863, when 310 acres of land were bought from six Amherst farmers for an agricultural school, one of several land-grant colleges enabled by the Morrill Act. The parcel's defining features were a large hill named Prexy's Ridge on the eastern side, a plateau known as Chestnut Ridge in the center, and a slope descending to the western boundary. The land was rich in wetland systems: a creek flowed north–south through the center and drained into a ravine that ran east–west to the Mill River. This river flowed south along the western edge of the campus toward its mouth on the Connecticut River, four miles to the west.[4] The existing roads consisted of two north–south routes: North Pleasant Street, which ran through the center, and East Pleasant Street, which followed the ridge on the eastern edge.[5]

The first class of students would not arrive until 1867, but soon after buying the land the board of trustees decided that the college should be located on the central plateau, with all of its facil-

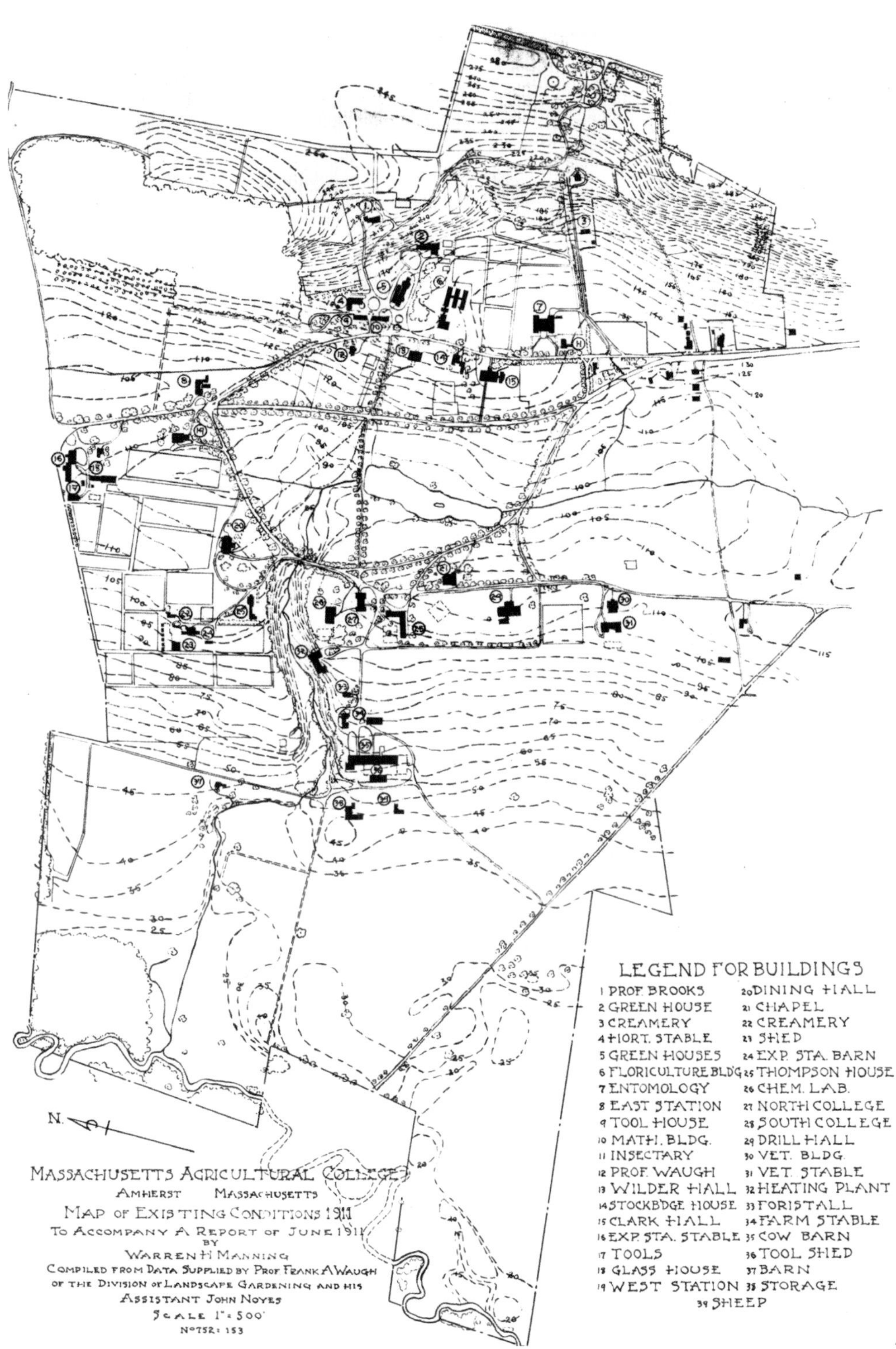

The map of existing conditions shows a disorganized arrangement of buildings—the college's original trustees had previously rejected campus plans by both Frederick Law Olmsted and Calvert Vaux. "Map of Existing Conditions," plan no. 752-153, 1911. Courtesy UMass Amherst Library Special Collections and University Archives (UMA SCUA).

ities housed in one large building.[6] In late 1865 or early 1866 Calvert Vaux and the architect Joseph Richards submitted a plan that proposed locating additional buildings and the campus core on the eastern plateau instead of in the geographic center of the campus, as the board preferred. The board rejected the proposal and solicited a plan from Frederick Law Olmsted in 1866, this time specifically requesting that the campus core be located on the central plateau. But Olmsted recommended the same site identified by Vaux and Richards, on which he proposed constructing a cluster of small buildings around a central green, as in a New England village. Olmsted also suggested damming the brook to create a pond just west of this site.[7] After some disagreement, the board and adminis-

Manning's proposed plan (1910) recommends dividing the campus into three zones (labeled Upland, Midland, and Lowland) and shifting the north–south axis to an east–west alignment running from a new administration building to the parklike core. "General Plan," plan no. 752-91-9, 1910. Courtesy UMA SCUA.

tration shelved Olmsted's plan in 1867, when William Smith Clark became the college's president. When Clark left office in 1879, the campus had expanded to include half a dozen residential-scale buildings on the central plateau and a new entrance on the eastern boundary street. In the following years, the landscape was laid out chiefly by Samuel T. Maynard, professor of horticulture, and James Draper, chair of the campus planning and landscape committee. The campus pond, which remains one of the landscape's most distinctive features, was created in 1892–93, during Draper and Maynard's tenure, by damming the brook, as Olmsted had suggested.[8]

The next two campus plans were submitted simultaneously on May 19, 1908, by Waugh and the architect F. I. Cooper. (Though the board had asked them to collaborate, a misunderstanding resulted in their each creating a separate plan.)[9] Both plans addressed campus expansion and reflected the board's proposal to cluster new buildings according to academic discipline—science, agriculture, and so on.[10] At the May 1908 meeting, the commissioners listened to the two presentations and, for unknown reasons, chose neither. Instead, they resolved to invite Manning to "study the arrangement of buildings and grounds . . . with a view to the establishment of a permanent plan."[11]

The campus in 1908 consisted of 484.5 acres, agricultural in character, surrounded by open fields for use by the agriculture departments. Thirty-nine buildings were clustered around a large lawn with the oblong campus pond, edged with specimen trees, at its center. The principal roads formed a circuit flowing north–south through and around the campus, consisting of North Pleasant Street, a busy public way, running north–south through the center, and two lanes to the east and west (Lincoln Avenue and Olmsted Road). The pond emptied into a small creek as it flowed into a ravine that ran east–west (near the present physical plant building). Then, as now, the creek emptied into the Mill River on the western edge of campus.[12]

Manning later wrote that in formulating his plan he "went back to the studies of Vaux and Richards in 1864, and to the very important report and plan of Frederick Law Olmsted Sr. in 1866."[13] In particular, Manning's plan reflects Olmsted's use of topography to organize the campus, his concern about pedestrian safety on the busy central street, and his vision of the campus green as a dominant landscape feature. In a color drawing dated September 1910, Manning broke out the three topographic regions of the campus, labeling them as the Uplands on the east, the Midlands at the center, and the Lowlands on the west. His final plan, dated September 1911, combined this topographical scheme with the board's request to group academic buildings by discipline. He also recommended preserving two tree-lined lawns enclosing the pond. Echoing Olmsted, he called them "greens."

The 1911 plan addressed concerns about the safety of pedestrians by closing the central street to all vehicles except electric streetcars, but it otherwise preserved the existing roads. Manning's plan was also the first to integrate new modes of transportation by expanding circulation on the perimeter, devising electric streetcar routes that anticipated present-day auto roads, and adding a new highway along the eastern edge of campus. He also proposed a scenic roadway along the Mill River as it flowed from campus to the Connecticut River, physically connecting the college to one of the area's most prominent natural features.[14] He suggested building a second pond (where the Campus Center now stands), which would have expanded the parklike core. The additional pond,

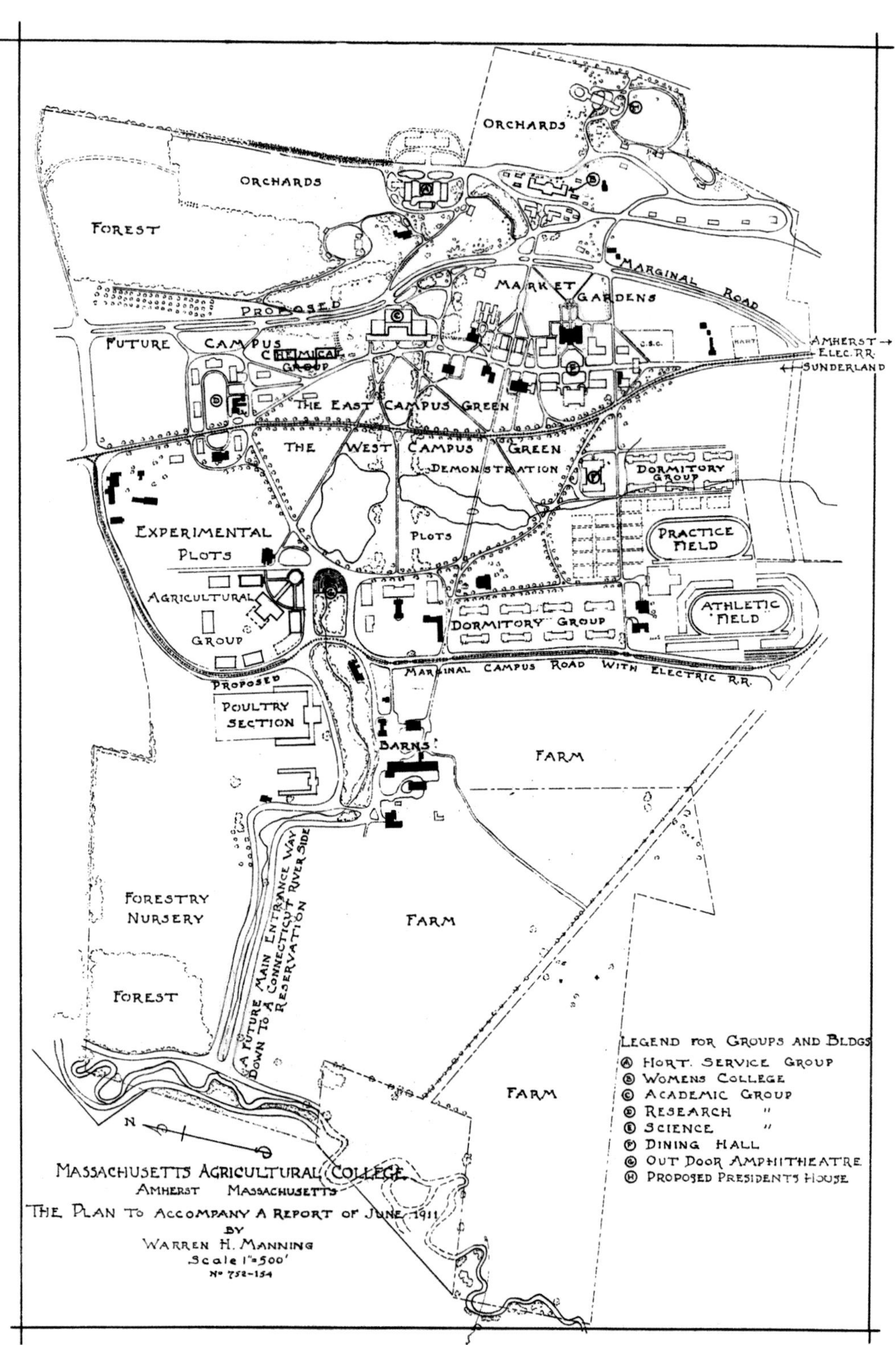

A revised plan submitted a year later proposed a more traditional campus green and the addition of market gardens and orchards in the upland section. Plan no. 752-154, June 1911. Courtesy UMA SCUA.

the scenic drive, and several other features of the 1911 plan were never executed, but Manning's influence can still be seen in the placement of buildings dating from his time.[15] Manning consulted periodically for at least another two years.[16]

The campus was renamed Massachusetts State College in 1931, and in 1947 it became the University of Massachusetts. Like many universities it saw a major growth in enrollment in the post–World War II era, but the green campus core remained relatively undisturbed until 1962, when a master plan by Sasaki, Dawson & DeMay located buildings much closer to the campus pond, reducing the green space that Manning had formalized, eliminating internal roads, and creating perimeter roads that bear more than a passing resemblance to routes Manning proposed.[17] Today, more than 350 buildings are densely arranged on a campus that has tripled in area since Manning's time to nearly 1,450 acres. In 2010 the university began another round of planning, with the firms Wilson Architects and Ayers Saint Gross. Their stated goals were to integrate neighborhoods within the campus, strengthen open spaces, improve connections, and create a more compact and sustainable campus. In April 2012 the university completed a new master plan that directs future growth to the campus core by moving all parking to several garages at the campus perimeter and clustering buildings within the primary road network. The plan, which is intended to guide development until the institution's bicentennial in 2063, also proposes increased pedestrian routes and a more effective connection among the open spaces within the campus core.[18]

Clement S. Houghton Estate

CHESTNUT HILL, MASSACHUSETTS

JAMES O'DAY

In 1906 the Boston financier Clement Stevens Houghton and his wife, Martha Gilbert Houghton, began building a new house on twenty-six acres on Suffolk Road in the Chestnut Hill section of Newton, Massachusetts, a suburb of Boston. The site's rugged terrain, with ledge outcrops overlooking the Charles River floodplain, held dramatic possibilities. The Houghtons chose the Boston architectural firm of Chapman & Frazer to design their house and Warren Manning to design the landscape.[1] Warren Manning and Horace Southworth Frazer shared similar aesthetic sensibilities and frequently collaborated on residential work.

Frazer, a socially prominent architect who had been trained at MIT, was best known for his refined Tudor Revival style, which distilled fifteenth-century architectural features into a cleaner and more modern interpretation. Yet for the Houghtons he designed a somewhat exotic (by Boston standards) Spanish Mission style house with stucco walls, quatrefoil windows, a loggia, balustraded terraces, and a barrel-tile roof. In front of the 8,200-square-foot house was a greensward, flanked by shrubs and mature trees. A circular driveway swept through the lawn, and a stucco arbor with a wide-eaved tile roof covered a walkway to the main entrance. A formal terrace and garden, classically appointed with columns and an Italian oil jar, lay to the rear of the house.[2]

Beyond this terrace garden, the designed landscape changed as precipitously as the topography. The house, perched on the brow of a steep slope with dramatic rock outcroppings, provided a panorama of the countryside and the surrounding marshlands, a pond, and two streams.[3] It was in these wooded lowlands that the Houghtons, likely with Manning's guidance, developed an extensive "wild garden." The term referred to a type of naturalistic garden (sometimes also called a nature garden) popular in this period.[4] The Houghtons' wild garden included flowering shrubs such as azalea, rhododendron, leucothoe, mountain laurel, and other native species, as well as meandering paths, rustic bridges, and a lagoon created by damming one of the streams.[5]

Scenes of ethereal beauty throughout the wild garden were created with combinations of native and introduced plants. Photograph by Herbert Wendell Gleason, 1928. Courtesy Robbins-Mills Collection of Herbert Wendell Gleason Photographic Negatives, Concord (Mass.) Free Public Library.

Manning dammed a stream to create Houghton Pond, the centerpiece of the Houghtons' wild garden. The pond's mirror surface redoubled the impact of the surrounding plantings. Photograph by Herbert Wendell Gleason, 1928. Courtesy Concord (Mass.) Free Public Library.

In 1918 Martha Houghton established a rock garden on the steep ledges overlooking Houghton Pond, a small water body that Manning created by damming Hammond Brook. The naturalistic rock garden held her expanding collection of alpine plants, including native ferns and primula seedlings imported from the gardens at Bodnant, in Wales.[6] At the garden's zenith, she hired the landscape photographer Herbert Wendell Gleason to document the garden.[7]

Like his wife, C. S. Houghton was an avid amateur botanist and gardener. A founding member of the Chestnut Hill Garden Club, he collected trees, with an emphasis on conifers.[8] Over the course of fifty years, the couple built an extensive plant collection in the wild garden, seeking guidance from several of the period's experts in horticulture and landscape architecture—not only Manning, but also the landscape architect Fletcher Steele, a former Manning employee;[9] the horticulturist Charles Sprague Sargent; and Reginald Farrer, the English alpine plant collector and author of *The English Rock-Garden*.[10] The Massachusetts Horticultural Society awarded the Houghtons a silver medal in 1928, proclaiming their gardens "the best example in this country of becoming design, proper construction, and desirable arrangement of flower and foliage" and "a wonderful pageant of Naturalistic beauty."[11]

C. S. Houghton died in 1949, and Martha Houghton lived at the property until her death in 1956.[12] The estate was sold, the property subdivided, and the wild garden below the house abandoned. But by the late 1960s, the community had grown to appreciate the site's historical and environmental significance. The Massachusetts Department of Natural Resources listed the pond and surrounding wetlands in a 1966 inventory. Between 1968 and 1979 the City of Newton acquired 114 acres to form the Webster Conservation Area and Hammond Pond Reservation, which includes a ten-acre portion of the Houghtons' wild garden. In the 1970s the Newton Conservation Commission and the Chestnut Hill Garden Club led a rehabilitation of the neglected garden.[13] Between 1999 and 2003 a combination of public and private funds provided for another rehabilitation, by Pressley Associates, a Boston-based landscape architecture and planning firm.[14]

Despite considerable research, no one has uncovered the extent of the role Manning played in the Houghton landscape design; although his office recorded sixty-one plans for the property, none have come to light.[15] In counterpoint, several published articles testify to the Houghtons' skill with plants, implicitly crediting them as the designers.[16] Martha Houghton's extant garden diaries note that she worked with Manning, but allude only to his building a small dam to create a pond.[17] The fact that the Houghtons consulted other horticultural and design experts further blurs the garden's design history. Yet the wild garden, especially, has Manning's signature water features, meandering woodland walks, and masses of native and naturalized plants, especially rhododendron and azalea.

Bancroft Park

HOPEDALE, MASSACHUSETTS

MATTHEW MEDEIROS

In 1896, shortly after leaving the firm of Frederick Law Olmsted Sr. and starting his own business, Warren Manning began planning a neighborhood of worker housing for the Draper Company in Hopedale, Massachusetts. The development, Bancroft Park, would consist of thirty duplexes on approximately seven acres when it was completed in 1903. During his first year of private practice, Manning made good use of his previous connections in the town, acquiring commissions for half a dozen projects in addition to the Bancroft Park housing.[1]

The Draper Company owned and managed almost all the property in the town, and built clusters of worker housing along the northern part of Hopedale Street as early as 1857.[2] Civil engineers planned this early company housing, siting the neighborhoods on relatively flat terrain and emphasizing functionality over aesthetics. Manning, the first landscape architect commissioned by the Draper Company, introduced design principles inspired by the garden city movement.[3] The houses were densely arranged to evoke the feeling of a small village, and workers could walk from the neighborhood to the factories in the town center. Manning used topography as an essential element of his overall design, arranging the houses at the base of a knoll around an elliptical road and envisioning an earthen berm on the east side of the neighborhood to screen views of the nearby Draper factories. The prominent Boston architect Edwin J. Lewis, who also designed a church for the Drapers, created the half dozen templates for the houses.[4]

The initial construction of Bancroft Park proceeded rapidly, and the fourteen houses on the inner loop of the ellipse were completed and occupied by 1897. Six years passed, however, before completion of the outer loop of houses along the ellipse.[5] The landscape, visible in maps and photographs from that period, consisted of closely grouped Colonial Revival duplexes along two streets that formed an oval. Alleyways were positioned along the backyards behind the outer loop and bisecting the inner loop of houses. The streets featured deciduous trees in evenly spaced rows at the edge of the turf front lawns, and residents parked their cars at a garage in the northwest corner of the neighborhood.[6]

Once Bancroft Park was built, the Draper Company diligently maintained it with assistance from the neighborhood improvement committee, an organization created by the manufacturer that encouraged tenants to appreciate the landscape by awarding prizes for plantings of trees or garden beds.[7] Although Draper valued employee management of the neighborhood landscape, administrators also enforced strict rules to preserve a consistent aesthetic character. Fences were strictly forbidden in Bancroft Park, creating the sense

The houses in Bancroft Park were densely sited to evoke a New England village character. By 1903, thirty had been built on seven acres. Lantern slide, n.d. Courtesy MPI.

Residents were encouraged to "beautify" their properties, as in other developments laid out by Manning. The Draper Company maintained strict design guidelines, which included a prohibition on fences. Postcard, n.d. Courtesy Daniel Malloy.

of an open parklike landscape. Street signs and house numbers were also banned, and the company fastidiously picked up garbage and removed trash from vacant lots.[8]

Bancroft Park was managed according to Draper rules until the company sold its stake in worker housing in the mid-1950s. Although private owners were free to make residential changes, the neighborhood landscape remains similar to that of Manning's day. Many mature street trees still stand along the sidewalks, and structural changes to the houses are minimal. The most significant change in the appearance of Bancroft Park occurred several decades ago, when the garage buildings were removed and residents began to park on neighborhood streets.

Frank Dutcher Estate (Oakledge)

HOPEDALE, MASSACHUSETTS

MATTHEW MEDEIROS

In 1889, the year after he joined the Olmsted firm, Warren Manning began working as a consultant on a landscape plan for a new high school in the central Massachusetts town of Hopedale. By 1890 he had taken on commissions for a mausoleum in the town cemetery for George Draper, the patriarch of the Draper Company, and a residential project for the company's supervisor, Frank Dutcher. Through the late 1920s, Manning would find a faithful client base in the Draper Company and its executives. In all, Manning worked on twenty-nine projects in Hopedale, ranging from plantings and paving construction to town-wide park planning.[1]

Hopedale, originally part of the town of Milford, was founded as a religious commune in 1841 by the preacher Adin Ballou and a dedicated group of followers from the local area. Ballou and his congregation bought a 238-acre farm with land on either side of the Mill River, a tributary of the Blackstone River, in the southwestern part of Milford called the Dale. After a financial crisis in 1856, brothers Ebenezer and George Draper, who owned 75 percent of the commune's shares, withdrew their investment, effectively dissolving the community. The Drapers then expanded their business and began acquiring textile companies, including that of Warren Dutcher, Frank Dutcher's father.[2]

When Manning began his landscape survey and planting plan for Frank Dutcher's house, many large homes intended for the second generation of prominent mill families were under construction on Adin Street. After Dutcher's house was struck by lightning and burned in 1901, Manning became the landscape architect for an ambitious project to build a new home on the site. Working in conjunction with the prestigious architectural firm of Chapman & Frazer, Manning integrated the lawn of the original Dutcher home with an old apple orchard and a small woodland to create a cohesive landscape over several acres. The design's incorporation of what Manning described as "ledges at and near the house with big white Oaks" gave rise to the property's new name, Oakledge. These large mature trees also framed the streetside lawn and screened the entry driveway. Additional features included a small pond on one of the ledges, planted with aquatic vegetation, and flower beds and a small kitchen garden along the sloping expanse of the rear yard. Beyond, there was an informal landscape of "sloping grass field passing up to an Oak, Maple, and Birch forest on ledgy uplands." Reflecting on the project, Manning remarked that he had never encountered "so many distinctive, closely associated, picturesque beauty and wild life values."[3]

In his autobiography Manning mentions over

Manning's c. 1901 design for Frank Dutcher's large home (by Chapman & Frazer) integrated existing white oaks with boulders, ledges, and an old apple orchard. Photograph, n.d. Courtesy Daniel Malloy.

The design emphasized a sense of wildness, apparent even in this winter photograph. Manning described a "sloping grass field passing up to an Oak, Maple, and Birch forest on ledgy uplands." Photograph, n.d. Courtesy Daniel Malloy.

The lot has since been subdivided, but the original house stands, along with remnants of Manning's landscape design, including some of the old oaks. Photograph by Carol Betsch, 2010.

a half dozen projects that were the result of Frank Dutcher's advocacy and praises his patron for adding "so much to the efficiency, beauty, service, and recreation values of Hopedale."[4] The original lot of the Dutcher house was later subdivided, and the grassy field and wooded areas now contain several homes. The pool is gone, and the house has undergone multiple expansions that extend into former garden areas. A few of the large white oaks remain, along the entries at the hilltop ledges and lining a fieldstone wall beside the entrance drive.

General Draper High School

HOPEDALE, MASSACHUSETTS

MATTHEW MEDEIROS

In 1926 the school committee in Hopedale, Massachusetts, hired Warren Manning to create a landscape plan for General Draper High School. By this time, Manning had designed more than sixty school landscapes, including several for Hopedale schools.[1] The new high school was located on the site of the former home of its namesake, General William Draper, head of the Draper Company from 1887 to 1906.[2] After Draper's death in 1910, the family property at the intersection of Adin and Dutcher Streets passed to his daughter, Margaret Preston Boncompagni, and in the 1920s Boncompagni donated it to the town, directing that the property be used for a school.[3] The Draper mansion was demolished and replaced by a Colonial Revival school building with a cupola designed by Chase Roy Whitcher, a Manchester, New Hampshire, architect.[4]

In his autobiography, Manning described his overall concept for the school grounds as "open lands with play space at the back and planting about the building and on boundaries."[5] Manning's design wove remnants of the mansion landscape, such as four European beech trees, into his new design. The building featured a portico with four full-height Ionic columns, and Manning laid out walkways from each side of the portico, leaving the central space to be planted with a scattering of shrubs and small trees. Open land at the rear of the building became a recreation area and was dotted with a grid of specimen trees; the east perimeter of the property included a small woodland.[6]

Manning's General Draper High School landscape has been greatly altered since the 1920s. In 1932 an adjacent property north of the original school grounds, donated by a Dutcher descendent, was designed to mirror the grounds along the south side of the school.[7] A garden bed was added near the portico, and several of the original beech trees and shrub plantings have been removed. Parking lots have expanded into formerly open areas on both the north and south sides of the school, as well as into woodlands on the north perimeter of the property. Additions to the schoolhouse, made over more than eight decades, extend the building out into areas that were originally open fields.

Manning's c. 1926 design for General Draper High School specified a rich and varied planting of trees. Photograph, n.d. Courtesy Daniel Malloy.

Many changes have occurred on the school grounds since the 1920s, but a few of the old trees, such as this beech, still survive. Photograph by Carol Betsch, 2010.

Hopedale Parklands

HOPEDALE, MASSACHUSETTS

MATTHEW MEDEIROS

Warren Manning's first major public park project began in 1891, when he was consulted on the design for a new park system for Hopedale, Massachusetts. Although he had not yet established his own practice and was still working for Olmsted, Olmsted & Eliot, Manning was known in the community because of his recent work on the landscape plan for George A. Draper's home. On October 30, Manning submitted a report to the park committee suggesting the purchase of forty acres of forested land on the southeast side of town and an additional twenty acres around the Draper millpond. Because the forested tract included land owned by many of Hopedale's wealthiest residents, the committee decided against this plan.[1]

In November 1898, however, the town passed a resolution to acquire parkland through eminent domain and move forward with park planning. In March 1899, under a newly created park commission that included another member of the extended Draper family, George Otis Draper, along with Charles F. Roper and Manning's client Frank J. Dutcher, Manning was chosen to determine the boundaries of the new park system.[2] With the help of surveyor Gordon H. Taylor, he made field visits to assess potential park locations and in July submitted a map that delineated the park borders along the shore of the Draper Company millpond and designated a site for a recreational area northeast of Draper's factory. The Draper Company and Draper family owned almost half of the acreage; the remainder belonged to the town and eight individuals. The Hopedale Park Commission approved the plan and immediately appropriated $12,000 for project expenses over the next year.[3]

Manning's 1899 design included a six-acre park with ball fields on the corner of Freedom and Dutcher Streets, as well as a naturalistic park that encompassed over 187 acres along the majority of the Draper Company millpond shoreline. Water and islands composed almost 57 acres of the park, and the west side of the property included a substantial portion of the highest topography in town, Darling Hill. The Draper Mills and Milford–Mendon electric streetcar lines were located along the south side of the pond. Streetcars crossed a steel bridge over the pond and then ran along the Grafton & Upton Railroad tracks at the west edge of the park. The park's eastern boundary extended along the shoreline, which faced the backyards of a row of houses on Dutcher Street, and the northern boundary ran though the wetlands, the headwaters of the millpond.

From 1899 to 1914 the town financed the park system through $2,500 allocations each year. To prioritize construction, the commission divided the project into two phases: the naturalistic Parklands dedicated to hiking and aquatic recreation, and a playground and recreation fields known as Town Park.[4] Hopedale completed Town Park first, as land acquisition for the Parklands took several years and public opinion at the meeting to approve the project favored completing the playgrounds and athletic fields sooner.[5] Construction of Town Park began in 1899, with initial work beginning at the Parklands in 1900, when the Draper Company drained the pond for dredging and removed several large boulders. At this time Manning directed the town to install a rustic bridge in the northern reaches of the Parklands, at the former location of Rawson's Bridge.[6]

During the construction of Town Park, fieldstone was excavated from the property and shaped into a wall along Dutcher Street and retaining walls along the park's north and east perimeters. By the end of 1900 the walls, drainage, grading, and turf lawn were complete, and Manning proposed enhancing the grass fields by lining the perimeter with shrubs and trees and adding baseball diamonds at the center of the park.[7] A dirt tennis court, two ball fields, and a bandstand

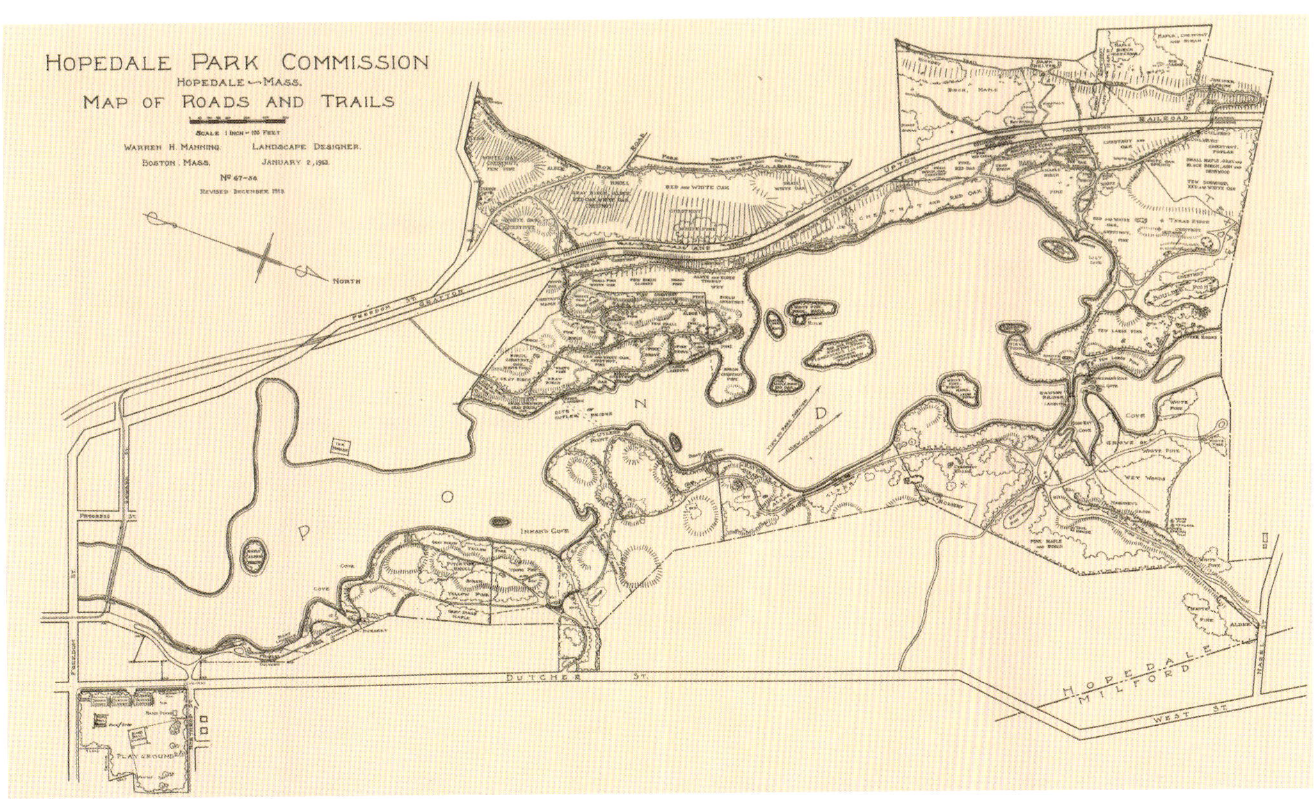

The 1913 plan included intricate details of tree species, views, boat landings, trails, islands, and other natural and designed features. "Map of Roads and Trails," plan no. 67-58, January 1913. Courtesy MCL.

were completed in the spring of 1901. The woods along the north edge of the property created a natural boundary that was further emphasized by a new stone retaining wall along the north and east edges of the park. On July 4th the Draper Company held its field day in Town Park for the first time. Businesses shut down and the community enjoyed "bag races, pole vaulting, high jumping, broad jumping, bicycling, canoeing, and something called tub race."[8]

"Town Park Field Day," 1919. Town Park, inaugurated on July 4, 1901, provided areas for active recreation and was the site of annual field days. Photograph, n.d. Courtesy American Textile History Museum, Lowell, Mass.

The Parklands offered opportunities for quiet enjoyment of nature. Postcard courtesy Daniel Malloy.

As work on the Parklands continued in 1901, the town confronted various obstacles, including litigation over a land parcel on the east side of the pond, while Manning focused on creating a gathering space and circulation routes in areas north of the disputed property.[9] Clearing and grading began along the course of a mile-long roadway around the park, passing over the newly constructed Rawson's Bridge. Manning also directed town officials to clear undergrowth from Maroney's Grove, in the northeast part of the park, and designed a picnic area among the old trees. With the roads, bridge, and a gathering space in place, the framework for the park was established.

Throughout the process of creating the Hopedale Parklands, Manning displayed his characteristic ambition and vision. He used his extensive horticultural knowledge in siting the plantings, creating lush stands of a wide variety of primarily native trees including maple, chestnut, ash, hickory, yellow pine, hemlock, white pine, gray and black birch, tulip tree, red oak, white oak, Carolina poplar, and black alder. In order to manage such intensive planting, the town built a temporary nursery within the park and hired a nurseryman to tend it in 1902.[10] The next year, when Hopedale officials acquired land that included a portion of the Old Saltbox Road and several ruins of early homesteads on the west side of the Grafton & Upton Railroad, Manning incorporated these existing landscape elements into his plan. The Old Saltbox Road, enclosed by stone walls and lined with historic cellar holes, became a picturesque trail leading to the open vistas along Darling Hill.[11]

Around this time Manning documented the landscape topography, views, and conditions in the park through a series of photographs. Many show the abandoned fields of the Rawson and Cutler Farm enclosed by scenic fieldstone walls and filled with stands of gray birch, red cedar, and juniper. The open areas of former farm fields provided expansive views of the hillsides to the east and west of the pond. In contrast, dense forests are visible in many of Manning's photographs, including one of a notable geological formation known as Texas Rock. He also documented the area's urban character by including images of residences and boathouses along Dutcher Street and the streetcar bridge and Draper factory on Freedom Street.[12]

The picturesque beauty of the naturalistic Parklands was much valued in Hopedale. In this postcard scene, the perimeter trail is visible, as are nearby homes. Postcard courtesy Daniel Malloy.

Woodland trails continue to offer park visitors opportunities for quiet, intimate experiences of nature. Photograph by Carol Betsch, 2010.

Over the next eight years, Manning worked with the Hopedale Park Commission and gradually completed his vision of a naturalistic park along Hopedale's millpond. New features were added each year: a train stop along the Grafton & Upton tracks in the north end of the park (1903); a bathhouse and sandy "beach" that became the primary swimming area (1904–1905); roads along the north and west side of the park (1903 and 1912); a network of several miles of footpaths throughout the pond shoreline (1904–1914); and "the Lookout," a stone shelter positioned at the summit of Darling Hill (1908). The park system continued to evolve after Manning completed his work on the project in 1914.[13]

During the 1920s, the town made a number of structural adjustments, erecting additional stone structures at Fisherman's Island and Maroney's Grove and replacing the wood and stone Rawson's Bridge with a fieldstone version that came to be known as the Rustic Bridge. Other alterations occurred over the years, such as replacement of the bathhouse and lookout shelter, repairs to existing structures, and new plantings. Although the streetcar line stopped operating in the 1920s, the bus system that replaced it continued the practice of dropping schoolchildren at the park during the summer for swimming lessons and other recreation. In September 1938 the Great New England Hur-

Manning's design for Hopedale Parklands emphasized the irregular beauty of the millpond, with its islands, wetlands, and surroundings woods. Photograph by Carol Betsch, 2010.

Wetlands at the pond edge contribute to the complex natural beauty of the park. Photograph by Carol Betsch, 2010.

ricane devastated the Parklands, requiring the clearing of all the trees at Maroney's Grove. In 1945 Hopedale acquired forty-four additional acres along the southwest edge of the park. The Grafton & Upton Railroad in the 1970s ended regular service on the tracks that run through the west side of the park, and the Draper Corporation, as it was by then called, finally shut down during the 1980s.[14]

From 1904 to 1987, seasonal visits to the pond averaged between four and thirteen thousand. Although attendance records were not kept over subsequent years and swimming was discontinued in 2002, the park remains a popular attraction.[15] Since 2012, LALH's Warren H. Manning Project has inspired community activists and the town's parks commission to advocate for the restoration of the Parklands to Manning's original vision.

Galen L. Stone Estate (Great Hill)

MARION, MASSACHUSETTS

JANE ROY BROWN

Great Hill, the summer estate of Galen L. and Carrie Gregg Stone, occupies six hundred acres in Marion, a coastal resort town in southeastern Massachusetts. The property encompasses the town's highest point, for which it is named: a glacial landform (elevation 127 feet) rising from a peninsula in Buzzards Bay. Galen Luther Stone, a self-made Boston financier, bought the land in 1908 and razed a former hotel to build the thirty-room Tudor Revival mansion, designed by Chapman & Frazer of Boston.[1] From the top of Great Hill, the terrain slopes gradually to the sandy shoreline of the bay, two and a half miles of which lie within the Stone estate.

In 1909 Warren Manning assigned his young associate Fletcher Steele to oversee the estate's development, which involved locating "the house, the road, farm buildings, stables and garages, the place for gardens and wharves for the yacht and boats, [and] where to cut vistas [through] the woods," as well as "planning for reservoir and saw mill and gate lodges."[2] Reporting on the project decades later, another Manning associate, Egbert Hans, noted that the ocean exerted the strongest influence on the estate design, beginning with the siting of the mansion. After deliberating over various locations, the Stones, Manning, and the architects agreed to locate the building near the base of the hill, just high enough to capture southwest views of the water across a sloping lawn. This site also exploited "an opportunity to open a wood vista from an important outlook of the house in an inland direction," Hans wrote.[3]

This feature, the Rhododendron Vista, a straight allée of rhododendron, cuts through an oak and pine forest for roughly a thousand feet, terminating in a glade of purple beech that could be seen from the main terrace as well as from the mansion's west wing.[4] At its far end the Rhododendron Vista meets another allée, the Azalea Vista, at an almost 90-degree angle. From there the Azalea Vista cuts northwest to intersect a secondary drive.[5] The azalea walk could not be seen from the house, so visitors exploring the Rhododendron Vista were treated to the surprising

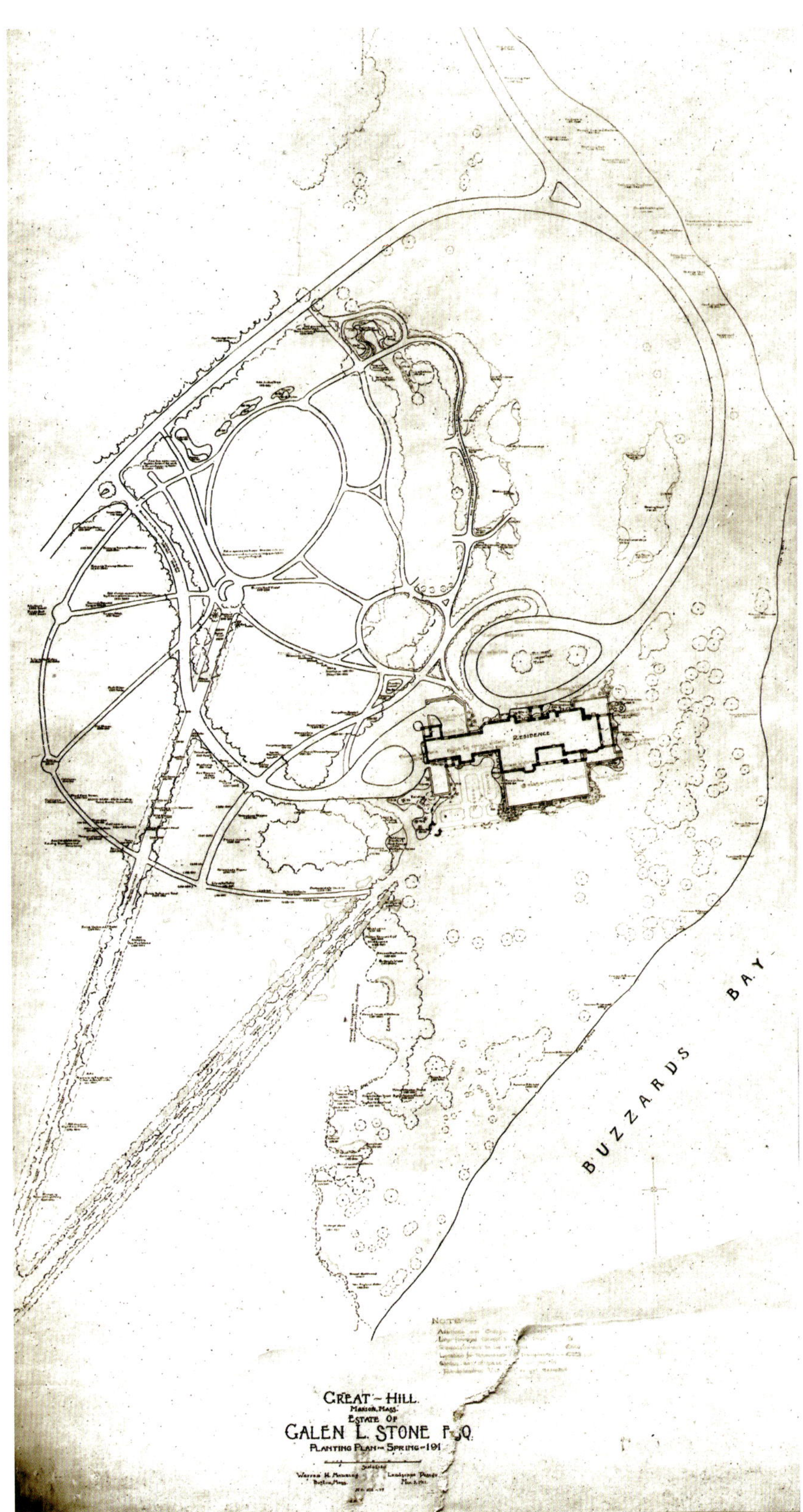

The thirty-room house by Chapman & Frazer was sited close to the water, approached by a long entry drive set below the ocean view. "Planting Plan," plan no. 812-79, March 1911. Courtesy MCL.

The one formal feature near the residence was a large rose garden (right). Manning's landscape plan, supervised by Fletcher Steele (then his employee), left great swaths of the existing woodland intact. Photograph courtesy Catherine Stone.

The grandest landscape feature of the plan was a thousand-foot rhododendron allée that stretched from the house into the woodland. Photograph courtesy Catherine Stone.

The view toward the mansion was dramatic, with the building's roofline silhouetted. Photograph courtesy Catherine Stone.

Although redesigned to reduce its size, the house retains an arresting presence in the landscape. Photograph by Carol Betsch, 2011.

The Rhododendron Vista continues to flourish, having narrowed as the large stands of shrubs have matured. Photograph by Carol Betsch, 2011.

sight of this woodland corridor of pink and white bloom once they reached the end.

Aside from these linear plantings, Manning's design responded to the ocean as the site's powerful *genius loci*. He and his clients decided to create only one formal garden near the house, a partially enclosed and intensively cultivated rose garden. The entry drive, laid out in a wide arc below the mansion's sightlines, showed off the carefully enhanced natural features of the site, culminating in the spectacle of the bay. Looping trails and bridle paths outlined irregular wooded spaces northwest of the house, including a signature Manning wild garden. Hans's account of its creation aptly described Manning's approach to the wider landscape: "The existing growth was developed by careful trimming and enriched by new plantations such as rhododendrons, azaleas and their companions."[6] Rhododendrons, in particular, were planted extensively throughout the property.

A road linked the mansion grounds to an extensive farm complex south of the entry drive. Here the Stones raised Guernsey cows, pigs, and chickens. In addition to an elaborate vegetable garden, workers tended orchids, acacias, espaliered fruit trees, melons, grapes, and other tender plants in a cluster of greenhouses, which included a palm house. Galen L. Stone II, a grandson of his namesake, remembered a "battery of beehives" behind the vegetable garden. "We were almost completely self-sufficient and free of the privation

A secondary allée of azalea intersects with the rhododendrons in the woods. Photograph by Carol Betsch, 2010.

Handsome old trees on the lawn, seen here from the roof of the house. Photograph by Carol Betsch, 2011.

Great Hill, now a family compound, is surrounded by about two and a half miles of shoreline. Photograph by Carol Betsch, 2010.

that most people experienced in the Second World War," he recalled. Behind the greenhouses, spruce hedges enclosed rectilinear flower gardens with a central circular fountain. Stewartia and dogwood lined gravel paths with iris and mallow borders. Galen Stone II recounted that each of his parents claimed a space and competed "to see who could make the most beautiful flower garden. His was blue and yellow, hers pink and white."[7]

Today Great Hill remains within ten acres

of its original size. Members of the Stone family still own and manage the property. To reduce expenses, most of the mansion was torn down in 1950, followed by several barns, the greenhouses, and other outbuildings.[8] But the Stone family's extraordinary stewardship has preserved many landscape features, including the Azalea and Rhododendron Vistas, mature beeches, mounds of rhododendrons, and the formal garden spaces and fountain near the former greenhouses. A wisteria-covered pergola still marks the entrance to the overgrown wild garden.

The Stone family has traditionally opened portions of the landscape to the public on certain days of the week.[9] Experiencing the beauty of the estate firsthand, community residents have come to appreciate both its historical importance and its grandeur.

The entry to the old wild garden is marked by a pergola near the tennis courts. Photograph by Carol Betsch, 2011.

Billerica Garden Suburb

NORTH BILLERICA, MASSACHUSETTS

MATTHEW MEDEIROS

In 1913 the small town of Billerica, Massachusetts, became the site of America's first residential development for workers based on Ebenezer Howard's garden city model. Warren Manning's involvement in Billerica Garden Suburb was almost inevitable, as he ran his landscape architecture practice from the Manning Manse, his ancestral homestead in North Billerica, and was involved in local politics as well as serving as the town tree warden. The town's board of trade, of which Manning was a member, had encouraged the Boston & Maine Railroad to locate its new maintenance facility in Billerica. Working with the support of the Massachusetts Homestead Commission, the board planned a development intended to house over twelve hundred employees and their families, potentially doubling the town's current population of three thousand. Manning consulted on the project with the landscape architect and planner Arthur Coleman Comey.[1] A 1907 graduate of Harvard, Comey brought to the Billerica project the practices he learned as a student of Frederick Law Olmsted Jr. and his experience as a city planner based in Cambridge, Massachusetts.[2]

In June 1914 the Billerica Garden Suburb began to take shape in the northern village of the town, on fifty-seven acres of riverfront plateau along a bend in the Concord River. The site was both attractive and convenient, being near several schools, the library, churches, a post office, and a free train to the Boston & Maine rail shops.[3] In contrast to tenements typical of the time, the plan provided for only five to six single-family houses per acre, which was even less dense than garden cities previously constructed in England. The houses, all based on a few prototypes designed by Comey, were set close to the road, and the curving streets were relatively narrow compared to modern standards, ranging from thirty-two feet on the main street of Letchworth Avenue to twenty-four feet on the secondary roads. As Comey explained in a 1914 article, the suburb embodied the "five essential elements of [a garden city]—site planning, limited number of houses per acre, wholesale operations, limited dividend, and participation by residents." In garden city terms, "wholesale operations" were the standardized templates used to create many similar homes; "limited dividend" and "participation by residents" referred to the practice of "co-partnership" financing, in which mortgagees also owned a minimum of 10 percent of their property value in the corporation's stock.[4]

The plans for Billerica Garden Suburb were never fully realized, however, because the Massachusetts Homestead Commission disbanded in 1919, leaving many of the three hundred houses in the suburb still under construction.[5] As it exists today, the Billerica Garden Suburb is essentially a bedroom community of greater Boston. A commuter train to Boston now stops at the same train

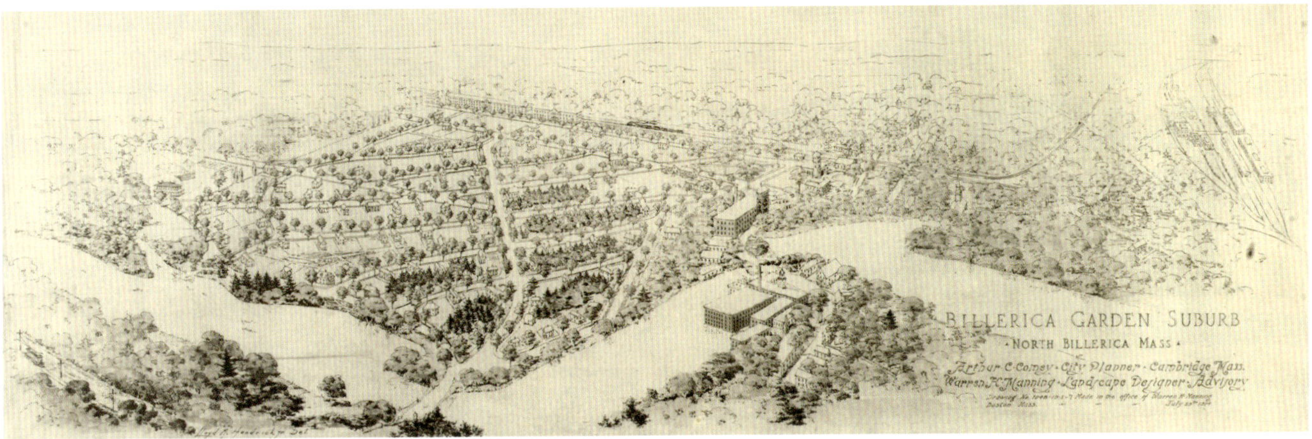

Manning collaborated with Arthur C. Comey on the layout of Billerica Garden Suburb, the first residential development based on Ebenezer Howard's garden city model. Drawing no. 1048-19-5-7, July 1914. Courtesy MPI.

Mature trees throughout the neighborhood create a parklike atmosphere. Photograph by Carol Betsch, 2010.

The Billerica Garden Suburb neighborhood is largely intact, situated behind the old mill buildings of T. C. Talbot & Company (now the Middlesex Canal Museum). Photograph by Carol Betsch, 2010.

station where residents of Billerica Garden Suburb once caught the train to the Boston & Maine rail shops. This is a logical evolution of the garden city movement's emphasis on the importance of accessibility to mass transit. A feeling of spaciousness remains, along with the original housing density, road widths, and housing setbacks from the road. The most significant change is that the neighborhood is no longer affordable for the working class.

The Billerica Garden Suburb represents an early attempt in the United States to implement Ebenezer Howard's garden city concept—predating Radburn, New Jersey, and Greenbelt, Maryland.[6] The neighborhood is also a notable precursor to Manning's work in environmental planning and resource-based design. In 2005 the Billerica Garden Suburb received a National Planning Award from the American Planning Association, recognizing its roots as an important site in the history of residential planning.

Houses were set close to the street, with five to six per acre. Photograph by Carol Betsch, 2010.

Manning Manse

NORTH BILLERICA, MASSACHUSETTS

MATTHEW MEDEIROS

In the late 1890s, Warren Manning began to stabilize and restore his family's ancestral homestead in North Billerica, Massachusetts, a project that would become a passion over the next four decades. Built by the family in the late seventeenth century, the Manse represented qualities Americans were celebrating two hundred years later embodied by the Colonial Revival then sweeping the nation. In his efforts to assure the preservation of the homestead, Manning helped establish the Manning Association of America, published its newsletter, *The Manning Manse Messenger,* and organized yearly reunions at the ancestral property. As he explained to readers of the *Messenger,* the Manning Association was working "in cooperation with the national government in the development of higher standard[s] of life, ideas and patriotic accomplishment for the American people."[1] The Manse, and its collection of thousands of Colonial artifacts, documents, and relics, would become a shrine both to the Manning family and to the American ideals it represented.

Manning's ancestors built the original portion of the Manse, a traditional two-and-a-half-story saltbox structure, about half a mile west of the Concord River in 1696.[2] The house was located on approximately twenty-five acres of farmland along the south side of Chelmsford Road near Black Brook, with American elms positioned at the corners of the building. Over time, the farm expanded to include a barn and another forty-seven acres of land. In 1752, when William Manning opened the Manning Tavern at the homestead, the building took on a prominent role in the region. Local Minutemen visited the tavern frequently during the Revolutionary War, and a small factory operating in a structure west of the house made saltpeter, an ingredient in gunpowder.[3] Business at the tavern continued to grow, especially once a stagecoach route between Boston and Amherst, New Hampshire, began passing along Chelmsford Road in 1795.[4]

The last Manning descendent to reside in the Homestead died in 1880, leaving the house and surrounding eighty acres to a group of trustees.[5] In the early 1890s, members of the family became interested in saving the decaying homestead, but little was accomplished until the fall of 1898, when Warren Manning organized a preservation effort. That winter, a group of descendants assessed the property and determined a course of action during successive meetings in North Billerica and Boston; by May 31, Manning had become so involved in the homestead's preservation that he leased the property himself. Over the next few months, he supervised a team of hired workers and family members, including his wife, Henrietta Hamblin Pratt Manning, and his brother J. Woodward Manning, in restoring the clapboards and roof and repairing the floor, walls, and ceiling.[6] Work on the landscape involved grading to drain water away from the structure and planting new garden areas with plants appropriate for a Colonial-era farm. By 1900 a kitchen garden was established in the field west of the house and a line of white pines separated the vegetables from the meadow beyond. In the yard near the house, Manning added mature "lilac bushes and clumps of old-fashioned flowers" that he found in cellar holes and nearby gardens of other historic homes.[7]

Manning's ancestral homestead, seen here before restoration, dates to 1696. Two centuries later, he galvanized a preservation effort among members of his family to restore the decaying structure. Photograph courtesy William C. Manning.

In 1921, when the project was substantially complete, *House Beautiful* featured an article about the Manse and its restoration. Photograph by Arthur G. Eldredge. Courtesy MCL.

With the structures stabilized and gardens progressing, Manning shifted his attention to developing a preservation plan for the homestead, which he had named the Manning Manse.[8] In June 1900, at an unveiling of the restoration, a group of descendants formed the Manning Association in order to buy and maintain the Manse. The association formally incorporated at a second Manning reunion that June and immediately began fundraising to buy the property.[9] After securing this group commitment, Manning began purchasing adjacent land near the Manse, adding new structures to the homestead and his own property, and clearing vegetation to achieve views of the house. By 1902 Manning had purchased a parcel of adjacent land, where he constructed a building using experimental techniques, including a roof "with the shingles set far enough apart to save about one-quarter of the shingles."[10] During this period, Manning spent vacation time at the property and appears to have considered the Manse his summer home. Around 1907 he built a one-and-a-half-story house, Juniper Cottage, on land across Chelmsford Road from the main house. The front yard of the cottage included tufts of juniper and two birch trees in the lawn.[11] By 1908 Manning had removed birch trees at the edge of the woods southeast of the house and from a pine grove along a meadow west of the house to create additional views. He later wrote that the yard near the house, though cluttered with undergrowth, still contained a mixture of elm and locust trees and the former gardens included "stumps of lilacs" and "a few struggling plants of bouncing Bet, tansy, and flowering spurge."[12] The cluster of structures comprising the homestead was surrounded by six acres of open fields, with woods covering the remainder of the property.[13]

Despite the house's museumlike interior, Manning and his family used it as a summer home. Manning also kept his professional library there, and for a period he required members of his staff to work on the grounds each day. From *House Beautiful,* July 1921. Photograph by Arthur G. Eldredge. Courtesy MCL.

Although the Manning Association served as caretaker of the Manse, Manning was contributing large amounts of time and money to its maintenance and by June 1915 had come up with a plan to operate a "Tea Tavern" on the property to help defray expenses. At this time Manning also decided to move much of his professional practice from the Tremont Building in Boston to a site near the Manse.[14] In December 1917, after the

The Manning Association still owns the Manning Manse and maintains portions of the interior; a later addition houses a restaurant. Photograph by Carol Betsch, 2010.

A peat bog lies behind the homestead, which in 1908 provided the subject for a *Country Life in America* article by Manning, "The Two Kinds of Bog Gardens." Manning's other bog, which featured non-acidic plants, is across Chelmsford Road. Photograph by Carol Betsch, 2010.

construction of "a large octagonal office building," Manning completely relocated the firm to North Billerica, where it remained until a final move to Cambridge in September 1923.[15]

At the North Billerica office, Manning required his employees to spend an hour each day learning about landscape design through work around the Manse and in the surrounding woods.[16] By 1921 the firm had added masses of rhododendron along the entry drive and among the elms bordering Chelmsford Road, as well as large lilac bushes along the south facade of the house. A bog was enlarged south of the Manse by damming Black Brook.[17] Manning continued to experiment with structures in the landscape, creating a small amphitheater of concrete benches and, in 1930, building an addition west of the Manse to accommodate new kitchen and toilet facilities for the Tea Room.[18]

Manning held the Manse dear to his heart, writing to his wife that it was "where, as you know, I can enjoy myself better than anywhere else." By the end of his life, he had secured the future of the homestead and sold the 150 acres of surrounding woods to the state for part of what would become the Warren H. Manning State Forest.[19] After Manning's death in February 1938, his son Harold inherited the remaining property near the Manse. Although Harold owned Juniper Cottage throughout his life, by 1939 he could not pay taxes on the office and tore it down, donating the land to the state forest.[20]

The Manning Association continued enlarging the restaurant adjacent the Manse, adding a new entry vestibule in 1952 and an expansion in 1960.[21] In 1982 the Manse was named to the National Register of Historic Places. After a 1994 fire that destroyed the restaurant and damaged the historic house, the family rebuilt the restaurant and painstakingly restored the Manse. Today, formerly open areas, including the kitchen garden and surrounding meadows, are dense woods. The bog survives, and massive evergreens in the woods west of the house mark an earlier division between the original vegetable garden and meadow.[22] Juniper Cottage is still across the street, and a stone marker nearby notes the location of Manning's former office. Although preservation of the Manse was a deeply personal project, Manning made a significant contribution to conserving land in Billerica by contributing to the state forest. He also left his country a shrine to Colonial America that reverberates on many levels—as an artifact of its time and as an example of the national nostalgia for the past that characterized the Colonial Revival period.

Arthur A. Houghton and Alanson B. Houghton Estates

SOUTH DARTMOUTH, MASSACHUSETTS

JAMES O'DAY

In 1911 Arthur A. Houghton and Alanson Bigelow Houghton, grandsons of Amory Houghton Sr., the founder of Corning Glass, commenced building the family's summer compound overlooking Apponagansett Bay in South Dartmouth, Massachusetts.[1] The Meadows, a thirty-five-acre estate that included two Shingle style cottages, was nestled into the ridge of a moraine—a peninsula-like glacial landform—offering a panorama of the Elizabeth Islands and Martha's Vineyard. The Houghtons likely found the location attractive for its rural charm and its proximity to the established nineteenth-century summer colonies of Nonquitt, Salter's Point, and Mishaum Point, where elite New Englanders idled away the hottest months.

The Houghtons hired Warren Manning and the Boston architectural firm of Chapman & Frazer. Manning had collaborated with Horace Southworth Frazer on earlier projects, among them the summer residence of financier George Herbert Walker in Kennebunkport, Maine (currently the George H. W. Bush compound), in 1902, and the five-hundred-acre estate of investment banker Galen Stone, in Marion, Massachusetts, in 1909. Although Frazer's designs for the Houghton houses were substantial (22,434 and 16,694 square feet, respectively), they were more understated than Galen Stone's baronial mansion.[2] At The Meadows, Frazer designed the two shingle-clad "cottages" in the Craftsman style, evocative of the New England vernacular.

Manning's landscape design for The Meadows, much of which is extant, took advantage of the site's existing conditions and topography. Consistent with his standard practice, Manning would also collaborate with the architect to determine the optimal building site.[3] By tucking the houses into the hillside, Manning and Frazer used the land's contours to shield them from the weather and render them invisible from the road, only five hundred feet away. Formidable fieldstone gateposts mark the estate's entrance. The drive traverses orchards and meadows, descending a gentle slope and passing a Tudor Revival Episcopal chapel, St. Aidan's, built by the Houghtons in

The plantings in the formal beds of the Houghton estate were unusually robust, a mixture of shrubs, roses, and perennials. Eastern cedar and white birch planted at the end of the garden eventually formed a screen. Photograph by A. D. Taylor, June 1913. Courtesy MPI.

The turf paths set with stepping stones offered an informal alternative to stone or brick. Photograph by A. D. Taylor, June 1913. Courtesy MPI.

The property retains the geometry of the formal garden layout and the irregular beauty of the surrounding meadows. Photograph by Thomas Wedell, 2012.

As in Manning's original design, plantings provide a foil for architectural features. Photograph by Thomas Wedell, 2012.

1917.[4] Passing the meadows, the drive splits, and a branch leads to each house, becoming a hedged corridor that recalibrates the vista and the landscape's spatiality. Each house reveals itself at the driveway's terminus, set off by a teardrop-shaped cul-de-sac encircling a grass panel. Dense plantings of mature shrubs and trees envelop both entrance courtyards.

Set among the boulder-strewn and wooded terrain, the estate grounds embrace the natural landscape. The A. A. Houghton house had two designed landscapes located within the larger grounds: a small formal garden and an adjacent terrace. Both are extant, although the terrace has been modified. The formal garden, rectangular and approximately 60 by 120 feet, extends from the house's southern facade. Photographs taken around 1913 reveal that it had an axial *tapis vert* (12 by 100 feet) bordered by square stepping stones and terminating in an exedra with a pair of stone benches. A mixed herbaceous border, twelve feet wide, was planted with drifts of perennials, roses, and other shrubs. Around the perimeter, another perennial border framed the space. The garden was screened by a belt of eastern red cedar and European white birch, along with shrubs to create shelter and privacy.

The terrace, located along the eastern facade, overlooks Apponagansett Bay. Early photographs show the terrace as a grass panel (24 feet by 60 feet) enclosed on three sides by a Doric-columned loggia, paved with brick, and two wings projecting from the main block of the house. A stone retaining wall defines the terraced lawn along the eastern edge and is punctuated by semicircular stone steps descending to the greensward beyond.

In 1928 A. A. Houghton Sr. died, and his son, Arthur A. Houghton Jr., and daughter, Gratia Houghton Rinehart, inherited their father's portion of the estate. Like his father, Arthur Jr. served as president of Corning Glass and was an important patron of the arts.[5] His family continued summering at The Meadows and made changes over time. In 1935 Gratia Houghton Rinehart and her husband, Alan G. Rinehart, a Hollywood producer, built an additional summer residence on the property. In 1937 the younger Houghton commissioned Ellen Shipman to redesign Manning's original 1911 formal garden. She altered Manning's design by reapportioning and formalizing the planting beds, creating a design for a "white garden."[6] At the far end of the formal garden, Shipman's design incorporated a previously installed rectangular ornamental pool dating from 1918, replete with a small bronze fountain sculpture. It was cosseted by large evergreen shrubs to create a tranquil and sheltered focal point.[7]

Through the years, the Houghton heirs retained control of The Meadows, with the descendants of A. A. and A. B. managing their respective shares. The A. A. Houghton house remained in the family until 1982, when his heirs relinquished their share of the family compound. Since that time the A. A. Houghton house has had four owners.[8] The current owners acquired the house in 2004 and appreciate the property's architectural and historical significance. They are aware of Ellen Shipman's 1937 plan and are currently working to rehabilitate both the house and the gardens.[9] The A. B. Houghton house remains in the Houghton family, and the property retains much of its design integrity.

Fuller Brook Park

WELLESLEY, MASSACHUSETTS

MATTHEW MEDEIROS

In 1897 the town of Wellesley hired the firm of Olmsted, Olmsted & Eliot to make recommendations for new parks. John Charles Olmsted submitted a report to the town outlining a plan for a park system similar to the Emerald Necklace the Olmsted firm had devised for Boston. Wellesley was then a rural community free of the dense urban development of nearby Boston, and the plan proposed to set aside an eighth of the town's total acreage for a unified system of outdoor public spaces connected by parkways. Specific recommendations included preserving the town's highest hills, the Charles River bank, and Lake Waban, as well as acquiring lowlands for flood control and municipal trolley and sewer lines. The Olmsted firm recommended that the channel in the lowlands, which would become Fuller Brook Park, be widened and deepened to increase the capacity for storm drainage, and that this scenic waterway be used as a linear park with pathways following the route of the brook as it flowed eastward to the Charles River. The park would also create a corridor that could connect recreational amenities such as ball fields and playgrounds and possibly serve as the route for a municipal sewer and a trolley line. The report specified a parkland corridor a minimum of 150 feet wide, increasing to 300 feet in places of notable natural beauty. At the time of the report the proposed park was a swampy forest of about seventy-five acres surrounded by farms.[1]

Warren Manning was involved with Fuller Brook Park from 1899 to 1907, likely obtaining the job through his past connection with the Olmsted firm.[2] His chief responsibility was to recommend specific parcels for the town to acquire and to create the infrastructure and engineering to improve storm drainage. His surviving drawings for the project, dated April 1900 to August 1903, show land acquisitions, designs for altering the streambed's course and elevation, and plans for bridges and culverts at street crossings. No planting plans have come to light, and some of the extant plans were clearly never built (such as one that shows a separate bikeway running parallel to the pedestrian path).[3] Most of the drawings, however, are consistent with the few extant records of the park's development from this period, which document clearing unwanted vegetation, acquiring land, and grading the stream channel.[4]

The last record of Manning's involvement was in 1914, when he briefly consulted on a proposed quarter-mile expansion of the park's western end (which took place in 1920, after land purchases were made). By 1914 Fuller Brook Park encompassed about seventy-five acres and two miles of linear watercourse that varied in width between 150 and 300 feet. The brook's channel had been lowered and straightened, improving drainage of swampy areas. As swamp was supplanted by dry parkland, Manning created expanses of lawn edged with shade trees and rambling shoreline

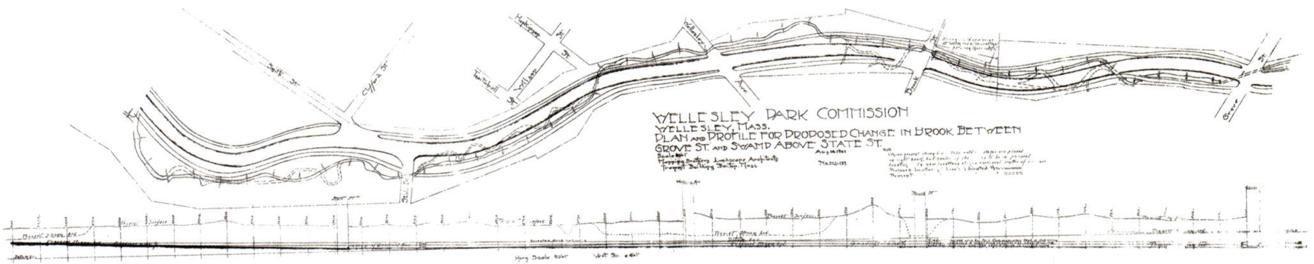

Manning's 1903 rendering depicts the course of the stream, along with proposed bridges, culverts, roads, and bicycle and walking trails. "Plan and Profile for Proposed Change in Brook," plan no. 262-139, August 1903. Courtesy Wellesley Park Archives.

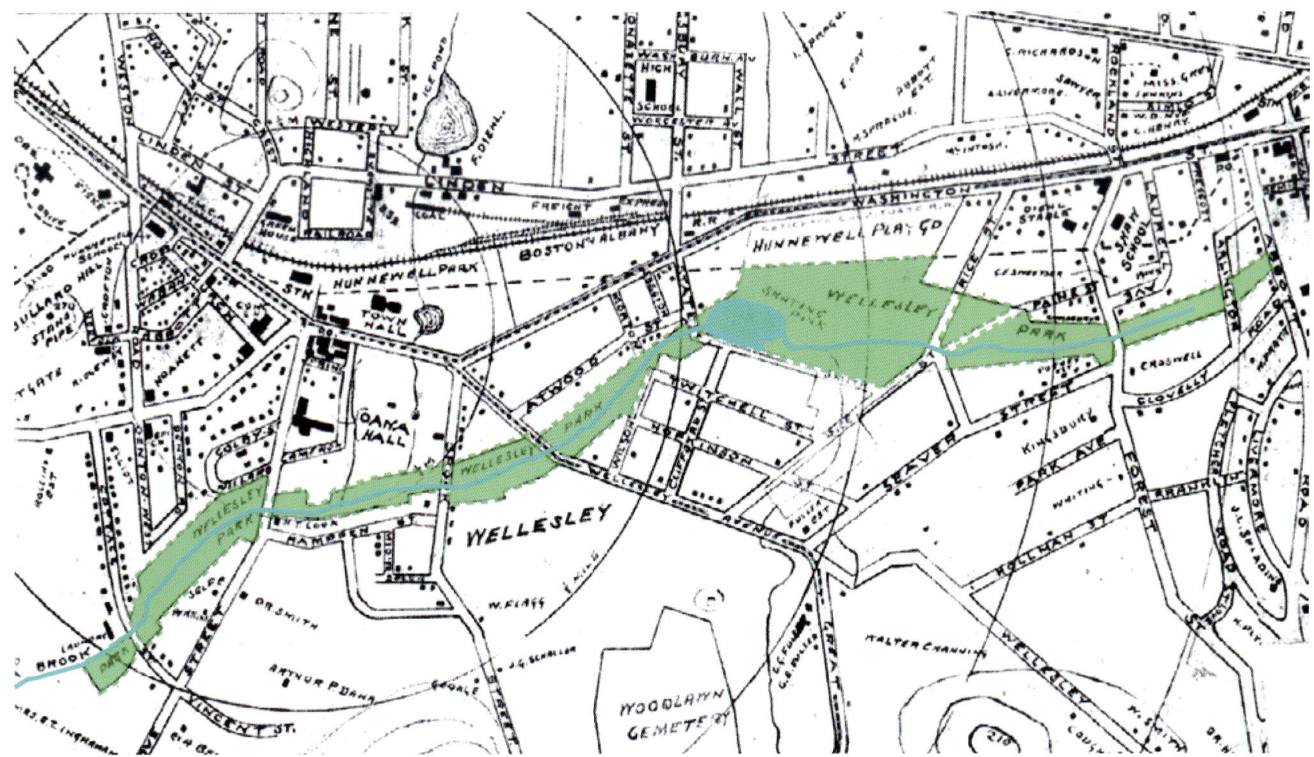

Fuller Brook Park (here identified as "Wellesley Park") winds through a heavily settled neighborhood on this 1910 map. Courtesy Wellesley Historical Society.

The stream, with its heavily vegetated banks, provides a rural setting to the backyards that border it. Photograph by Carol Betsch, 2010.

At some locations the park widens to about three hundred feet, a suggestion made in the original Olmsted, Olmsted & Eliot report. Photograph by Carol Betsch, 2010.

walks. Then, as now, the park was segmented by many roads, as well as the public athletic fields at Hunnewell Field. In contrast to later years, however, the stream flowed uninterrupted until very near the end of the park.[5]

The first subsequent design changes took place between 1915 and 1921, when engineer and landscape architect Ernest Bowditch integrated the city's new municipal sewer into the park and then redesigned substantial areas that were destroyed during the sewer construction. Documents and photos from that period show a naturalistic park in the Olmstedian tradition. In 1936 twelve acres south of Hunnewell Field were removed from the park, and the stream was diverted underground for the first time to accommodate the new Wellesley High School. In the 1950s and 1960s Fuller Brook Park was redesigned again by officials at the Wellesley Department of Public Works to reverse neglect that had occurred in the 1940s, when park budgets were lean. First, in 1958, they deepened the western segment of the brook channel, cleared it of vegetation, and lined it with concrete retaining bricks, and they also built three new roadway bridges. In the following years they worked with the Wellesley Garden Club to soften this section's engineered appearance with new plantings of dogwoods, evergreens, and maples. In 1950, when a new skating rink was constructed, and again 1961 and 1972, the stream was channeled underground at several points in Hunnewell Field to create more space for recreational facilities and fields.[6] Despite these changes, the park retained its storm-drainage function and its form as a linear park corridor.

Today Fuller Brook Park is a lush, two-and-a-half-mile water corridor through twenty-three acres in the Wellesley Hills neighborhood, where it is a popular spot for walking, running, and biking. Large shade trees and ground cover create an open and lush landscape. The pedestrian pathway crosses the roads at grade. Where roads intersect the brook, it flows underground through culverts

Areas of the park are dominated by large trees, a few of which date to Manning's period of work on the park. Photograph by Carol Betsch, 2010.

or on the surface below scenic bridges, each distinct in its design, imparting a unique character to the adjacent area of the park. In the urban areas in the western portion of the park, the bridges and the watercourse are transparently engineered, with a concrete channel and concrete retaining wall. In residential areas, openings in backyard fences allow neighbors to enter the park. Other stretches are wilder, with rugged terrain and dense vegetation. After the brook passes through an underground culvert at Hunnewell Field, it resurfaces in the eastern portion of the park in a more naturalistic channel without retaining walls or other obvious engineering features. Though the park is a half-mile longer than it was in Manning's time, its north and south boundaries are unchanged. Fuller Brook Park has yielded ground to three other public spaces, losing its legibility as it passes through them: the twelve acres of grounds at Wellesley High School, thirty acres of public athletic fields at Hunnewell Field north of the high school, and, east of the school, the half-acre playground at Phillips Park. In each of these areas the Fuller Brook corridor dwindles to little more than a pathway, and a culvert diverts the water underground.

In 2006 the town of Wellesley began a revitalization of Fuller Brook Park, structured by a master plan created by Halvorson Design Partnership and Shary Page Berg, a landscape preservation consultant. The plan identified key areas in need of improvement and recommended strategies, such as restoring plantings and bolstering erosion control, for these places. In 2011 Pressley Associates began the ongoing second stage of master planning, creating specific designs for new and restored features in the park. In 2013 the park was named to the National Register of Historic Places.

Because Fuller Brook Park has gone through so many changes, it is doubtful that specific elements of Manning's design, such as plantings, culverts, and bridges, have been preserved. But the aesthetic principles the park embodies remain close to those envisioned by the Olmsteds and executed by Manning. In his unpublished autobiography, Manning observed, "Many times, most attractive bodies of water can be made in mosquito-breeding swamp areas by establishing dams that appear to be the work of Nature. There will be the opening up of footpaths along lanes of special plant interest to attractive views, also bridle paths . . . and bicycle ways."[7] Since the 1930s, when Manning wrote this, science has established the importance of leaving wetlands intact, both for wildlife habitat and for flood control. But the idea of enhancing a particular type of environment for human use and enjoyment through naturalistic design is clearly articulated in Fuller Brook Park, and subsequent design changes, including the current renewal of the park, have stayed true to this vision.

Agassiz Park

CALUMET, MICHIGAN

LYNN BJORKMAN AND ARNOLD R. ALANEN

Upper Michigan's Keweenaw Peninsula contains one of the world's richest deposits of copper, and efforts to extract the mineral for industrial uses began there in the late 1840s and continued into the 1960s. Historically, the Boston-based Calumet & Hecla Mining Company (C&H) dominated Michigan's copper industry. Crucial to the company's success was the leadership of its longtime president, Alexander Agassiz, who directed the mining enterprise for more than forty years. With profits from the company's Michigan mines, Agassiz, son of the famed naturalist Louis Agassiz, supported his own primary work as a natural scientist, achieving international recognition for his research in marine biology and oceanography.

In 1917, seven years after Agassiz's death, C&H employed Warren Manning to design a park in memory of the late president, for use by the residents of Calumet—then a community of about 25,000 people that had developed around the company's mines. The park was not the first project that brought Manning to Calumet; in 1915 he designed a garden (no longer extant) at the residence of C&H general manager James MacNaughton. This commission marked the beginning of an association between the landscape architect and C&H that would continue until 1932. Most of Manning's work for the firm consisted of planting plans for company properties; Agassiz Park represents his most extensive and important project in Calumet.[1]

The idea for the park likely originated among Agassiz family members, including Alexander's two sons, Rodolphe, who became C&H president in 1915, and George, the donor of the cast bronze statue of Agassiz that was the park's centerpiece. (The noted American sculptor Paul Wayland Bartlett received the commission for the monument.) Manning evidently completed an initial set of plans for the park soon after he was hired, but work on the ground was delayed by the company's "rush to get out copper" during World War I. In 1919 MacNaughton wrote to Manning that C&H was ready to begin the project, and the two men directed the park's construction between 1919 and 1923.[2]

The site selected for the park was a wedge-shaped parcel of C&H-owned land, about twenty acres in size, bordered by the commercial area of what is now Calumet Village, a neighborhood of miners' houses, and the edge of the company's industrial complex. C&H had left the area undeveloped to act as a firebreak, but used the land over the years in a variety of ways—as pasture, industrial storage space, and a baseball field. In 1916 the company improved the grounds with pavilions and paths in preparation for events celebrating its fiftieth anniversary.[3]

In 1920 Manning produced a final park plan that featured eight pathways, all focused on the Agassiz statue; two led out of the park to the industrial and mining area, two ran along the perimeter of the industrial properties, and four passed through the park and connected with streets in the village. All but one pathway were designated as a "walk," each distinguished by an allée of mixed tree species: ash, basswood, elm, hard maple, red maple, white birch, and yellow birch. (Manning also designated an Oak Walk elsewhere in the park.) At one end, where space between the walks was limited, he created several intimate, wooded planting areas; the other

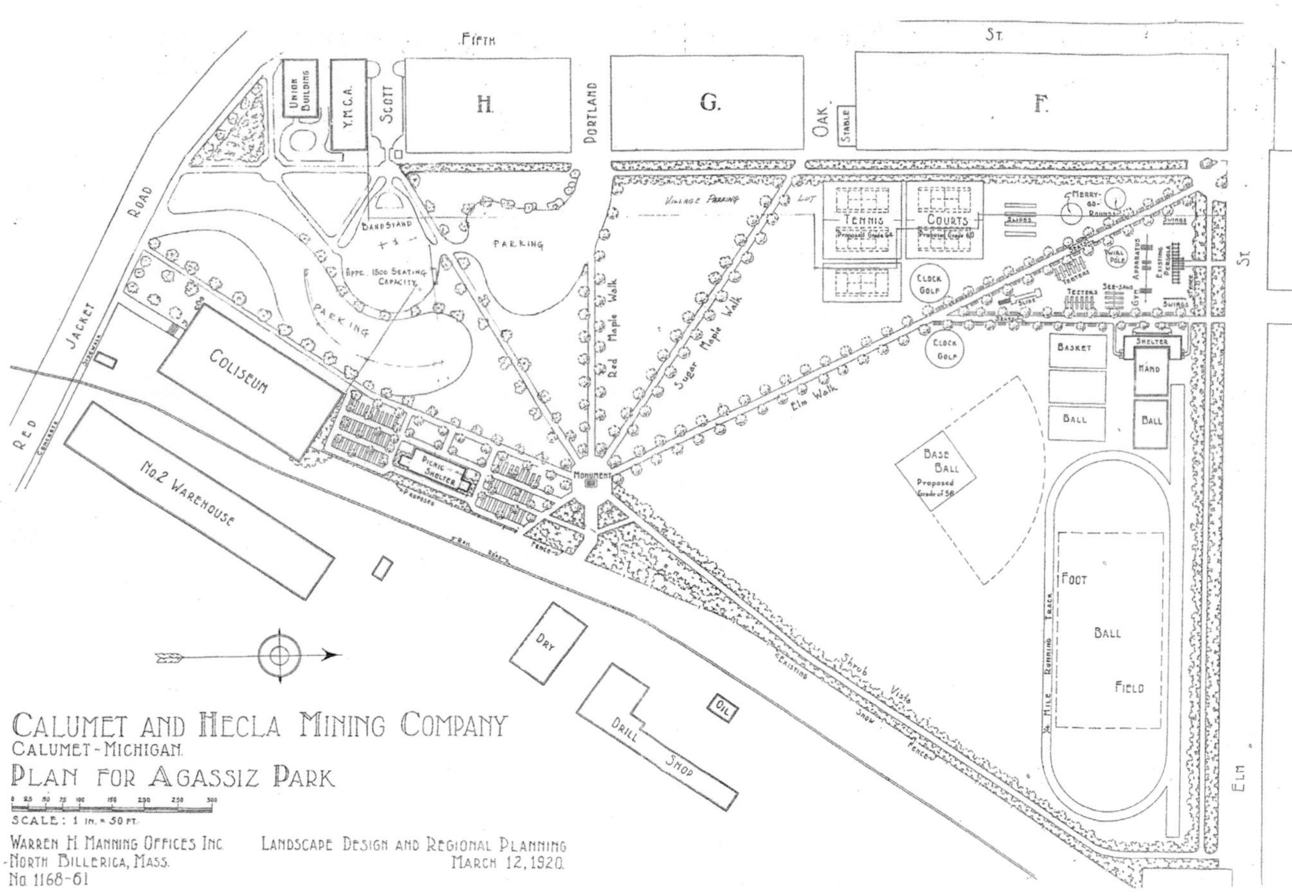

The 1920 plan for Agassiz Park was structured by a framework of long walkways bordered with trees and a wide planting belt of native trees and shrubs underplanted with wildflowers, ferns, and mosses. Proposed areas for active recreation included tennis, basketball, clock golf, baseball, and football. "Plan for Agassiz Park," plan no. 1168-61, March 1920. Courtesy National Park Service, Keweenaw National Historical Park.

Park plantings were installed by volunteers over two Community Days in 1922 and 1923. Photograph, 1930. Courtesy Foster Oversized Photos Collection, National Park Service, Keweenaw National Historical Park.

end was characterized by larger open spaces suitable for group activities. To accommodate these events Manning designed an amphitheater for five thousand people, a bandstand for fifty musicians, a rustic picnic shelter, and a "Playground House" for children and mothers. None of these structures was built, but the proposed baseball and football fields, running track, and tennis and basketball courts were eventually developed.[4]

Manning's planting program was detailed, giving special emphasis to the native species of the region: "[Those] who live in a northern region with a long cold winter," Manning wrote in 1920, "have a wealth of beautiful native woody plants, the beauty of which few can fully realize until they are brought together in masses where the flowers and the fruits and the variations in spring, summer and autumn foliage can be readily seen, as the plan provides in Agassiz Park." Around the park's borders Manning proposed a "wide belt of planting," with "native trees, shrubs and herbs." These included a range of species, some of which were non-native: cedar, fir, mountain ash, elder, thimbleberry, bush honeysuckle, buffaloberry, barberry, and dogwood. The understory, Manning wrote, would be made up of ferns, mosses, clubmoss, trilliums, violets, anemones, hepaticas, and other spring flowers seldom seen by some of the town's residents.[5]

The border between the park and industrial grounds was designed to reveal "the more brilliantly colored and showy garden flowers and shrubs," and to appeal to "the infirm or older people, or mothers with babies" who would find enjoyment in the "elements of beauty and comfort" offered by plants. These plantings included a mixture of shrubs and flowers—lilacs, spiraeas, roses, peonies, loosestrife, day lilies, hollyhocks, and "many other favorites"—all set against a backdrop of Lombardy poplars.[6]

C&H provided miners to complete the site preparation and construction work involved in developing the park. Much of the planting, however, was accomplished during two "Community Days," volunteer work sessions that Manning staged in 1922 and 1923 to foster personal interest in the park among the townspeople. A simple public ceremony marked the unveiling of the Agassiz statue and dedication of the park in September 1923.[7]

Manning's involvement with Agassiz Park did not stop with the formal dedication. Until his contract with C&H ended in 1932 he made at least one visit each year to Calumet, making recommendations for improvements and maintenance. C&H continued to maintain Agassiz Park for community use until the early 1950s, but as the company's fortunes declined the park became increasingly neglected. The termination of company mining operations in 1968 by C&H's new corporate owner led to the removal of the Agassiz statue and the sale of the parkland for the construction of a supermarket, an insurance company building, and a public housing complex. The former athletic field was sold to the local school district; though it has been

The ornamental centerpiece of the park design was a bronze statue of Alexander Agassiz, president of the Calumet and Hecla Mining Company, who was also a renowned marine scientist. Postcard courtesy Michigan Technological University Archives and Copper Country Historical Collections.

The park was dedicated September 1923 at a ceremony attended by local citizens and workers of the C&H Mining Company. Photograph, 1923. Courtesy Brockway Photograph Collection, Michigan Technological University Archives and Copper Country Historical Collections.

Manning's characteristic emphasis on intimate experiences of nature—despite the open plan—is evident in old photographs. Photograph courtesy Calumet and Hecla Photograph Collection, Michigan Technological University Archives and Copper Country Historical Collections.

modified, its original use continues. Most of the park's remaining land was purchased by Calumet Village in the 1990s. To meet the community's recreational needs, a shelter building, parking lot, and sports fields have been completed, along with the rehabilitation of remnants of the original tree-lined paths. The intrusion of new buildings and the resulting loss of original design features have obscured the park's associations with Manning. Nonetheless, some of the allées and Lombardy poplars along the site's eastern edge remain as evidence of his efforts.[8]

Gwinn Model Town

GWINN, MICHIGAN

ARNOLD R. ALANEN AND LYNN BJORKMAN

In the early years of the twentieth century Warren Manning designed three communities for mining and manufacturing industrialists who sought to accommodate their workers in model company towns: Warren, Arizona, for the Calumet & Arizona Copper Company; Goodyear Heights, in Akron, Ohio, for the Goodyear Tire & Rubber Company; and Gwinn, Michigan, for the Cleveland-Cliffs Iron Company (CCI; now Cliffs Natural Resources). The Arizona and Ohio communities were built next to larger cities, but Gwinn—sponsored by William Gwinn Mather, president of CCI from 1891 to 1931—functioned as a stand-alone settlement on the Marquette Iron Range of Michigan's Upper Peninsula.

At the time that Gwinn was founded, many captains of American industry, including William Mather, sought to attract desirable workers by offering attractive housing and recreational facilities, as well as medical and pension benefits. European industrialists led the way in developing these programs, and Mather garnered first-hand knowledge of them by visiting model towns in England, Germany, and Sweden during the 1890s. In 1898, when Mather announced that the design and management of European factories and housing were "far ahead" of what was occurring in the United States, he supported the development of CCI's welfare department, which offered employees safety instruction, medical programs, and clubhouses. A year later Mather hired Manning to prepare landscape designs for the company's northern Michigan shaft houses, office buildings, and executives' homes, and to assist in the development of housing, school, and community beautification programs for several towns where CCI operated.[1]

When iron ore was discovered in a remote district of the Marquette Range in 1902, CCI officials realized that it would be hard to attract dependable workers to this isolated area unless "provision is made for their accommodation." To offer them comprehensive housing and community services, Mather commissioned Manning to select a site and prepare a plan for a model company town that the industrialist named Gwinn.

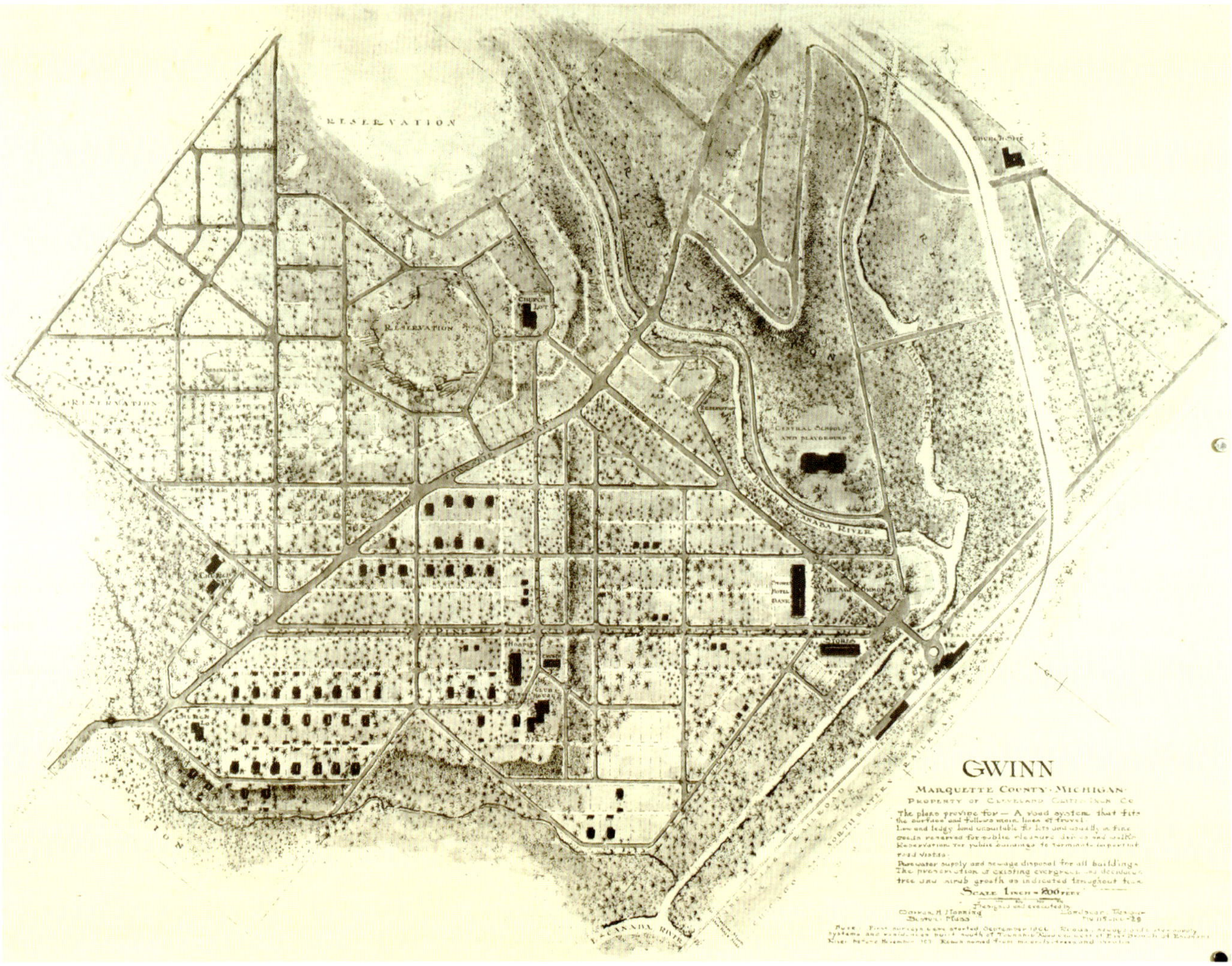

Manning's plan for Gwinn was dense with information. It specified low and "ledgy" land unsuitable for lots reserved for public pleasure drives and walks; the location of public buildings to terminate important road vistas; and the preservation of existing evergreen and deciduous tree and shrub growth. "Gwinn," plan no. 715-100-29, n.d. Courtesy MPI.

Manning visited the district in March 1907 and chose a site at the fork of the Escanaba River and its East Branch. Because three feet of snow covered the ground, he was unable to do any survey work, but two of his employees later put on snowshoes and staked out the 440-acre property. By early spring preliminary work—clearing trees and brush, grading streets and alleys, and laying out water and sewer lines—was under way.[2]

Manning designed a compact grid plan for Gwinn, placing the main streets at a 45-degree angle to the existing rectilinear township and range lines, thus distinguishing the model town from other nearby settlements. The design also provided space for a town common that served as both a public park and a focal point for several of Gwinn's most formal features. Three avenues, each lined with pines on both sides and with a row of trees along the median, were planned to extend from the common; sites for several public buildings were also proposed as "effective terminals to the main streets of the town." The residential streets were relatively narrow, with dwellings located close to the roads to increase the size of house lots and create ample room for backyard gardens. All of these attributes, Manning contended, would "not only make the town more attractive, but will give unlimited pleasure and comfort to the miners and their families."[3]

Manning called for the use of native vegetation throughout the site, and he sought to preserve trees that were "suitable to afford shade and

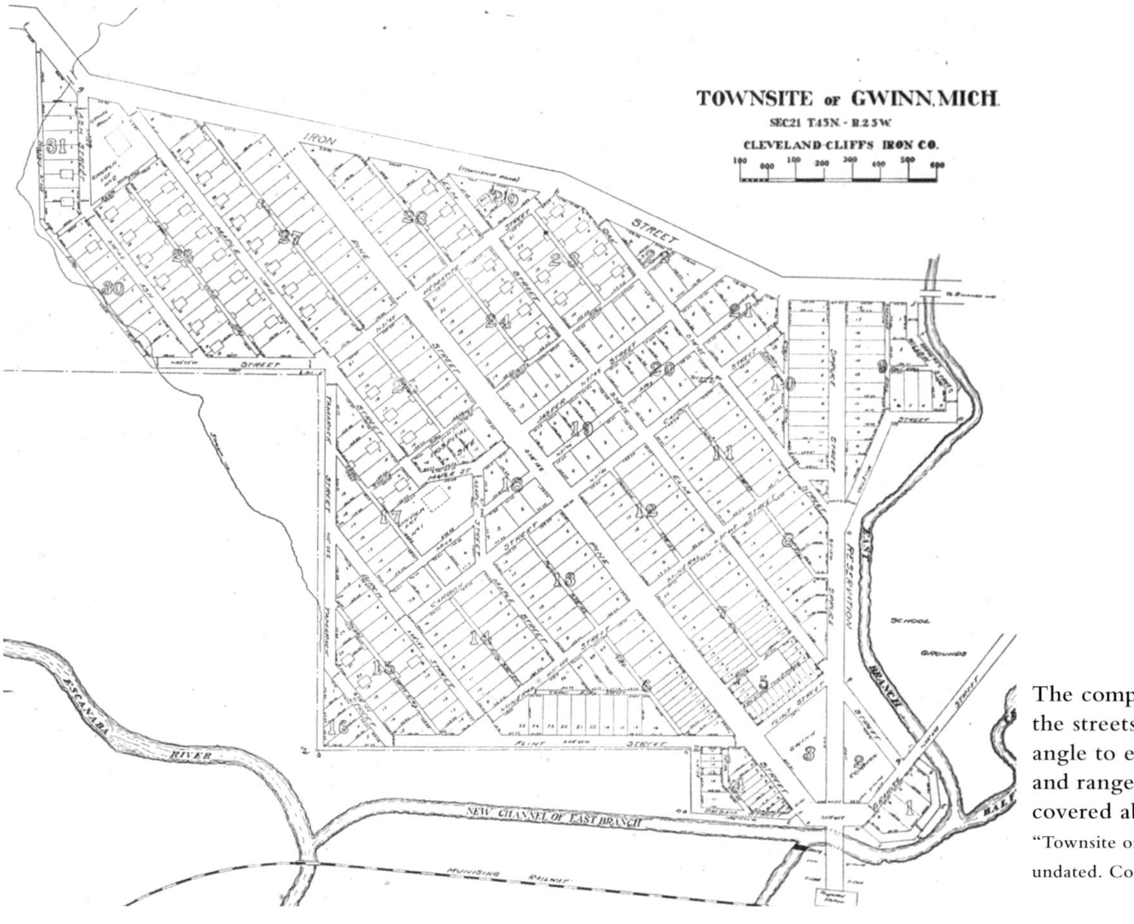

The compact plan placed the streets at a 45-degree angle to existing township and range lines. The town covered about 440 acres.
"Townsite of Gwinn, Mich.," undated. Courtesy MPI.

Manning sited the town at the fork of the Escanaba River and its East Branch. Photograph, n.d. Courtesy Forsyth Township Historical Society, Gwinn, Mich.

Houses were set close to relatively narrow streets, increasing lot size and space for backyard gardens. Photograph, n.d. Courtesy Forsyth Township Historical Society.

In time, the white pines bordering Gwinn's boulevards grew to maturity. Photograph, n.d. Courtesy Forsyth Township Historical Society.

Manning's plans called for native vegetation throughout the town. Wooded recreation areas were easily accessed. Photograph, n.d. Courtesy Forsyth Township Historical Society.

Residents remain proud of their "model town." Gwinn Model Town Historic District. Photo by Andrew Jameson, 2009.

beauty to the streets of the new town." Eight percent of all land development costs were devoted to landscape-related work, which allowed for the planting of one thousand trees and the transplanting of another thousand aspen seedlings from nearby forests to the town site. According to Manning, the greenbelt of trees and vegetation that encircled Gwinn allowed all residents to be "within ten minutes of extensive wild wood and river reservations," permitting miners and their families to "spend more of the outdoor life which they need, as their work in the mines keeps them most of the day where sun and fresh air can never penetrate."[4]

Gwinn's company-built housing for the miners consisted of fifty-five duplexes of one and a half stories, with four to six rooms each; supervisors and professional employees resided in larger and better-built single-family houses. By 1908 the *Detroit Free Press* reported that the emerging town offered "a distinct and individual appearance compared to the usual mining towns." Between 1907 and 1915 CCI also constructed a bank, a hospital, and a clubhouse and provided funding for several churches and other buildings.[5]

Manning worked with Mather to carry out a number of social planning objectives, many intended for Gwinn's foreign-born population. (By 1910 almost half of the one thousand residents were immigrants, primarily Finns, Italians, and Scandinavians.) Manning believed that most ethnic groups were "clannish and gregarious" and shouldn't be mixed together, while CCI sought "to split up the various nationalities in order to make congenial living conditions." As in other model company towns throughout the nation, CCI officials attempted to limit vice in Gwinn by requiring all prospective residents and business operators to sign contracts that banned "any bawdy house . . . or place for lewd or immoral purposes."[6]

The community prospered while the mining industry thrived, but during the economic depression of the 1930s CCI sold most of its residences and buildings in Gwinn. Mining continued to decline, and after World War II Gwinn saw the end of its mining enterprise. The community received a significant boost in 1956 when the K. I. Sawyer Air Force Base opened nearby. The influx of new residents contributed to a building boom that resulted in the construction of new housing, schools, and commercial establishments. Gwinn's population peaked at 2,350 in 1990, but the decommissioning and closing of the airbase in 1995 caused a downturn in local economic conditions and resident numbers.[7]

While the decline of Gwinn's economy contributed to the erosion of its architectural character, many landscape and planning features initiated by Manning have been maintained to the present, notably the public character of the common and the wooded areas along the rivers. Indeed, the Gwinn Model Town District was listed in the National Register of Historic Places in 2002 because many of its original landscape design and physical planning features had been maintained over time. The significance of Manning's landscape plan was recognized once again in 2006, when the community applied for and received a major grant from the Michigan Department of Transportation to restore the trees and plants formerly in the median of Pine Street, the major corridor serving the model town. Today Gwinn, which still calls its high-school athletic teams the "Model Towners," remains as one of Warren Manning's best preserved planning projects.[8]

William G. Mather Estate (Cliffs Cottage)

ISHPEMING, MICHIGAN

STEVE BRISSON

Warren Manning first met William Gwinn Mather when he was employed by the Olmsted firm, and he later recalled an enduring friendship with his client through "all the years of my independent practice" that followed.[1] In 1896 Manning had worked on projects for Mather's business, the Cleveland-Cliffs Iron Company (CCI), and on a plan for the model town of Gwinn in Michigan's Upper Peninsula. As early as 1899 Manning's private firm took on two projects for Mather in Ishpeming, Michigan, the private estate of Cliffs Cottage and nearby industrial grounds.[2]

The year after becoming president of the CCI in 1890, Mather built a cottage to serve as a headquarters during his frequent visits to the mine locations. Cliffs Cottage and its 1903 addition were designed by the architect D. Fred Charlton, who was based in nearby Marquette and was also responsible for several other CCI buildings, including the Ishpeming offices on the shore of Lake Bancroft and public buildings for the town of Gwinn.[3] Located on a broad ledge of the hill overlooking the town, the cottage site offered commanding views on three sides. The rambling, Shingle style residence features a central two-story, gable-roofed section with the first story built of logs and the gable ends shingled. A hexagonal sun porch on the east and a one-story west wing are constructed of rubble stone and mine waste rock with local Jasper ores.

Although no landscape plans for Cliffs Cottage survive, records in the CCI archives show that Manning provided further designs as late as 1912.[4] Fragmentary records and a property survey indicate that an extensive landscape plan was implemented. Manning stated that the conditions of the site provided for "rock gardens, and other growths that were extremely varied and attractive for such a small acreage."[5] The property is approached along Jasper Street, which borders it to the northeast, and is enclosed by a combination of solid masonry mine waste rock walls and wrought iron fences that date to 1906–1909.[6] At the juncture of Jasper and Bluff Streets, a curving road leads up to the cottage; to the right is an entrance gate to the agent's house grounds.

Across Jasper Street from the cottage property, the abandoned "Schoolhouse" mine pit remains, its upper sections incorporated into the masonry walls bordering the street.

The Cliffs Cottage site is roughly arranged into four regions: the ledge around the cottage; the hillside to the north below the house; the hillside to the south above the house; and "Mather Grove" beyond the south hillside. The entrance drive entered the ledge from the east and terminated in a carriage turnaround to the west. Lawns surrounded the cottage on all sides, with a variety of shrubs and planting beds adjacent to the building and along the edge of the northern slope. This turf area also contained a flower and vegetable garden and a maintenance shed.[7] A bowling green was located on the northwest lawn, surrounded by a semicircular stone wall with a bas-relief panel on the east end and a Doric-columned trellis on the west.[8] Sandstone steps bordered the green on the south. Other landscape features included a sundial on the east lawn and several Lake Superior sandstone benches. A retaining wall at the foot of the south slope incorporated a catch basin for a waterfall.

The slope below the house, bordered by the entrance drive and Jasper Street, merged seamlessly into the grounds of the agent's house to the northwest. The hillside was broken up by natural outcroppings of rock and stone retaining walls.

Manning began working on Cliffs Cottage, William G. Mather's Ishpeming, Michigan, summer home, in 1899. He met Mather while still an Olmsted employee. Photograph c. 1925. Courtesy MCL.

The house and a 1903 addition were designed by the Marquette architect D. Fred Charlton. Manning's plan for the property included a bowling green, vegetable gardens, and a sixty-acre grove open to the public for picnicking. Photograph by Lucy Weller, 2009.

The pedestrian entrance, composed of stone piers and Gothic-arched wooden gates, provided access from Jasper Street. Immediately past the gate, a series of stone steps bordered by stepped walls ascended to a switchback path leading up the hill to the cottage. The path terminated at the eastern end of the cottage lawn.

The hillside behind the house was treated similarly to the north slope, with stone retaining walls and switchback paths. A waterfall (or series of waterfalls) flowed down this slope, terminating in the stone basin. Mather Grove lay beyond the south hillside. Encompassing more than sixty acres, it included picnic areas and was open to the public. Manning mentioned introducing "numerous plants . . . to determine how they would behave" in this "public reservation."[9] In 1912 Manning recorded work completed for "Cliffs Cottage Woods," including "opening vistas for picture gallery" and "stepping stones around pond," and this likely referred to the grove.[10]

The octagonal sun porch overlooks a bowling green, edged by stone retaining walls and great stands of goat's beard. A wall fountain, originally designed for Mather's Cleveland home, Gwinn, was integrated into the Ishpeming grounds, probably around 1912. Photograph by Lucy Weller, 2009.

Although Cliffs Cottage is still used by Cliffs Natural Resources to house visiting officials and other company guests, the original layout of the landscape design is impossible to discern. A variety of non-native ferns, ground covers, and other plants grow throughout the hillside areas. Larger trees dating from the first half the twentieth century are now intermixed with numerous smaller trees, saplings, deadwood, and brush. The agent's and manager's houses were razed decades ago and the grounds there are also returning to wilderness. Surviving landscape elements include the gates and walls along Jasper Street, although portions are in ruins. The stone portions of the bowling green and the adjacent steps, several stone benches, and the catch basin for the waterfall are intact. The original carriage turnaround is now a parking lot. On the lower hillside, the pedestrian entrance gate and steps remain, and portions of the retaining walls are also visible. Well-trodden footpaths along the slope appear to follow the original routes. The upper hillside is even more overgrown, with only occasional portions of the retaining walls visible. Mather Grove has likewise returned to nature, perhaps as Manning would have intended.

Mackinac Island State Park

MACKINAC ISLAND, MICHIGAN

STEVE BRISSON

A major crossroads of the Great Lakes, the Straits of Mackinac was a Native American fishing ground for centuries. After the establishment of a French mission on the north side of the straits in 1671, the area rapidly developed into the main fur trade depot of the upper Great Lakes, passing into British hands in 1761. Mackinac Island was first settled in 1780, when the British moved Fort Michilimackinac from its vulnerable mainland location to the island. The island remained a center of the fur trade into the American period. By the 1850s, it was developed as a summer tourist destination and in 1875 was named the nation's second national park. Twenty years later, with the closure of Fort Mackinac and consequent loss of federal personnel to maintain the park, it was transferred to the state, becoming Michigan's first state park, administered by the newly created Mackinac Island State Park Commission. Originally about 50 percent of the three-by-two-mile island was included in the park; this has grown to 83 percent today.

In 1913 Warren Manning, with Morgan H. Wright of Marquette, Michigan, mapped the island for the Mackinac Island State Park Commission. The Wright–Manning map served as the commission's base map until the end of the twentieth century. Later that year the commission hired Manning under a two-year contract to provide "professional advice and plans for permanent beautification and detail in landscape work" on the island.[1]

No written report from Manning's project survives, but the commission's archives contain a topographical map and a large plan titled "Mackinac Island . . . A Plan for Its Future Development."[2] Both documents use the 1913 Wright–Manning map as their base. The topographical map provides a highly detailed analysis of existing vegetation on the island, with more than seventy numbered features that were likely keyed to Manning's lost report. The development plan shows numerous proposed improvements to park property. Among the most significant were expanding cottage rental lots throughout the park and developing public amenities in the former

A 1913 map drawn by Manning in collaboration with Morgan H. Wright of Marquette recorded information related to tree species, caves, land holdings, and historical events, such as the site of the British landing. "State Park & Private Claims," plan no. 1028-20-41, December 1913. Courtesy MCL.

army pasture west of Fort Mackinac. Cottage lots had been available for lease since 1885, during the national park era, originally around the east and west bluffs. After 1895 a handful of other lots were added to the leaseholds, and Manning's plan would have expanded this practice throughout the park. His extensive suggestions for the former army pasture included developing a baseball diamond, a football field, basketball courts, a bowling green, a running track, sand boxes, and an amphitheater. He called for a second amphitheater behind Fort Mackinac, on the slope of Fort Holmes hill.

The Manning plan was in keeping with recent activities by the park commission, but on a grander scale. For example, in 1898 the commission had developed the former army vegetable garden immediately below the fort. The east portion of this area was divided into three leased cottage lots, and the west part was converted into a public park named in honor of the seventeenth-century explorer Père Jacques Marquette, with gravel paths, flower beds, benches, and a bronze statue of Marquette. The Manning plan also recommended improving the shoreline boulevard, begun by the commission in 1896, and expanding it throughout the dock areas of the downtown district.

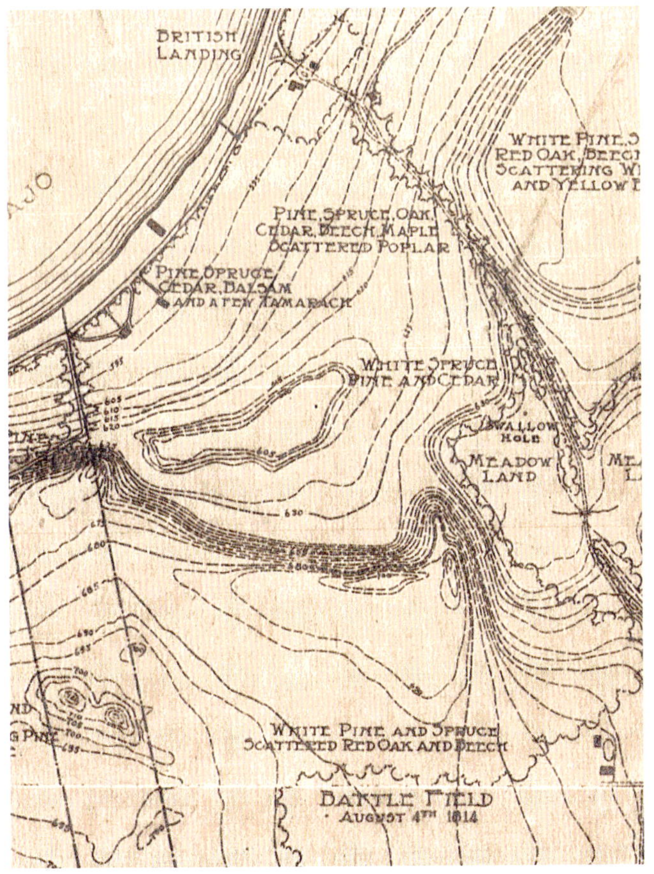

Detail of plan no. 1028-20-41.

None of the major components of the Manning plan was built. Whether any of the recommendations on forest management, scenic vistas, or other issues were followed is unknown; the commission minutes and other records make no further references to Manning's lost plan. The expansion of cottage lots on the scale suggested in the plan would have prevented public access to large portions of the park and likely would not have been economically feasible. And although Manning's plans for the former pasture would have added several public amenities, within months of his presentation the commission leased the pasture to Grand Hotel for use as a golf course.[3] Throughout the next several decades, the park commission made improvements to the shoreline boulevard, but it is not clear if Manning's specific suggestions were followed. The boulevard was never extended through the downtown.

During Manning's contract period, the commission consulted him on a number of other projects, including the construction of a swimming pool (which was never built) and the restoration of buildings at Fort Mackinac.[4] Manning did, however, complete two additional projects that remain unchanged today. The first, the Woolson Memorial or Anne's Tablet, is described in his unpublished autobiography.[5] Erected in the park

In 1915 Manning documented his bench design in a photograph he took of park superintendent Frank Kenyon. Courtesy Mackinac State Historic Parks, Mackinaw City, Michigan.

on the bluff directly to the east of Fort Mackinac, the monument was funded by another of Manning's clients, Samuel Mather of Cleveland, and given a separate project number. It honors Mather's cousin Constance Fenimore Woolson, a novelist and travel writer, who set one of her novels on the island. Consisting of a bronze plaque mounted to a base of embedded rocks, it pictures the novel's title character, Anne. A semicircular stone curb and three granite benches engraved with the titles of Woolson's works enclose the plaque.[6]

The other project, completed for the park commission, was the design of massive concrete benches, which were used throughout the park as well as at the commission's mainland Michilimackinac State Park. Large numbers of them were produced for both parks beginning in 1913, and in 1915 Manning documented his design in a photograph he took of park superintendent Frank Kenyon sitting on one of the benches.[7] The distinctive seats, still in use on the island and recently reintroduced in the mainland park, are the only other tangible signatures of Manning's work here.

Michilimackinac State Park

MACKINAW CITY, MICHIGAN

STEVE BRISSON

Michilimackinac State Park is located on the south shore of the Straits of Mackinac, a passage connecting Lake Huron and Lake Michigan. The area was the site of the French (and later British) Fort Michilimackinac from 1715 until 1780, when the fort was moved to nearby Mackinac Island. When the village of Mackinaw City was platted in 1856, the fort area was preserved as a public park, and in 1889 a U.S. lighthouse was established in the eastern portion. It is not clear if Mackinaw City had developed the park to any extent prior to 1907, when the village transferred the thirty-seven-acre site to the state. Two years later, the state designated the property as Michilimackinac State Park and placed it under the care of the Mackinac Island State Park Commission.

In 1914 the park commission hired Warren Manning under a two-year contract to consult on landscape development at Mackinac Island.[1] As a separate project during this period, the commission also asked Manning to make similar kinds of recommendations for Michilimackinac State Park. Little documentation survives to illuminate Manning's specific recommendations or design here. Although two original Manning plans exist in the commission archives, apparently he also produced at least two other sheets and likely a written report. Manning presented his final draft for both state parks to the commission in July 1915. He noted in his autobiography that "the recommendations were to have the old fort restored, to save the attractive forest growth about it, opening paths and trails, and provide for picnic parties."[2] The plan included a new shoreline walkway featuring outlooks with seats, a designated picnic area, a reconstruction of the fort on its original location, and a museum.

The commission began developing the park, adding concrete benches designed by Manning's office as early as July 1914. The shoreline trail was established by 1918, just as envisioned by Manning, connecting to a larger footpath system in the village. The park superintendent also reported that a picnic pavilion, an oven, a pump, and toilets were installed.[3] A rustic stone entrance gate was built over the main entrance. Since we do not

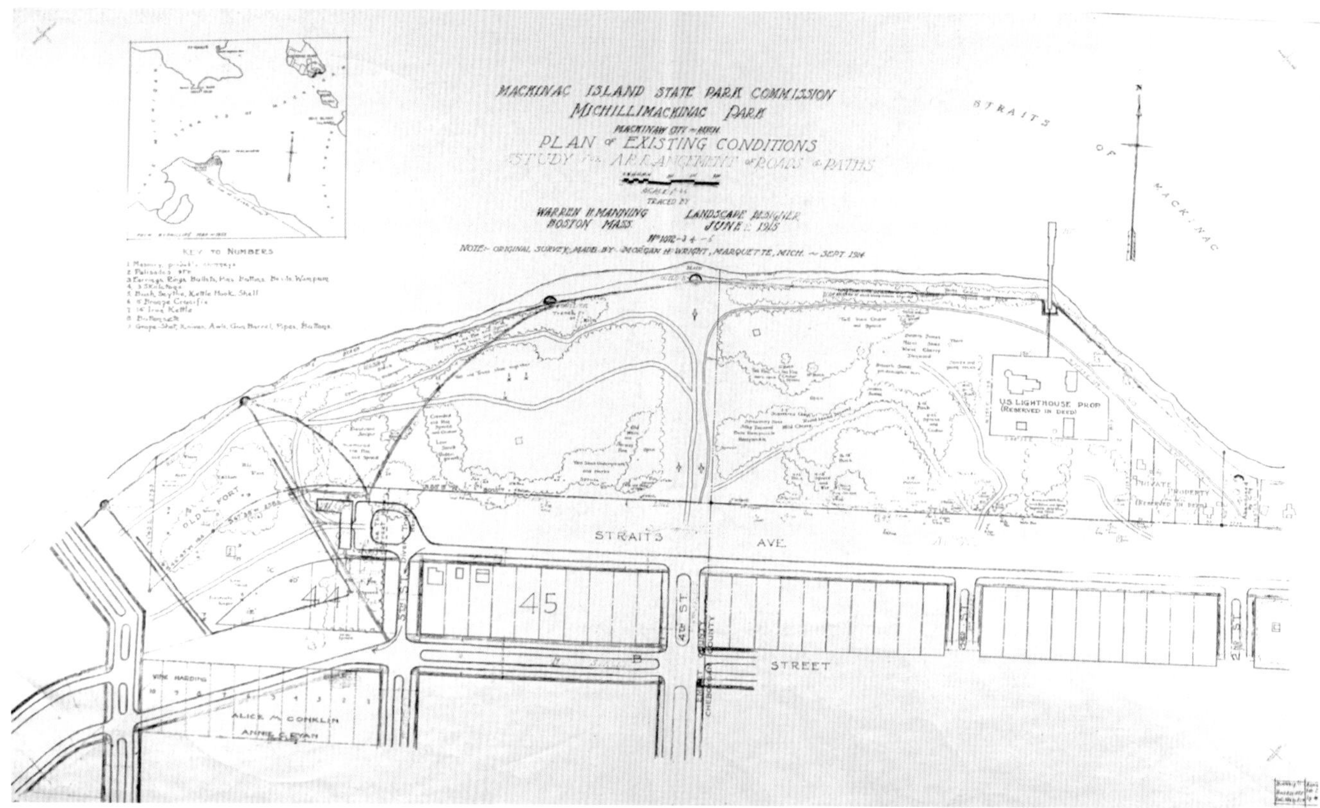

In 1915 Manning created a detailed map of Michilimackinac State Park before suggesting improvements. He recorded the site of the old fort, which he recommended restoring, as well as individual artifacts uncovered during the mapping process. "Plan of Existing Conditions," plan no. 1072-34-5, June 1915. Courtesy Mackinac State Historic Parks, Mackinaw City, Mich.

have detailed plans or a written report, however, it is not known if these conformed to any specific recommendations beyond Manning's suggestion to "provide for picnic parties."

During the 1920s the park became a popular campground and developed along lines not necessarily foreseen by Manning. By the 1930s roads, trails, and amenities, including a dance hall, shower buildings, and a bandstand, were scattered throughout the park. In 1933 another of Manning's recommended alterations was completed—a crude reconstruction of the eighteenth-century fort. In spite of these additions, much of the forest stayed intact.

In 1957 the south approach of the five-mile Mackinac Bridge, which crosses the straits to connect Michigan's two peninsulas, cut through the center of the park. Two years later the park commission launched an ambitious historical museum and professional archaeology and reconstruction program at the fort site (replacing the 1930s replica), which continues to the present. The lighthouse ceased operation shortly after the bridge was opened, and in 1960 the park acquired the property from the federal government and eventually created a maritime park surrounding the lighthouse. The commission banned camping in the area and removed the early campground-related buildings. The maritime park closed in 1990.[4]

Today the park is divided into two quadrants, with the Mackinac Bridge approach crossing

Among the most distinctive elements of the new design were Manning's stone benches, which the state park continues to replicate. Photograph, n.d. Courtesy Mackinac State Historic Parks.

Manning's 1913 report called for picnic facilities for visitors, including a pavilion, which was constructed by 1918. Postcard, n.d. Courtesy Mackinac State Historic Parks.

The concrete walk Manning laid out is still extant. Postcard, n.d. Courtesy Mackinac State Historic Parks.

over the center. The park's western end, containing the reconstructed fort, is fully enclosed. The park charges admission to this site, which is now a National Historic Landmark. Visitors enter by way of a visitor center and parking lot below the bridge approach. To the east is a free picnic ground set among trees. Within this area is the restored Old Mackinac Point Lighthouse (also a ticketed attraction), which is listed on the National Register of Historic Places. The concrete walkway in the eastern quadrant, designed by Manning, continues to be maintained, and a gravel walkway from the visitor center to the fort follows the original path. Although the commission long ago removed the original Manning-designed concrete benches near the entrance to the lighthouse, in 2005 it installed several new ones replicating his design.

John Gates Williams Estate

LADUE, MISSOURI

JANE ROY BROWN

Warren Manning designed the estate of John Gates Williams and his wife, Mary Randolph, in the St. Louis suburb of Ladue between the winter of 1923 and the summer of 1925. This was a productive period for Manning in St. Louis. During the mid-1920s he received twenty-eight local commissions, most of them for country estates, but also including the St. Louis Country Club, an amusement park, and a residential subdivision.[1]

Ladue is about five miles west of the city center, on a plateau between the Mississippi and Missouri Rivers at the northern edge of the Ozark Mountains. The Williams property lies near the top of a gently sloping hill. Williams, a financier with a seat on the New York Stock Exchange, hired Manning to design the landscape on this 150-acre property while the house was already under construction.[2] Local architects Jamieson & Spearl had completed the northeast portion of the building, and the unfinished northwest wing would have doubled the footprint.[3] Manning's October 1924 plan shows the unbuilt wing and the existing building.

The property's chief asset was its elevation. The entry drive surmounted the more gradual eastern slope through an allée of American elms that ended at an oval forecourt at the front of the house. The building's hilltop location also provided a panoramic view of the Ozark foothills from the southwestern facade. By exploiting the hilltop location and the fan-shaped meadow on the hillside below the house, Manning's design provided maximum exposure to this view.[4] The meadow ran about 350 feet from the house to the tree line at the end of the slope, widening toward the bottom, which exaggerated the panorama. This dramatic prospect is reflected in the name the Williamses chose for their country place, Far Meadows. Forest trees, which Manning faced down with specimen evergreens and understory shrubs, provided naturalistic edges. In the far southern corner of the property, the Williamses, who were avid equestrians, expanded an existing barn for their horses and asked Manning to design an adjacent paddock.[5]

In the first stages of the design process, Manning suggested new gardens near the house. On plans from October 1924, a 150-foot walk through a straight allée of plum and peach trees extends into the meadow, on axis with the center of the unbuilt wing of the house. The feature terminates in a circular pool, outlined in trees. A linear garden extended from the end of the wing. A ha-ha and retaining wall curve in a loose semicircle from the end of that garden to the wooded edge near the opposite end of the house, intersecting the allée. A stretch of turf—designated as "the perfect lawn" on one plan—and the ha-ha wall would have created a low pedestal for the entire house, magnifying it when seen from below and extending the views from inside.

When the wing construction did not occur, Manning altered his plan to realign the major garden development to the west, creating a long vista that contrasted with the dominant—and immediately apparent—horizontal view of the hillside meadow to the south. Presumably because this straight avenue of turf was about fifty feet wide,

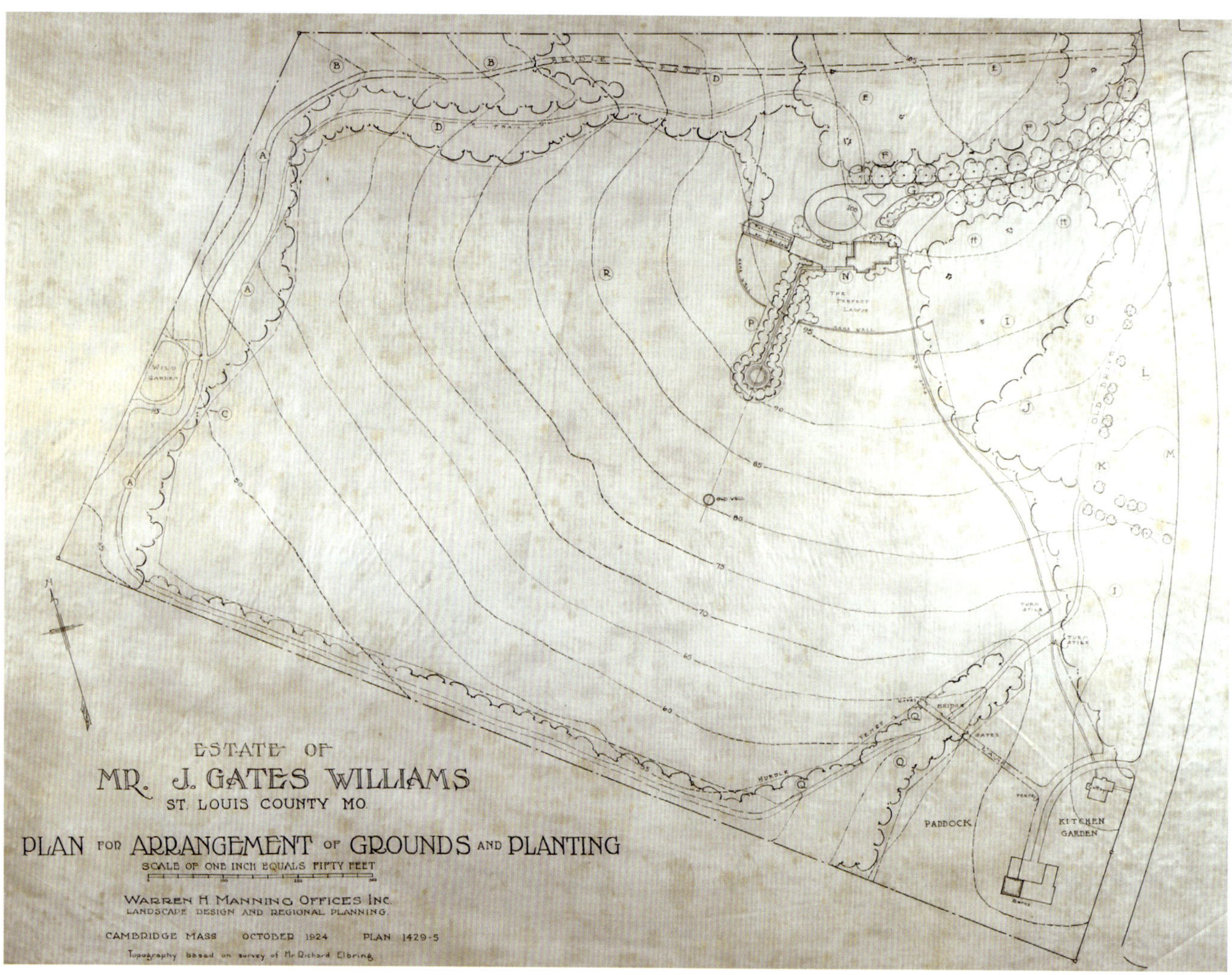

A 1924 plan showed the major garden developing from the still unbuilt wing of the house; neither the wing nor the gardens shown were constructed. "Plan for Arrangement of Grounds and Planting," plan no. 1429-5, October 1924. Courtesy MPI.

he called it "the mall." Manning bordered the woods with perennials, shrubs, and deciduous trees (including redbud and dogwood) chosen for spring bloom and bright autumn foliage. About two hundred feet down the slope, a rectangular swimming pool, set on a terrace a few steps below grade, crosses the grassy mall.[6] The grade change exaggerates the length of the main axis, creating, on a smaller scale, the illusion of an "infinite view" associated with Baroque gardens.

At cross-axis to the mall, two contrasting gardens extended from the short ends of the pool. Off one end lay a rectangular turf panel bordered in boxwood and white peonies, with a circular wishing well and a balustrade. (The wishing well was later replaced with a poolhouse.) Off the pool's opposite end, a path led to a warren of rustic, rocky gardens, a circular children's swimming pool edged in boulders, and stepping-stone paths, all complementing a log cabin built for the site. A grass path meandered east from the cabin landscape, looping through woods back to the house.

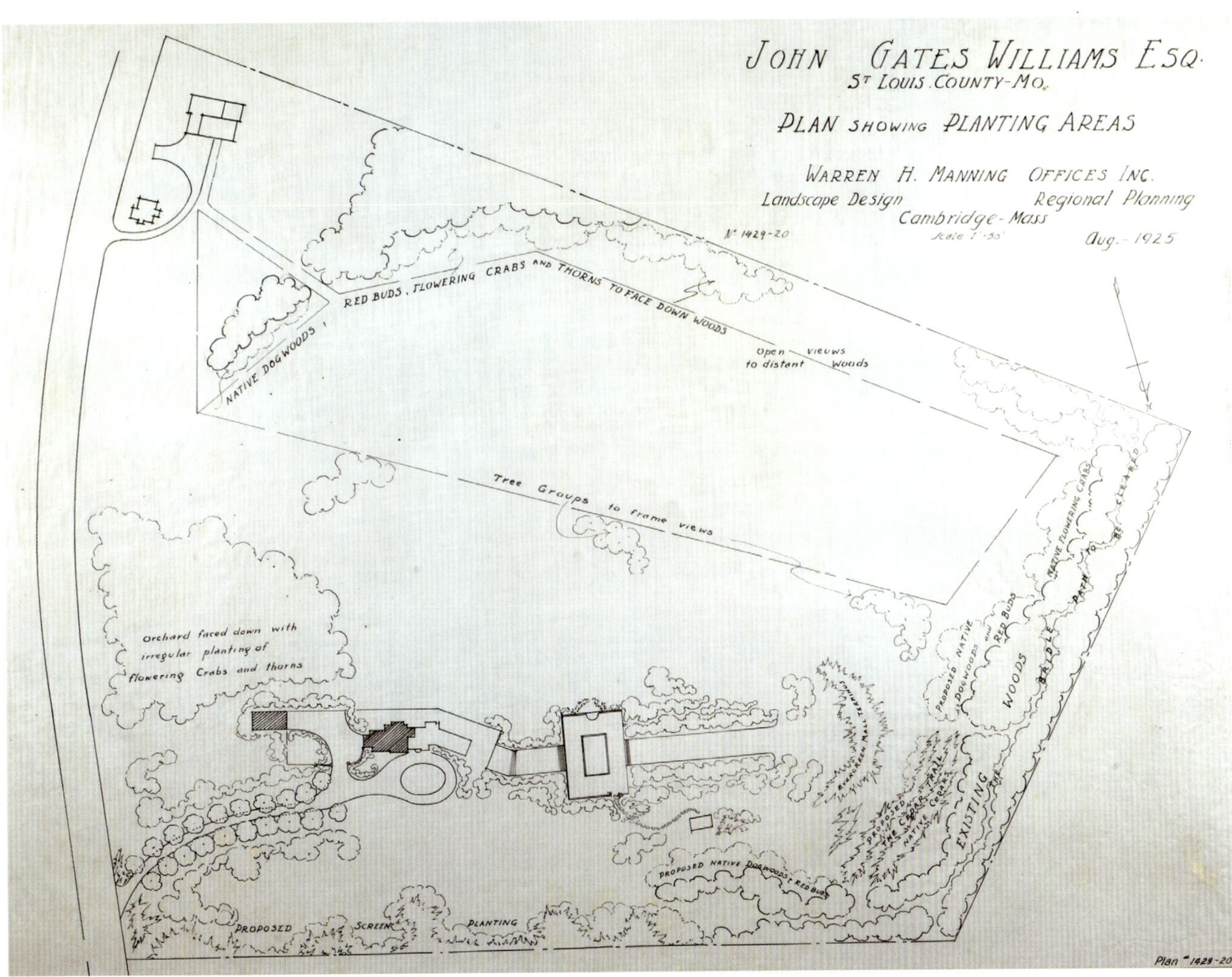

The 1925 general plan of the estate records the large groups of trees Manning used to frame views. New plantings of redbud, dogwood, hawthorn, and crabs were indicated to create an edge to existing woods. "Plan Showing Planting Areas," plan no. 1429-20, August 1925. Courtesy MPI.

The main garden view was developed to the west, across a long stretch of lawn ("the mall") intersected by a pool. "Sketch for Mall & Swimming Pool," plan no. 1429-10, August 1925. Courtesy MPI.

To the west, the path continued to a wild garden. A bridle trail encircled the entire property along its wooded edges, intersecting pedestrian trails.

Williams's fortune was among the casualties of the 1929 stock market crash. The architects completed only part of the unbuilt portion of the house, and Manning never built the gardens around the building—the allée walk, the ha-ha wall, and the rectangular garden on the northwest end. He did, however, complete the gardens in the woods—the mall and swimming pool, the log cabin and its rustic landscape—as well as the paddock near the horse barn in the property's south corner.[7] Between the 1930s and the 1960s, members of the family subdivided and sold portions of the property, and the state took twenty-five additional acres by eminent domain for a highway in 1945, leaving the estate at approximately thirty acres. Currently owned by the granddaughter of the original owners, the remaining property contains the Manning-designed landscape. Its spatial features, paths, pools, and the cabin remain largely intact. Although most of the original perennials have vanished, the trees planted by Manning have matured to provide the intended enclosure shown in his drawings, and a sense of expansive, pastoral beauty remains.[8]

The handsome house, by Jamieson & Spearl, was prominent in the view back across the pool. Photograph by Arthur G. Eldredge, c. 1928. Courtesy MCL.

Manning planted the dry-laid stone steps with a wide range of herbaceous plants. Photograph by Arthur G. Eldredge, c. 1928. Courtesy MCL.

Leonard Tufts Estate

CENTER HARBOR, NEW HAMPSHIRE

MARTHA LYON

Warren Manning was introduced to the Tufts family in 1895 while an associate at the firm of Olmsted, Olmsted & Eliot assigned to oversee the development of Pinehurst, the North Carolina health resort created by James Walker Tufts.[1] Manning retained the job when he opened his own landscape architecture practice in 1896.[2] When Tufts died in 1902, the resort was passed on to his son Leonard, who would engage Manning in many expansion projects at Pinehurst and at other sites in North Carolina. Leonard Tufts and Warren Manning became close professional associates and also sustained a forty-year friendship, taking frequent walks and motoring throughout the landscape surrounding Pinehurst.[3] In 1911, for example, they set out on a twelve-day car trip, accompanied by a doctor and a black servant, to Center Harbor, New Hampshire, and Keewaydin, the summer home of Leonard Tufts.[4]

Ten years earlier, Tufts had purchased land from the Piper family with an existing farmhouse, two barns, and a boathouse near the southern end of Squam Lake, New Hampshire's second-largest lake, located near the geographic center of the state. Over the next twelve years he acquired additional parcels, bringing the total to over four hundred acres.[5] In addition to creating a summer retreat, Tufts was interested in proving that farming in New Hampshire could be a profitable business. He had purchased a herd of milking shorthorns to fuel operations at Pinehurst, and he transported calves born at the Pinehurst dairy to Keewaydin for pasturing, believing they would grow stronger there.[6] He also established a kennel near the lake where he bred pointers and setters, shipping them to Pinehurst for use in quail-hunting. A sketch of the property prepared by Tufts's son, Richard, documents a serpentine series of drives and more than twenty structures, including several farmhouses, barns, an ice house, and boathouses, as well as a stone "office" and a large Federal style brick house (built around 1904) perched on a north-facing hillside, overlooking the lake.[7]

In 1912 Manning prepared a boundary and

Manning's precise involvement with the design is not known. In 1912 he created a detailed map of the four-hundred-acre property, indicating the location and composition of the woods that covered much of the site. Photograph, n.d. Courtesy Tufts Archives, Given Memorial Library, Pinehurst, N.C.

topographical survey of the property, which he updated in 1926.[8] The impetus for the survey is somewhat unclear, although it is possible that Tufts intended to document his holdings and confirm the property boundaries. The plans do not indicate that Manning played a role in designing any part of the property, but they demonstrate his deep understanding of the existing landform and his appreciation of the flora. Woodlands covered a significant portion of the acreage, and Manning identified the composition and size of each distinct woodland area.

The property remained in the family until 1943, just two years prior to Leonard Tufts's death.[9] It subsequently passed through a series of owners, including a small liberal arts college, an inn, and a musical organization, and in the process diminished in size to approximately forty acres. The structures and landscape fell into a state of disrepair, but remnants of the Tuftses' occupation remain, including the serpentine drives, several barns, the office, and the brick house. In 2013 a new owner acquired the estate at auction and is in the process of restoring the house.

Ambrose Swasey Plot, Exeter Cemetery

EXETER, NEW HAMPSHIRE

MARTHA LYON

In April 1915 Warren Manning communicated with Ambrose Swasey about the layout of a new portion of a privately owned burial ground, the Exeter Cemetery, located along the north bank of the Little River in Exeter, New Hampshire.[1] A native of the town, Swasey became a pioneer in the manufacture of telescopes, and although he resided in Cleveland, he maintained a summer home in Exeter and was active in the Exeter Cemetery Association.[2] A number of Swasey's Cleveland friends had worked with Manning, and Swasey assured the association's trustees that Manning would "work out the whole problem in a very satisfactory manner." Swasey agreed to put up $500 for detailed surveys and plans.[3]

The site consisted of low-lying land along the river edge rising northward to an upland area, which Manning believed could be drained with tiles placed far enough below the surface to accommodate new burials. The river edge, he suggested, should be planted with pines to create a forest. His July 1915 plan called for laying out a new cemetery entrance connecting to an elongated oval of burial lots, and for shaping the low-lying land into two lagoons.[4] He suggested plantings of native tree species throughout, including sugar and red maple, tulip, elm, and basswood. Plantings at the edges of the lagoons were to be a palette of native species transplanted from the "wild land," including shadbush, elder, maple, viburnum, arrowwood, silky dogwood, beech, wild rose, wild spiraea, and virgin's bower. His plan also addressed the existing cemetery, calling for the old paths to be filled with loam and seeded to establish a "lawn appearance," widening the main entrance on the east side, and closing two secondary entrances on the south.[5] To accompany the plan, Manning developed a set of "rules and regulations" he hoped would be adopted by the trustees. He recommended that the roads and paths take the names of plants, and monument heights be restricted as a means of maintaining "openness of the central areas." The document also outlined procedures for landscape maintenance and burials.[6]

In 1916 Swasey purchased the entire new oval

section, reserving fourteen lots for burial and re-deeding eight lots to be used for ornamental purposes.[7] For the oval, Manning prepared detailed plans for grading and road construction and specified plantings of flowering dogwood, arborvitae, and Lombardy poplar.[8] Soon afterward, Swasey acquired a half-moon-shaped plot at the oval's northern end and retained Manning to lay out a semicircle one hundred feet in diameter for a family plot.[9] The New York–based architect Henry Bacon, best known as the designer of the Lincoln Memorial, contributed to the plot design, proposing that four shrubs be planted as a backdrop to the Swasey monument.[10]

Manning's recommendations for Exeter Cemetery included a new entry and plantings on an oval plot belonging to Ambrose Swasey. Photograph by Martha Lyon, 2015.

Today, most of the plants specified by Manning for the "new portion" do not exist in the landscape, and no documentation has been found to confirm that planting took place to the extent proposed. Similarly, the lagoons shown in Manning's 1915 plan may have been altered over time by the shifts in the course of the Little River, or they may not have been constructed at all. The Swasey plot, however, remains in its half-moon configuration at the northern end of the entrance oval, set against a backdrop of arborvitae and offset by mature evergreen trees.

The Swasey plot, from the west. The handsome monument is by Henry Bacon. Photograph by Martha Lyon, 2015.

The Swasey plot, from the east. Mature conifers provide a sense of enclosure and a dramatic backdrop to the columnar monument. Photograph by Martha Lyon, 2015.

Wilton Lloyd-Smith Estate (Kenjockety)

HUNTINGTON, NEW YORK

PAMELA HARTFORD

In 1924 Wilton and Marjorie Lloyd-Smith commissioned Warren Manning to work on their newly purchased property on the shore of Lloyd's Neck, Long Island.[1] Over a five-year period, Manning collaborated closely with the Lloyd-Smiths, preserving as many of the native trees as possible and providing a habitat for game and a setting for outdoor recreation.[2] The estate's name, Kenjockety, was said to have been taken from the Algonquin word for a place "on the edge of the woods, far from the multitude."[3]

Marshall Field III, a friend and business associate of Lloyd-Smith, had introduced the couple to Lloyd's Neck, an isthmus of 5,700 acres along Oyster Bay, where he owned 1,725 acres of woodland, meadows, and waterfront property. The Fields and Lloyd-Smiths enjoyed a sporting lifestyle that included small game hunting and dog breeding. In July 1923, with help from Marjorie's father, the Lloyd-Smiths purchased 67 acres on the southwestern shore, a short commute to New York City.

Forested with mature oaks and chestnuts, the property featured half a mile of beachfront at the base of twenty-foot-high bluffs and a seven-and-a-half-acre spring-fed lake on the southwest boundary, near the waterfront.[4] Sloping gently downhill from the shore almost a mile inland, the narrow parcel ended two hundred feet from the north–south road abutting Field's property. The high bluffs, a well-known landmark along the otherwise low-lying North Shore of Long Island, afforded views across Cold Spring Harbor to neighboring Center Island and across the Sound to the Connecticut shore. With beach and protected waterfront, fresh water, and deep forest, the site fulfilled the Lloyd-Smiths' desire for "favorable conditions for a game preserve or sanctuary and for many forms of summer and winter recreation."[5]

Marjorie's father, Arthur Fleming, provided the funds to build a house and develop the property, insisting on Bertram Goodhue as the architect.[6] Goodhue's design for the house drew substantially on the English Tudor–inspired vocabulary he had used for other East Coast residences. The forty-six-room house featured brick

Guests arrived at Kenjockety through a walled courtyard, which screened the 46-room Tudor-inspired house, designed by Bertram Goodhue. Photograph by Arthur G. Eldredge, c. 1928. Courtesy MCL.

with half-timbering, steep gables, tall chimneys, tall leaded glass windows, and a timber-framed porte-cochere that created an ell connecting the servants' wing to the main house.

Shortly after his initial site visit, Manning proposed a layout that he believed would maximize engagement with the most compelling aspect of the site: the extensive mature woodland. Establishing the entry point to the site, which was bounded on all sides by private property, was key to his plan. Although an existing dirt road crossed midway through the parcel, he urged the Lloyd-Smiths to obtain thirty-six additional acres that would connect their property to the north–south road in the center of Lloyd's Neck.[7] From this entrance he created a mile-long drive through the woods to the house.

Prior to construction, Manning cleared only the dead underbrush and the house site. When plans were further advanced, he selected viewpoints, laid out trails, and "developed" the unique native plants throughout the property.[8] With a garage, water tower, boathouse, bathhouse, tennis court, and tea house clustered around the main house, Manning had over three-quarters of the property in which to edit views and amplify the horticultural beauty of woodlands, wetlands, and lakeshore. His work included shaping the drive to promote glimpses of the lake, lacing the woods with walking and equestrian trails, building habitat for pheasant runs, and accommodating ducks with a bridge over the road.

The woodland, and its high canopy, surrounded the house, reducing the impact of the imposing structure. In a gesture that further deemphasized the grand residence, Manning brought visitors not to the front door, but to the outside of the well-screened, timber-framed porte-cochere. Only after passing through the porte-cochere into the arrival court was the full scale of the house revealed, and only after entering the front door would a sweeping view of the Sound appear through the two-story-high window. The courtyard was populated with understory trees, vines planted against the house, and specimen trees left in the center of the turnaround.

As Manning explained to the first site superintendent, the property was "not in any sense to be a show place with many gardens and expansive lawn areas."[9] The majority of the work involved opening new views, thinning the forest, and enriching native flora by adding wild and exotic flowers. Manning's planting plan for the "Vicinity around the House" featured 104 varieties of native trees, shrubs, perennials, and ground covers. Culling the site for evergreens, he found pine, hemlock, and cedar to screen the garage and water tower from both the road and the house. He increased the existing population of rhododendron, bringing in a thousand seedlings of hybrids that he had collected in North Carolina. Trees were decorated with wistaria, "climbing roses, the Japanese bittersweet, actinidia (with its white flowers and edible fruit), akebia, Fox grape (with its fragrant flowers and small fruit), and edible grape vines at posts on the fence." The woodland

Manning's design left much of the wooded tract intact. Photograph by Arthur G. Eldredge, c. 1928. Courtesy MCL.

At the outset of the project, Manning encouraged the Lloyd-Smiths to acquire adjacent land so that he could lay out a mile-long driveway to the house. Photograph by Arthur G. Eldredge, c. 1928. Courtesy MCL.

The property featured a half mile of beachfront at the base of high bluffs and a seven-and-a-half-acre spring-fed lake on the southwest boundary, near the waterfront. Photograph by Arthur G. Eldredge, c. 1928. Courtesy MCL.

floor was carpeted with white clover, forget-me-not, and eleven thousand bulbs from Holland.[10]

Manning also took advantage of the wealth of native flora by exchanging it with plants from his other job sites. A boxcar-load of dogwood, benzoin, wax myrtle (bayberry), Japanese evergreen honeysuckle, pink marshmallow, grapevines, maple-leaved viburnum, seaside goldenrod, and buttonball bushes was sent to Walden (the estate of Cyrus H. McCormick II in Lake Forest, Illinois) in exchange for "grey-leaved grass, growing in the sand on the lake shore," red-stemmed rose, and red-berried elder, among other plants.[11] To Calumet & Hecla Consolidated Copper Company in Michigan he shipped ten small dogwoods, two hibiscus, a few seaside goldenrods, and raspberry plants for two quarts of Sweet William seed. The Cleveland-Cliffs Iron Company, also in Michigan, received small dogwoods in exchange for Russian rose for beach planting. Native bearberry, collected from locations along the North Shore, were used to augment the existing plants on the steep banks. After studying the neighbors' properties, Manning added Japanese barberry and rosa rugosa to the mix.

Manning devoted exhaustive attention to the layout of the long entrance, working on "saving all large trees . . . , fine-tuning [the] location of the road, shifting curves to save more trees."[12] The view to the pond specifically determined the layout of a portion of the road. Wilton Lloyd-Smith came up from the city several times a week to make sure nothing was being cut without his approval. Where retaining walls might have been required because of changes in grade, Manning provided drawings detailing how to use stumps in place of walls. Stumps would not only stabilize good soil, but also fertilize trees, "an economy and effect embraced by the client."[13]

The one flower garden was walled and viewed exclusively from the loggia. Plantings were modified yearly until Manning recommended altering the garden's scale and extent. He suggested "belts of magnolias," beyond which he would introduce "large leaved and large flowered varieties that make broad spreading low trees," further connecting the garden to its larger woodland setting.[14] An old orchard discovered on the newly purchased property adjacent to the entrance road became the location of a vegetable garden and small farm. Manning wanted to save the existing dogwood, sassafras, and sumac.[15] The attendant's cottage, diverse new additions to the orchard, and a cyclopian arbor draped with grape vines greeted visitors as they drove past the stone entrance gates and entered Kenjockety.

After Wilton Lloyd-Smith's death in 1944, Marjorie and the children continued to use the house for summers, weekends, and parties. It was sold in 1952 to a lawyer who subdivided the property into twelve parcels, retaining 3.75 acres around the main house, which had been reduced by removing the library and loggia wing. Though now marked by multiple driveway entrances, the road to the main house remains intact, with views across the lake and toward the harbor. Subsequent owners have rehabilitated the neglected trees and shrubs, while adding ornamental gardens carefully arranged within Manning's spatial layout.[16]

Cayuga Heights

ITHACA, NEW YORK

JACOB BROWN

Cayuga Heights is a residential development of approximately one thousand acres located north of downtown Ithaca and Cornell University and overlooking Cayuga Lake to the west. Over the last century, many prominent Ithacans and Cornell professors have made their homes in this upscale neighborhood. Several creeks run through the hilly terrain, cascading over ledges and cutting gorges into the underlying sedimentary rock on their way to the lake. Though largely bare of vegetation at the time of development, today the lots are densely planted with evergreens, and the topography and plantings give the neighborhood a distinctive local character. Warren Manning played a role in the layout of the lots, though much of the work is attributable to other landscape professionals as well as the developers, Jared Treman Newman and Charles Hazen Blood.

Newman and Blood, Ithaca attorneys turned real estate developers, ventured into the project following Edward Wyckoff's success in developing the Cornell Heights subdivision, which abuts the northeast corner of the Cornell University campus. Two new bridges suddenly made the land north of the campus accessible and attractive to developers. Newman and Blood decided to lay out a new residential community on the northern edge of Cornell Heights. They worked on the Cayuga Heights subdivision for nearly four decades, beginning in 1901 when they purchased 657 acres of farmland, and continuing to add parcels and manage the development until their deaths, in 1937 and 1938, respectively. The venture never succeeded financially, and the partners lost considerable money on it.[1]

Houses in the community are distinctive yet highly complementary. Although the subdivision includes several houses in the Spanish Colonial Revival and Mission styles, most were in the Arts and Crafts style, with exposed half-timber framing, stucco walls, and tile roofs of terra cotta or slate.[2] Local materials such as bluestone are prominent in many of the structures, retaining walls, and walkways throughout the neighborhood. The developers initially hired the New York City landscape architect Harold A. Caparn to assist with planting plans and lot subdivisions. Ithaca engineer Carl Crandall also played an important role in surveying the land and creating lot drawings.[3]

According to his client list, Manning produced drawings for the subdivision from 1906 to 1910 and again from 1914 to 1916. He divided the land into lots, created planting plans, and laid out the road network.[4] The majority of the more than sixty extant drawings relate to grading, reflecting the challenge of building on such irregular terrain. In addition to overall planning, Manning's client list shows that he also prepared landscape plans for several individual lots within Cayuga Heights, including the estates of J. H. Tanner, Charles H. Blood, and Robert H. Treman. The neighborhood retains its character and charm.

Manning laid out the road system and planting plans for Cayuga Heights from 1906 to 1910 and 1914 to 1916. Photograph by Carol Betsch, 2009.

Many of the houses in the upper-class development were Spanish Colonial Revival and Mission style. Large lots and old plantings contribute to the parklike ambience. Photograph by Carol Betsch, 2009.

Cornell University Campus

ITHACA, NEW YORK

DANIEL KRALL

Warren Manning began his professional involvement with Cornell University in 1910, through his friend and associate Liberty Hyde Bailey, then the dean of the College of Agriculture, and continued as landscape consultant to the university until his death. Among Manning's many projects, arguably the most important for the university are the two campus master plans he completed, in 1910 and in 1930, with the landscape architect Bryant Fleming.

Although the 1910 plan was Manning's first professional commission for Cornell, his relationship with the university through Bailey began much earlier. As a world-famous horticulturist, author, and educator, Bailey had a long-standing interest in landscape design and began teaching courses in "outdoor art" soon after his arrival at Cornell in 1888.[1] He and Manning learned of each other's interests during the 1890s, perhaps through their respective work on the Columbian Exposition, but certainly through the American Park and Outdoor Art Association. Both attended the initial meeting of the organization in Louisville, Kentucky, in 1897, and they served together on the committee to draft its constitution and bylaws. Bailey was also one of the first honorary members of the American Society of Landscape Architects, of which Manning was a founding member.[2]

Bryant Fleming, a 1901 graduate of Cornell's unofficial landscape program, represented another key connection.[3] Following his graduation, Fleming worked in Manning's office for three years before returning to Buffalo to open his own firm. In 1904, responding to a request from Bailey, Fleming organized the first official curriculum in Cornell's newly established Outdoor Art program.[4] This was part of the expansion of the School of Agriculture into a college, for which Bailey served as the first dean. Manning was also involved in the early years of the Outdoor Art program, although his actual role is difficult to ascertain.[5]

By the end of the decade, the College of Agriculture was entering a period of rapid growth. To guide the design of the expanding campus,

Bailey recommended that the university hire Manning as site planner. He was to work with Fleming, by then a professor in the Department of Rural Art, and with professors in the College of Architecture to develop plans for the College of Agriculture within a master plan for the entire Cornell campus.[6] Three design options, based on an array of statistics and data collected by the two landscape architects, were presented to Cornell's board of trustees. Extant records do not clearly indicate what was decided. But the statistical studies accurately anticipated campus expansion: today buildings occupy all the sites identified in the 1910 studies.[7]

Manning, with assistance from Fleming, continued to advise the university on campus planning during the following decades, adhering to the suggestions they had advocated in 1910. In early 1930, following a partial revision by Fleming in 1925, the university asked Manning and

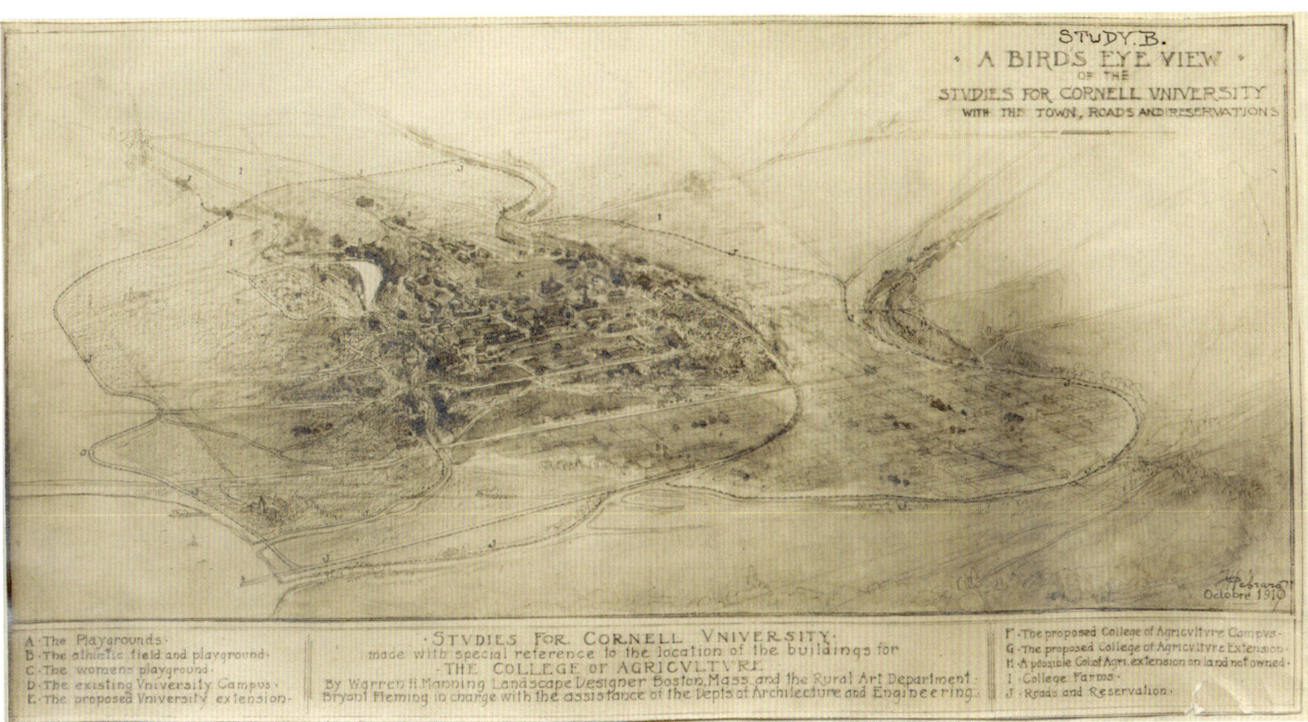

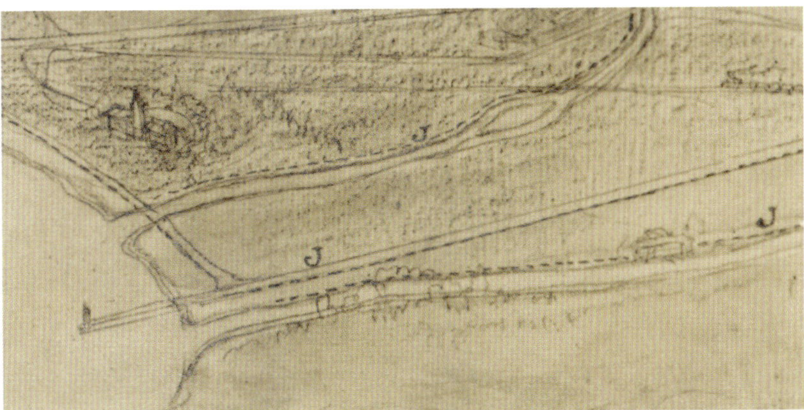

ABOVE: In 1910 Manning was commissioned to create a master plan for Cornell that would accommodate an expansion of the College of Agriculture. He collaborated on the plan with Bryant Fleming, a former employee who was then a professor in Cornell's Department of Rural Art. LEFT: (detail) Fall Creek and Cascadilla Creek are visible running almost parallel. "A Bird's Eye View of the Studies for Cornell University," October 1910. Courtesy Warren H. Manning Landscape Architecture Blueprints and Drawings, Division of Rare and Manuscript Collections, Kroch Library, Cornell University.

Fleming to undertake a major update of all previous campus planning options. At this time changing conditions presented new topics for study, among them traffic flow and parking, plans for an expanded arboretum, and the need for larger library facilities. Extensive consideration was given to problems of local and regional traffic and the width of roads. For his part, Fleming focused on the principal landscape features and building groups of the university's lower campus. By far the most radical proposal of Manning's 1930 report was his suggestion to build garages and an access tunnel under the university campus. Another interesting proposal, which indicates that Manning's farsightedness was not entirely out of focus, was his suggestion to lay out an airfield near the existing country club in Cayuga Heights.[8]

Today Manning's legacy on the Cornell campus is evident in the efficient circulation, particularly the main spine of Tower Road running from the eastern entry to the heart of the original campus, which Manning and Fleming first highlighted in their 1910 plan. Manning's suggestions for building locations, his proposal to add the second of two entrances from downtown Ithaca (now Campus Road), and his insight into changing needs demonstrate his ability to anticipate future conditions. In one campus historian's view, the plans "prepared by Fleming and Manning in the 1930s are probably the most imaginative and perhaps the most effective overall plans prepared in the history of planning for the development of Cornell's campus. Their research and analysis provided a realistic basis for the proposals. The grouping of buildings, the disposition of roads, and the carefully conceived presentation of ideas set a high standard for future campus planning."[9]

Enfield Glen State Park (Robert H. Treman State Park)

ITHACA, NEW YORK

DANIEL KRALL

When Warren Manning first met Robert H. Treman, in 1900, he could not have envisioned the long and productive relationship that would ensue. Edward B. Green, a Buffalo architect with whom Manning had worked and a Cornell classmate of Treman's, introduced the two. After graduation Green had remained in Ithaca to work with William H. Miller, the first graduate of Cornell's architecture program. In 1881 he moved to Buffalo and established his own office.[1]

With a lifelong interest in the natural beauty of upstate New York, Treman and his wife, Laura, sought to preserve the magnificent landscapes of the Finger Lakes region and make them accessible to others. One of their earliest efforts focused on Lucifer Falls, a popular tourist destination near the small village of Enfield Falls, just southwest of Ithaca. By the early twentieth century the trails and bridges providing access to the falls, which had been tramped by tourists since the mid-1850s, were badly deteriorated. Visiting the village and adjacent glen during the summer of 1914, Treman was dismayed by the site's condition. Determined to improve the situation, the Tremans purchased roughly forty acres that encompassed the small community and the nearby gorge and waterfall.[2]

To address the numerous landscape challenges, Treman turned to Manning, who, over the next several years, assisted in upgrading and further developing the site. The Tremans covered the cost, which came to several thousand dollars.[3] Manning's specific interventions during this period are unclear, as much of his initial work focused on improving paths and bridges that had been in place for years. One of his major contributions, however, was expanding Treman's vision for the site. Treman's daughter Elaine later recalled "walking down through Enfield with Father, who for many years was chairman of [the] Buildings and Grounds [Committee] at Cornell, and in connection with it had employed [Manning]. Father wanted to get his ideas for improvement of the ravine." On that hot summer day, Elaine, her father, and Manning "walked from the bottom to the top of the ravine."[4]

During that walk, Manning helped Treman to

In 1916 Robert Treman hired Manning to advise on a plan to restore badly deteriorating trails and bridges around Lucifer Falls. The Tremans had purchased the waterfall and surrounding forty acres to protect the area from further degradation. Undated stereopticon card, from The Artistic Series, No. 36, E. & H. T. Anthony & Co. Courtesy William C. Hecht, http://nytompki.org/hecht_index.htm#3.

see the potential of the larger landscape surrounding Lucifer Falls, which included other waterfalls, rare flora, and stunning views up and down the ravine. Embracing this expanded vision, Treman quietly began acquiring additional properties adjacent to the glen. In May 1920, following the initial work by Manning and the Tremans' acquisition of almost four hundred acres in and around the glen, the Tremans presented the entire Enfield Glen property to New York as a state reservation. Enfield Falls Reservation was the second of the sites—after Watkins Glen, acquired in 1906—that would become the Finger Lakes Regional Parks system.

The Treman gift highlighted the growing interest in the nascent state parks movement in New York. When the Finger Lakes State Parks Commission was established in 1924, Treman was named its first chairman, a position he held for many years. In this role he repeatedly encouraged the state to hire Manning as landscape consultant for the commission, an annual process determined by available state funding. Over the next several years Manning traveled to various sites, inspected isolated gorges and streams, and identified locations of unique native flora in the course of pursuing what was one of his most important and least recognized roles as a professional landscape architect. Manning's vision and professional expertise laid the groundwork for the extensive

CCC workers built trails that gave visitors dramatic access to the falls. Unknown photographer. Courtesy New York State Office of Parks, Recreation and Historic Preservation, Finger Lakes Region.

Even casually attired visitors could enjoy the hike to Lucifer Falls. Unknown photographer. Courtesy New York State Office of Parks, Recreation and Historic Preservation, Finger Lakes Region.

Prospects from the bluff tops still provide spectacular views. Photograph by Carol Betsch, 2014.

Steep gorge walls shelter a wide variety of rare plants; the concentration of rare species was of particular interest to Manning. Photograph by Carol Betsch, 2014.

Complex rock formations, rushing water, and delicate foliage combine to create settings of great poetic force.
Photograph by Carol Betsch, 2014.

The Gorge Trail that runs along the northern edge of Enfield Creek offers dizzying prospects of Lucifer Falls, seen here below. Photograph by Carol Betsch, 2014.

Finger Lakes Parks system, which remains one of the most outstanding state parks organizations in the nation. Producing extensive reports on the opportunities and challenges for individual properties, Manning was instrumental in establishing standards of preservation and development for parks that continue today.[5]

That Manning understood Treman's devotion to their shared efforts is clear in a tribute he wrote for a dinner honoring Treman in 1925: "In my association with men and women in nearly 1500 projects that I have been asked to give advice or prepare plans for in some 30 years, I know of no person who has given a larger portion of their attention or means to work that is distinctly in the interests of the public."[6] Upon Treman's death in 1937, the State Parks Commission changed the name of the park to Robert H. Treman State Park.

Finger Lakes State Parks

FINGER LAKES REGION, NEW YORK

JACOB BROWN

Warren Manning served as consulting landscape architect for the creation of the Finger Lakes State Parks system from 1916 through 1929, and possibly later. Making specific site recommendations as well as conducting a broad-based survey of the entire region, he was influential in shaping the park system, which included Enfield Falls Reservation (later Enfield Glen State Park, now Robert H. Treman State Park) and Buttermilk Falls, Taughannock Falls, Fillmore Glen, Keuka Lake, and Watkins Glen State Parks. Manning secured the consultancy through his relationship with Ithaca philanthropist and conservationist Robert H. Treman, who was the largest single force in the development of the Finger Lakes State Parks; he served as chairman of the Enfield Falls Reservation and Finger Lakes State Parks commissions from their inception, in 1920 and 1924, respectively, until his death in 1937.[1] Treman and his wife, Laura, had bought and donated the land for the Enfield Falls Reservation and Buttermilk Falls State Park. The Finger Lakes State Parks system would become one of the most enduring monuments to Treman's devotion to conservation. For Manning, the long-term project also served as an opportunity to add to his nationwide resource-based initiative known as the National Plan (1913–1923).

Treman began acquiring property for the Enfield Falls Reservation in 1916. The site was a likely choice for a park because of its scenic grandeur and close proximity to Ithaca, but it also possessed a historical importance as the site of the Enfield Falls Mill, constructed by Treman's great-uncle, Jared Treman.[2] Much of the park's current character comes from the massive stone walkways, walls, terraces, and staircases completed by the Civilian Conservation Corps between 1933 and 1941. Although Manning's involvement with the project had ended before these extensive stoneworks were built, the layout of the features owes much to his initial recommendations.[3]

Shortly after Treman assembled the properties for Enfield Falls Reservation, he and his group of Finger Lakes conservationists began to envision a network of parks in the region. In 1923, supported

Taughannock Falls, in Ulysses, N.Y., is also part of the Finger Lakes State Parks system. Undated stereopticon card from The Artistic Series, No. 95, E. & H. T. Anthony & Co. Courtesy William C. Hecht, http://nytompki.org/hecht_index.htm#3.

The falls were a popular tour destination even in the nineteenth century, but poor planning and the threat of industrial development had put them at risk by the time of Manning's 1916 involvement. Undated stereopticon card from The Artistic Series, No. 14, E. & H. T. Anthony & Co. Courtesy William C. Hecht, http://nytompki.org/hecht_index.htm#3.

Many of the trails in Enfield Falls Reservation (now Robert H. Treman State Park) suggested in Manning's report were later constructed by CCC workers. Photograph, n.d. Courtesy New York State Office of Parks, Recreation and Historic Preservation, Finger Lakes Region.

Taughannock Falls today is accessible via a trail system that accommodates wheelchairs and strollers. Photograph by Carol Betsch, 2014.

by New York State's conservation commissioner, Alexander MacDonald, and Robert Moses, secretary of the New York State Association, the group assigned Manning to create a survey of the Finger Lakes region that would guide investment and support the long-term planning of a regional recreation system. The survey was to include physical mapping of the region, park site recommendations, transportation improvement suggestions, property ownership research, and land acquisition strategies.

Exceptionally fine stonework is still maintained today. Buttermilk Falls State Park. Photograph by Carol Betsch, 2009.

Manning's method, as applied in previous surveys, was to travel and document the entire region by rail, automobile, and boat.[4] Specifically, Manning pledged to personally travel 610 miles of railroad, 3,000 miles of dirt roads and improved highways, and the 150-mile total length of the seven Finger Lakes in the course of compiling the survey.[5] In 1924 the Enfield Falls Reservation Commission disbanded, and the Finger Lakes State Parks Commission was formed to assume responsibility for

Buttermilk Falls State Park. Photograph by Carol Betsch, 2009.

park planning across the ten counties that compose the Finger Lakes region. Again Robert Treman served as chairman. Manning continued as the consulting landscape architect to the commission and made recommendations for trail layout, plantings, bank stabilization, wall placement, swamp dredging, signs, parking and programmatic siting, architectural styling, entrance schemes, and other design elements.[6]

Throughout his involvement with the Finger Lakes State Parks, Manning advocated expanding both the scale and the scope of planning. He envisioned a statewide—and, eventually, nationwide—survey of natural, social, economic, and cultural resources to guide transportation and land-use planning. With this ambitious National Plan, as he called it, in mind, he sought to use his work in the Finger Lakes region to secure additional planning resources from Commissioner MacDonald and Robert Moses. Moses respected Manning's work and thought him the most suitable consultant to undertake regional planning in the Finger Lakes, but he was quick to point out that in seeking to expand planning beyond the Finger Lakes, Manning had "overreached himself." Ross Kellogg, director of the Finger Lakes State Parks Commission, agreed that Manning's expansive tendencies were "running wild,"[7] but Manning continued to develop the regional survey and serve as landscape consultant to the commission. There is no clear end point in Manning's involvement in developing the Finger Lakes State Parks, though the final mention of his name in commission minutes appears on August 13, 1929.

Ithaca Improvement Plan

ITHACA, NEW YORK

JACOB BROWN

Warren Manning completed a variety of studies and plans for the City of Ithaca between 1906 and 1919. As with most of his other projects in the area, the commissions initially came from his relationship with local hardware magnate, banker, philanthropist, and conservationist Robert H. Treman, for whom Manning had designed a private estate in 1901. Archived drawings show that Manning contributed to many City of Ithaca projects over the course of thirteen years as a consultant, several of them tangentially related to Treman's development plans and public-land contributions.[1]

Much of Manning's early work for Ithaca appears to have been related to Treman's developments around Cascadilla Gorge, in the east-central part of the city. One of his first commissions came in 1906, when he was asked to resolve the complex intersection of Willow and Lake Streets at the base of the gorge, where Ithaca's street network met the foot of East Hill.[2] The roadwork was likely done in preparation for new development that was about to take place around the intersection. Shortly thereafter, Treman and several partners formed the Hillside Development Company and began planning a small Arts and Crafts neighborhood known as Cascadilla Park, to be wedged on a steep hillside between Cascadilla Gorge, University Avenue, and the historic City Cemetery. Over the next ten years, Manning worked on the neighborhood layout for the corporation, and he was also engaged by the city to plan how the development's new streets would connect with existing roads and the City Cemetery. Treman donated the gorge itself to Cornell University to be maintained as a natural area, and he deeded the small park at the gorge's base, now called Treman Triangle, to the city. Manning left his mark here too, recommending that this space be left open except for a few specimen trees, as it still is today.[3]

Also at Treman's request, Manning began to conduct regional recreation planning surveys for the City of Ithaca.[4] Some of the earliest maps, made in 1907–8, show local and regional road networks and their relation to various scenic

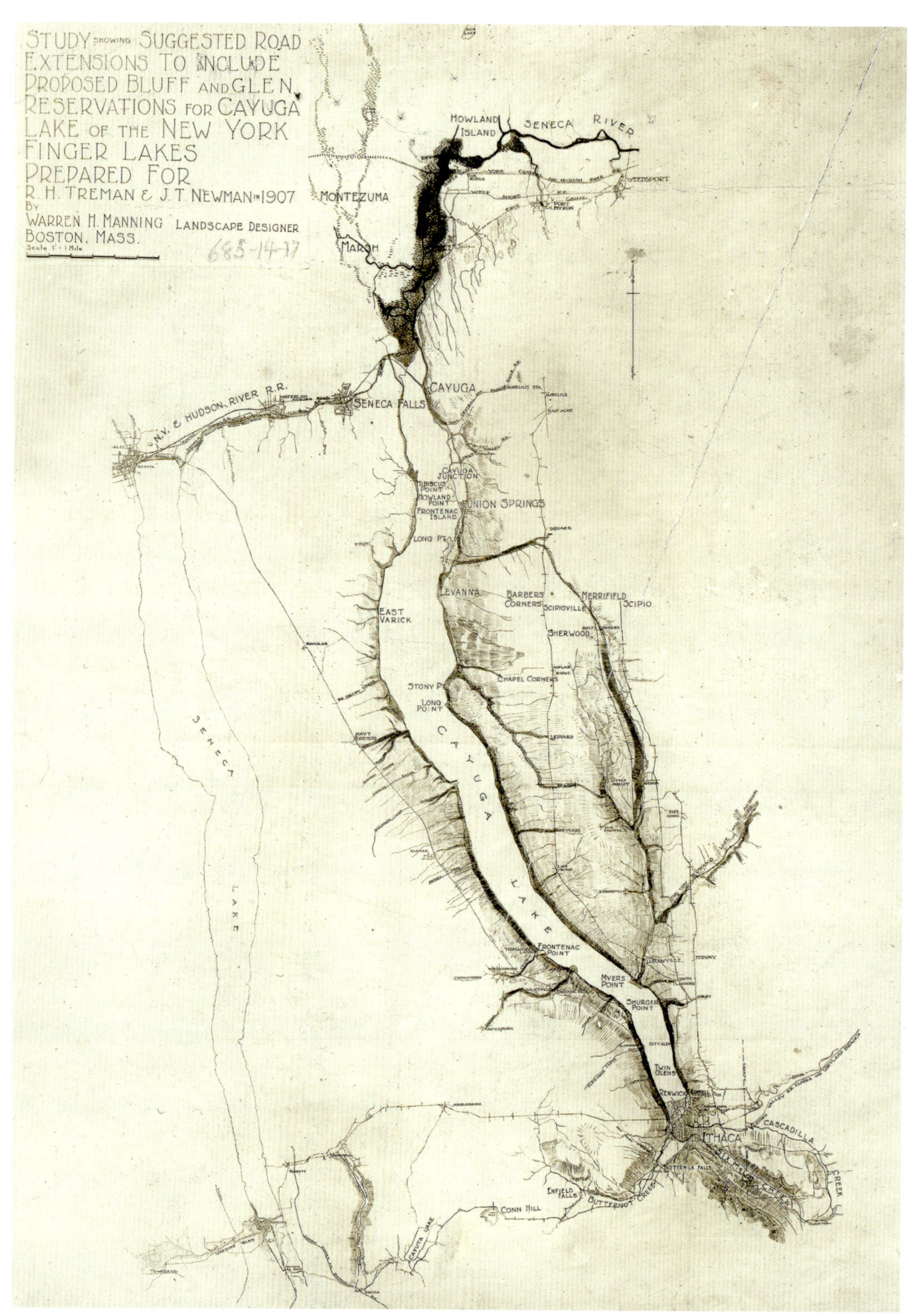

When Manning began work on the Ithaca Improvement project in 1906, he had already begun identifying scenic reservations in the region and transportation routes to reach them from the city.
"Study Showing Suggested Road Extensions," plan no. 685-14-17, 1907. Courtesy MPI.

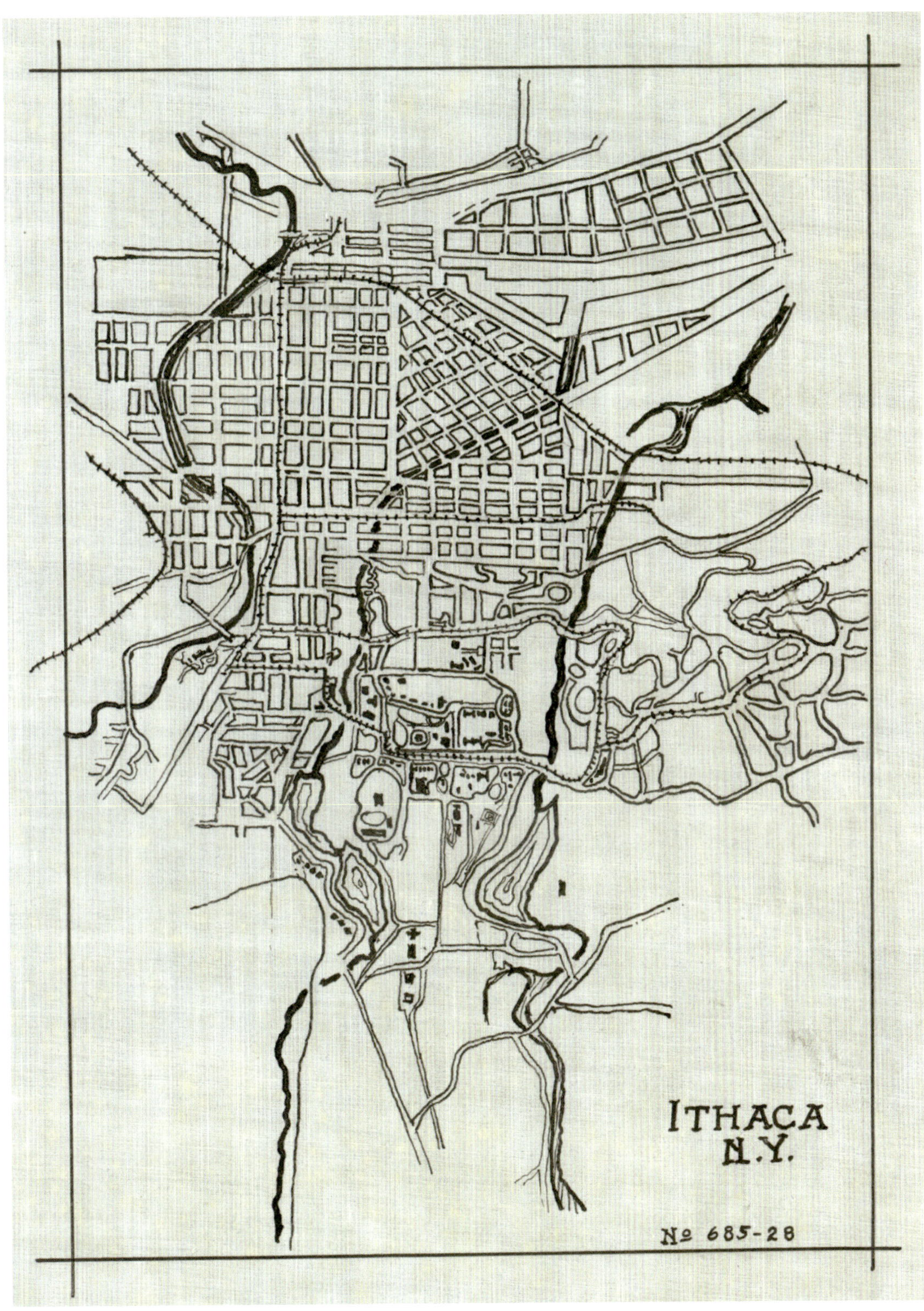

This undated plan depicts the Cornell campus, the Cayuga Heights neighborhood, and the creeks that defined their boundaries. "Ithaca, N.Y." plan no. 685-28. Courtesy MPI.

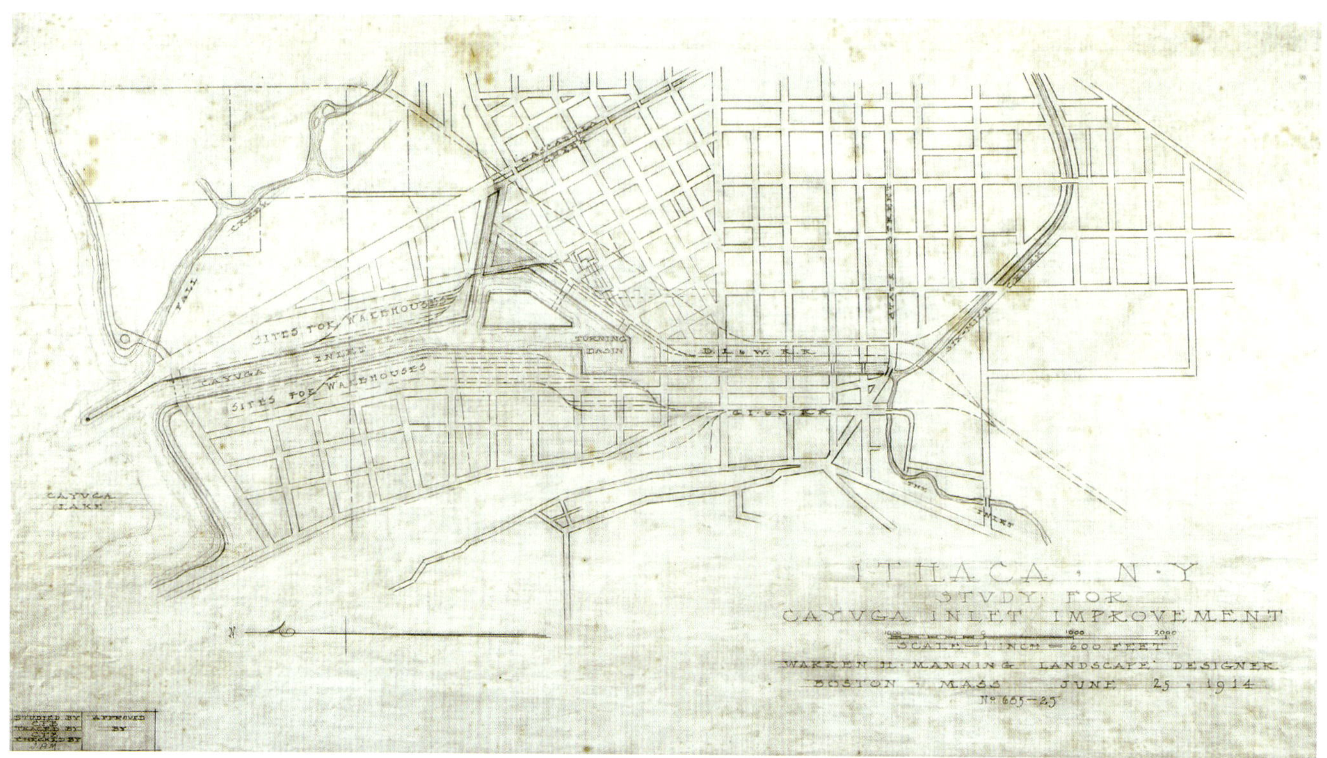

One of the major areas of improvement Manning proposed was the inlet on Cayuga Lake. "Study for Cayuga Inlet Improvement," plan no. 685-25, June 1914. Courtesy MPI.

In this undated drawing, grain elevators are sited in proximity to the canal and railroads. Plan no. 685-26c, August 1914. Courtesy MPI.

As part of the improvement, Manning laid out Cascadilla Park, a small Arts and Crafts–influenced neighborhood developed by Robert H. Treman and several business partners. Photograph by Carol Betsch, 2009.

The winding roads and steep driveways of Cascadilla Park add interest and charm to the development. Photograph by Carol Betsch, 2009.

Over ten years, Manning worked on the layout of streets in Cascadilla Park and their connections to existing roads and City Cemetery, pictured here. Photograph by Carol Betsch, 2009.

and natural resources.[5] Manning's regional-scale studies made early recommendations for the locations of large parks and reservations, while his smaller-scale plans focused on making gorges and waterfalls accessible within the city. These initial studies laid the groundwork for a much larger regional survey that Manning would conduct as a consultant to the Finger Lakes State Parks Commission.[6]

While much of Manning's initial involvement in the city related to Treman's endeavors, he soon began to consult on other landscape issues throughout the city. He created layout and planting plans for DeWitt Park as early as 1906, and planting plans for State and West Buffalo Streets in 1908.[7] His unpublished autobiography notes that he made recommendations to widen the city's three stream channels for flood control, incorporating plantings for beautification. In May 1913 the *Ithaca Journal* published an interview with Manning regarding plans for the beautification of Cascadilla Creek. He suggested planting American elms along the street and Japanese tree lilacs along the creekside walks. He also recommended dwarf spiraea for continuous summer color, golden bell (for seasonal interest), and Japanese barberry as a slope stabilizer along the Cascadilla's banks. He insisted that this relatively minimal plant palette be utilized for the length of the creek, so that the visual continuity would create a larger effect. Manning continued to consult on city projects through at least 1917, with some of his later drawings relating to proposed reconfigurations of the canals, railroad lines, and shipping yards surrounding the Cayuga Inlet at the southern tip of Cayuga Lake.[8]

Stewart Park

ITHACA, NEW YORK

JACOB BROWN

Situated at the southern end of Cayuga Lake, Stewart Park has been a popular lakefront park on and off since it first opened to the public in 1894. Then it was known as Renwick Park, a modest amusement park developed by the Cayuga Lake Electric Railway Company, which operated a trolley line to it. The company dissolved in 1908, but Renwick Park remained open until 1915, when trolley service was discontinued. A pair of silent film producers, Leopold and Theodore Wharton, then leased the property for use as a movie studio for the next four years. In 1920 Ithaca's mayor, Edwin

Stewart Park was created at the base of Cayuga Lake on the site of Renwick Park, an amusement park developed by the Cayuga Lake Electric Railway Company in 1894. Undated photograph. Courtesy William C. Hecht, http://nytompki.org/hecht_index.htm#3.

Manning's involvement in Stewart Park came in 1922. He wrote that he created plans for "recreational buildings and grounds, distinctive trails, plantations, and canoe ways." Photograph by Carol Betsch, 2009.

C. Stewart, sought to reopen the park as a public amenity. The city purchased the park in 1921 and opened it to the public that year on July 4, a month after Stewart's death.[1] It was renamed in his honor.

By this time, Warren Manning had been working in Ithaca for nearly twenty years on a variety of projects for private developers, the state park system, and the City of Ithaca. Manning's client list notes that he did planning for Stewart Park in 1922, the year after the park's opening, and his autobiography reports that he added "recreational buildings and grounds, distinctive trails plantations, and canoe ways."[2] No working documents have surfaced to confirm the extent or results of his involvement. An uncompleted, unsigned 1934 master plan represents many elements of the park as it exists today.[3] It is not known whether this is the plan begun by Manning in 1922, or whether it represents elements of his design.

Park grounds are now maintained by the City of Ithaca. Photograph by Carol Betsch, 2009.

Robert H. Treman and Charles E. Treman Estates

ITHACA, NEW YORK

JACOB BROWN

Warren Manning's landscape design for the site of three Treman family estates on Ithaca's East Hill was noteworthy upon its completion in 1901. In a break with convention, it included a sheep pasture in the foreground of an estate landscape, and Manning and his clients planned to allow the pasture to gradually grow into a forest. These concepts were innovative, even radical at the time.

In the eyes of his client, the wealthy local businessman Robert H. Treman, such originality may have marked Manning as a kindred spirit, because this would prove to be the first of many commissions from Treman. He subsequently hired Manning for jobs involving Cornell University, the City of Ithaca and surrounding area, and the Finger Lakes State Parks Commission. Manning found in Treman a long-term collaborator who shared his vision of the importance of public access to natural areas and of planning at the regional scale. Together, the two shaped much of present-day Ithaca and its surrounding environment.

The Treman family name is prominent in the history of Tompkins County, of which Ithaca is the seat. In 1790 Abner Treman received, in repayment for military service, a six-hundred-acre allotment that would eventually become the village of Trumansburg, northwest of Ithaca. Generations of Treman heirs prospered through business and escalating land values and maintained high status by assuming prominent community roles. By 1901 the three great-grandchildren of Abner Treman who remained in the area—Charles Edward and Robert Henry Treman and Elizabeth Lovejoy Treman Van Cleef—were ready to build family homes. Unlike their predecessors, who had built houses in the urban grid near their places of business, the Treman siblings decided to build on Ithaca's East Hill.[1] At the time, East Hill was home to a relatively new and prestigious neighborhood on the southwestern edge of the Cornell University campus. Improvements in telephone technology, transportation, and utilities made development on the hill more feasible, creating a building boom between 1870 and 1920.[2]

The Treman family bought a large lot on Ithaca's East Hill and in 1901 commissioned Manning to lay out three conjoined estates. His design specified a sheep meadow on the shared sweep of lawn, only a portion of which survives. Photograph by Carol Betsch, 2009.

The three Tremans chose to group their homes on a single nine-acre lot, demonstrating their status not through individually grand residences—the houses themselves were relatively modest—but in their collective presence, situated naturalistically in the landscape.[3] The prospect over the city also signified the owners' social prominence, while the view of the Cayuga Lake valley reflected their taste for picturesque scenery. Construction of the houses took place between 1901 and 1903. Robert Treman was the first to build, hiring a prominent local architect, William Henry Miller, to design a modified Arts and Crafts style house with exposed half-timbers framing bluestone and Ohio brick, sited on the southern end of the lot and angled slightly northward to capture the view up Cayuga Lake. Charles Treman selected the local firm of Clinton L. Vivian and Arthur N. Gibb to design a complementary Tudor house of similar scale.[4] It stood at the northern end of the site, angled to face slightly to the south, overlooking the inlet at the southern end of Cayuga Lake and the city of Ithaca. The central house, belonging to Elizabeth Van Cleef and her husband, Mynderse, faced due west over the valley. Miller also designed this house, though it differed in style from the other two; the Colonial Revival building with stone walls and a terra-cotta roof reflected the couple's more conservative taste.[5] The cohesive positioning and complementary design of the three houses clearly aimed to create a unified presence on the slope, but it was the landscape that would become the ultimate unifier.

Robert Treman, who knew of Manning's work through the architect E. B. Green of Buffalo, invited him to prepare a landscape design for the joint property in July 1901.[6] Manning's plan called for a lawn below the buildings, descending to a high stone wall, giving the homes a grander appearance when viewed from below and preventing the "belittling effect" of the Cornell University buildings in the background. The wall inflected slightly between each property to delineate the individual terraced yards. The most significant feature of the design, however, lay below the stone wall. Here a large pasture formed a pool of undifferentiated space that extended across the width of the family compound and served as a unifying pedestal. No driveways interrupted the pasture's expanse; the three residences appear to have shared a single winding carriage drive that departed from University Avenue and curved around the pasture's southern edge to provide access to entrances at the rear of each structure. The *Ithaca Daily News* called the pasture "an odd feature" and reported that it was inspired by "some of the beautiful manors in the South and in Pennsylvania."[7]

In keeping with his naturalistic aesthetic, Manning intended the pasture to be left untended,

The site was chosen for its location and views. Photograph by Carol Betsch, 2009.

The property returned to forest and was later donated to Cornell University, whose students enjoyed it as Redbud Woods. Almost all of the woodland was razed in 2005 to make way for a parking lot. Photograph by Carol Betsch, 2009.

creating a striking contrast with the manicured lawns and gardens surrounding the houses. If desired, he suggested, the pasture could at first be maintained by grazing sheep, but eventually it would be "left to nature as the best gardener," gradually becoming a forest.[8]

Members of the Treman family resided at their hillside estates until 1942. Cornell began negotiations to purchase the Treman properties in 1944, and in time would acquire all three estates. Two of original residences still stand, now housing university facilities; the third burned and was replaced by a university building.[9] The sheep pasture that Manning intended to grow into a forest did so over the course of a century, becoming known as Redbud Woods because of the large number of eastern redbud trees that bloomed in the understory each spring. Neighborhood residents valued the forest both for its beauty and for the buffer it created between their homes and university dormitories.

In 2001 Cornell announced plans to build a 176-space parking lot on the site of Redbud Woods. In the ensuing controversy, Ithaca's city council granted historic district status to Redbud Woods in the hope of saving it, but the Appellate Division of the New York State Supreme Court sided with Cornell, and the Manning landscape was sacrificed. Nevertheless, the debate spawned useful discussion of Manning's design intent, sustainable parking-lot design, and the protocol for preserving a historic landscape.[10]

Greensboro Normal and Industrial College (University of North Carolina at Greensboro)

GREENSBORO, NORTH CAROLINA

MATTHEW MEDEIROS

Warren Manning's involvement in campus planning at North Carolina's State Normal and Industrial College, now the University of North Carolina at Greensboro, began through connections he made while planning Pinehurst, a resort village about seventy-five miles south of Greensboro. During the Pinehurst project Manning met Kittie Dorcas Dees, a secretary at the Pinehurst hotels, and around 1899 he hired her for an administrative position in his Boston office. By 1900 Dees was handling the firm's business affairs. Dees apparently asked Manning to redesign the landscape of her alma mater, and by 1901 he had begun consulting with the State Normal and Industrial College on the project, which was Dees's gift to the school.[1]

In the early stages, Manning produced drawings of the existing campus, including a bird's-eye view of the college and a topographical map of the grounds. Through periodic visits and correspondence with the college's president, Dr. Charles D. McIver, Manning began suggesting landscape improvements. By May 1902 he had completed initial proposals for a central boulevard called College Avenue. The new road created a strong axis from a proposed rail station north to the college's Peabody Park.[2] New buildings along the boulevard were organized according to use, in a manner similar to the plan Manning later developed for Massachusetts Agricultural College. Although Manning's correspondence with the college seems to have fallen off after 1904, his recommendations continued to be implemented throughout the campus. By 1905 construction of the dirt roadway, wide planting beds, and pedestrian walkways was complete in the section north of Spring Garden Street, and a wooden bridge was built over Walker Avenue. A line of evenly spaced evergreens was planted in the beds between the walkways and road by 1907. During the next year, stone pillars were installed, marking the entrance to College Avenue from Spring Garden Street. New buildings specified in the plan were also in progress, including the Carnegie Library (now the Forney Building), and North and South Spencer Residence Halls.[3]

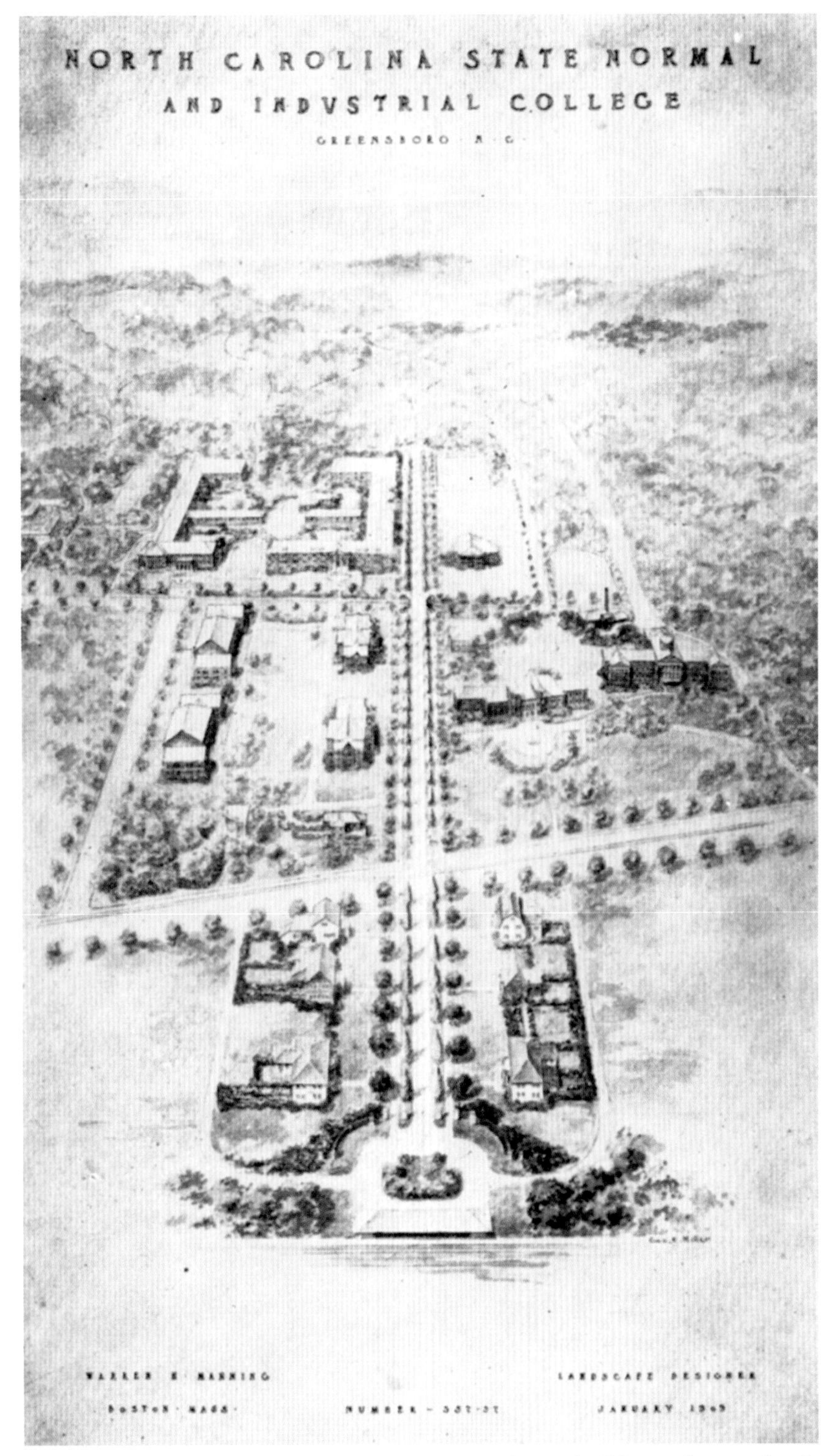

Manning's 1909 bird's-eye-view plan organized new buildings along a dominant axis. "North Carolina State Normal and Industrial College," plan no. 337-97, January 1909. Courtesy MCL.

In 1908 Manning resumed consulting with the college through correspondence with Dr. Julius I. Foust, who took over the position after the death of Dr. McIver in 1906. From this period until 1921, Manning and associates from his firm worked on a variety of projects, including the development of Peabody Park, which would eventually include over five miles of roadways and walking trails through its fields and woods.[4] Manning associate Fletcher Steele visited the campus in early 1910 to consult on a proposed "Arts and Crafts Village," where students would learn skills like pottery, metalworking, weaving, and woodworking.[5] A surviving plan from January 1912 indicates Manning's suggestions for locating a statue of McIver south of the McIver Science Building, where it was unveiled to the public on October 5 of that year.[6]

In a December 1917 report on campus planning, Manning also suggested land for future acquisition and locations for dormitories, a community house, a power house, an auditorium, and athletic fields. He repeated his recommendation, suggested on earlier plans, of creating a grand entrance to the campus by extending College Avenue into the area between Spring Garden Street and the rail-

Students in Peabody Park, c. 1905. Photograph courtesy Martha Blakeney Hodges Special Collections and University Archives, University Libraries, University of North Carolina at Greensboro (MBH UNC).

College Avenue, c. 1910. Photograph courtesy MBH UNC.

Summerhouse at entrance to Peabody Park, c. 1920. Photograph courtesy MBH UNC.

View of campus, 1907–8. Note the pedestrian bridge over the road. Photograph courtesy MBH UNC.

road tracks.[7] After consulting on additional minor projects—commemorative benches for alumni and road arrangements—Manning concluded his work at the college by the end of 1921.[8]

Despite the addition of many buildings to the formerly rural campus, the core of Manning's design is still present. Although College Avenue has changed over the years—from Manning's broad unpaved boulevard with lush landscape elements to an automobile route with minimal greenery to most recently a brick-lined pedestrian mall—it is still a central feature of the campus.[9] Peabody Park remains, though campus development has reduced it from seventy to thirty-four acres. Renewed interest in the remaining woods led to a renovation project, conducted from 2003 to 2005, that included eliminating roads and creating new bridges and walkways through the landscape Manning planned one hundred years earlier.[10]

Pinehurst Village

PINEHURST, NORTH CAROLINA

MARTHA LYON

In June 1895 the Olmsted, Olmsted & Eliot firm received a call from James W. Tufts, who announced that he had "800 acres of land three miles from Southern Pines and Aberdeen, North Carolina, 100 of which he intended to lay out as a village for consumptives," and that he wanted their assistance with a landscape plan. The firm offered to make a plan without visiting the site for $300 and in July signed an agreement. Within a few weeks, however, it became clear that designing a village on an unseen site would not be feasible. By September the Olmsted firm dispatched its associate Warren Manning to meet Tufts and inspect the property.[1]

James Walker Tufts was born in Charlestown, Massachusetts, and began his professional life at the age of sixteen as an apprentice in an apothecary. By twenty-one, he had purchased his own shop and created the Tufts Soda Fountain Company. The operation later merged with other manufacturers to form the American Soda Fountain Company, providing him with the capital to finance a new venture.[2] A man of less than robust physical condition, Tufts set his sights on developing a health resort for ailing individuals—including early stage tuberculosis patients, whom he mistakenly believed were not contagious—seeking a warm, dry climate in which to heal. Learning quickly that all stages of tuberculosis could spread, he decided to develop the village into an outdoor sporting venue, with recreation as its primary business.[3]

When Manning returned from visiting Tufts, he described the site as dominated by sand hills. (The region had been covered with longleaf pine, but most of the trees were harvested for the production of turpentine.) The broadly rolling landscape included "summits, long ridges, and valleys," with "springs, streams, and narrow irregular wetlands" as well as small trees, shrubs, and herbs.[4] Manning worked with John C. Olmsted to come up with a general plan for the village. It featured an egg-shaped central "Village Green," two-thirds of which was surrounded by serpentine roads hugging the natural grades; adjacent to the Green was a pine grove that was often filled with deer. Buildings included the Holly Inn, a casino, a general office building, and a home for the *Pinehurst Outlook,* the local newspaper. Cottages were situated on lots lining the roads, and plantings of evenly spaced trees stood between the houses and the roads.[5] Variegated clay, obtained from a local pit, was used for the roads and footpaths.[6]

After working with Tufts through the winter of 1895–96, Olmsted, Olmsted & Eliot turned the project over to Manning in February 1896. A letter to Tufts from the firm stated: "As we understand it, you are not likely to ask of us any further general or working plans. On the other hand, it seems to us that you will desire some competent person concerning the new plantations of trees and shrubbery," and went on to recommend Manning for that position.[7]

Over the next year, Tufts's vision swelled. He established a nursery to store and propagate plants for the village and added a farm, with a large barn housing a herd of Jerseys and Holsteins.[8] In 1897 he opened a nine-hole golf course, marking the beginning of a tradition that would make Pinehurst into an internationally renowned venue for the sport. Tufts recruited Donald Ross to oversee golfing operations in 1900, and the Scotsman went on to design four courses at the resort, launching his career as a golf course architect. Pinehurst's courses became some of the most famous in the world. The Carolina Hotel, located to the west of the Green, was built in 1900 and created a new focal point within the village. Manning advised Tufts on the details of several of these additions.

When Tufts died in 1902, his son Leonard inherited the resort, developing a close relationship with Manning. Over the next three decades,

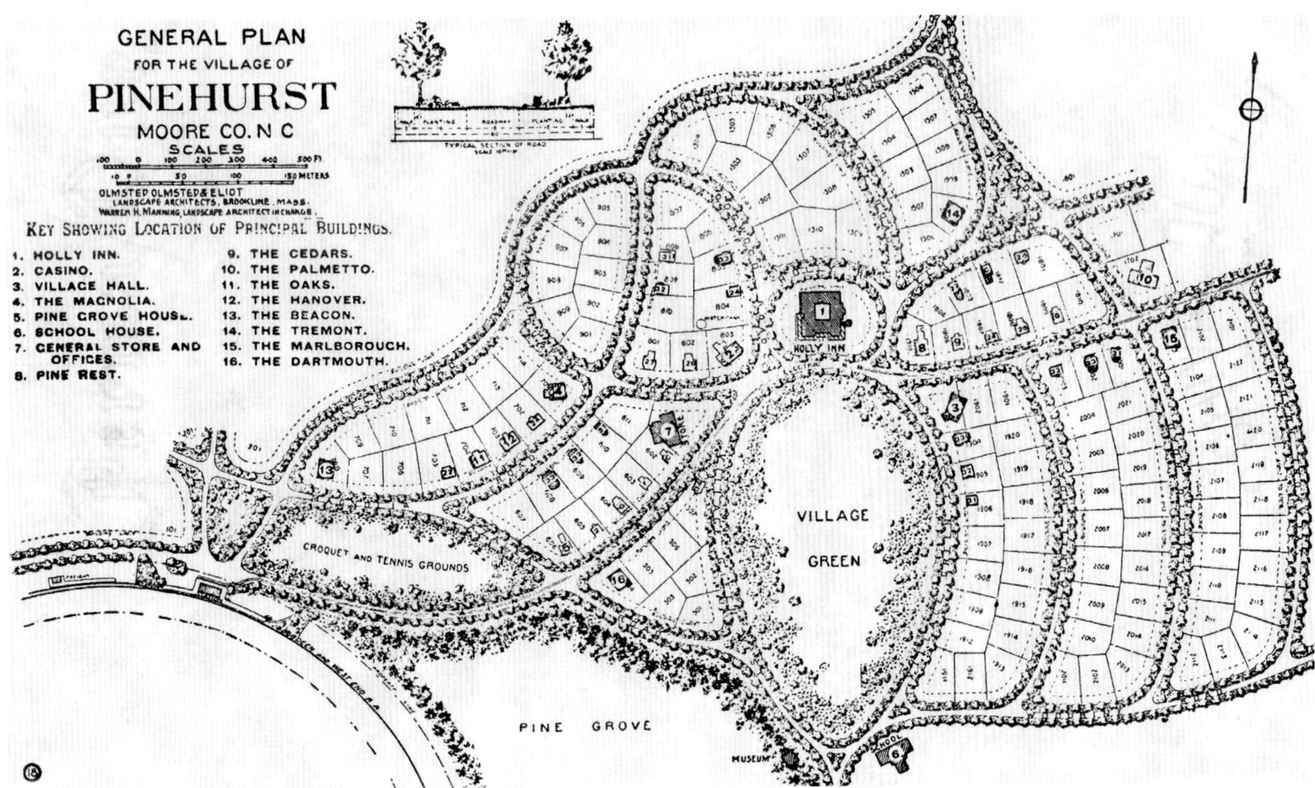

"General Plan for the Village of Pinehurst." Olmsted, Olmsted & Eliot, Warren H. Manning, Landscape Architect in Charge, 1895. Courtesy Tufts Archives, Given Memorial Library, Pinehurst, N.C.

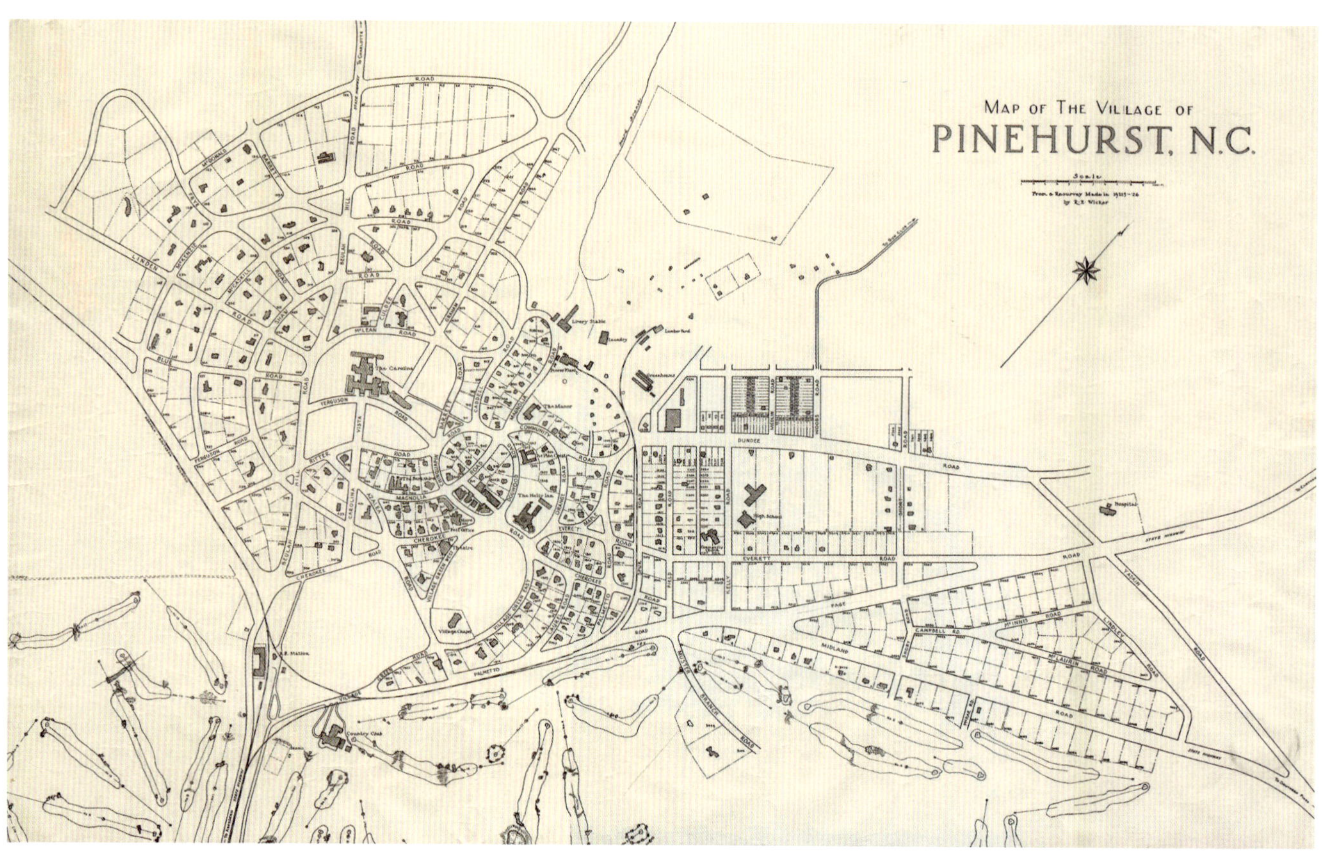

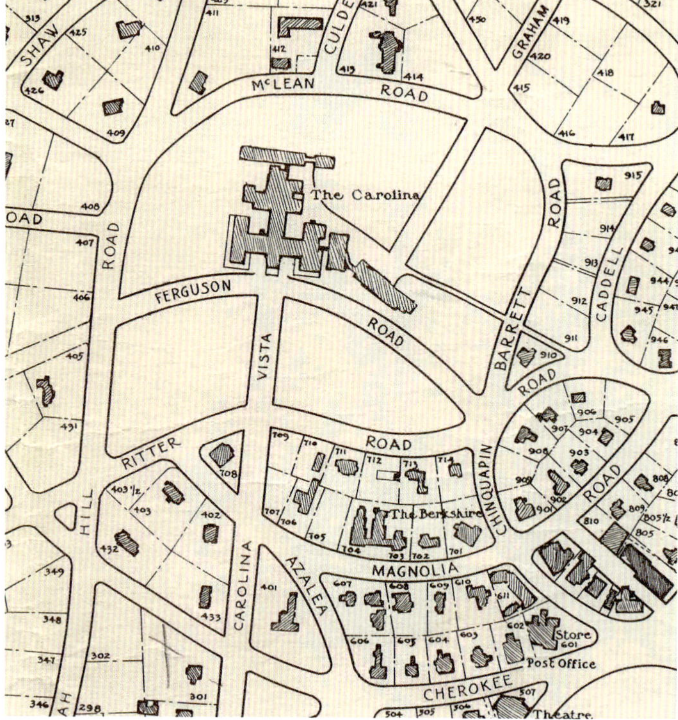

"Map of The Village of Pinehurst, N.C.," 1925–26. Manning's expansion of house lots appears west and east of the village, with the Carolina Hotel as focal point. Courtesy Tufts Archives, Given Memorial Library, Pinehurst, N.C.

Looking east, Village Green on right. Photograph courtesy Tufts Archives, Given Memorial Library, Pinehurst, N.C.

The village within a few years of its establishment (Holly Inn at right; Village Green at left). Photograph courtesy Tufts Archives, Given Memorial Library, Pinehurst, N.C.

Manning worked with Leonard to extend his client's vision of the Sandhills region. As Pinehurst continued to develop, Manning designed a fairground and race track, collaborated with Ross on at least one of the golf courses, laid out extensions to the village on the west and east sides with more house lots, and envisioned a ring road for the village periphery.[9]

In 1920 Leonard Tufts purchased several thousand acres between Pinehurst and Southern Pines and began planning a new residential and recreational development he named Knollwood. That July, he sent a letter asking Manning if he would "tackle the job," in collaboration with Ross and the architect Aymar Embury II, who would design the clubhouse.[10] Tufts and four other investors financed the venture with the intention of connecting Southern Pines and Pinehurst by "an unbroken stretch of residential properties and golf courses [that] will jointly comprise the greatest winter playground in the world."[11]

In letters to Tufts, Manning detailed his thoughts about the Knollwood site, suggesting that Midland Road, the main highway connecting Pinehurst to Southern Pines, serve as the "trunkline" from which branch roads would radiate to a village center. He noted the numerous evergreen and flowering plants growing in wetlands along creeks and recommended establishing a "reservation"—a twenty-foot buffer from the wetland—to be used by foot passengers, horseback riders, and possibly horse-drawn vehicles. On steep slopes, he suggested routing the trail along the ridges, allowing for views across the reservation. He emphasized that "these reservations with their great natural beauty, held for the benefit of the public, and made accessible by trails along the edges of paths leading out between lots to the highways, . . . will give Knollwood a unique distinction." The general concept behind Manning's design appeared in an October 1920 plan.[12] Distinct residential developments emerged around Donald Ross's two golf courses, which divided Knollwood into two private developments, Mid Pines (south of Midland Road; opened in 1921) and Pine Needles (north of Midland Road; opened in 1928). Embury's clubhouse was completed in 1921 and operates today as the Mid Pines Inn.[13]

The year before the Knollwood commission, Tufts asked Manning to review the building footprint for his new Pinehurst residence, which

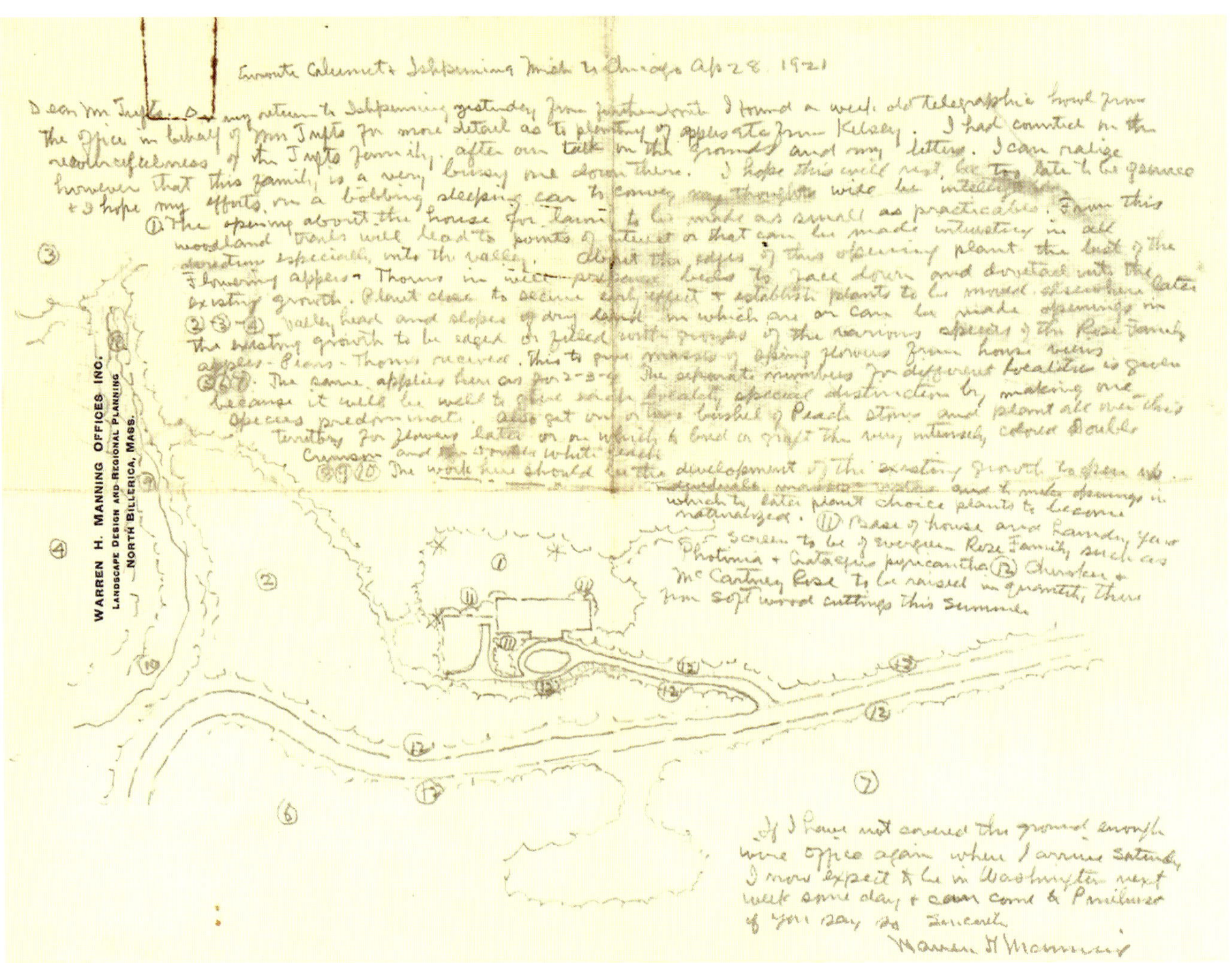
WARREN H. MANNING OFFICES, INC.
LANDSCAPE DESIGN AND REGIONAL PLANNING
NORTH BILLERICA, MASS.

Enroute Calumet & Ishpeming Mich to Chicago Ap 28. 1921

Dear Mr Tufts. On my return to Ishpeming yesterday from [illegible] I found a week old telegraphic [illegible] from the Office in behalf of Mr Tufts for more detail as to planting of apples etc from Kelsey. I had counted on the [illegible] of the Tufts family, after our talk on the grounds and my letters. I can realize however that this family is a very busy one down there. I hope this will not be too late to be [illegible] & I hope my efforts on a bobbing sleeping car to convey my thoughts will be intelligible.

[illegible]

If I have not covered the ground enough wire Office again when I arrive Saturday. I now expect to be in Washington next week some day & can come to Pinehurst if you say so. Sincerely

Warren H Manning

Letter from Manning to Leonard Tufts, April 28, 1921, with general recommendations for planting areas at Tufts's home, written while Manning was aboard a train in Michigan. Courtesy Tufts Archives, Given Memorial Library, Pinehurst, N.C.

Swimming pool, Leonard Tufts's home, 1920s.
Photograph courtesy Tufts Archives, Given Memorial Library, Pinehurst, N.C.

included a circular outdoor terrace and swimming pool.[14] Manning's reaction to the exterior features was both humorous and less than positive: "Your architect suggested an opportunity for a pool [on the terrace], into which a guest could conveniently tumble when he backed away from the front door in giving you his partial greeting. There are some guests that deserve such as fate, it is true."[15] In April 1921 Manning sketched his vision for the property while en route from Calumet and Ishpeming, Michigan, to Chicago in a "bobbing sleeping car." He suggested massing flowering trees, including apples, pears, peaches, and thorns, to provide springtime color at the edges of existing vegetation, and enhancing the edges of the driveway and road with Cherokee and McCartney roses. About the base of the house, he recommended evergreens such as scarlet firethorn as well as photinia and hawthorn.[16] The Colonial Revival residence was constructed in 1922 at 25 Muster Branch Road, overlooking the third hole of Pinehurst's signature No. 2 golf course, which was designed by Ross in 1920. Photos of the grounds dating to the early twentieth century show the evergreens, roses cascading over the entrance portico, and the swimming pool set away from the house on a broad terrace, all indicating that Tufts followed Manning's suggestions.

Although Manning clearly influenced both the details and overall layout of the village, his most remarkable contribution to Pinehurst was planting. Photographs of the village during its initial development illustrate the extent to which mature trees had been removed, leaving a sterile, barren, inhospitable landscape. Manning not only revived the site but made it into an attractive place for people to live. He specified and located trees, shrubs, and ground covers throughout, with the initial order consisting of over 200,000 plants, some of which came from France and nine American nurseries.[17] He arranged the plants to frame views from cottages

The Knollwood Clubhouse, designed by Aymar Embury II, opened in 1921. Embury also designed several buildings at Pinehurst. Photograph courtesy Tufts Archives, Given Memorial Library, Pinehurst, N.C.

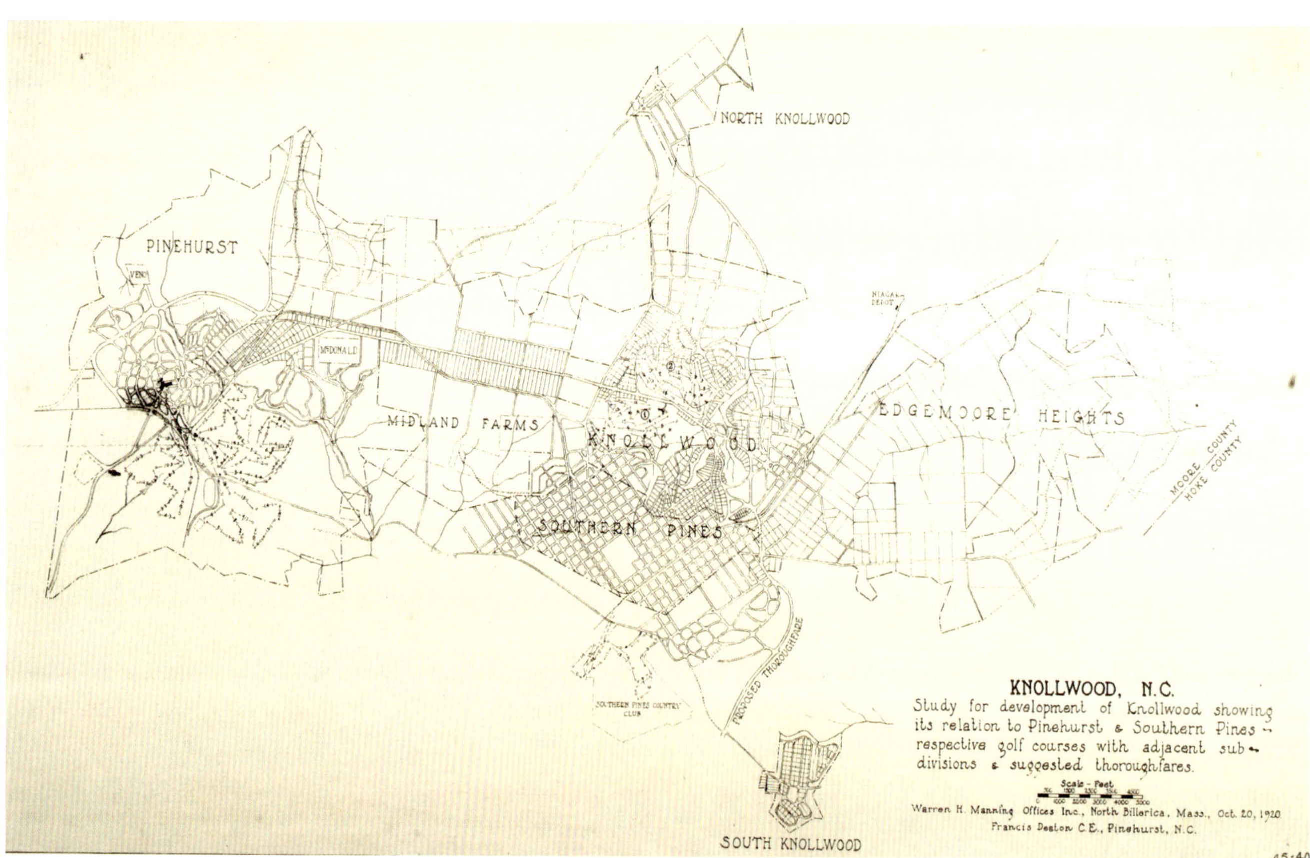

"Study for development of Knollwood, showing its relation to Pinehurst and Southern Pines and the respective golf courses with adjacent subdivisions and suggested thoroughfares." Plan no. 45-407-13, October 1920. Courtesy MPI.

and hotels across the village landscape, providing a lush appearance every season, especially in winter, with native species—mountain laurel, sweet magnolia, fothergilla, winterberry, southern magnolia, Carolina laurel cherry—and evergreen oaks (willow oak, live oak, swamp water oak) as well as boxwood, scarlett firethorn, American holly, inkberry, honeysuckle, and English ivy, augmented by non-native exotics such as deodar cedar, cedar of Lebanon, Bhutan pine, quince, heavenly bamboo, Scotch broom, and many varieties of roses.[18]

Manning remained connected to Pinehurst and to the Tufts family until his death in 1938; the relationship was one of his longest with a single client.[19] In the 1920s he designed a peach orchard, advised on an expansion to the Holly Inn and construction of a village chapel at the southern end of the Green, and commented on development of an airfield.[20] By 1929 he had prepared drawings and cross sections for 150 to 200 miles of bridle paths traversing lands surrounding the village.[21] On one of his last visits Manning walked the village, noting that the plantings of native trees had fared best and that only two exotic non-natives had succeeded, the heavenly bamboo and the deodar cedar.[22]

Pinehurst was added to the National Register of Historic Places in 1973 and named a National Historic Landmark in 1996. Since the late 1930s, changes have been made to accommodate a growing population and the expanded use of automobiles. The original sixteen-foot-wide roads were broadened, the adjacent planting beds were narrowed, and portions of the Green became sand parking areas. Traffic circles sited at the edges of the village eased congestion but introduced modern features into the historic landscape. Despite these changes, Manning's imprint on the village remains visible through the layout of roads and amenities, and through the thousands of trees, shrubs, and ground covers continuing to flourish throughout Pinehurst.

Glendale Park

AKRON, OHIO

GLORIA SCHREIBER

The improvement of Glendale Park was one of Warren Manning's later commissions for Frank and Gertrude Seiberling in Akron, Ohio. The park, a 6.4-acre parcel of land on Glendale Avenue near the city's historic Glendale Cemetery, was essentially an open space in 1925, when Gertrude Seiberling saw the property as an opportunity for the Akron Garden Club to "beautify" the cemetery entrance.[1] The park was located on both sides of Glendale Avenue and bounded by Locust Street on the west and Cherry Street on the east. Manning, who had been employed by the Seiberlings on various projects for more than a decade, received the commission for its design in 1928.

Manning presented his ideas for the park at a garden club meeting on January 8, 1929, and by May had submitted a plan and report.[2] In an effort to involve local residents in the planning process, he suggested hosting a community planting day and scheduling a July meeting in which property owners and concerned citizens could express their views. Although Manning's plan may have been implemented, the only significant element remaining is a long flight of stone steps and terraces built into the steep hillside of the park's northern boundary, intended to provide access to the park for residents of the neighborhood along South Walnut Street.

The steps begin as a series of wide stairs, which then divide into two smaller parallel stairways; the rectangular spaces between were intended for plantings. The stairs meet at a terrace midway down the hillside before separating again to circumvent a stone wall with a niche, which serves as the focal point of the design. As they continue down the slope, the stairs create two halves of a semicircle from an aerial perspective. In the final descent, the parallel steps break at small landings before continuing diagonally toward the street and meeting at a set of wider stairs leading to a grassy area in front of Glendale Avenue.

Although the onset of the Great Depression delayed construction of the steps, the Akron Garden Club introduced five thousand plants to the park during the early 1930s. Spruce, elm, black locust, mountain ash, and pine trees stood on the hillsides, and witch hazel, chokecherry, and honeysuckle inhabited the areas around the steps. Flowers included native lupine, phlox, and iris. A garden club fundraising event in support of the park was held at the home of H. B. Stewart Jr., chairman of the Akron, Canton & Youngstown Railroad. It attracted fifteen hundred guests and raised more than $2,000.[3]

From 1936 to 1937, the Federal Works Progress Administration constructed the 242 steps and surrounding stonework using locally quarried sandstone. In the ten years following the completion of the steps, the park featured popular community events including theatrical performances on the terraced landing. Local preservation groups have been concerned with preserving the steps since the early 1980s, and in 1992 a coalition of local preservationists formed a nonprofit group dedicated to that cause, Save Our Steps. The Glendale Steps became an Ohio Historical Marker in 2007. Today, the property is cared for by the city, the Preservation Alliance of Akron, and other local groups.

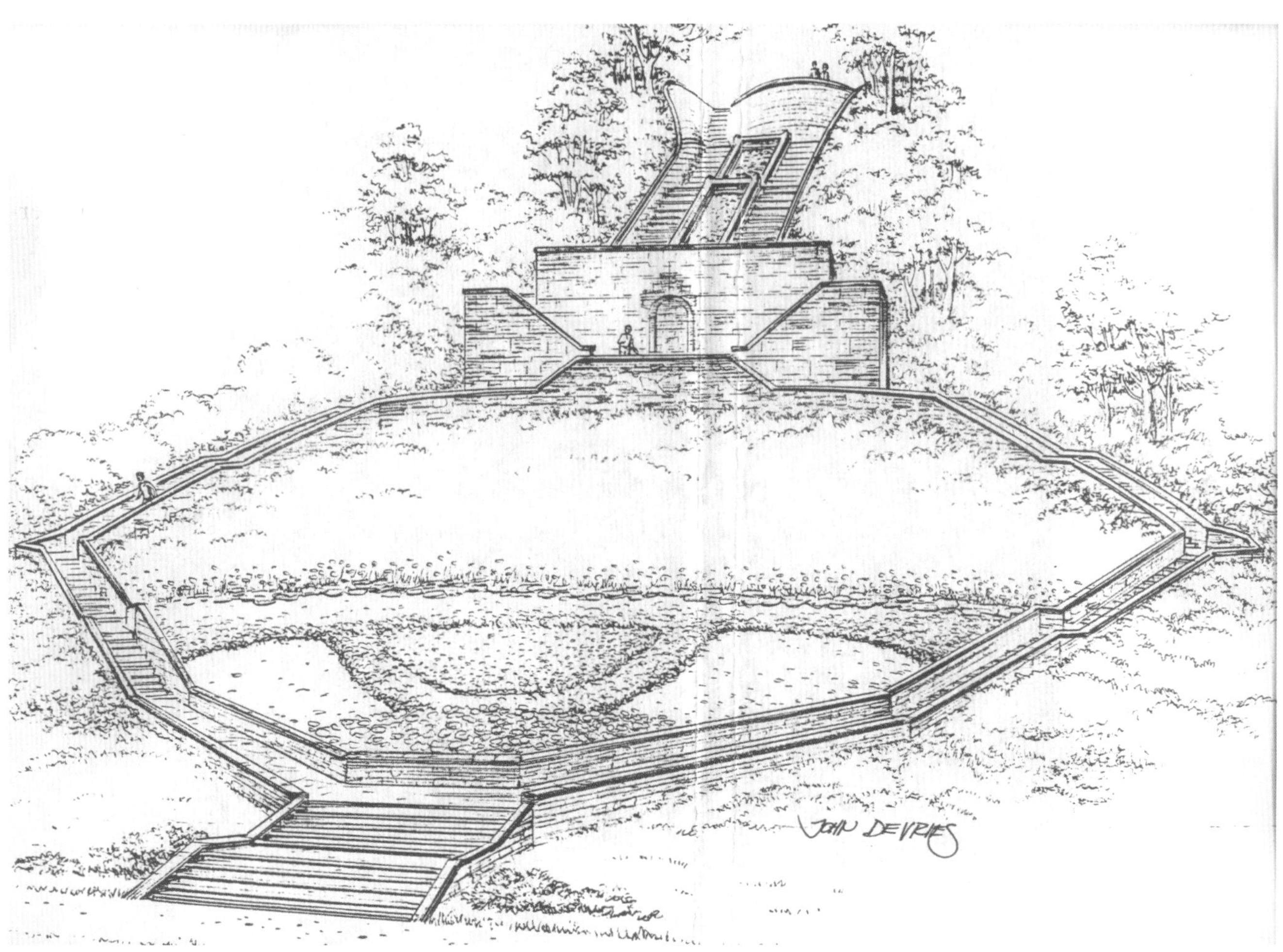

Manning designed the Glendale Steps in 1928 as a feature of Glendale Park. Owing to the rapidly declining economy, the 242 sandstone steps were not constructed until 1936–37. The stylish staircase, in time, became a popular site for dramatic performances. Drawing by John DeVries. Courtesy Progress Through Preservation of Greater Akron.

Goodyear Heights

AKRON, OHIO

GLORIA SCHREIBER

Warren Manning was an experienced planner of company towns by 1912, when Frank Seiberling commissioned him to design a housing development for employees of the Goodyear Rubber Company. Designed to increase in size alongside the expanding rubber industry, Goodyear Heights became a "city for Goodyearites" featuring a modern transportation network, a community park capable of entertaining thousands, and a variety of civic amenities. Manning used his experience from previous company town plans, including the Draper Company's worker housing in Hopedale, Massachusetts, the Calumet & Arizona Copper Company's town of Warren, Arizona, and the Cleveland-Cliffs Iron Company town of Gwinn, Michigan, to develop a comprehensive two-phase plan in anticipation of over three thousand residents.

Akron became a center of rubber manufacturing beginning in the later decades of the nineteenth century, with the founding of B. F. Goodrich in 1870, and grew rapidly alongside the development of the automobile and airline industries. Seiberling founded the Goodyear Tire & Rubber Company in 1898, and just ten years later was supplying tires for the Ford Company's Model T. Between 1900 and 1920 employment opportunities in Akron attracted a steady flow of new residents; the city grew from about 42,000 to over 200,000. By 1930 Akron was known as "the rubber capital of the world."[1]

Manning's association with Frank Seiberling began in 1911, when he was commissioned to design the landscape for Stan Hywet, the Seiberling home. As his company expanded, Seiberling became concerned with the lack of worker housing in the area and hired Manning to consult on buying land suitable for this purpose. By July 1912 Seiberling had purchased about four hundred acres in the eastern part of Akron, just a quarter mile northeast of the Goodyear plant. A few months later, Seiberling was forced to confront growing discontent over labor conditions. The Industrial Workers of the World, which had organized workers in Lawrence, Massachusetts, moved into Akron to aid the rubber workers,

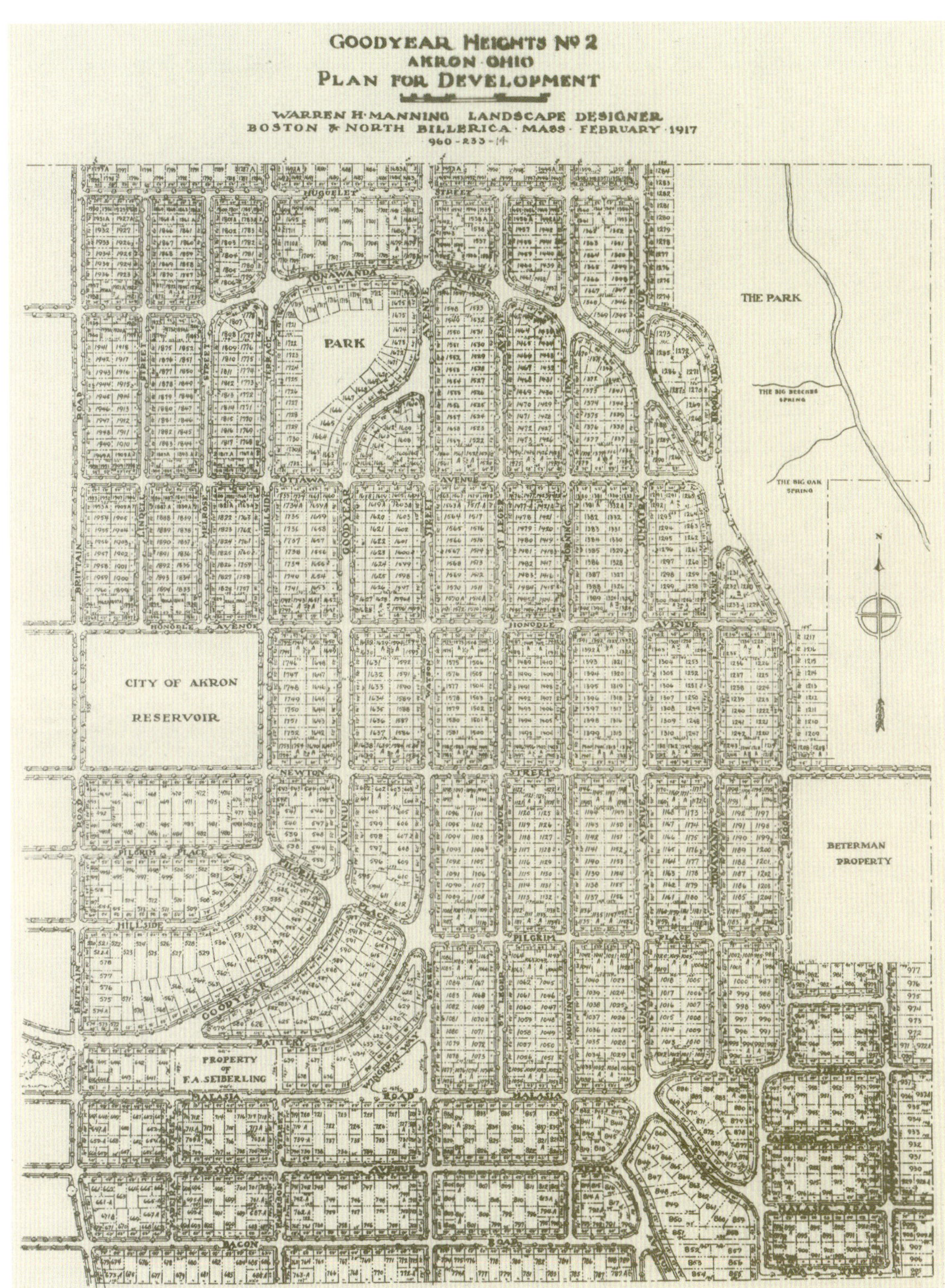

Manning's densely platted plan for Goodyear Heights featured curving roads that followed the rise and fall of the hilly site. "Plan for Development," plan no. 960-233-14, February 1917. Courtesy MPI.

facilitating strikes at the Firestone and Goodyear plants. The planning of the "Goodyear allotment," later known as Goodyear Heights, became an immediate necessity as Seiberling struggled to maintain productivity in his workforce.

The site for Goodyear Heights was about two and a half miles from the center of Akron, and Manning laid out the development to eventually merge with a seventy-foot main street intended as an "extension" of Akron's principal street, with an electric railroad from the city to the factory and housing development. In 1913 Manning described designing a "great 100-acre rectangle" with twenty-one streets and a bridge over the railroad that led to what would become Blue Pond Park and Playground, a twenty-eight-acre area featuring a pond, ball fields, a play area, and, eventually, a public school. Manning's design emphasized street views, shade trees, and the inclusion of "useful plants," such as fruit trees, "each . . . grafted to an early, medium and late variety, and on each house . . . a grape-vine for

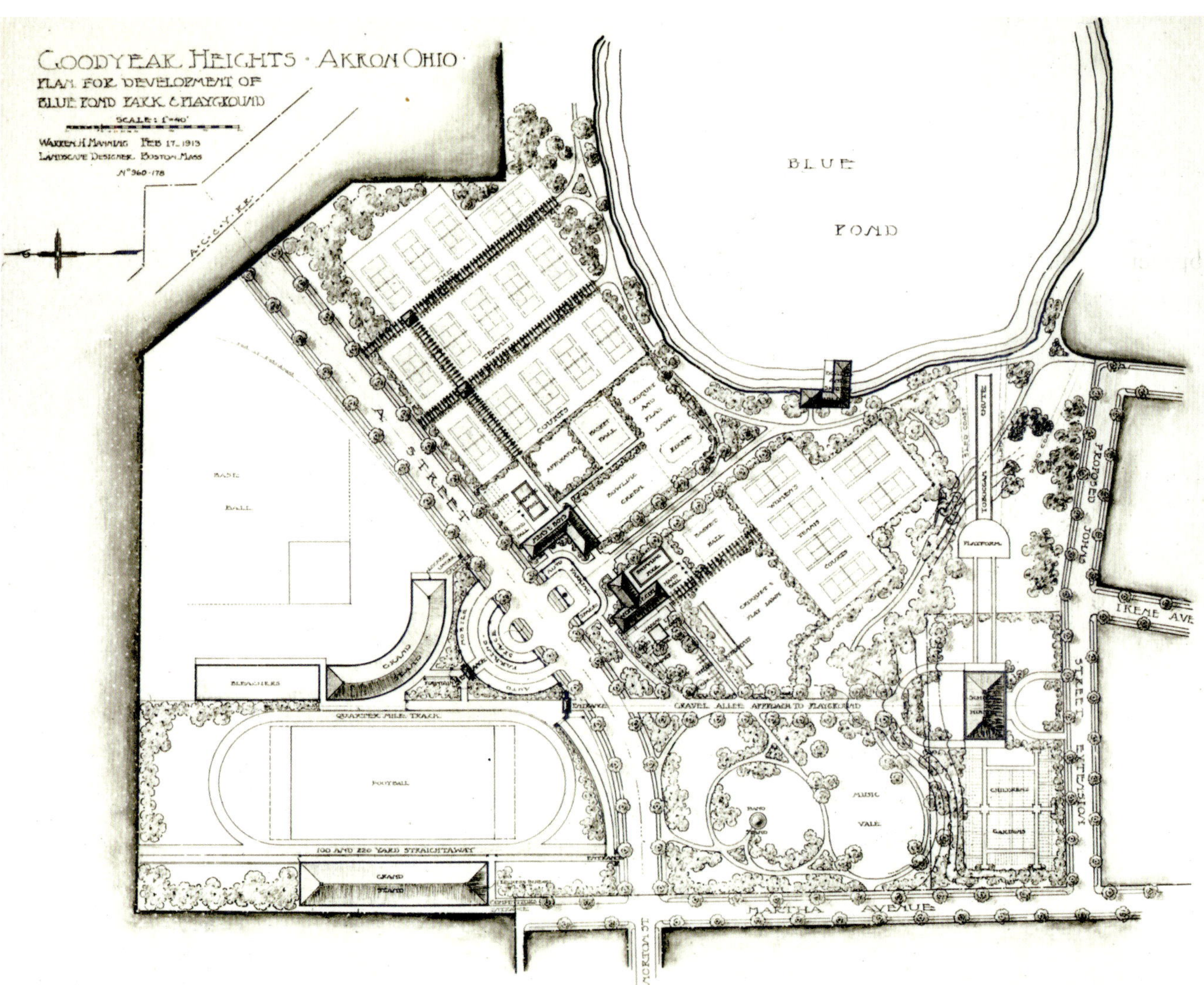

Designed primarily for active recreation, Manning's plan for Blue Pond Park specified facilities for tennis, football, baseball, tobogganing, boating, and ice skating. "Plan for Development of Blue Pond Park and Playground," plan no. 960-178, February 1913. Courtesy MCL.

shade, ornament and fruit." The plan included 436 lots and seven different house designs provided by the New York architectural firm Mann & MacNeille. In 1913 Manning declared that the allotment would "be a city in itself of some 500 homes and 3,000 inhabitants."[2] In fact, just three years later another 1,503 lots were created, as Goodyear Heights went into a second, even more impressive phase of development. Designed by the Pittsburgh architect George H. Schwan, the new houses came in nineteen styles, all created for single families to discourage overcrowding. Beginning in September 1915, residents of Goodyear Heights could pay three cents to board a double-decker bus and travel to work or the city.

The Goodyear Company's newspaper, *The Wingfoot Clan,* circulated 18,000 copies in 1918, the year it reported on the second phase of development. In addition to about sixteen small parks and green spaces located inside the Goodyear Heights neighborhood, the design included Reservoir Park, at the top of a hill in the center of the development, and Blue Pond Park and Playground, the "recreation grounds" on the western edge. In just five years, Blue Pond Park had become known for its baseball games and "gigantic track and field meets," one of which the paper claimed attracted over fifty thousand people. The playground was supervised by "three competent instructors," who not only watched the children but also taught classes in folk dancing,

Laying sidewalks in Goodyear Heights, c. 1913. Photograph, n.d. Courtesy University of Akron.

Manning's design included pocket parks throughout the development. Photograph by Carol Betsch, 2014.

calisthenics, and basket weaving. Reservoir Park, planned around what would become a city reservoir, included a stone building for community use. Goodyear Heights also featured its own church, stores (one of which included a branch of the American Express Company), and a school, which was already overcrowded and about to be replaced by a larger one.[3]

Although the English garden city model served as the precedent for Goodyear Heights, the development featured a centrally located town square, a community space inspired by early settlements in New England. In his usual way, Manning made a special effort to preserve existing trees and emphasize the natural beauty of the landscape. The 1913 plan for Blue Pond Park and Playground was never fully constructed, in part because of Goodyear's involvement in the World War II production effort.

Today, Goodyear Heights is a neighborhood of lower- to middle-class homes, and much of the park land has been compromised. Blue Pond was partially filled in to make room for the growing Goodyear Tire & Rubber facility, and most of the park and playground became parking lots, with the exception of a few ball fields. Reservoir Park has doubled in size, however, and is now the largest and primary park for the neighborhood. The stone building serves as a day care center and a location for community meetings, including those of a local group called RIGHT (Residents Improving Goodyear Heights Together). The sycamores planted ninety years ago still stand in the park, which now also includes a swimming pool, playground, tennis courts, and sports fields. Goodyear School (1918) is still in operation, and although Seiberling Elementary School was recently demolished, a new school will soon take its place.

A later expansion of the development featured an additional nineteen house styles by the Pittsburg architect George H. Schwan. Photograph by Carol Betsch, 2014.

Large trees provide a leafy canopy throughout Goodyear Heights. The architectural firm of Mann & MacNeille designed seven different house styles for the original development. Photograph by Carol Betsch, 2014.

Changes in topography and pockets of open space create a sense of parklike expansiveness, even when such areas are not visible from the street. Photograph by Carol Betsch, 2014.

Frank A. Seiberling Estate (Stan Hywet)

AKRON, OHIO

ROBIN KARSON

In 1910 Frank A. Seiberling, cofounder of the Goodyear Tire & Rubber Company, wrote to Warren Manning to tell him about a hundred-acre parcel of land he had recently purchased on the outskirts of Akron. Frank and his wife, Gertrude, were planning a country estate, and they would soon go abroad with their architect to study models for the Tudor Revival mansion they already had in mind. Manning visited Akron in June of the following year to assess the property and wrote to Seiberling approvingly, "Very few of the thousand or more properties that I have examined and made plans for, offer within a hundred acres so many and such varied incidents."[1]

Manning's letter noted mature fruit orchards (several established farms made up the bulk of the property), open forest with very fine individual specimens, and springs and wetlands at the base of an escarpment, a remnant of an abandoned sandstone quarry. The feature that would give the proposed estate its greatest distinction, in Manning's opinion, was the escarpment—"a great irregular pan, with one side a perpendicular rough wall face, capped by an old peach orchard." It would also give the place its name, Stan Hywet, Old English for "stone quarry."

Along with his letter, Manning sent a plan of existing conditions on which he had sketched a proposed arrangement of the estate. His preliminary scheme, which included new roads and a house site, divided the property into three general areas: a large lawn southeast of the house, a large wild garden to the northwest, and a farm. The plan put the house on the escarpment, an arrangement that recalled Charles Platt's siting of the house at William Mather's Cleveland estate, Gwinn, where Manning had designed plantings and an extensive wild garden a few years earlier.

In 1912 ground was broken for the mansion, designed by architects Charles S. Schneider and George B. Post (both of George B. Post & Sons).[2] Construction required improvements to city roads and water lines and a narrow-gauge railroad to bring building materials from the local rail line. Manning's representative on the job during the main period of landscape construction, from

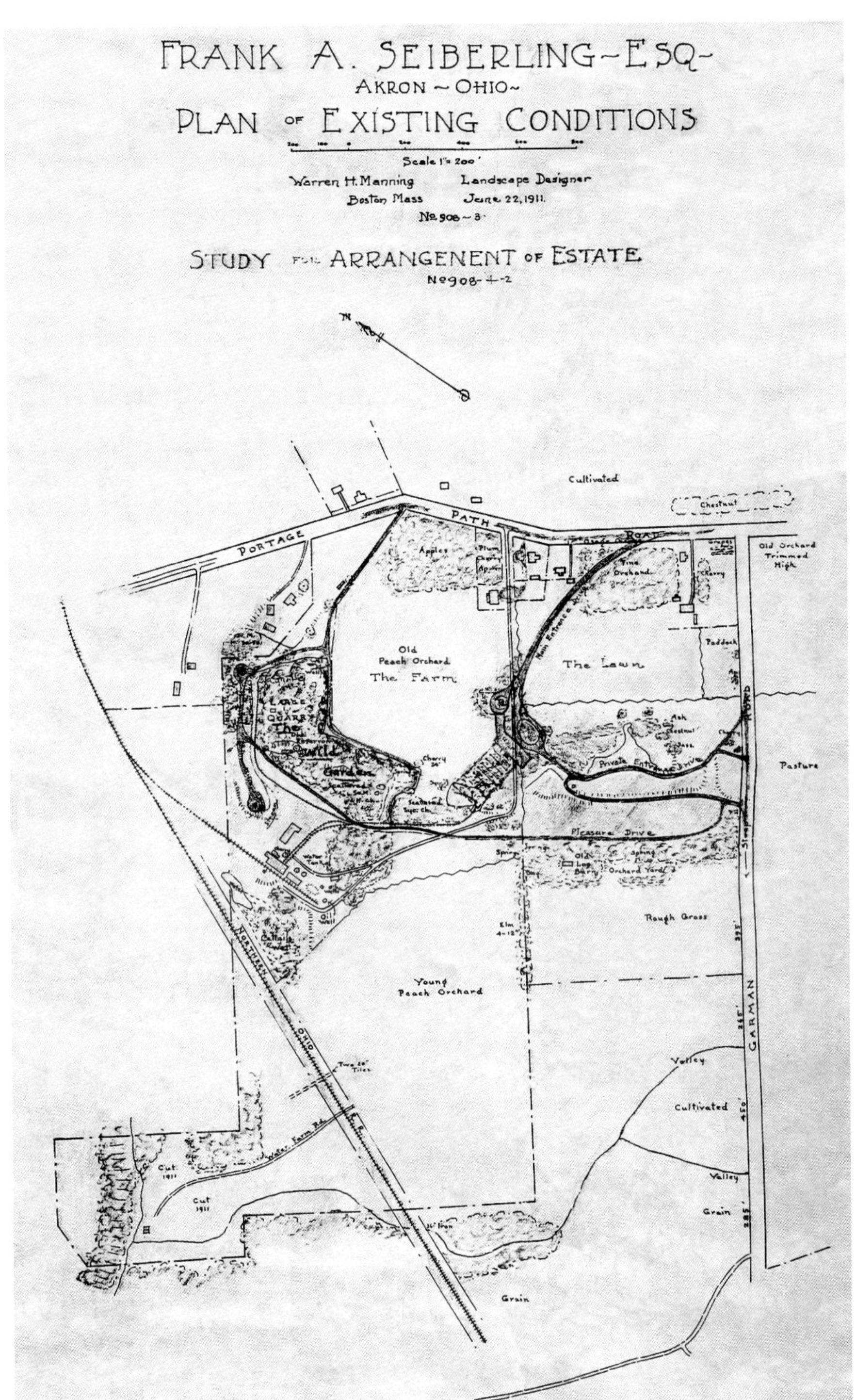

One of the very few surviving plans for Stan Hywet, this 1911 map shows existing conditions and Manning's early ideas about the layout of the estate. "Plan of Existing Conditions," plan no. 908-3, June 1911. Courtesy Stan Hywet Hall and Gardens.

1912 to 1915, was A. D. Taylor, who had also supervised work at Gwinn. An affectionate relationship quickly grew between the Seiberlings and Manning, who would come to work on several initiatives related to Goodyear, the source of Seiberling's rapidly increasing wealth.

Manning's design for the estate reflected the influence of two broad stylistic principles. The large wild garden, lagoon, vistas, and improved woodland emphasized naturalistic compositions. The rolling lawns and winding drive reflected the English Picturesque. Both were typical of Manning's preferred aesthetic approach. Buildings throughout the seventy-acre home grounds were designed by Schneider—these included a carriage house, stables, a gate lodge, a poultryman's house, and a gardener's cottage—sited according to Manning's plan. Schneider, who had resigned from Post's architectural firm at this point, also designed the house terraces and overlooks, in collaboration with Manning.

A view of the vast rolling lawn greeted visitors on the approach road, who then traveled through an old apple orchard, retained, in Manning's words, to "give the property a rural beauty and long-established character."[3] The house was screened from full view until the last turn, where it loomed imposingly. Manning's restrained planting scheme for the facade featured several towering American elms that overarched the geometric architecture.

The primary landscape feature was a lagoon that had been created by excavating and damming the pan below the escarpment, comprising

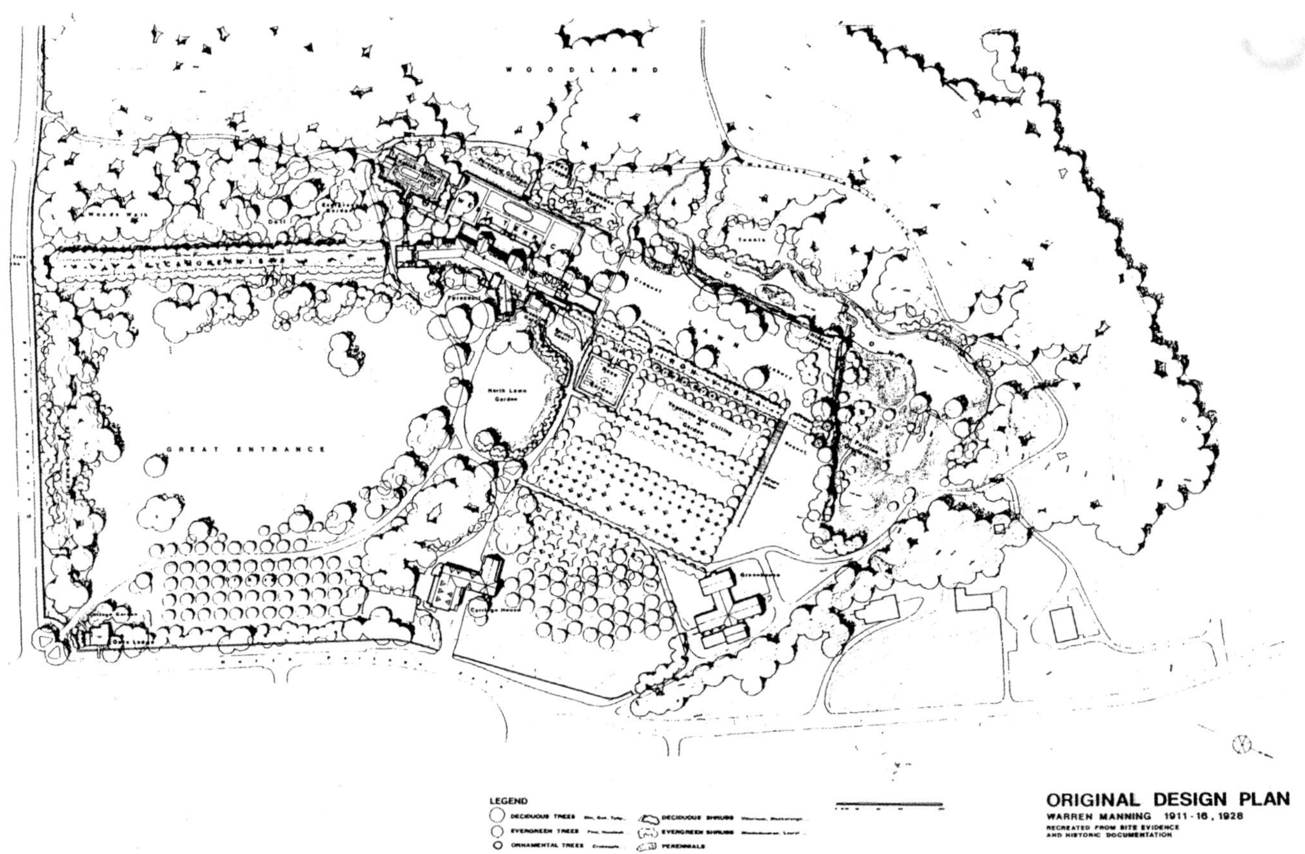

A plan showing the estate as it was developed. "Original Design Plan," created 1984. Courtesy Child, Hornbeck Associates.

One of Stan Hywet's most impressive features is the vast lawn across which approaching visitors catch glimpses of the large Tudor-inspired house. Photograph by Carol Betsch, 2006.

three sinuous pools with small islands linked to the shore by wooden bridges. The water provided a foreground to several long views, and it also offered recreation—the six Seiberling children were avid swimmers and skaters. The wild garden surrounding the lagoon featured an eclectic mix of trees, shrubs, and herbaceous plants—both native and exotic—selected for broad color effects. In Manning's 1911 letter he had envisioned "great carpets of color instead of little garden bunches." As in other examples by Manning in this genre, planting compositions were inspired by nature and, to some extent, his artistic imagination.

In two areas, however, Manning used a formal French device, the allée, as a means of connecting the sprawling house with the land. To the south, he laid out a 650-foot double row of plane trees on axis with the music room, underplanted with great stands of rhododendron. On the opposite end of the house, he planted a 550-foot pleached birch allée that leads to a high lookout giving long views over the wild garden and to the Cuyahoga

Vistas from the wild garden stretch over the lagoon and the Cuyahoga River Valley. Photograph by Carol Betsch, 1996.

The design of the outlook was a source of disagreement between Manning, who wanted the view left open, and the architect Charles S. Schneider, who proposed using it as a setting for a large sculpture. Undated photograph. Courtesy Stan Hywet Hall and Gardens.

Valley beyond. Rhythmically alternating pools of light and shadow enliven the vista down the tunnel formed by the native American tree.

Over the course of the project, aesthetic tension emerged between Manning and Schneider. They disagreed, for example, about a feature for the terminus of the birch allée. Schneider's letters argue in favor of a garden house sited in the center, where it would have been visible from the house but blocked the long view. Seiberling agreed with Manning that the view should remain open, and twin pavilions were subsequently created to frame the vista. Another topic of aesthetic dispute was the overlook that was to project from the center of the house terrace. Schneider suggested a large circular terrace featuring a significant sculpture, visible from inside the house; Manning won the day with his idea, a small terrace left open so that it could function as a viewing platform.[4]

At Gertrude's suggestion, a small Japanese garden was developed in 1915. Manning sited the feature over a large underground cistern, west of and below the house terrace and out of view. The work was supervised by the Japanese garden designer T. R. Otsuka, whom Manning had met at the World's Columbian Exposition in 1893.[5] Stone paths were laid, a small waterfall constructed, and decorative objects, including a stone lantern, added. Another request from Gertrude, a walled flower garden, led to the design of a 60-by-120-foot "English Garden" also sited below the house terrace, screened by a grove of trees. The garden's robust architectural detailing, local stone paving, and lych-gate entry suggest Arts and Crafts influence. Manning's 1915 plant list for the beds may have been similarly inspired. He specified a mix of maroon, pink, rose, white, scarlet, gray, violet, blue, yellow, and orange.[6]

A sense of expansive scale prevailed throughout the design process at Stan Hywet. At Manning's encouragement, the Seiberlings bought up several neighboring farms; in time, the estate came to encompass approximately three thousand noncontiguous acres, linked by a system of bridle trails. New farm buildings were constructed and meadows fenced for Frank's growing herd of

The lagoons were the scenic centerpiece of Manning's design, but they also were a setting for active recreation. Photograph, 1920s. Courtesy Stan Hywet Hall and Gardens.

The walled English Garden, designed collaboratively by Manning and Schneider, was the setting for many family gatherings, including Virginia Seiberling's 1919 wedding. Photograph, 1919. Courtesy Stan Hywet Hall and Gardens.

The old stone quarry was the setting for the lagoons Manning created by damming natural springs. The edges were planted with a wide range of native and imported plants. Photograph by Arthur G. Eldredge, c. 1928. LALH Collection.

The scale of the house terrace was a source of disagreement between Manning and Schneider, who prevailed in the somewhat grand scheme.
Photograph by Carol Betsch, 1997.

A sycamore allée underplanted with rhododendron stretches from the south end of the house to a woodland glade.
Photograph by Carol Betsch, 1997.

To the north of the mansion, Manning created the estate's most dramatic feature, a 550-foot pleached allée of native white birch. Photograph by Carol Betsch, 1997.

dairy cows. Like other American country places of its size, the layout also featured a formal rose garden, acres of vegetable and cutting gardens, and an extensive greenhouse complex.

In 1921 Frank Seiberling was forced to resign from Goodyear as a result of overreaching business loans made during the First World War. In response to the severe financial setback, the size of the staff at Stan Hywet was drastically reduced and maintenance on the many parts of the landscape was relaxed. In 1925 the Seiberlings donated one thousand acres to form the Sand Hill Reservation, the first section of the Akron Metropolitan District Commission, a new regional park system designed by Olmsted Brothers. The size of the estate was reduced again in 1929, when one thousand acres were subdivided into parcels for residential development, according to a plan created by Manning.[7]

Perhaps in compensation for the loss, Gertrude began a revision to the plantings in the English Garden that same year. Manning recommended that she commission Ellen Shipman to design the project, since he considered her, as he had declared years earlier, "one of the best, if not the very best, Flower Garden Maker in America."[8] It was a widely shared opinion. Shipman's finely detailed planting scheme soon provided a "glittering mosaic" of color to replace the somber hues of Manning's original plan.[9] Gertrude tended this garden until her death in 1946. Frank lived at Stan Hywet until his death in 1955.

Two years later, the Seiberling children established a nonprofit foundation to operate the seventy-acre core of Stan Hywet as a historic house museum and landscape. In an effort to attract crowds and increase income, the new site manager filled the English lawns with beds of brilliant annuals. The estate became known for its floral display of petunias, zinnias, marigolds, and the like. Parking lots were constructed and old roads widened to accommodate growing numbers of visitors.

By the 1980s, however, new appreciation for Manning's artistic stature was providing the impetus for a return to the original character-defining aspects of his landscape design. In 1981 Stan Hywet was awarded National Historic Landmark status, and two years later a master plan to restore the landscape was commissioned from Child, Hornbeck Associates. Under the direction of foundation president John Franklin Miller, obtrusive flower beds were removed, views reopened, lost trees replanted, and the widened drives narrowed to their former proportions.[10]

Stan Hywet Hall and Gardens, as it is known today, continues to operate as a museum and historic landscape, open to the public and heavily used by the local community for activities ranging from antique car shows to baseball games. Though altered in many respects, the core of the landscape remains one of Manning's best-preserved designs, a reflection of his most deeply rooted aesthetic principles.

Henry G. Dalton Estate (Edgewater)

CLEVELAND, OHIO

JOAN RANDALL AND MARY HOERNER

Edgewater, the Henry G. Dalton estate, sits on a bluff on the shore of Lake Erie, east of Cleveland in the village of Bratenahl, where wealthy local families built summer homes in the early twentieth century. Edgewater is situated approximately 160 feet east of Gwinn, William G. Mather's celebrated estate.[1] Henry George Dalton was a philanthropist and senior partner in the Cleveland firm of Pickands, Mather & Company, a major supplier of raw materials to the steel industry. He engaged local architect and presidential scion Abram Garfield to design his 1910 mansion, which is a blend of Neoclassical and Georgian Revival architecture, and asked Warren Manning to design the landscape.[2] After the landscape was constructed and planted, M. H. Horvath, a nurseryman and former Cleveland forester, served as Edgewater's gardener.[3]

The Edgewater estate comprises five acres on a lot approximately twice as long as it is wide. The residence is set back from the public road on the southern boundary of the property, about two-thirds of the way into the parcel. The main entrance is on this road, near the property's southwestern corner. Along the public road, decorative wrought-iron fencing and gates supported by low square brick bases and stone pillars open to a long, straight driveway that curves right to a turnaround containing a circular planting bed in front of the house entrance. Two short walkways lead east from the turnaround, one toward a small garden on the east side of the house and the other toward a long rectangular garden along the property's eastern boundary. These are the main gardens on the residence level. Mature trees line the inside of the fence, shielding the estate from public view. The long garden extends north toward Lake Erie for about 350 feet from the public road, ending in a portico. The rear lawn is level near the house, then slopes at least 300 feet down a bluff to a garden at the bottom.

These main landscape features, as well as steps on the bluff and a bridge to the edge of the water, appear on a 1934 plan, which also indicates plantings: a scattering of elm, oak, and maple trees throughout the front and back lawns, rhododendron around the house and gardens, and birch trees in the lower garden.[4] Low, clipped hedges outlined the rectangular, stone-lined beds of the long garden, which were planted with seasonal flowers, including tulips, begonias, heliotrope, calendulas, and Oriental poppies. The beds extend between a rectangular reflecting pool near the street, on the garden's south end, and the four columns of a portico at the north end of the garden, parallel with the end of the house. (This portico is extant, but the matching portico at the south end of the garden no longer exists.) The columns forming the portico are carved with delicate entwining garlands and tendrils, and crossbeams connect the columns at the top to form a pergola-like roof. Manning's office noted that the view is "looking over Lake Erie thru a 'window' at the end of a formal garden."[5]

Early photographs of the reflecting pool at the south end of the garden show that it once contained a fountain with a sculpture of a small figure standing on a sphere. Walks of herringbone-patterned red brick run along both sides of the beds. A narrow white-trellised

The house by the architect Abram Garfield was designed in 1910. Henry G. Dalton commissioned Manning to design the landscape at the same time, perhaps inspired by the beauty of the nearby Gwinn estate. Photograph by Arthur G. Eldredge, c. 1928. Courtesy MCL.

pergola parallel to the garden's middle section provides a sheltered, shady corridor "for cool leisure in the garden."[6] On the east side of the house, next to the portico, lies a small square pool with a wall fountain. The early garden comprised a few deciduous trees on low evergreen ground cover outlined by a rectangular herringbone-brick walk. At the pool, a cherub fountain was attached to the side of the portico. Today this garden is much the same, except for the absence of the cherub fountain and the addition of a clipped rectangular hedge enclosing perennials and ground cover.

A diamond-patterned brick path leads from the front of the house and curves around to the pool and from there through an iron gate to the back lawn. At the top edge of the bluff, flagstone steps supported by river-stone risers set in concrete curve down the gradual slope. Large boulders of eroded white limestone form cheek walls. The staircase once led to two "Panel Gardens," as Manning described them, "on either side of the stone bridge that leads from the center walk to the top of the Shore Breakwater." Here Manning, in a 1929 follow-up visit, spotted "a fine plant of the Winterberry, or Black Alder, at

Manning established large masses of rhododendron to provide year-round interest. Photograph by Arthur G. Eldredge, c. 1928. Courtesy MCL.

A "window" (in Manning's word) opened from the portico onto a view to Lake Erie, framed by luxuriant vines and climbing roses. Photograph by Arthur G. Eldredge, c. 1928. Courtesy MCL.

the top of the bank" and made a note that it was to be saved. The bridge is still in place, although without the gardens.[7]

The current owners, Peter and Victoria Broer, have revitalized the Edgewater landscape by preserving and rehabilitating the hard surfaces, which are otherwise unchanged. They have created viewpoints into the long garden by using clumps of rhododendron instead of the original solid bank along the west side. The Broers are maintaining the existing garden structures, such as the portico, and have recently repaired the reflecting pool fountain and the fountain at the east side of the house. To further preserve the existing historic design, they have resisted the urge to add new landscape features.[8]

William G. Mather Estate (Gwinn)

CLEVELAND, OHIO

ROBIN KARSON

In 1906 William Gwinn Mather, a wealthy iron-ore magnate based in Cleveland, wrote to Warren Manning to request help buying land for a small estate he wanted to build east of the city. The two were well acquainted as a result of Manning's extensive planning and design work for Mather's Cleveland-Cliffs Iron Company, begun in 1886 when Manning was still employed by the Olmsted firm (this work included a plan for the model town of Gwinn, in Michigan's Upper Peninsula). Within five days of receiving Mather's letter, Manning had visited Cleveland to inspect three sites Mather had selected. He immediately drafted a report recommending the purchase of a five-acre parcel on Lake Erie, citing dramatic water views and an unusual amphitheater-like bluff as particular advantages.[1] Mather was simultaneously consulting the nationally renowned architect Charles Platt about the same question.[2] Platt also saw advantages in the lakeside site, admiring not only its prospect but its roughly rectangular shape, which would support a cohesive landscape plan—the cornerstone of Platt's Italian-influenced design approach. Manning soon learned that Mather had selected Platt to design the grounds as well as the house, as was Platt's custom. At Mather's request, Platt agreed to collaborate with Manning on a planting design, and the project quickly got under way.

Platt's plan sited a handsome Georgian house at the edge of the clay bluff, at the midpoint of the shorefront lot. The architect's method was to conceive the layout as a whole, determining the location and proportions of each component of the plan in relation to the others. The scheme included (on the lawn side) a formal garden at the western boundary and, on the east side, a small bosco. For the lakeside, Platt designed a two-hundred-foot curving concrete seawall that regularized the contour of the cove. The predominant ornamental feature of the house was a circular portico reminiscent of the Temple of Vesta at Tivoli (and the south facade of the White House). From this enclosure, a pair of curving stairways led to a terrace below, and from there a second set of stairs led to a lower terrace. A single wide set of stairs led to Lake Erie. The spare, strong architectural elements framed the wide water view.

Manning's plantings for the lakeside reiterated the restraint of Platt's architectural scheme. Extreme weather conditions on the lake severely limited plant choices for this area. A carpet of barberry clothed the curving bank; a pair of fringe trees flanked the stairs; Lombardy poplars (short-lived but dramatically vertical) framed the portico. When Platt added gazebos to the ends of the seawalls in 1912, clipped allées of Norway maple were planted at Mather's suggestion. The trees were a compromise; Platt wanted pyramids of conifers, and Manning, weathered spruce. The polarity of tastes reflected in the clash colored many exchanges between the two designers during the course of the project, reflecting the differences in their design principles—one essen-

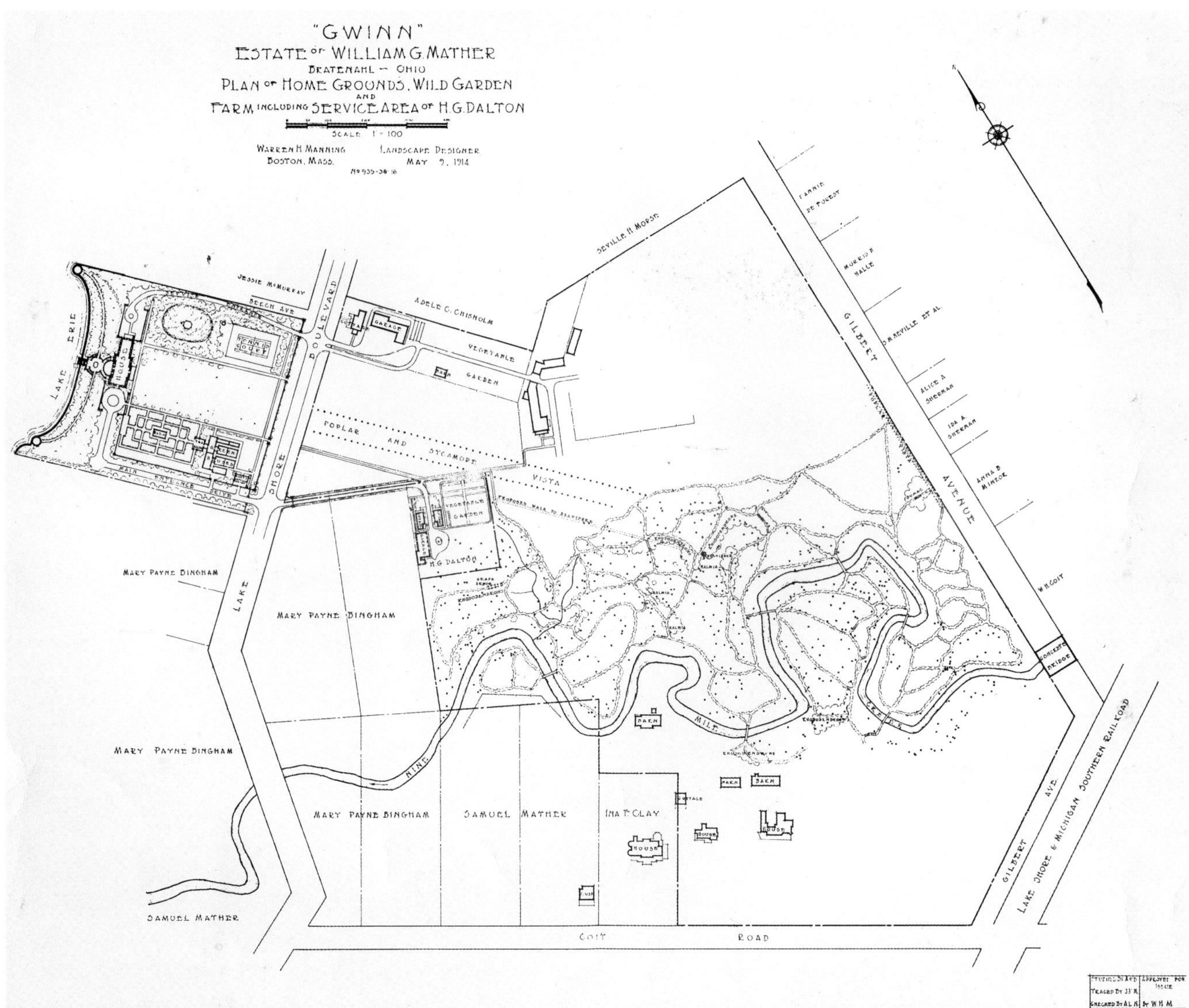

Platt's geometric layout for Gwinn's home grounds contrasted markedly with the irregular lines of Manning's wild garden. "Plan of Home Grounds, Wild Garden and Farm," plan no. 935-38-16, May 1914. Courtesy Charles Adams Platt Architectural Records and Papers, Avery Architectural and Fine Arts Library, Columbia University.

Manning's planting design for the front lawn called for the addition of several large trees to those already growing on the site. Photograph by Carol Betsch, 2007.

tially a classicist, the other a proponent of naturalistic design.

The park side of the grounds was less exposed to the effects of wind and water, but the cold, clay soil presented its own set of challenges. Manning's charge—in addition to the overall planting design—included protecting large existing trees, ameliorating the soil with humus to support new plantings, locating the sources of new plants, and making certain that they prospered. A. D. Taylor, hired by Manning as a young assistant in 1908, supervised some of this work. Mather's own grounds superintendent, George Jacques, proved key to the success of the scheme, from its implementation through long-term care.

Two rectangular garden areas framed the wide expanse of front lawn, which was planted by Manning in the style of the English Picturesque. The Italianate formal garden on the west, reminiscent of many others laid out by Platt during this period, was initially planted geometrically,

The cove on the north side of the house was cushioned with a carpet of barberry, one of the few plants that could withstand the wind and waves coming off Lake Erie. Photograph by Arthur G. Eldredge, c. 1928. Courtesy MCL.

Lake Erie is here framed by the foliage of a Norway maple allée, a feature suggested by William G. Mather. Photograph by Arthur G. Eldredge, c. 1928. Courtesy MCL.

Gwinn was one of Manning's most fully realized wild garden creations. The widely varying terrain, which included swamps and bogs, provided a setting for a great range of plants. Photograph by Arthur G. Eldredge, c. 1928. Courtesy MCL.

Meadows and glades, too, were heavily planted. The mix of treed and open spaces created striking effects of light and shadow. Photograph by Arthur G. Eldredge, c. 1928. Courtesy MCL.

Manning moved a group of old lilacs from an estate in Brookline, Mass., to form a boundary of the formal garden. Photograph by Carol Betsch, 1993.

according to a plan furnished by Platt's assistant Paul Rubens Frost.[3] In 1908 Manning suggested a lilac hedge to more fully separate the garden from the lawn, purchasing one hundred mature shrubs from an old Brookline estate that was likely undergoing subdivision.[4]

On the opposite (east) side of the lawn, Platt indicated a small woodland, also in the Italian tradition. There Manning retained a stand of large deciduous trees to provide enclosure and shade, adding an understory of rhododendron and a wide range of ferns and wildflowers. Dissatisfied with the result, Mather in 1909 asked both designers for improvements that would make the area look less "indefinite."[5] Here again, Manning's preference for native plants clashed with Platt's classical tendencies. Mather rejected Manning's suggestion (a small drip fountain to encourage the growth of new moss) in favor of Platt's bolder recommendation: a monumental fountain based on Italian villa prototypes Platt had photographed on his travels.

In 1910 Manning learned that Mather had purchased an additional twenty-one acres across Lake Shore Drive, enough land to provide a small farm for the estate and, most significant from Manning's point of view, a range of fields, bogs, and woods that would support a wild garden on a much larger scale than the original home grounds. Manning had designed wild gardens for several clients previously—one of the most notable of these was Dolobran, the quarry garden of Clement Griscom, which J. Horace McFarland had effusively praised in his 1899 article "An American Garden."[6] He would design other wild gardens, but few of them achieved the refinement, complexity, or beauty of that at Gwinn.

Mather's new acquisition had the advantage of a lively creek that had carved the parcel into topographically and horticulturally diverse areas. Manning's circulation system echoed the winding course of this stream, responding as well to the large trees that were nourished by it. As was

The lush, almost tropical density of Manning's wild garden at Gwinn recalled the planting compositions of Olmsted at Biltmore, where Manning had served as a planting assistant. Boxcar-loads of rhododendron were dug in the mountains of North Carolina and shipped to Gwinn. Photograph by Arthur G. Eldredge, c. 1928. Courtesy MCL.

his method, Manning had begun the project by mapping existing conditions: topography, vegetation (primarily large trees and masses of shrubbery), soil, and hydrology, including the bogs. The network of paths and plantings that structured the new plan was established in relation to these features. The scheme was implemented by the gardener, Jacques, and E. J. Cotter, Manning's Cleveland-Cliffs supervisor, brought down from Ishpeming, Michigan, to oversee a crew of forty local men.

Over the course of the next four years, tens of thousands of plants were installed in the new wild garden. While many came from nurseries (including thousands of bulbs from Holland), many were dug in the wild and transported by train. Others came from neighboring estates or were raised from seed in Gwinn's new nurseries. A series of photographs commissioned by Manning from Arthur G. Eldredge in 1927–28 record a sequence of carefully composed landscapes, arguably among the finest executed by Manning in the wild garden genre.[7]

Manning's motives at Gwinn were complex. Beyond his sense of artistic satisfaction, he came to envision Gwinn as a prototype for other private developments. Even toward the end of his life, the landscape architect continued to believe that private estates such as Gwinn could function as preserves, safeguarding scenic resources for future generations. But Manning was unable to persuade Mather to transform Gwinn into a public or (in his words) "semi-public" reservation open to visitors or to bequeath it for that purpose.[8] Mather continued to live at Gwinn until his death in 1951; his wife Elizabeth died six years later. In 1974, the property was listed on the National Register of Historic Places.

Soon after Elizabeth's death, Mather's descendants formed a nonprofit foundation to operate Gwinn as a conference center for Cleveland organizations, maintaining virtually all of the estate's original architectural features and many of its interior furnishings. (Most of the wild garden had been seized by eminent domain for the construction of I-90.) Eventually the nonprofit enterprise proved unsustainable, and the family put Gwinn on the market.

Since purchasing the estate in 2007, Gwinn's current owners have attempted to preserve the creators' original design intentions. New amenities are contemplated, such as a swimming pool located on the site of the former service court, but these are to be designed to respect the distinctive spatial and stylistic parameters of Platt's plan for the house and grounds. Extant plantings have been retained where possible, along with plantings refurbished in the spirit of Manning's original design. The home grounds of Gwinn remain one of the finest preserved examples of an American estate from the early twentieth century.

Harry B. Stewart Estate

HARTVILLE, OHIO

GLORIA SCHREIBER

The commission to design a landscape for the Harry Bartlett Stewart Sr. estate came to Warren Manning in the fall of 1928 through a recommendation from F. A. Seiberling, for whom Manning had designed Stan Hywet.[1] The 703-acre property had been amassed in 1914, when Stewart, a lawyer and cofounder of the Akron, Canton & Youngstown Railroad, bought up a series of land parcels in Hartville, Ohio, about eighteen miles southeast of Akron. The property, known as the Minnie Taylor Farm after Stewart's wife, included a log house built in 1842 that the family used as a country retreat. Around 1922 Stewart began construction of a Greek Revival addition to create the forty-room house that became the family's permanent residence. A three-story carriage house and servants' quarters were also built at this time. The estate was also an active farm, with cattle and hogs.

Following initial discussions with Stewart, Manning assigned Egbert Hans to direct the project. In November, the Manning office submitted a "sketch showing development of [the] estate" that focused on the areas around the house and outbuildings on the property.[2] Manning's design included more than fifty elm trees.[3]

For a garden of about one acre, Manning composed three distinct areas: a rock garden, a perennial garden, and a croquet court. A stone path east of the house led to a flight of stone steps down to the rock garden. On the north side of the entrance, a waterfall fed a small pool that flowed into a rock bed, crossing the lawn to the east. A hillside to the west included boulders of many shapes and sizes, suggesting a natural setting. Manning estimated that the 2,400 square feet of slope would require 2,400 alpine plants.[4] A grass path at the northeast corner of the garden led to the perennial garden.

Bordering the north edge of the rock garden and the croquet court, the garden was structured around a central path on an east–west axis and divided by stone walls into three sections. A formal herb garden occupied the central section. A path running north to south between the rock garden and the croquet court crossed the main axis and terminated in a stone arch covered with climbing roses. This junction of paths defined the eastern end of the garden, the location of a small fountain. Privet and crabapples accompanied the perennials along the interior walls, and broad-leaved evergreens, crabapples, cedars, and euonymus were used as exterior screening.

Minnie Stewart played a significant role in selecting plants for the garden, and Hans corresponded with her directly when discussing orders, cost estimates, and other details. During the planning of the herb garden in 1930, Hans sent Stewart a plant list and drawings that suggested a basic design, but also included "blanks" for trying

The original farmhouse on the Stewart property dates to the mid-nineteenth century. In 1922 the Stewarts created an addition to expand the house to forty rooms and also added a three-story carriage house. Photograph, n.d. Courtesy Quail Hollow Garden Archive, Quail Hollow State Park, Hartville, Ohio.

Views are carried across the shrub plantings to the bowling green and countryside beyond. Photograph, n.d. Courtesy Quail Hollow Garden Archive.

out "various patterns and color schemes."[5] Like Manning's client Gertrude Seiberling, founder of the Akron Garden Club, Stewart was involved in decisions throughout the project. Manning himself wrote a joint letter to Minnie Stewart and Gertrude Seiberling suggesting that they engage in plant exchanges.[6]

In his plan for the Stewart garden, Manning emphasized the role of screen plantings, such as deciduous shrubs and other plants collected from old homes or other sources, in blocking unwanted views from the garden rooms. Evergreens at the southeast corner of the garage served as a screen, and the eastern border of the croquet court was also screened by a wall of shrubs. Manning was intent on creating visual harmony between his design and its surroundings. He described a gradual transition from an exotic shrub garden adjacent to the garage, "to the natural shrub garden in the moist and wet meadow beyond." Trails were established to give access to the wider landscape.[7] Always a champion of the naturalistic garden, Manning advised the Stewarts to "set aside some fields and encourage and establish by planting and seeding the field flowers that will take care of themselves." The gardens were enclosed by three-foot stone walls. Groupings of arborvitae, spruce, mugo pines, and other evergreens structured the garden rooms. Despite the small size of the walled garden, the Manning office recorded over 650 hours on the project.[8]

The rock garden entrance, spring. Photograph, n.d. Courtesy Quail Hollow Garden Archive.

The Stewart family owned the estate until 1975, when they offered to sell it to the state for $1.7 million, half of the appraised value. Quail Hollow State Park was established that year: the parlor of the historic Stewart house now serves as a visitor center, and the carriage house as a nature center. In 2006, as a Manning Project volunteer research associate, I investigated the landscape surrounding the Stewart house and discovered the remains of the rock garden.[9] Since 2007, I have led a volunteer group in reconstructing and restoring the rock garden, based on Manning's overall design for its configuration, and launched an effort to preserve this important example of Manning's work.

Manning created dense screens of foliage to separate intensely designed gardens from the country setting.
Photograph, n.d. Courtesy Quail Hollow Garden Archive.

View from the bowling green, toward the house.
Photograph, n.d. Courtesy Quail Hollow Garden Archive.

Jeptha H. Wade Estate (Valley Ridge Farm)

HUNTING VALLEY, OHIO

CHRISTOPHER BOND

Between 1906 and 1921 Warren Manning worked with Jeptha H. Wade, a Cleveland-area philanthropist and businessman, to design the landscape at Valley Ridge Farm, the summer estate for Wade, his wife, Ellen Garretson Wade, and their three children. Wade was the grandson and namesake of the founder of the Western Union Telegraph Company, who was also a prominent Cleveland philanthropist. A successful businessman in his own right, the younger Wade was an executive in more than forty-five banking, railway, mining, and manufacturing firms during his lifetime. His many charitable activities included founding the Cleveland Museum of Art, where he served on the board, and supporting a host of other arts, educational, and children's organizations.[1]

In 1905 he purchased 470 acres in what is now Hunting Valley, then part of Orange Township, about fifteen miles east of Cleveland. The last glacier had sculpted the land into low hills, steep inclines, and stunning ravines; the Chagrin River meandered north–south through the property's eastern side. Wade would spare no expense in realizing the full potential of this land, on which he envisioned creating a gentleman's farm, or *ferme ornée,* complete with a grand house and numerous barns and farm buildings. To design it, he turned to the prolific Cleveland architectural firm of Hubbell & Benes, which had also designed Mill Pond, his estate in Thomasville, Georgia. (The firm later designed the Cleveland Museum of Art and Wade Chapel, a memorial to Wade's grandfather in Cleveland's Lakeview Cemetery.) After commissioning the architects, Wade hired Manning to lay out the landscape of his new estate. He likely knew Manning's work for Cleveland-Cliffs Iron Company, for which he served as vice president. And the company's owner, William G. Mather, was about to commission Manning for a design for his own Cleveland-area estate, Gwinn.[2]

Responding to Hubbell & Benes's architectural design and working from his own elaborate site notes and sketches, Manning made full use of the property's varied topography and existing plants, integrating the dynamic ridges, slopes, and ravines into a cohesive design. His plan incorporated ancient stands of maple and beech within the wooded site and provided views of these pristine passages. He also cut vistas through the forest so the Wades could enjoy views of the Chagrin River, as well as the ridges, streams, and even the mansion itself from the hilltop gardens and other points of interest. Still other viewpoints took in the lower farm fields, the estate's distinctive structures, and features such as the grape arbor and artificial lake. Directly across from the Wades' house, on the other side of a deep ravine, Manning designed an orchard oasis named the Garden of Eden, the principal garden at Valley Ridge Farm.[3] He filled it with fruit trees and berries—pears, apricots, plums, quince, apples, cherries, blackberries, raspberries, and strawberries—planted in clusters and long rows for floral display

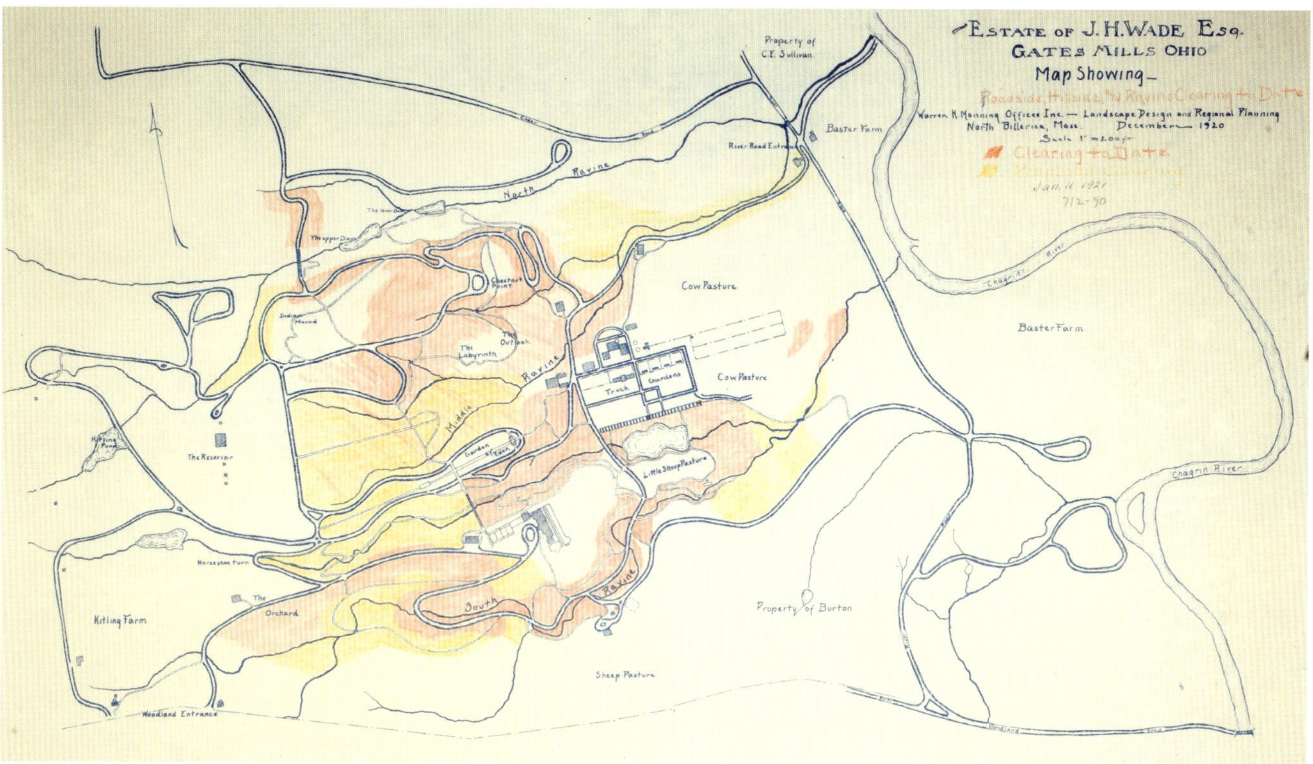

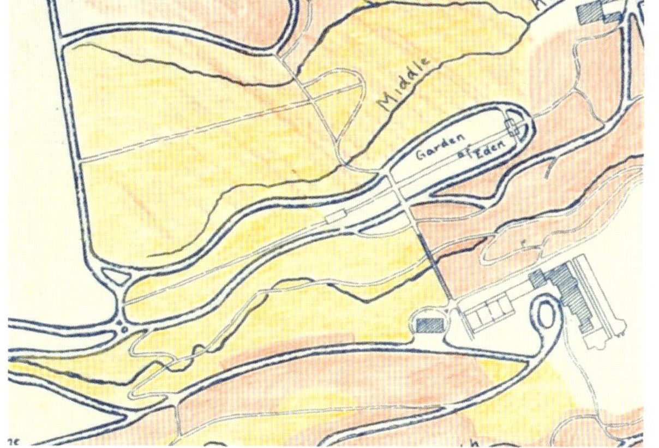

ABOVE: In 1905 Jeptha Wade bought 470 acres fifteen miles east of Cleveland and a year later commissioned Manning to lay out Valley Ridge Farm. This 1921 plan indicates the roads and other features that were developed in relation to river views and three large ravines on the site. LEFT: (detail) The principal garden at Valley Ridge Farm was the Garden of Eden, where flowering fruits and shrubs grew in abundance. "Map Showing Roadside, Hillside and Ravine Clearing to Date," plan no. 712-90, December 1920, January 1921. Courtesy MPI.

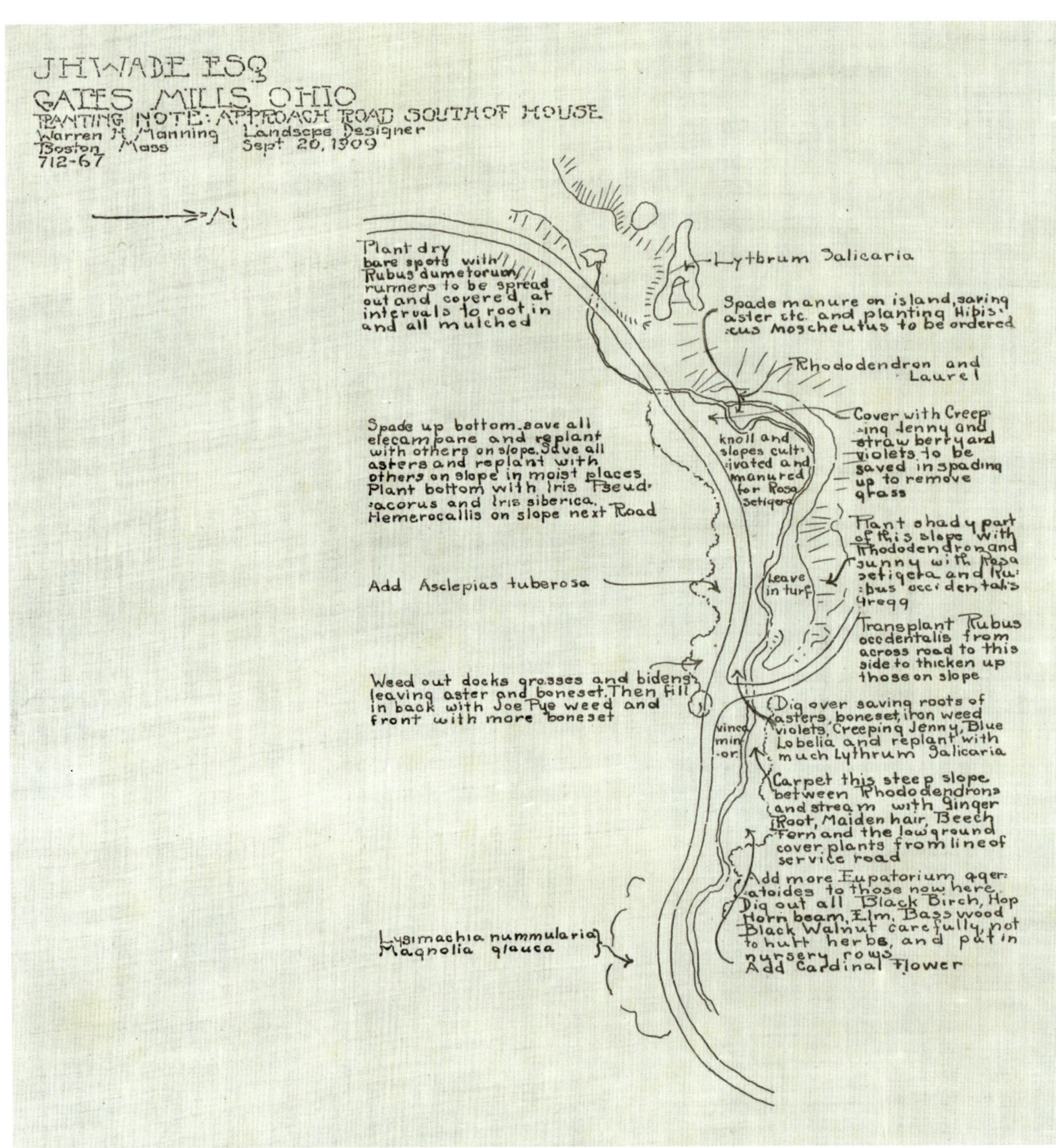

In this early plan, Manning specified plantings in characteristic detail along the new entry road. Plan no. 712-67, September 1909. Courtesy MPI.

Views to the Chagrin River determined fundamental aspects of Manning's landscape design. Photograph courtesy Case Western Reserve University Farm.

Abundant informal plantings surrounded the distinguished house. Photograph courtesy Case Western Reserve University Farm.

and ease of harvesting. A gazebo afforded a sheltered view of the surrounding scenic ravines, one of them straddled by an iron pedestrian bridge that connected the Wades to their private Eden.

Manning also designed plantings for such utilitarian spaces as pastures and barnyards, delineating them with masses of shrubs and small trees, including lilac, dogwood, rhododendron, azalea, and mock orange. He tied these areas into the overall estate design by scattering some species throughout the property.[4] Naturalistic masses of trees and shrubs, including magnolia, hawthorn, hemlock, sumac, honeysuckle, chestnut, and various roses, both blended with the existing landscape and drew attention to its dramatic topography. During Manning's more than fifteen-year collaboration with Wade, he created other landscape destinations—including Chestnut Point, Indian Mound, and the Labyrinth—features that enhanced the natural beauty of the land and determined a circulation system through the rugged terrain.[5]

In 1926 Wade died at his estate in Georgia; his wife had died nine years earlier. In 1929 the house at Valley Ridge Farm burned to the ground. Wade family members owned the farm until the late 1970s and employed a year-round staff to care for it. In 1977 Wade's heirs sold much of the land for private development and donated to Case Western Reserve University the remnants of the original estate, including two houses, barns, and other original farm buildings.[6] The university's holdings now include the 389-acre University Farm complex, also comprising Squire Valleevue Farm (formerly owned by Wade's neighbor to the west), and ten acres donated by another landowner to the north. The covenant with the Wade heirs requires the university to maintain stewardship, perpetual preservation, and use for education and research.[7]

Over time, the encroaching forest has reduced Manning's work at Valley Ridge Farm to a trace; only about 5 percent of the designed landscape

Some of the original landscape features have been restored, including this grape arbor and summer house. Photograph by Carol Betsch, 2014.

Traces of Manning's plantings can be discovered throughout the site. Photograph by Carol Betsch, 2014.

is recognizable today.[8] Thick masses of periwinkle carpet acres of the forest, as does snow-on-the-mountain (also known as bishop's weed or goutweed).[9] Outside the ruins of the mansion, on the southeast edge of University Farm, clusters of barberry, spiraea, and hydrangea are other likely survivors of original plantings. Original vistas from the gazebo in the former Garden of Eden are evident as corridors of younger trees within the older forest. A restored gazebo, part of the massive grape arbor, overlooks the ravine that once contained the lake, adjacent to the vegetable fields. An irrigation pipe under the gazebo is all that remains of a water system that fed a stone reservoir which spilled into the lake. This water feature was another destination in the estate's circulation system.

Case Western Reserve University Farm staff members, students, and volunteers are taking steps to recover features of the designed landscape. In 2010 the grape arbor, with many of its original posts, was fully restored. In the spring of 2012 workers replanted grapes along the posts according to Manning's 1910 plan. The university's engineering school has also advised on how to rebuild ruined structures. Available funds and human resources will dictate how much of this once grand property can be restored.

Henry S. Sherman Estate

LYNDHURST, OHIO

JOAN RANDALL

Henry Stoddard Sherman, a great-nephew of Civil War general William Tecumseh Sherman, was an engineer, an industrialist, and the president of the Society for Savings in Cleveland. He also served as board chairman and foundation president of the Cleveland Clinic.[1] After the 1899 extension of the Cleveland & Eastern Railroad line encouraged commuting between the city and its eastern suburbs, Sherman, like many other wealthy Cleveland businessmen, decided to build an estate outside the city.[2] He purchased a lot in the Mayfield Country Club Estates, a new project that Warren Manning was commissioned to plan.[3]

In laying out the new subdivision, Manning displayed two of his signature strengths by taking full advantage of the natural elements of the land and encouraging native growth as he developed the lots, both individually and in concert with one another. In their 1918 prospectus for the development, Manning and local real estate agent Frank C. Newcomer wrote that their goal was to produce a "community of homes" with a "spirit of co-operation between owners," "individuality in home grounds," and an "appreciation of natural beauty." Manning laid out the roads and lots and sited the structures with regard for views, features, and existing vegetative screening for each lot. He also advised on additional plantings. The prospectus indicates that the Sherman estate was one of the first two in the development to be built; the other was Franchester, the estate of Chester C. and Frances Payne Bolton, which is used today as a guest house by the Cleveland Clinic. By 1918 six other lots (38–43) had been purchased but not yet developed.[4] Notable among them was the estate of Dudley S. and Elizabeth B. Blossom, which was constructed around 1922 on lots 40 and 41 and demolished in 1993.[5] A 1951 aerial photograph suggests that by the mid-twentieth century, aside from the numerous smaller lots in the far northeast corner of the community, only a few of the Mayfield Country Club Estates sites had been developed and were extant.[6]

The Sherman estate comprised a large stone Tudor Revival residence and grounds with "a

One of the primary features of the Sherman estate was a circular walled garden, whose central ornament was a sundial. Manning retained an old pump house as part of the design, here seen covered with a bower of roses. Photograph by Mattie Edwards Hewitt, n.d. Courtesy Ohio History Connection.

great variety of landscape incidents" and "formal and informal gardens, sheep pasture and wild gardens," in Manning's words.[7] A photograph of the mansion's exterior, taken around 1917, shows it set in an expanse of close-cropped grass with a flagstone path to the entry, a mass of trees in the background, and gardens west and southwest of the house.[8] The 1918 prospectus map suggests that a large rectangular bed or pool and tennis court were planned east of the house, with a smaller square garden on the north, a circular garden to the southwest, and trees along the property perimeter.

The house and landscape, save for a circular walled garden eighty feet in diameter, were demolished during the commercial redevelopment of the property in 1985, and the garden was altered at that time.[9] Sometime before 1957, however, Ethelwyn Harrison, a local landscape architect who collaborated with Manning on several projects in northeast Ohio, commissioned the New York architectural and garden photographer Mattie Edwards Hewitt to photograph the Sherman walled garden.[10] The photographs show the large circular garden enclosed by a low, squared-and-coursed stone wall; still present, the wall is approximately thirty-one inches high and eighteen inches deep, with four openings for entry and exit. A wide perennial bed lined the interior. An irregular dry-laid flagstone path led from the southeast opening to the center of the garden, which was marked by a rustic sundial: a gnomon mounted on a craggy boulder about twenty inches high, with a circular base of irregular dry-laid flagstone. From there the path continued toward the northwest opening. Aside from the stone path and the circular perennial border, turf covered the ground inside the enclosure.

The Hewitt photographs show distinctive architectural features at each of the garden's entry points. The one on the southeast incorporated a circular squared-and-coursed stone Tudor Revival pump house. Its plank door had pointed arches, flanked on either side by six-light windows, also with pointed arches; a conical thatched roof supporting a climbing rose; and a battered stone chimney. At the east breach, the photographs show a wooden pergola and rectangular beds filled with trees and perennials. A straight flagstone stairway down an adjacent slope provided entry from the northwest. At the western entrance, a robust pergola of stone and wood led to a stairway of four flagstone steps.

In 1985 TRW, Inc., completed construction of its 350,000-square-foot world headquarters building on combined portions of the former Bolton and Sherman properties in the Mayfield Country Club Estates development.[11] TRW hired Massachusetts-based Sasaki Associates to fit the massive new building onto the ninety-four-acre site while conserving as many trees as possible and making good use of other existing features. Sasaki recast the Sherman walled garden in a Japanese style but retained the older garden's form and most of its built features.[12] A comparison with archival photographs shows that the garden is well preserved: the stone wall with four openings, the two flights of stairs, the pump house (still used as such by the Cleveland Clinic), the stone and wood pergola, the beds along the inside wall, and the central sundial all remain.[13]

The changes, however, are also readily apparent. Grass has replaced the flagstone paths that intersected the grassy interior space. The sundial rock has been truncated to a height of approximately sixteen inches, with a clock face etched into the cut surface. The gnomon is gone, and the circular flagstone base has been replaced by a much larger circular bed of wood mulch edged in stone. While the conical pump-house roof of the early photographs appears to be genuine thatch, today the roof is made of concrete tiles. The interior perimeter beds now hold thirteen small deciduous trees and assorted hostas and grasses instead of the more diverse flowering perennials shown in the Hewitt photographs. Wooden benches occupy four niches that were cut into the perimeter beds during the Sasaki redesign. TRW donated its headquarters and grounds to the Cleveland Clinic in 2002, when the company changed hands.[14] The Cleveland Clinic has maintained the Sasaki-era walled garden (now known as the Japanese Garden) as it was when it acquired the property.

Mill Creek Park

YOUNGSTOWN, OHIO

REBECCA ROGERS

Between 1910 and 1912 Warren Manning and Volney Rogers explored opportunities to expand parkland within Mahoning County, in northeastern Ohio. Rogers, a Youngstown attorney and an advocate for conservation and urban parks, was particularly interested in the possibility of enlarging 460-acre Mill Creek Park in Youngstown, which he had helped to establish a decade earlier. During the time he worked with Manning, Rogers was serving both as a Youngstown Township park commissioner and as a trustee of the Tod Homestead Cemetery, which had just hired Manning to design the landscape—the project that initially brought Manning to Youngstown.[1]

Rogers was deeply engaged in the urban parks movement and had traveled to other growing American cities to see examples firsthand. In 1891 he led the push to establish Mill Creek Park after witnessing industrial development consume much of the Mahoning River Valley during the last two decades of the nineteenth century, when Youngstown was becoming a steel boomtown.[2] Rogers chose the initial parcel of parkland to conserve the creek's dramatic sandstone gorge, a popular local attraction, and also because the site remained relatively free of the air pollution that clouded the skies closer to the industrial center. Rogers was also concerned with reserving a place for outdoor recreation and relaxation.[3]

In the 1890s Rogers had brought in two other distinguished landscape architects to design elements of Mill Creek Park, H. W. S. Cleveland of Minneapolis and Charles Eliot of Boston. Working separately during the same period, Cleveland and Eliot laid out drives and trails and consulted on vistas and other features that Rogers and his brother, Bruce Rogers, later designed.[4] Manning became involved in 1910, proposing several ideas to enlarge and improve Mill Creek Park; however, the park commission lacked the funds to undertake the work proposed by Manning. In 1920, the year after Rogers died, park commissioners invited Manning back to plan a new phase of park development in response to the growing need for more parkland; in particular,

H. W. S. Cleveland and Charles Eliot were hired (separately) before Manning became involved in the Youngstown, Ohio, project. They designed the original woodland drives of Mill Creek Park. Photograph by Arthur G. Eldredge, c. 1928. Courtesy MCL.

they wanted to build more playgrounds and other spaces for active recreation.

Manning presented his earlier ideas and found them well received by the park commissioners and park superintendent Hugh Imlay, himself a landscape architect.[5] The commissioners responded promptly to Manning's suggestion that the park spend most of its funds on land acquisition. In July 1921 the commission added important connecting parcels comprising thirty acres to the west. These included Bear Creek valley, three quarry sites, and a wild, sandstone-boulder ravine that was already one of Youngstown's favorite camping and picnic sites. The next year, Imlay and Manning began planning to acquire more land on which to create another lake (to be called Lake Newport), and by 1924 the commissioners had added 270 acres, including the lake site.

Manning's first contract called for six annual visits (later reduced to four) for three years starting in 1920, relying on park staff to prepare drawings and perform any required engineering work in advance of his visits. The park commission would renew his contracts through 1932. Manning's office created new designs, leaving tracing paper sketches and schematic drawings with the park staff or sharing designs Manning had created for other city parks. During visits, he fleshed out the designs by walking the land with members of the park staff, and he followed up with letters summarizing each visit and directing the work to be done before his next arrival.[6]

Manning's initial recommendations included creating a more defined entrance at the park's north end, near the Mahoning River (this was never built); extending the park south, to include the new Lake Newport, and west, to encompass the sources of Mill Creek's four tributaries; cre-

Mill Creek and its tributaries were the defining natural elements in the layout. Photograph by Arthur G. Eldredge, c. 1928. Courtesy MCL.

Between 1920 and 1932, Manning succeeded in significantly extending the park's southern boundary. Photograph by Arthur G. Eldredge, c. 1928. Courtesy MCL.

Damming Mill Creek to form Lake Newport (1923–1928) was one of Manning's major contributions to the park design. Photograph by Arthur G. Eldredge, c. 1928. Courtesy MCL.

One of three lakes in the park system, Lake Newport still provides expansive views from the roadways and picnic areas bordering it. Photograph by Carol Betsch, 2014.

ating space for active recreation at the top of the dramatic sandstone gorge conserved in the initial parcel of parkland; and adding another picnic area near the amphitheater, a service area, and two viaducts to direct traffic east–west across the Mill Creek gorge. Between 1920 and 1932 Manning succeeded in extending the park's southern boundary by two and three-quarters miles, adding a total of about a thousand acres. His design contributions included many facilities for active recreation, including the fifteen-acre Volney Rogers play fields (1921), a new, Moderne-style park office building (1922), a designed landscape near the Falls Avenue entrance that encompassed a statue of Volney Rogers (1922), a massive stone retaining wall known as the "Big Cut" (1922–1927), and land for two eighteen-hole golf courses. Between 1921 and 1937 Manning added the eighty-five-acre Bear's Den area, comprising three landscaped sandstone quarry sites, two picnic areas, and two stone auto bridges.[7]

In 1922 Manning and one of his associates, Egbert Hans, prepared bird's-eye renderings of Lake Newport for the Youngstown Planning Commission. The renderings also showed an adjacent suburban "village" located beyond the east boundary of the park. North of the "suggested village center" and east of Lake Newport on the plan, Manning proposed another residential development, the Forest Glen Allotment. South of the planned Lake Newport village and east of the golf course lay the Ridgewood Allotment, also slated for suburban development.[8] Although the lake itself was created between 1923 and 1928 and some of the suburban roads developed during the same period, the Great Depression tabled these planned residential developments.

Damming Mill Creek to create the hundred-acre Lake Newport was a major engineering feat and one of Manning's most significant contributions to the park. During the dam construction, Manning worked with Imlay, park engineer Ralph Ingram, and county engineer Luther Fawcett to work out the least expensive way to give the dam "a picturesque surface" in keeping with the park's dramatic natural terrain. They decided to build the dam of concrete, configuring each side differently. On the side holding the lake, the wall was vertical and smooth, but on the downstream side the wall sloped toward a wide base. The team selected large stone slabs and blocks with "as much weathered surface as could be secured," as Manning described to Imlay in a letter. His intention was to "break the flow of water into tumbling, foamy cascades and ripples and make a very attractive fall without the heavy added cost beyond actual engineering."[9] According to other letters and photographs, Manning's efforts to maintain naturalistic landscape effects extended to designing Lake Newport's shore by

Working with the park superintendent Hugh Imlay, Manning designed the dam to create Lake Newport. He created an irregular concrete surface to "break the flow of water into tumbling, foamy cascades and ripples." Photograph by Carol Betsch, 2014.

The headwaters of Lake Newport are now managed as wetlands. Photograph by Carol Betsch, 2014.

tying fabric strips to plants to show the location of the waterline and the roads, removing native plants before construction, and subsequently returning them to islands and the lake edge.[10]

Manning also advised on the siting and landscape design of two golf courses (1928 and 1932) south of Lake Newport, designed by Donald Ross Associates. (By 1939 the park had a third Ross course.) Ross, one of the greatest golf course designers in the United States, sent two associates from his firm to supervise the construction. The golf complex also included a field house (1929) and a maintenance and watering pump station (1935) designed under Manning's direction. Other Manning-era park enhancements included the Daffodil Meadow (1932), and four new gardens (1920, 1922, 1929, and 1932). Throughout all of the park projects, Manning worked carefully with the existing topography to minimize the expense of moving earth. Park records reflect a warm, collaborative effort by staff, administrators, and landscape architects during Manning's twelve years of coordinated work in the park.[11]

After 1932 development of new parkland within Mill Creek Park continued, following Manning's recommendations.[12] Most of his proposed suburban streets, constructed after 1932 to guide future development, are extant. Some original plantings in the garden spaces and other parts of the park still survive. The upstream end of Lake Newport has become a wetland. The bones of the Manning-era additions, such as the "Big Cut," the Falls Avenue entrance and all drives, most of the golf course holes, the active recreation area, bridges, and numerous related structures are still extant and in good condition. Mill Creek Park Historic District is listed on the National Register of Historic Places.

Tod Homestead Cemetery

YOUNGSTOWN, OHIO

REBECCA ROGERS

George Tod, the scion of a prominent Youngstown family, set aside 256 acres of the family homestead in his will, to be used as a cemetery for residents of Youngstown and the Mahoning Valley. It was to be called Tod Homestead Cemetery, in honor of Brier Hill Farm, which the family had occupied for three generations, since 1801.[1] George Tod chose the members of the cemetery's board of trustees, including Volney Rogers, an attorney and a Youngstown Township park commissioner.[2] Rogers interviewed two landscape architects, O. C. Simonds of Chicago and Warren Manning, about laying out the cemetery.[3] The board authorized Rogers to commission plans from Manning in December 1909, and the earliest extant plans from Manning's office, for the "east section of the cemetery," are dated March 17, 1911. That September, Rogers asked Manning to prepare detailed maps of gravesites, tombstones, and other features.[4]

The Brier Hill Farm site, on the east side of the Mahoning River, stretched from the Youngstown–Warren Road along the river, up the steep bank (through briers), past the limestone quarry, and onto the bluff, where it flattened into farmland. A Federal style house looked out across the valley two hundred feet below. With the Boston architect Julius Schweinfurth, whom he selected for the project, Manning created an elegant, stylish, and dramatic urban design on this level portion of the hilltop. To create the entry drive for the cemetery, Manning modified a city street (renamed Tod Lane) to align on axis with the entrance on the eastern side of the cemetery property. This design introduced a grand vista along the east–west axis and abandoned the long driveway from the Youngstown–Warren Road that scaled the steep riverbank on the west side. Manning planned the arrival sequence to begin at the west end of Crandall Park and follow Tod Avenue, crossing Belmont Avenue through the tall arch of the entry gate to focus on the Tod family plot, with a sandstone mausoleum at its western end. The sandstone structure was never built; instead, a far more modest granite mausoleum was built on the far side of a slightly sunken acre of lawn designed by Manning. Schweinfurth designed the imposing two-story entry gate, built of coursed blocks of rough limestone and embellished with a campanile and bas-relief angels on either side of the arch. The gate structure houses a chapel on the south side of the arch and offices on the north. When the chapel and entry gate were completed, in 1918, Manning laid out the cemetery lots in the northeast–southwest arrangement of burial "blocks," separated by turf paths, shown on the 1911 plan. He located the slightly sunken one-acre Tod family plot opposite the entry arch. Early photographs show deciduous shrubs and trees surrounding the sunken area, a circular flowerbed on axis with concentric plantings of annuals.[5]

Tod Homestead Cemetery was Manning's first project in Youngstown and among his first nonresidential works in Ohio. This project showcased Manning's professional design skills to the

Manning's 1911 design for Tod Homestead Cemetery featured an entrance spanned by a monumental gatehouse. Postcard, c. 1920. Courtesy Trustees of Tod Homestead Cemetery.

Vines covered the gatehouse loggia, anchoring the large building in the landscape. Postcard, c. 1920. Courtesy Trustees of Tod Homestead Cemetery.

The Tod family plot was located on axis with the cemetery entry. Postcard, c. 1920. Courtesy Trustees of Tod Homestead Cemetery.

Youngstown Township park commissioners, who, through Volney Rogers, subsequently hired him to design large additions to Mill Creek Park.[6] The Schweinfurth entry gateway, with the chapel and office wings, was placed on the National Register of Historic Places in 1976 and survives today.[7] Some of Manning's original grid of cemetery plots remains intact, as does the organizing feature of his design, the dramatic vista of the entranceway from the east.

Bellevue Park

HARRISBURG, PENNSYLVANIA

ROBIN KARSON

Warren Manning's association with Harrisburg began in 1901 with his plan for the city park system, and it soon came to include designs for other types of landscapes, most of which were private estates. Among the most noteworthy of these is Breeze Hill, the home of J. Horace McFarland, who achieved wide renown for his achievements as a conservationist, publisher, and horticulturalist.[1] Breeze Hill was the first property in Bellevue Park, a 132-acre subdivision that Manning had been commissioned to lay out on the site of an old vineyard. He was hired in 1907 by the Union Real Estate Company, undoubtedly on the recommendation of McFarland, who was secretary of the company and one of eight investors in it. Manning's task was to create lots on the hillside parcel for 276 new homes.[2]

Manning based his 1909 plan for the development on the same principles that had informed his park system for Harrisburg, primarily a strong regard for nature. He laid out roads to closely follow the lay of the land and provide varied views. He dammed a small brook to create a chain of ponds. He saved great trees whenever possible. He set aside a large percentage of land for parklike reservations and planted street trees in great quantity. Utilities were buried to further preserve the rural ambience.[3]

The company's promotional booklet emphasized the salutary and moral benefits of living close to nature: "Looking over the hills and valleys, the parkways and ponds, the roads and drives, the walks and lanes of Bellevue Park, considering its height, its freedom from smoke, its proximity to the city's best pleasure-ground, no one will deny that here life may be best lived."[4] The new subdivision had been conceived and was marketed in counterpoint to life in the city, where factories spewed heavy black smoke and worker tenements proliferated.

The entrance to the new subdivision was on Market Street, across from Reservoir Park, "the city's best pleasure-ground." Lots varied in size and shape. The larger, more expensive ones were located nearest the center, closest to the ponds and reservations. Buyers hired architects of their own choosing, but house plans were reviewed by the company and a minimum cost was enforced.[5] The majority of the houses constructed in the development were Colonial Revival style; the second most popular style was Tudor Revival, reflecting widespread aspirational tastes of the period. Streets were planted with single tree species to achieve impressive display. Manning specified both native (including American elm and locust) and exotic (Chinese elm and ginkgo) species.

By 1910 sufficient infrastructure was in place to begin putting lots on the market, and a sales office designed by the Philadelphia architect Miller I. Kast opened at the end of the trolley line.[6] Sales were initially brisk, but they fell off sharply in the years during and after World War I. To recoup losses, the investment company sold a portion of the parcel to the city for a new high school in 1923. Sales languished again during the Great Depression, and in 1938 the Union Real Estate Company declared bankruptcy.

Despite its failure as an economic venture, Bellevue Park was, from the first, a vibrant and desirable place to live, and it remains so today. Manning's plan has not been significantly altered

In 1907 Manning was commissioned for landscape advice at Breeze Hill, the home of the civic leader and horticulturalist J. Horace McFarland. The house is extant but McFarland's extensive trial gardens vanished long ago. Photograph by Carol Betsch, 2012.

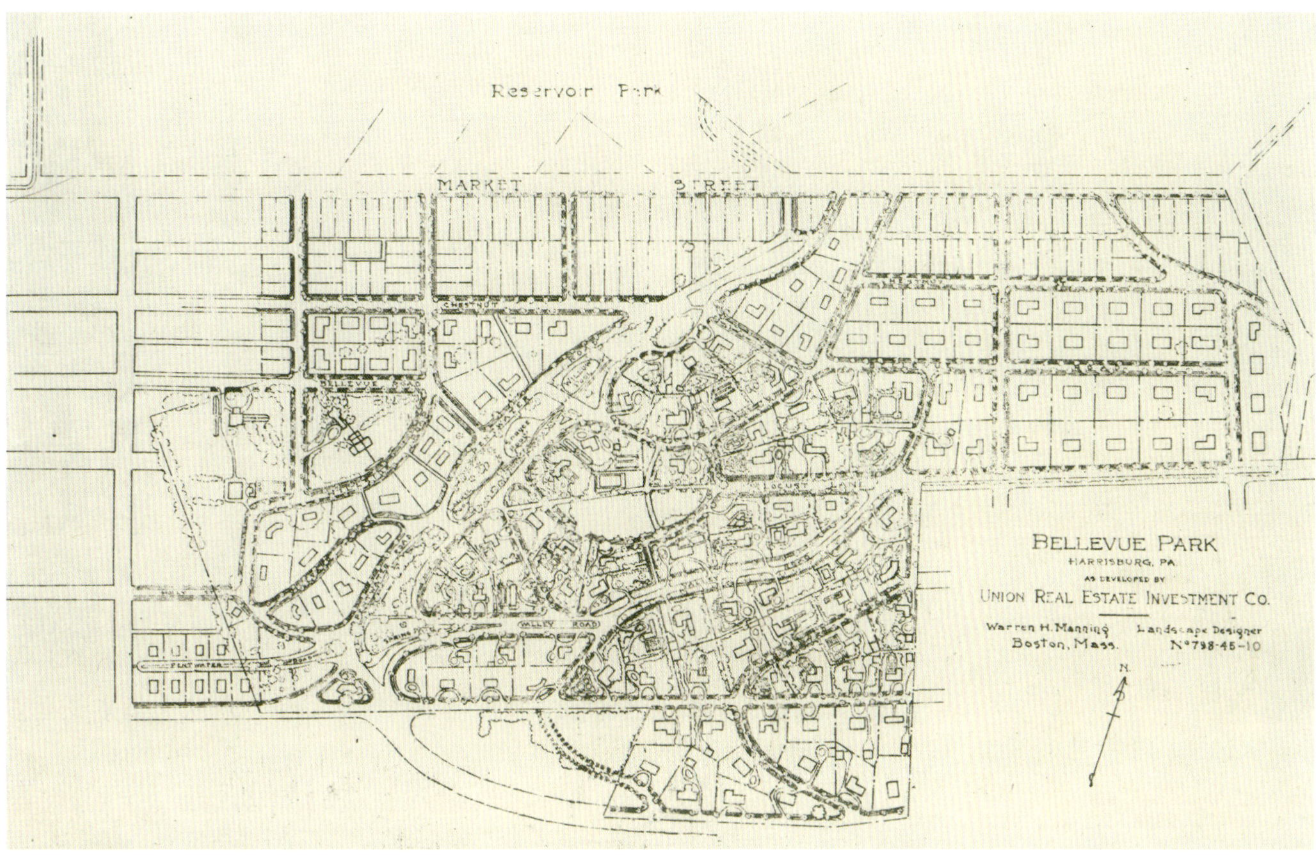

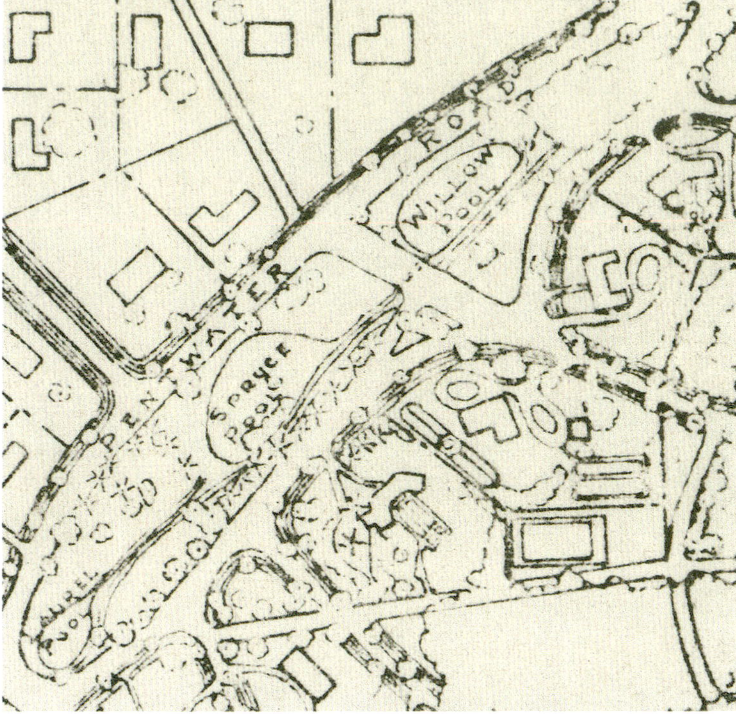

ABOVE: The plan for Bellevue Park provided lots for 276 houses. These were sited on a road system that responded to the curves of the hillside terrain. LEFT: (detail) The layout included several small wooded reservations and two ponds. "Bellevue Park," plan no. 798-45-10, n.d. Courtesy MPI.

Early photographs of Bellevue Park capture the charm of lush, informal plantings. Postcard, n.d.

One of several reservations, Oak Woods provided a parklike setting with benches throughout and paths. Postcard, n.d.

The ponds suggest a sense of countryside and also bring reflections of sky into the common landscape. Photograph by Carol Betsch, 2012.

Pedestrian ways cut through common land in the development. Photograph by Carol Betsch, 2012.

Some of the main roads in Bellevue Park were designed as parkways. Photograph by Carol Betsch, 2012.

since its 1910 implementation. Two ponds still form the centerpiece of the stylish enclave, where many of the old street trees have grown to great size, and five wooded reservations continue to offer a haven for birds and other wildlife. One is these is named for the landscape architect who created the plan.

Harrisburg Parks

HARRISBURG, PENNSYLVANIA

ROBIN KARSON

In 1901 Warren Manning began planning a park system for Harrisburg, a project he would later identify as one of the most important of his career.[1] His initial report proposed acquiring a mile of privately held river frontage for a new public park and building a parkway loop of about thirteen miles. He also recommended creating several small city parks and playgrounds, doubling the size of forty-six-acre Reservoir Park, acquiring several small islands and portions of Hargest's Island (later, City Island) for parkland, and creating a large "country park" (Wildwood Park) on a five-hundred-acre tract north of the city. Most of these proposals were implemented.[2]

Manning had been recommended for the job by J. Horace McFarland, an impassioned civic reformer who was the driving force behind a beautification initiative McFarland dubbed the "Harrisburg Awakening." The newly formed Harrisburg League for Municipal Improvements also hired James H. Fuertes, a sanitary engineer, and M. R. Sherred, a highway engineer, to collaborate on the citywide beautification effort. A massive public campaign overseen by McFarland and supported by the local press promoted the salutary, aesthetic, and economic benefits of the "awakening," which would begin with a restoration of the severely polluted Susquehanna River, the source of the city's drinking water and the centerpiece of Manning's plan.[3]

In 1902 Vance C. McCormick was elected mayor, running on the "anti-typhoid ticket," and a $1.1 million bond issue in support of the beautification effort was approved by voters. At Manning's encouragement, several private landowners donated tracts of land for the new parks, and work began on the riverfront. That enterprise included building a new intercepting sewer and dam to control water levels and installing new plantings on the bank. Manning also designed the entry to the new Harrisburg Bridge, which featured a pair of columns from the old state Capitol.[4] By 1906 much of the riverfront park work was complete. The degraded site had become a "splendid strip of green more than a mile long."[5]

Work on several sections of the parkway was

also begun at this time. On Manning's recommendation, temporary roads were created at low cost. The new pleasure roads followed the lay of the land, connecting new parks with existing ones and with other open space, such as Prospect Hill Cemetery.[6] In his concept for this feature, Manning had been influenced by his years with Frederick Law Olmsted, who, with Calvert Vaux, had created the first parkway system in the world in Buffalo, New York, and gone on to transform Boston with a complex system of parks and parkways. Harrisburg's parkways, however, lacked the financial underpinnings of the park initiatives in Buffalo or Boston. They appeared to be scarcely improved roads, naturalistically planted.

Manning regarded (already extant) Reservoir Park as the most important landscape feature outside the city center—citing in particular its fine

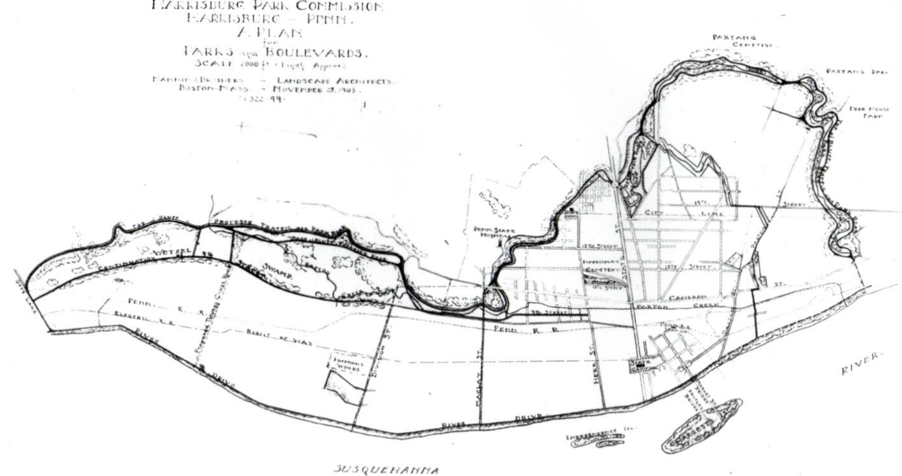

Manning's plan for the Harrisburg parks incorporated the Susquehanna River, river islands, Wetzel Swamp, and several creeks. His system of parkways linked green space, such as Reservoir Park and Paxtang and Prospect Hill Cemeteries. "A Plan for Parks and Boulevards," plan no. 322-99, November 1903. Courtesy MPI.

Reservoir Park provided visitors with clean air, breezes, and long views toward the city and river below. Manning's plan added many acres to the park. Photograph by Arthur G. Eldredge, c. 1928. Courtesy MCL.

The system's parkways were constructed at low cost with temporary roads that utilized existing roadside scenery. Photograph by Arthur G. Eldredge, c. 1928. Courtesy MCL.

Amenities such as benches and drinking fountains were added to parkways that wound through woodland in a thirteen-mile circuit around the city. Photograph by Arthur G. Eldredge, c. 1928. Courtesy MCL.

Manning's initial work on the park system focused on the Susquehanna River and the small island (now City Island) accessed from the city via a bridge. Photograph by Carol Betsch, 2012.

Reservoir Park still provides city dwellers with an escape from urban pressures. Photograph by Carol Betsch, 2012.

Views to the west take in the State Capitol. Photograph by Carol Betsch, 2012.

One of the most dramatic additions to the park system was the creation of two-and-a-half-mile Wildwood Lake, formed by damming the wetland known as Wetzel's Swamp. Photograph by Carol Betsch, 2012.

Wildwood Park still offers trails around the lake and through managed wetlands. Photograph by Carol Betsch, 2012.

panorama of distant mountains, river, city, and ridge—and he recommended its enlargement. On his advice, the city acquired the entire summit and one-half of the northerly slope of the hill on which it sat.[7] Still, Reservoir Park was a "holiday park," too far from the city center to offer citizens a daily getaway.[8]

For this purpose, Manning proposed developing a new park on about five hundred acres of swamp, meadow, and upland, a parcel north of the city that he deemed a "natural park." Manning described the site (known locally as Wetzel's Swamp) as "framed in with wooded bluffs on one side and a line of fine old willows along the [canal] on the other." He emphasized the relative ease with which the comparatively level and dry upland could be made ready for picnickers, and he praised the beauty of the meadows, where masses of brilliant wildflowers already flourished.[9]

The centerpiece of the new country park was to be a narrow, two-and-a-half-mile-long lake created by damming Paxton Creek. By 1907 a loop trail had been laid out, and a year later, a dam was constructed to make the new lake. According to city records, eleven thousand people visited the Wildwood Park that year. Old photographs attest to the splendor of Wildwood Lake and the appreciative visitors who came there to boat.[10]

Manning's Harrisburg park work brought him a wide range of local commissions. These included private estates (one, Breeze Hill, was McFarland's own country place), Bellevue Park (an upscale subdivision), Harrisburg High School, Harrisburg Hospital, Harrisburg Country Club, Harrisburg Light and Power Company, and improvements to the Capitol grounds. Plans for most of these projects have not been recovered.[11] As a result of McFarland's lectures, Manning's work in Harrisburg also brought the landscape architect new commissions beyond the Susquehanna River Valley, and it increased his standing in the profession. In 1906 the city planner Charles Mulford Robinson praised Manning's "broad grasp and far-seeing vision" for Harrisburg. Robinson and others saw the value in Manning's plan, a scheme that made rich use of scenic resources while addressing a host of urban dilemmas.[12]

Manning's Harrisburg legacy lives on most tangibly in Wildwood Park and in the work of the Capital Area Greenbelt Association. Founded in 1990, this organization has successfully developed a twenty-mile walking and bike loop that traces Manning's original park system, Harrisburg's own Emerald Necklace.[13]

Clement A. Griscom Estate (Dolobran)

HAVERFORD, PENNSLYVANIA

MAUREEN S. THOMPSON

In 1896 Clement Acton Griscom, a shipping magnate, hired Olmsted, Olmsted & Eliot to design the landscape for his summer residence in Haverford, Pennsylvania, approximately nine miles from Philadelphia. Warren Manning oversaw the project, using abandoned quarries on the site to create one of his most dynamic wild gardens.[1]

The year before, the well-known Philadelphia architect Frank Furness had completed a major expansion of Dolobran, the house he had designed for Griscom in 1881.[2] Because the structure was built on a slope, five distinct levels were incorporated into the design, the first floor of which covered half an acre and featured a fireproof underground art gallery. Dolobran's surroundings included woodlands, grassy glades, marshes, streams, and a small lake used for swimming and boating. The property's undulating topography presented welcome challenges for Manning, who incorporated a wide range of features into his design, including a woodland walk along a ravine, complete with "crow's nest" lookouts and rustic benches for admiring the views.[3]

After purchasing neighboring land in 1900, Griscom increased his property from 62 acres to almost 150 acres.[4] The parcel included sizable deposits of Wissahickon mica schist, which had been quarried and used throughout the renovation projects, as well as Soapstone Farm, a working dairy, and a golf course. Rather than seeing the quarry as an eyesore and filling it in, Manning used this feature as the basis for a wild garden with native plant species imported from throughout the country. The various quarrying sites offered opportunities to create forest pools that nourished water lilies and other aquatic plants.[5] Dolobran's essence was admiringly described in a 1903 *Country Life* article written by J. Horace McFarland: "We do not all at once come into this garden, through an entranceway; we are unconsciously in it before we know it, and seeing objects of interest at every step." McFarland had championed the garden in a previous article for *Outlook* in 1899, focusing in particular on the vast number of native plants that Manning had woven into the quarry garden design. Writing in *The Fern Bulletin,*

An old quarry was the site of one of the Manning's largest wild gardens, Dolobran. The name was derived from the Welsh for "meadow bird." Unknown photographer, 1897. Courtesy MPI.

Manning clothed the rock walls with vines and carpeted the ground with wildflowers. Unusual rock formations contributed drama and provided a range of habitats for the thousands of plants installed there. Unknown photographer, 1897. Courtesy MPI.

Manning's assistant F. W. Barclay described the importance of Dolobran's quarries as model gardens for native plants and noted the successful growth of a particular species of fern, *Pellaea atropurpures* (purple cliffbrake), nestled in the rock wall crevices.[6] Manning regarded Dolobran as one of his most successful wild garden creations and used its example in efforts to persuade other clients to commission similarly "wild" designs.

Griscom lived his later years in semiretirement at Dolobran. He and fellow agriculturalist Alexander J. Cassatt, president of the Pennsylvania Railroad, embarked on a friendly rivalry by competing in state fairs. After Griscom died in 1912, most of Dolobran's land was sold and subdivided, but a 1915 article in the *Minnesota Horticulturist* still listed Dolobran as one of the "largest and best wild gardens in America." The house has had a succession of owners. It remains under private ownership.[7]

As in his other wild garden creations, Manning combined native trees and an understory of ferns and wildflowers with masses of rhododendron to provide a structural framework through four seasons. Unknown photographer, 1897. Courtesy MPI.

Wilcox Park

WESTERLY, RHODE ISLAND

MARTHA LYON

In early March 1899 the trustees of the Memorial and Library Association in Westerly asked Warren Manning to examine the former grounds of the Rowse Babcock estate as a potential site for a park.[1] The property abutting the library had been proposed as a possible town park the year before, but town meeting voters rejected the idea. A few months later, Harriet Hoxie Wilcox purchased seven acres of the estate as a gift to the community in memory of her late husband, Stephen, a leader in the founding of the library in 1892.[2]

As Manning noted immediately, the parcel was ideally located in the center of the prosperous town. Westerly's business district was to the west and the civic center to the south, with established neighborhoods clustered to the north, east, and southeast. The Memorial and Public Library, on Broad Street, abutted the southwestern edge of the park. Christ Church stood nearby on Broad and Elm, and the old town hall just a block away on Union Street. Manning's plan would make use of this proximity to the town by focusing on pedestrian access, while also surrounding the green space with dense plantings to create an escape from the urban center.

Within a few weeks of his initial visit, Manning submitted a plan and report for the "public library grounds." He noted that "the principal topographical features are the broad valley with a water course passing near its centre and the slopes bounding the east and west sides."[3] Growing along the brook were many species of woody plants, including spruce, maple, oak, linden, lilac, and dogwood.[4] Observing that the northwestern property line bisected the bottom of the valley, Manning urged the trustees to extend the park holdings to include the entire valley. "With such an addition to the property," he wrote, "you will have a tract of land having natural features and an extent unsurpassed by any similar property that I am acquainted with so immediately in the centre and thus so accessible to the citizens of a large town."[5]

In his plan, Manning suggested preserving the best existing landforms and plants, while subtly adding the amenities needed for a park facility. He reserved the valley for an open meadow, "free from all artificial structures," allowing a few large trees to grow into dominating features. Around the meadow edges at the top of the slopes he planted a dense border of trees, shrubs, and native flowering plants. On the slopes he placed trees individually and in groups, and at the back of the meadow, abutting existing houses on the northeastern park edge, he sited evergreen trees underplanted with rhododendron, trillium, lungwort, bleeding heart, orchid, and fern. Along the east edges at the top of the slopes he added a wall, "made of good, big boulders with the mortar kept well back in the joints."[6] He created a system of paths rimming the base of the meadow slopes underneath the shade of trees, with branch walks leading to the top of the slopes in several spots, so visitors could view the meadow from above. Manning objected to carriage roads and bicycle paths, as the park was "so near the centre of town that the majority of frequenters are likely to come to it on foot."[7] Finally, he designed a formal entrance from Broad Street, next to the library, including a promenade leading to an oval-shaped overlook terrace, with steps cascading from the terrace down into the meadow.[8]

Construction of the park began in 1899, with small additions made by Manning over the next five years.[9] Many of the plants were sourced locally, including native viburnum, holly, and spicebush from a "collection ground" located eighteen or nineteen miles from Westerly, and mountain laurel

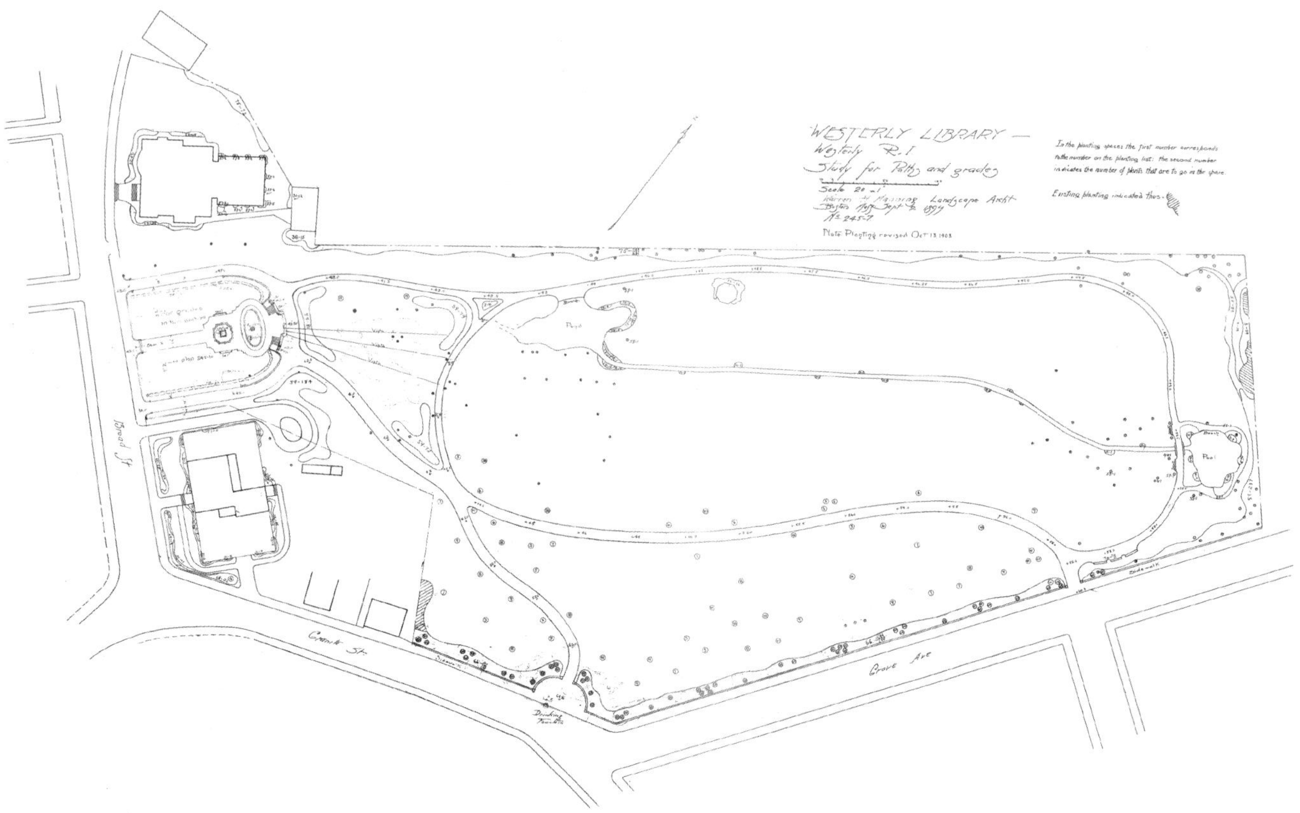

Manning's plan specified an overlook near the Broad Street entrance, a circulation system around the perimeter, and the small brook that bisected the property. He reserved the valley for an open meadow, "free from all artificial structures." "Study for Paths and Grounds for the Westerly Library," September 1899. Courtesy Memorial & Library Association, Westerly Library and Wilcox Park.

The drop in elevation from the entrance to the park (at left) is visible in this postcard view, taken c. 1905. Postcard courtesy William C. Manning.

Manning retained the existing pond, which fed the brook that ran through the valley. Postcard courtesy William C. Manning.

Today the pond and brook are gone, but the old stone bridge still adds architectural interest to the north end of the park. Photograph by Carol Betsch, 2009.

Park stewards have retained the concept of an open meadow for the park interior. Photograph by Carol Betsch, 2009.

Many of the trees planted during Manning's tenure were lost during the Great Hurricane of 1938; replanting began almost immediately. Photograph by Carol Betsch, 2009.

from the immediate vicinity.[10] Manning's planting specifications stated that "bids are to be only upon American grown nursery stock . . . or collected stock."[11] Planting continued through 1904.

In 1905 the trustees implemented Manning's recommendation to secure the remainder of the valley by purchasing the nine-acre Hannah B. W. Brown estate, located along the park's northwestern boundary. The New York City–based landscape architect Frank Hamilton oversaw the expansion, which included a comfort station (c. 1906), the pond (1907), and the extension of walkways and perimeter wall in keeping with Manning's original 1899 vision for a larger park. In the 1920s Westerly constructed a new town hall across Broad Street from the park entrance, and hired the Boston-based landscape architect Arthur A. Shurcliff to revise the park entrance. Shurcliff replaced Manning's oval terrace with a rectangular bluestone plaza, balustraded overlook, and fountain, all placed on axis with the front entrance to Town Hall.[12] In 1937 Shurcliff and his son Sidney designed the Westerly War Monument, located at the southeast corner of the park outside the mortared boulder wall.[13] Contributions of other professionals to the park landscape include John Copley and Associates, authors of a 2004 master plan, and Elmore Design Collaborative, landscape architects for a 2006 planting master plan.

The trustees have continually invested in Wilcox Park since its inception, and as a result the property retains much of Manning's design intent. The Great New England Hurricane of 1938 tore through Westerly, taking down 198 of 525 park trees, but replanting began the following spring.[14] In 1973 the Wilcox Park Historic District was added to the National Register of Historic Places, and in 1999 the American Society of Landscape Architects honored the property with an ASLA Centennial Medallion.[15] In 2001 the Rhode Island Historical Preservation & Heritage Commission featured the property in *Heritage Landscapes of Rhode Island,* noting that it is "the largest and best example of a Warren Manning landscape in Rhode Island."[16]

Fairyland Estates

CHATTANOOGA, TENNESSEE

MATTHEW MEDEIROS

When Warren Manning first visited the future site of Fairyland Estates, overlooking Chattanooga, Tennessee, he is quoted as proclaiming that it could "never be used for homes"; he thought that the area's scenic beauty, which "rivals the Garden of the Gods in Colorado . . . must be preserved just as it is."[1] Although Manning did not attempt to stop the homes from coming to Lookout Mountain, his efforts at incorporating the native plants, scenic views, and unusual rock formations into the planned development helped to preserve these aspects of the site. His work on a residential commission in the Chattanooga area as early as 1914 may have played a role in his garnering the commission.[2]

Inspired by the real estate boom in Florida, Chattanooga residents Garnet and Freida Carter and Oliver B. Andrews first envisioned Fairyland Estates in 1923, when they decided to transform three hundred acres of stony woodland on nearby Lookout Mountain into a resort community. Fairyland Estates, a name derived from Freida's love of fairytales, was to be an idyllic retreat from the city. In addition to its carefully planned subdivision, the development featured the Fairyland Inn (now called the Lookout Mountain Fairyland Club), the ten cottages associated with it, a full-size golf course, and the first miniature golf course in America. Suggested by Freida Carter in 1927–28, the Tom Thumb golf course offered a variety of obstacles, including hollow logs and rock features, watched over by plaster gnomes and fairies.[3] The resort's fantasy theme was further extended by the addition of Mother Goose Village, ten two-bedroom cottages constructed near the clubhouse in 1928.[4]

The highest point of the Cumberland Plateau at 2,388 feet, Lookout Mountain encompasses the northwest corner of Georgia, the northeast corner of Alabama, and the southern border of Tennessee near Chattanooga, and it offered Manning the unprecedented challenge of designing on a mountainside with a historic past. The slope below the Fairyland subdivision site had seen action in the Civil War and became part of Chickamauga & Chattanooga National Military

Park during the 1890s. This conserved land culminated at Point Park, at the northern edge of a plateau, in a designed landscape with monuments commemorating the historic battles. Since the nineteenth century the mountain had also been a scenic wilderness attraction notable for its picturesque views of the Tennessee River Valley, springs, and unique rock outcroppings. Over the years the popular geological formations acquired names, such as Sunset Rock (located in Point Park), Rock Village, and Rock City (both located on the Georgia side of the eastern brow of the

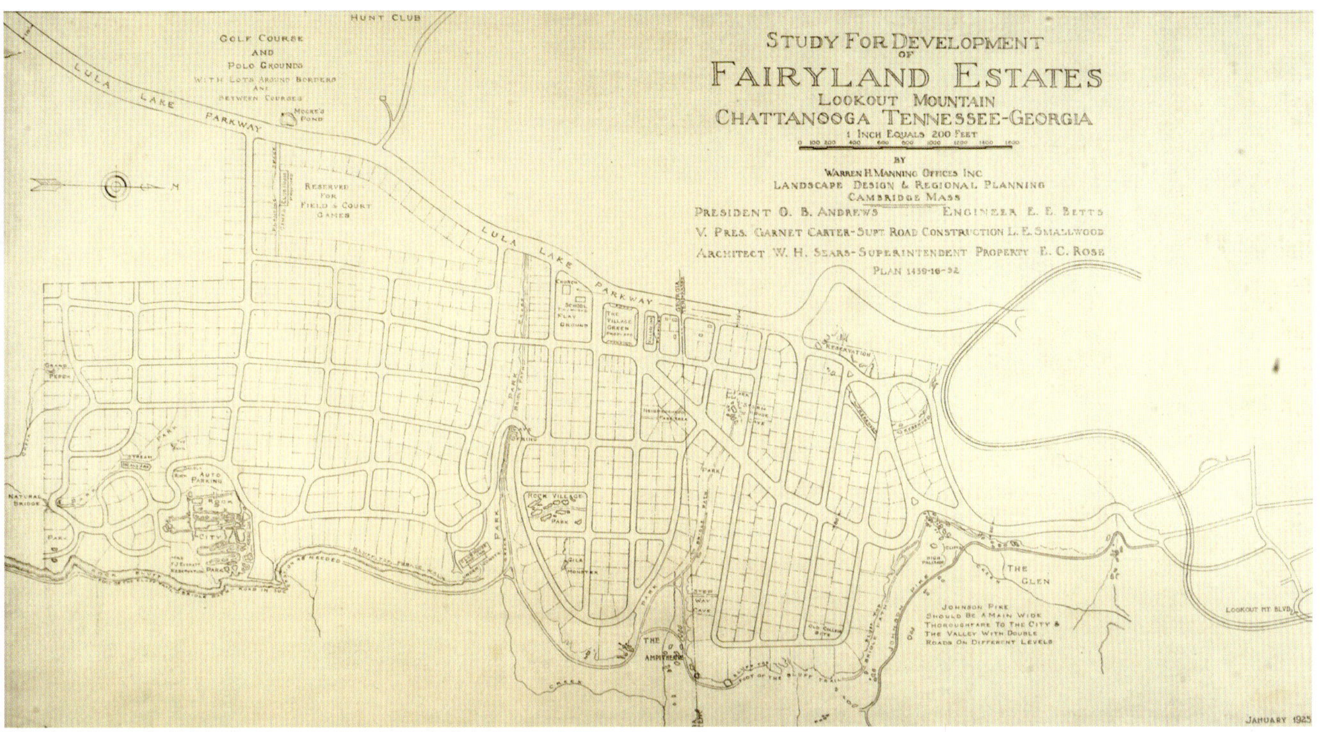

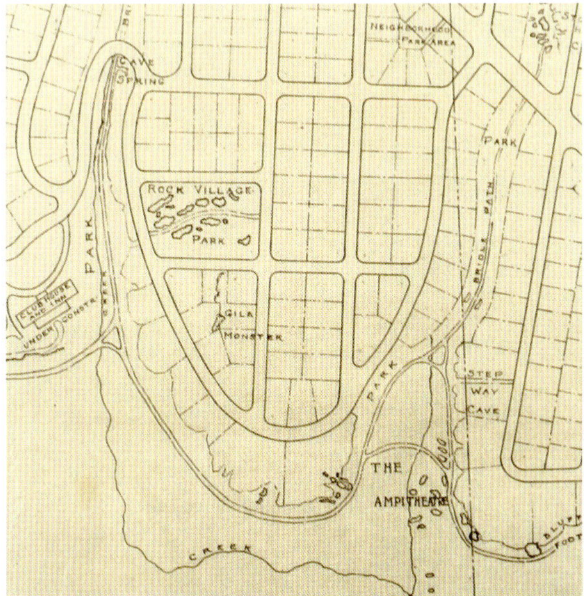

ABOVE: Manning's 1925 plan for Fairyland Estates records a creek and bridle path cutting through the center of the development, near the inn, then under construction. LEFT: (detail) In addition to new roads for house sites, the plan details rock formations, caves, and other natural features. "Study for Development of Fairyland Estates," plan no. 1439-16-92, January 1925. Courtesy MPI.

mountain). Walking trails ascended the slopes, but the only vehicular routes were the mile-long Lookout Mountain Incline Railway and a narrow, unpaved road called Johnson Pike.[5]

Manning and his clients shared a commitment to preserving the existing features of the mountain, including views, rock ledges, and unique topography, and incorporating these natural amenities into the resort landscape.[6] By November 1924, work had begun on the foundation of a Tudor Revival hotel, designed by a local architect, William Hatfield Sears. Situated on the eastern brow of the mountain, the Fairyland Inn was the centerpiece and clubhouse of the Lookout Mountain Fairyland Club. Two large rock formations framed the entry drive adjacent to the building. A new paved highway, the Lookout Mountain Scenic Parkway (Tennessee State Route 148) would connect Chattanooga and the homes on the mountain. A golf course by the renowned designer Seth J. Raynor was also in the early planning stages.[7] Workers were clearing trees from the property and staking out lots, with 160 acres completed in advance of the first public offering of lots on December 6, 1924. That same month Manning visited Fairyland Estates to supervise road construction and surveying at the site.[8]

By January 1925 Manning had completed his first plan of the subdivision, encompassing four hundred acres (though by this time his clients had expanded the project to six hundred acres), with home lots on what Manning described in a November 1925 letter as "very rugged and interesting topography" with "remarkable views."[9] Much of the design involved working with this topography: grading roads, positioning retaining walls, and locating home lots favorably within the landforms of the plateau. On the Tennessee side of the subdivision, home lots along the outer roads backed up to the precipitous drop of the plateau's edge, providing stunning views down the moun-

The Lookout Mountain Fairyland Inn, with its ten cottages, provided spectacular views to the east. Photograph courtesy Chattanooga History Center.

East cliff terrace at the Fairyland Inn, c. 1926. The Fairyland Club remains an active dining, social, and recreational center for its members. Photograph courtesy Chattanooga Public Library.

tain. Cross streets connected these cliffside roads and wound around existing gullies and hills. This district was organized around a town common, with the newly completed Scenic Parkway along its eastern edge. The flatter terrain on the Georgia side of the subdivision led to a more consistent grid of roads clustered around the large rectangular parcel devoted to the Fairyland Golf Club.[10]

Although much of the planning of Fairyland Estates was completed by 1925, Manning remained a presence in the new community for several years. As residents began building homes in Fairyland, Manning was called upon to design the landscapes for many properties; his client list notes fifteen residential design projects between 1925 and 1926, as well as projects for the Lookout Mountain Garden Club and the town of Lookout Mountain, Tennessee. Meanwhile, with the opening of the Fairyland Golf Club (now the Lookout Mountain Golf Club) and the Lookout Mountain Fairyland Club in 1927, and the luxurious Lookout Mountain Hotel in 1928, Fairyland Estates was quickly developing into the sort of resort community envisioned by its developers. Manning continued to work on Lookout Mountain as late as 1929, when he consulted on a subdivision for the Lookout Mountain Holding Company.[11]

With the onset of the Great Depression, development on Lookout Mountain came to a standstill. Many of the roads in the Georgia portion of Fairyland were left incomplete, and newly opened resort facilities on the mountain temporarily closed. Manning's work planning the conservation of the mountain's natural features proved a key element in the area's revival during this period. The Carters renewed their fortunes by developing a number of trails and gardens on their property at Rock City, opening it for tours in 1932. The business proved to be a successful tourist attraction and, along with other nearby attractions like Ruby Falls, gave Lookout Mountain a reputation for outdoor tourism as well as luxurious resort living. Civilian Conservation Corps camps were established in multiple locations to work on improvements to the Chickamauga & Chattanooga National Military Park.[12]

As the economy improved over the years, the Fairyland Golf Club and Lookout Mountain Fairyland Club reopened. In 1990 the Fairyland Club was placed on the National Register of Historic Places. Although the rise of tourism changed the character of the original subdivision, the spatial layout was not altered. Despite new road development, especially in the Georgia portion, Fairyland Estates is surrounded by conservation land that continues to evoke the woodland feeling appropriate to its name. The road network, with its winding roads and stunning views down the mountain, retains a high level of integrity today.[13]

The Fairyland Inn swimming pool, 1947. Photograph courtesy Chattanooga Public Library.

University of Virginia

CHARLOTTESVILLE, VIRGINIA

CHRISTOPHER PATZKE

When Warren Manning was commissioned to produce a master plan for the University of Virginia in 1908, he lent his vision to a project that was conceived by Thomas Jefferson around 1814. For Manning, who considered Jefferson the nation's first regional planner, landscape designer, architect, and builder, "no project could be more inspiring."[1] By the time Manning came to work at the university, Jefferson's original design had been modified, and it lacked the space needed for an evolving architectural program. Although his master plan was not fully implemented, Manning's work introduced a circulation system for the twentieth century while respecting Jefferson's original spatial layout. His work would help to shape future planning decisions for generations to come.

After a devastating fire in 1895, the university hired the architectural firm of McKim, Mead & White to restore the Rotunda. The disaster prompted a review of the university's needs, which resulted in the design of several new buildings and, by June 1908, Manning's commission to develop a master plan. Manning submitted his plan on October 8; the next month he received a four-year appointment as consulting landscape architect.[2]

Manning approached this project by dividing the university into four sections: Observatory Hill, with its dense forest, to the west; the university farms to the south and west; the recreation areas to the north of Ivy Road; and the main academic core with Jefferson's original buildings. He limited the master plan to this central core, where he focused on vehicular and pedestrian circulation, planning for additional buildings, and plantings. He noted that the pavilions surrounding the Lawn were focused on the central space, with service and access to the rear of the buildings. The East and West Ranges, which contained student housing and dining halls (known as Hotels), faced outward and lacked the monumentality of the core structures. The best views of the Rotunda were from Carr's Hill to the north and from the far end of the Lawn, recently enclosed by three buildings. Manning's analysis helped him under-

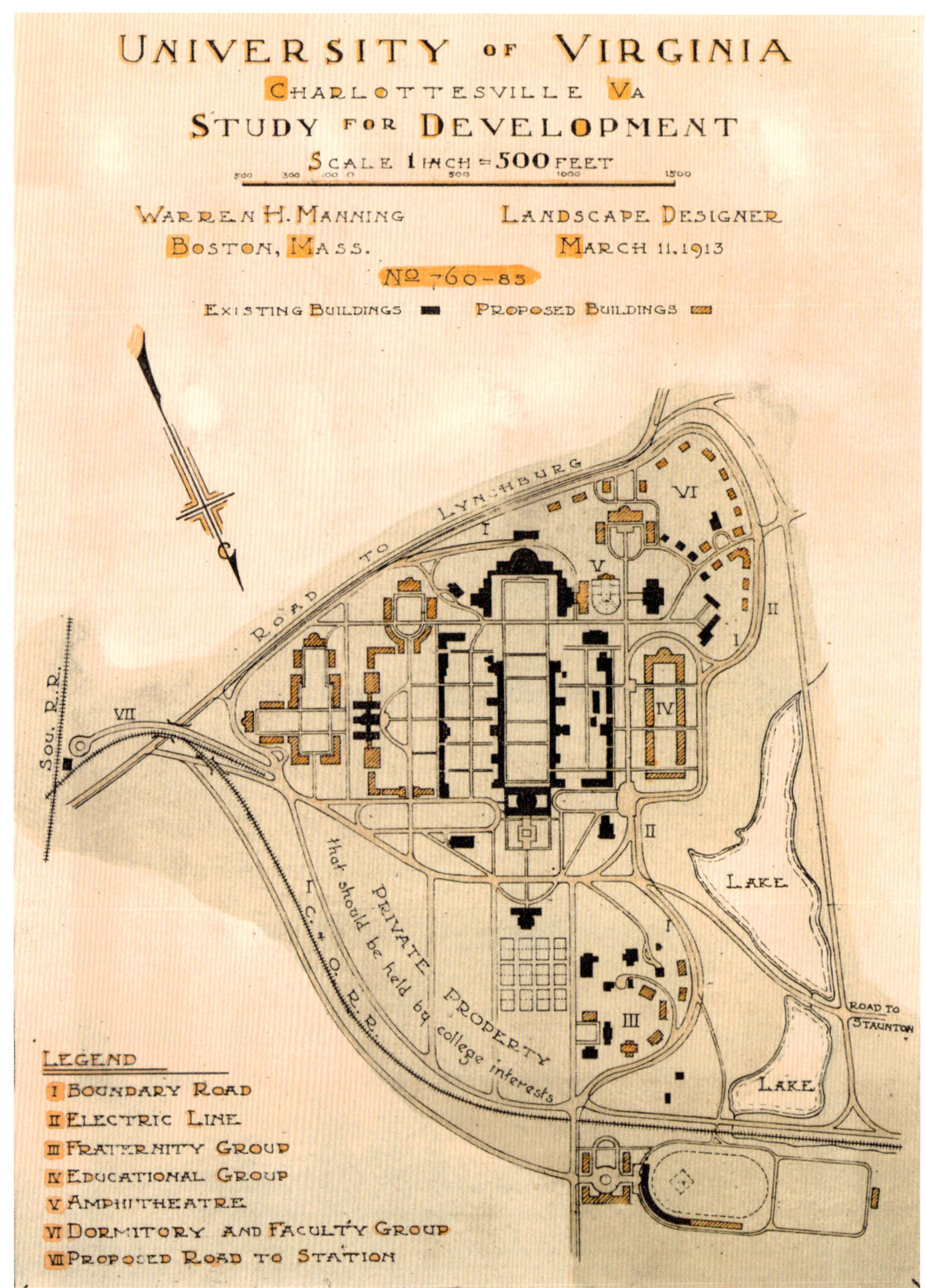

Manning's plan for the University of Virginia focused on the core of the campus. He proposed eliminating interior roads, adding a new perimeter road, increasing the size of nearby ponds, and strengthening transportation links to nearby towns and the rail station. "Study for Development," plan no. 760-85, March 1913. Courtesy MCL.

stand Jefferson's intentions for "outlook, orientation, intercommunication, architectural and landscape composition" and guided his proposed additions.[3]

After analyzing the approaches to the university, Manning envisioned a boulevard from the train station as the major entrance route and suggested adding a road adjacent the existing train tracks, to be divided into three sections: a lane accommodating slow traffic, an electric streetcar line in the middle, and a highway on the outside.[4] As one traveled along the new road from east to west, the view of the Rotunda would change from an oblique angle to the preferred view from Carr's Hill. To the west, Manning proposed an adjustment to Ivy Road that would ease the ascent to Carr's Hill and serve as a dam, which would triple the size of the existing pond. To the south, he suggested enlarging the road to Lynchburg into a boulevard. After the implementation of the boulevard and the ring roads, Manning recommended abandoning four centrally located roads that limited the growth of the university. He felt that his new roads would not only better follow the public's desired routes, but also be built and maintained at public expense, thus relieving the university's financial burden.[5]

The proposed roads also served to create new boundaries. Manning suggested buying the private land to the northwest of the Lawn and the land south of the road to Lynchburg, which could be used for storage, stables, and consolidating the area around the university's power plant.[6] Despite the expense, Manning argued for the new roads in his report, insisting that they were necessary to ensure the growth and cohesiveness of the university and analyzing the costs and requirements.

The circulation changes Manning proposed also allowed for access to three new quadrangles—one proposed for the west and two for the east—that would double the university's built space. He avoided adding quadrangles to the north that might compete with the Rotunda and to the south near the newly completed buildings closing off the Lawn. In all of his proposals for the university, Manning's guiding philosophy

A model of the campus core from 1912 emphasizes the proposed boulevard to the west of the Academical Village. From this perspective, the view is to the north, with the Rotunda at the top and the pavilions with their individual gardens (defined by serpentine walls) flanking the central Lawn, at the bottom. Photograph courtesy MCL.

was that "all new buildings . . . should follow the Jeffersonian design and construction so faithfully as to appear to be his work."[7]

The proposed quadrangle to the west was to be "intimately connected" by topography to the Lawn while respecting the privacy of the original grouping. A further connection would come from a proposed east–west cross axis at the north edge of the quadrangle that aligned with the Rotunda and one of the proposed quadrangles to the east. The cross axis would be anchored by a ceremonial overlook above the enlarged ponds in the west valley and a loop road that connected the overlook with the base of the Rotunda. The quadrangle would also be aligned on the east side with a road on axis with the recently constructed President's House. This road would pass by a proposed amphitheater and enlarged faculty and student housing to the southwest. The proposed quadrangles to the east were similar, but limited by the steep slopes and existing buildings. Instead of using fill to bring the buildings level with the East Range, Manning placed them lower in elevation to maintain the view to the campus along the proposed entry boulevard. He also suggested height restrictions on buildings to preserve the views of the original campus. The university's law school was sited to the southeast of the Lawn.[8]

At the University of Virginia, Manning envisioned himself building a "Garden University of America." Noting that the existing gardens were beautiful but accidental, he proposed the restoration of the garden spaces behind each of Jefferson's pavilions. His plan encouraged selectively pruning and removing trees to clear views to distant vistas and buildings. He suggested removing existing plants, except for the Indian strawberries, forsythia, hollyhocks, perennial pea, and evergreen Japanese honeysuckle. To this plant palette he advised adding trees and shrubs native to the region.[9] The plantings were to be installed at low cost and designed with a concern for maintenance. By April 1910 several grading projects were finished, including terracing areas around the existing dining hall and on Carr's Hill, which was also graded and covered with grass for the first time. Plantings were added throughout the grounds, and "hedges . . . planted on many boundaries in order to break up the random and unsightly paths."[10] The master plan included an arboretum for the benefit of students studying natural history and engineering.

In 1913 Manning became involved in a dispute with a board member who wished to demolish a building Jefferson had designed near the Rotunda. Manning objected and rallied three prominent architects, Henry Bacon, J. Randolph Coolidge, and Charles Platt, to join him in pleading the case for preservation. "After this," Manning dryly notes in his autobiography, "I was not continued as an adviser to the University." His account books list his last bill, sent on July 1, 1913, as "doubtful."[11]

Although few of his ideas were realized, Manning's master plan respected Jefferson's original intentions and shaped planning decisions for succeeding decades. In 1921 Fiske Kimball designed the classically detailed McIntire Theatre and located it at Manning's suggested site. The plan was also consulted in 1922, when Chi Phi Fraternity petitioned to build a new house.[12] Edmund S. Campbell, dean of the School of Architecture, studied the plan when he advocated locations for new academic and residential buildings, including Peabody Hall, which would anchor a quadrangle to the west of the Lawn, originally proposed by Manning. Manning's legacy also lives on in the heart of Jefferson's Academical Village with his executed designs for the gardens behind pavilions 8 and 10.[13]

Jamestown Exposition

NORFOLK, VIRGINIA

JANE ROY BROWN

The Jamestown Tercentennial Exposition of 1907 marked the three-hundred-year anniversary of the founding of Jamestown Colony in Virginia, the first English settlement in America. Warren Manning had received the commission to design the exposition grounds by October 1904.[1] How he obtained the commission has not yet come to light, but various connections and opportunities positioned him well. As a veteran of the influential World's Columbian Exposition in Chicago in 1893, when he was employed by the Olmsted firm, Manning could claim prestigious qualifications. He also happened to be designing a campus in neighboring Hampton in 1901, when Norfolk businessmen began campaigning to host the exposition in their city.[2] Finally, the exposition's advisory architect, Robert S. Peabody of the prominent Boston firm of Peabody & Stearns, had worked on some of the same projects as Manning.[3]

In the early years of the twentieth century, such large-scale expositions, or world's fairs, were still popular ways to showcase advances in industry, agriculture, and domestic life. The precedent for the trend was London's Great Exhibition of 1851, featuring the Crystal Palace. Collectively, exhibits at these events blended commerce, education, and spectacle, drawing tens of thousands of visitors from all over the world. By emphasizing their educational mission, expositions (and their organizers) not only reflected prevailing cultural currents and social anxieties but also attempted to shape the future and ease the prevailing social anxieties of the day. The 1904 St. Louis World's Fair, for example, celebrated the moral rightness of Manifest Destiny, just as America was trying to annex the Philippine Islands.[4] In the case of the Jamestown Tercentennial, America was then competing with Japan to control the Philippines and other Pacific islands. To show off America's naval might, President Theodore Roosevelt commissioned the "Great White Fleet" (four squadrons of battleships painted white, with gilded scrollwork adorning their bows). Roosevelt appeared on the exposition's opening day, and twenty battleships passed the fair's coastal site in a preview of the fleet's world tour, which would

Manning created the plan for the Jamestown Exposition of 1907, a celebration of the three-hundred-year anniversary of the founding of the first English settlement in America. Postcard, 1906. Courtesy William C. Manning.

Borrowing key design elements of the World's Columbian Exposition of 1893, Manning organized the plan around a great basin on the waterfront. The feature was defined by two piers extending into the harbor, with a bridge connecting them. Postcard, 1906. Courtesy William C. Manning.

Manning sited the pavilions, roads, gardens, and open spaces of the main section in a grid. The Colonial Revival pavilions were ornamented with white quoins, triangular pediments, and a dome that recalled Monticello. Postcard, 1907. Courtesy William C. Manning.

launch from the same site in December.[5] Other exhibit themes included the common English ancestry of northerners and southerners, and Virginia's claim to the nation's founding myth. This was also the first U.S. world's fair to dedicate a pavilion to the contributions of African Americans to the country's development.[6]

Cities vied to host these high-profile fairs, not only for prestige but also for profit. Yet, as Manning pointed out in a 1902 lecture at the Massachusetts Horticultural Society, expositions did not always live up to their promise. His remarks did not address the ideological content of expositions, but more pragmatic concerns, especially financial results. Tangible proceeds were unpredictable, unevenly distributed, and difficult to assess, which led Manning to conclude that overall, for host cities "the loss is probably much greater than the gain." He predicted that after the 1904 St. Louis World's Fair, this financial calculus would defeat "any attempts at a great World's Fair for a long time."[7]

The organizers of the Jamestown Exposition would have done well to heed Manning's words. A day after the fair ended, on November 30, 1907, the *New York Times* deemed it "the most colossal failure in the history of expositions," only slightly exaggerating the prevailing opinion. The exposition closed with a debt of $2.5 million, which the *Times* blamed on tardy federal funding, poor management, and worse transportation. Specifically, the organizers delayed construction by changing the program at the last minute and drastically underestimated the capacity of the two streetcar lines built to shuttle visitors to and from the fairgrounds. Backup transportation by steamship was slow and irregular. When the fair opened in April, two-thirds of the grounds and buildings were incomplete, and some exhibits remained unfinished by early August.[8] For some critics, these and other failures overwhelmed the exposition's brighter notes: "superb" plans and exhibits, "magnificent" construction, an "ideal" location, and landscapes that "were veritable dreams." One opening-day visitor found no concessionaires, plans, maps, or any other information, but then concluded that "it did not really matter whether this Exposition were finished or not—the beauty of the location, the historic interest, and the delightful Spring weather made it a pilgrimage worth having taken."[9]

The location—about forty miles southeast of the original Jamestown settlement on the James River—was a peninsula called Sewell's Point, which offered nearly a mile of shoreline fronting Chesapeake Bay, the largest estuary in the United States. The point protrudes from the south shore of Hampton Roads, a channel at the confluence of the Elizabeth, James, and Nansemond Rivers. The 340-acre fairgrounds site was largely flat. On the north it faced the sheltered water of Willoughby Bay and on the east a tidal estuary called Bousch's Creek. Marshes flanked the steep banks of the creek, which forked into two branches that meandered into the site. The terrain here was so wet as to be impassable in places.[10] Near the western boundary, saloons and boardinghouses sprawled on the shores of the Elizabeth River and Hampton Roads. At Manning's urging, the exposition organizers purchased adjacent land to screen these buildings from view and buffer the fairgrounds from competing attractions.

A road remaining from an abandoned subdivision formed the property's southern boundary. Visitors arriving from the north and west could choose from numerous routes and modes of travel, but the peninsula, though settled and cultivated, was less accessible overland from the south. Visitors from this direction would travel on the two streetcar lines built for the purpose. The rail company engaged to build the lines bought this road and surrounding land.[11] With the site protected on all sides, the designers enjoyed the unusual advantage of being able to create a world unto itself.

Manning sat on the exposition's official board of design, which also included architects Parker & Thomas of Boston and Baltimore and John Kevan Peebles of Norfolk, with Robert S. Peabody of Boston in an advisory role. It is unclear to what degree Manning collaborated with the architects, but he apparently helped select the fairgrounds and created an existing conditions plan on a local survey map, indicating the locations of important views, trees, shrubs, and herbaceous plants. (Later, in choosing sites for the exposition buildings, Manning took care to preserve or move distinctive plants.) He also created a site plan and a town plan, because the exposition company intended to convert the site into a town after the fair. Manning envisioned the exposition's central compound of open courts, parade grounds, and larger buildings as the future town's civic center after the fair structures were torn down, and his town plan laid out streets and systems for drainage and sewers. Construction of these, along with extensive drainage of the wetlands, began as soon as the organizers approved the plans, probably in 1904.[12]

The designers exploited the waterfront for both access and views. Manning's initial plan featured two parallel piers extending into the harbor, bridged at the far end to form a vast water basin. Subsequent schemes presented variations on the pier theme, but Manning's concept prevailed. The center of the basin was dredged to allow boats to enter it from the harbor, and the bridge was designed to allow passage. The geometric layout followed an axis that traced the highest point of land, a ridge that intersected the shoreline at right angles. Manning's first plan extended the width of the basin into the grounds to form a court flanked by two wings, and the buildings behind nearly reached the site's southern boundary. Budget cuts later eliminated the court's wings and rear section, and several iterations of the layout ensued. Eventually, the main auditorium building headed a court along the main axis. With state buildings vying for positions on the waterfront, which was not tenable, Manning created a linear park containing a series of oval spaces along the shore to preserve water views for the state buildings, most of which he pushed back a block from the shoreline. The main buildings and open spaces occupied rectangles in a horizontal grid whose western section was more than twice the size of the eastern section. These buildings shared similar architectural features and materials: brick walls with prominent white quoins on the corners, triangular pediments, and Monticello-like domes.[13] The grid dissolved into a more naturalistic landscape on the far eastern edge, near Bousch's Creek. There Manning used an exedra-like semicircle of old trees between the

Trim, geometric lawns and fruit trees dominated the plantings around the primary buildings. At the last minute, native rhododendron were added to mask still bare foundations. Further inland, plantings became more naturalistic. Postcard, 1907. Courtesy William C. Manning.

The influence of the Arts and Crafts style was evident in the architecture of smaller pavilions and plantings. Postcard, c. 1907. Courtesy William C. Manning.

Manning's plans called for an entire Arts and Crafts Village. In 1917 the U.S. Navy built a base on the site of the exposition, incorporating infrastructure (such as this curving road) and several buildings from the original layout. Postcard, 1907. Courtesy William C. Manning.

arms of the creek to form the outer edge of an Arts and Crafts village. Formal gardens, edged by low hedges of California privet, filled curving spaces between the concentric streets.[14]

In 1905 Manning established a nursery on the site and started gathering a large variety of native species from the local area to plant throughout the grounds, both to reduce costs and to "lead the people of the South to recognize the beauty and value of the plants about them." He transplanted hundreds of pin, willow, and water oak, red maple, dogwood, cherry, and locust to line the parade grounds and cedar to ornament the interior courts. He chose a species of tree or shrub to distinguish each street, using French mulberry on one, evergreen bayberry on another, mountain laurel on a third, and so on. To complement the woody plants along the streets, he designed gardens of native perennials (including goldenrod, marsh mallow, sneezewort, and penstemon) that provided a succession of bloom. Instead of grass, which was difficult to establish on the site, he transplanted vinca, strawberries, ferns, and other native species growing on various parts of the property, filling in with annuals and fast-growing vines in the spring of 1907. With construction continuing up to and beyond the fair's opening date, Manning installed native rhododendron around the buildings and terraces at the last minute.[15]

Among the sideline events that took place at the Jamestown Exposition was a Congress of Horticulture convened by the National Council of Horticulture. Manning and John C. Olmsted were among the speakers during three days of sessions. Manning, who likely was instrumental in organizing the meeting, included a pitch for a "national system of public reservations" in his remarks on the topics of civic horticulture and civic improvement. For maximum public benefit, he proposed, such reservations should be part of comprehensive planning, based on the opportunities afforded by existing natural features and systems. Following this course, civic horticulture could achieve efficiency, economic benefits, and aesthetic unity. While these comments expounded on the regional planning concepts advocated by Charles Eliot more than a decade earlier, they also hint at Manning's growing interest in planning on a national scale.[16]

Paradoxically, and despite Manning's early start in designing and building the site, contemporary critics and present-day historians point out that it was the lack of coherent planning and leadership among the exposition organizers that doomed the Jamestown Tercentennial Exposition to failure. Though a land-development company bought the site after the fair, no town arose on the former fairgrounds as the organizers had planned. States exhibiting at the fair sold their buildings either to the development company or to private citizens to be used as houses. But the fair raised awareness of the strategic location of Sewell's Point, and in 1917 the U.S. Navy built a base there, incorporating the infrastructure and several buildings. Today, nineteen of the state buildings, most used as private residences for officers, form "Admirals Row" on Dillingham Avenue.[17] Aerial photos suggest that much of Manning's layout has been altered, but the semicircular streets of the former Arts and Crafts village near Bousch's Creek remain intact.

Milwaukee Parks

MILWAUKEE, WISCONSIN

WILLIAM GRUNDMANN

Between 1890 and 1892 the Milwaukee Board of Park Commissioners acquired several parcels of land for the city's first park system. The board chose the sites with an eye to their distribution throughout the city, envisioning that eventually boulevards would connect them.[1] In 1892 city engineer Edward Kuhlmann supervised the preparation of the sites, conducting surveys and clearing trees to prepare for laying out roads and installing water and sewer systems. The park commissioners soon recognized, however, that they needed the skills of a landscape architect to fully exploit the land's potential.[2]

Warren Manning was an employee of Frederick Law Olmsted's firm in 1892, when the park commissioners contracted with the firm to design Lake and West Parks over a period of three years.[3] The firm completed preliminary plans in 1895, and city crews, with the help of local contractors, began building Lake Park. Manning made several trips to Milwaukee to supervise construction and planting. After he started his own practice, in January 1896, Manning continued to supervise the work on Lake and West Parks for the rest of that year. The park board commissioned him for further park projects, and of the eight parks in the original Milwaukee system, he eventually worked on five.

In 1901 the board hired Manning to begin renovating and planning new development on recently acquired land at Mitchell Park. The commissioners boasted that when his new design was completed, the park would be "one of the prettiest in the city."[4] Among the features of Manning's design were a lake and a sunken space ornamented with elaborate formal flower gardens planted in the popular Victorian carpet-bedding style. The crowning embellishment was a rectangular "water mirror," or reflecting pool, in the center of the sunken garden space. The water mirror—18 inches deep, 360 feet long, and 82 feet wide—extended from the existing conservatory to South Pierce Street.[5] By 1902 workers had completed excavation, grading, and some of the planting. Crews planted more than a hundred young trees, raised in nurseries at Mitchell and

Humboldt Parks, along the edges of the water mirror and the extensive garden walks. Work continued the following year on the walks, stone walls, steps, and lookouts in the garden. Most of these features and the formal plantings (including 2,400 roses, 7,500 lilies, and 20 poplar trees) were completed by 1904.[6]

Meanwhile, in 1903 the park commissioners hired Manning to make a topographical survey of Kosciuszko Park in preparation for improving an addition to it and altering portions of the old grounds.[7] Manning, who was then practicing with his brother J. Woodward Manning under the name Manning Brothers, submitted a plan for

Manning became involved with the Milwaukee parks while still working for the Olmsted firm, and he took the project with him when he opened his own practice in 1896. Mitchell Park, which he completed about 1904, featured a spectacular sunken garden with a "water mirror" 360 feet in length. Postcard courtesy Milwaukee County Historical Society.

Manning began improvements to Kosciuszko Park in 1903. These included an artificial lake for boating and ice skating. Photograph courtesy Milwaukee County Historical Society.

the work, which began the following year. The improvements to Kosciuszko Park, which was relatively small compared to those built earlier, included an artificial lake for boating and ice skating, with a pavilion on the north side.[8]

By January 1905 the Manning Brothers partnership had dissolved, and Manning had resumed practicing under his own name.[9] Simultaneously, Manning's park design and planning in Milwaukee ended. By then most of the planning and construction of the existing city parks was finished, and the commissioners were not contemplating adding more parks to the system. Earlier, beginning in 1902, Alfred C. Clas, a local architect who joined the Board of Park Commissioners that year, was hired for design and planning. Clas's firm, Ferry & Clas, subsequently designed several structures in Lake Park, and during his tenure on the board Clas did most of the planning for additions to other existing parks.[10] With the appointment of Charles

Most of Lake Park had been laid out during the Olmsted tenure, but Manning continued to design plantings throughout, some of which survive today. Photograph courtesy Milwaukee County Historical Society.

One of Lake Park's most dramatic features was the Grand Staircase, which still exists. Photograph courtesy Milwaukee County Historical Society.

Lake Park was sited on high bluffs overlooking Lake Michigan. Deep ravines through the bluffs necessitated several bridges, including this one, known as the Lion Bridge. Photograph courtesy Milwaukee County Historical Society.

The central section of the locally renowned Lion Bridge was eventually transformed into a park, open to pedestrians and bicyclists only. Plantings in the ravine have matured to form a woodland. Photograph from the Library of Congress, Prints and Photographs Division.

G. Carpenter as the first superintendent of parks in 1903, the board may have viewed the services of a landscape architect as redundant.[11]

By 1905 the city's park system had reached a turning point. The park board's fifteenth annual report reviewed the commission's work to date and pointed out that the existing park system was too small to meet the needs of the growing city. The commissioners urged the city to consider buying additional land to meet demand. Two years later, the Milwaukee County Park Commission was formed and purchased park land outside the city limits.[12]

While the Olmsted firm outlined Milwaukee's original park system in broad strokes, it was Manning who filled in the details. Some of those details are still extant, especially the stands of trees in Lake, Washington, and other city parks.[13] Most of the myriad shrubs and flowers Manning planted throughout the parks are gone, as is the water mirror and its sunken garden in Mitchell Park. As the twentieth century progressed, the Olmsted and Manning "pleasure ground" designs absorbed many modern recreational amenities: golf courses, tennis courts, athletic fields, and playgrounds.

Despite the changes that have taken place in Lake and Washington Parks during the last century, the roads, paths, and tree plantings preserve the original spatial structure. Washington Park still has its lake and its undulating topography, although freeway construction claimed a large area on its western side in 1962.[14] Kosciuszko Park retains many of its trees, but the lake designed by Manning has been filled.[15] With its ravines, bridges, and bluff overlooking Lake Michigan, Lake Park is the best-preserved example of the city's early parks.

Afterword

ROBIN KARSON

Warren Manning's career spanned vast territory, and it is our hope that the portion we cover in this volume will inspire others to create an increasingly comprehensive view of Manning's life's work. The information collected by contributors to the LALH Warren H. Manning Research Project is available as an online database through our website, lalh.org. It provides survey data on many sites for which only scant traces have surfaced—a source of clues for further explorations.

Among Manning's most significant park design and planning projects still to be investigated are examples in Minneapolis (1903); Wilkes-Barre, Pennsylvania (1905–11); Flint, Michigan (1904–19); and Miami, Florida (1924). In some cases, we know that Manning prepared a sizable number of plans for these projects, but they have not yet been located. Manning's records also list at least four Olmsted firm park projects in which he remained involved after leaving that practice, none of which is documented in his archives: Jackson Park, Chicago (1897), the Louisville, Kentucky, parks (1896–99), Audubon Park in New Orleans (1897–98), and the Bronx Zoo (1898).

Important campus planning projects by Manning that deserve future investigation include the University of Minnesota (1902–8); Richmond (Virginia) College (now Richmond University, 1898, 1911–18); George Peabody School for Teachers (now Vanderbilt University, 1911–12); Pennsylvania State University (1924); and Asheville University (now UNC Asheville, 1924–25). Manning's extensive railroad work, some of which was purportedly executed by "conducting" arrangements of plantings from a moving train, is certainly worthy of research. The Parks Library at Iowa State University holds a large collection of circa 1903 plans related to "Pennsylvania Railroad Grounds," in which Manning specified plantings for station grounds in forty towns and cities, from Washington, D.C., through Maryland, Delaware, and Pennsylvania.

We know that Manning was involved in several suburban developments beyond those covered here, including Fairlawn Heights in Akron, Ohio

(1915–18), and New Bern Country Club Resort in New Bern, North Carolina (1924). The Parks Library holds a particularly large collection of plans relating to the latter. Manning's work on several residential landscapes in St. Louis, some of which were executed in conjunction with his design for the St. Louis Country Club (1924), should also receive closer attention. Among his clients in St. Louis were Joseph Pulitzer, Oliver Anderson, August Busch, J. D. Lambert, and A. Wessel Shapleigh, all listed in 1925. A splendid collection of archival photographs by Arthur G. Eldredge held by the University of Massachusetts Lowell includes a number of the St. Louis commissions.

By our estimate more than half of Manning's career projects—which total approximately 1,600—were private estates. Those covered in this volume were selected according to their significance to Manning's development, the availability of archival documentation, and their condition (the estates of William G. Mather, Frank A. Seiberling, J. H. Whittemore, and Galen L. Stone, for example). Among the many luminaries on Manning's private client roster not covered here, besides Pulitzer and Busch, are John D. Rockefeller Sr. of Pocantico Hills, New York; William H. Moore of Pride's Crossing, Massachusetts, and Lake Geneva, Wisconsin; and John J. Albright of Buffalo. One of the most illustrious names on Manning's client roster was Charles W. Eliot, president of Harvard University, whose renowned son had been a partner in the Olmsted firm. The intriguing circumstances of that 1909–10 Cambridge, Massachusetts, residential project, as for so many others on Manning's extensive list, remain to be discovered.

APPENDIX 1

Employees Listed in Manning's Financial Records

Frank Hartley Anderson 1917
K. E. Barker 1922
Albion Abraham Blinks 1926
E. H. Bodfish 1913
Charles F. Boehler 1913
Louis Brandt 1913
A. F. Brinkerhoff 1900–1902
Helen Elise Bullard 1921–1926
A. P. Bursley 1913
Clarence Cornelius Combs 1926
Wilbur David Cook, Jr. 1914
Louis P. Croft 1930
Frank Hamilton Culley 1913
Ralph W. Curtis 1913
Bryant Fleming 1900–1903
Herbert L. Flint 1910–1916
Harry E. Fraser 1927–1930
J. Martin Frisell 1931
Charles Freeman Gillette 1909–1912, 1914
Alfred V. Hall 1906–1912
Stephen F. Hamblin 1912–1918
Egbert Hans 1917–1934
Arthur K. Harrison 1898–1911
Violet Ethelwyn Harrison 1916–1921
Joseph H. Hayner 1924
Orlando D. Holmes 1916
Daniel Urban Kiley 1932–1938
Frederick S. Kingsbury 1912–1913, 1915–1916
Thomas LeNoir 1928–1929
D. Carl Lutender 1916–1934
George Leslie Lynch 1927
J. Woodward Manning 1897–1904, 1918–1921
A. Chandler Manning 1903–1905, 1918
Guy Gerald Manning 1918–1919, 1928–1929
William Manning 1918
May Elizabeth McAdams 1916
Warren B. Meixner 1917
George H. Miller 1906
John Barstow Morrill 1925
George L. Nason 1913
Samuel Pike Negus 1902–1905
Kenneth H. N. Newton 1924
Chester W. Nichols 1929
Tell W. Nicolet 1913
Arthur L. Norton 1900–1917
John Noyes 1911–1912

Victor G. Otto 1924–1926
Irving W. Payne 1915
Joseph Peterson 1908
Carl F. Pilat 1898–1901
William H. Punchard 1896
Charles Henry Ramsdell 1897–1910
Henry Bond Raymore 1918
Frank Asbury Robinson 1913
Roland Rogers 1919
Arthur F. Rosenbaugh 1924
Howard R. Sebold 1924
Marjorie Sewell (Cautley) 1917
George Otto Shaffer 1913
Arthur H. Sharp 1913
H. E. Smith 1916
J. Fletcher Steele 1908–1913
William A. Strong 1925
Arthur Clayton Sylvester 1930–1938
Arthur S. Talbot 1926
Albert Davis Taylor 1908–1913
Arthur S. Tupper 1913
Harold Stanley Wagner 1914–1918
Richard K. Webel 1924
G. Weir Wilson 1925
Elizabeth H. Wood 1925
Elizabeth Wooley 1926
Charles Ernest Woolverton 1909
Alanson Phelps Wyman 1897
Alfred Boyd Yeomans 1903

APPENDIX 2

U.S. Map of Projects

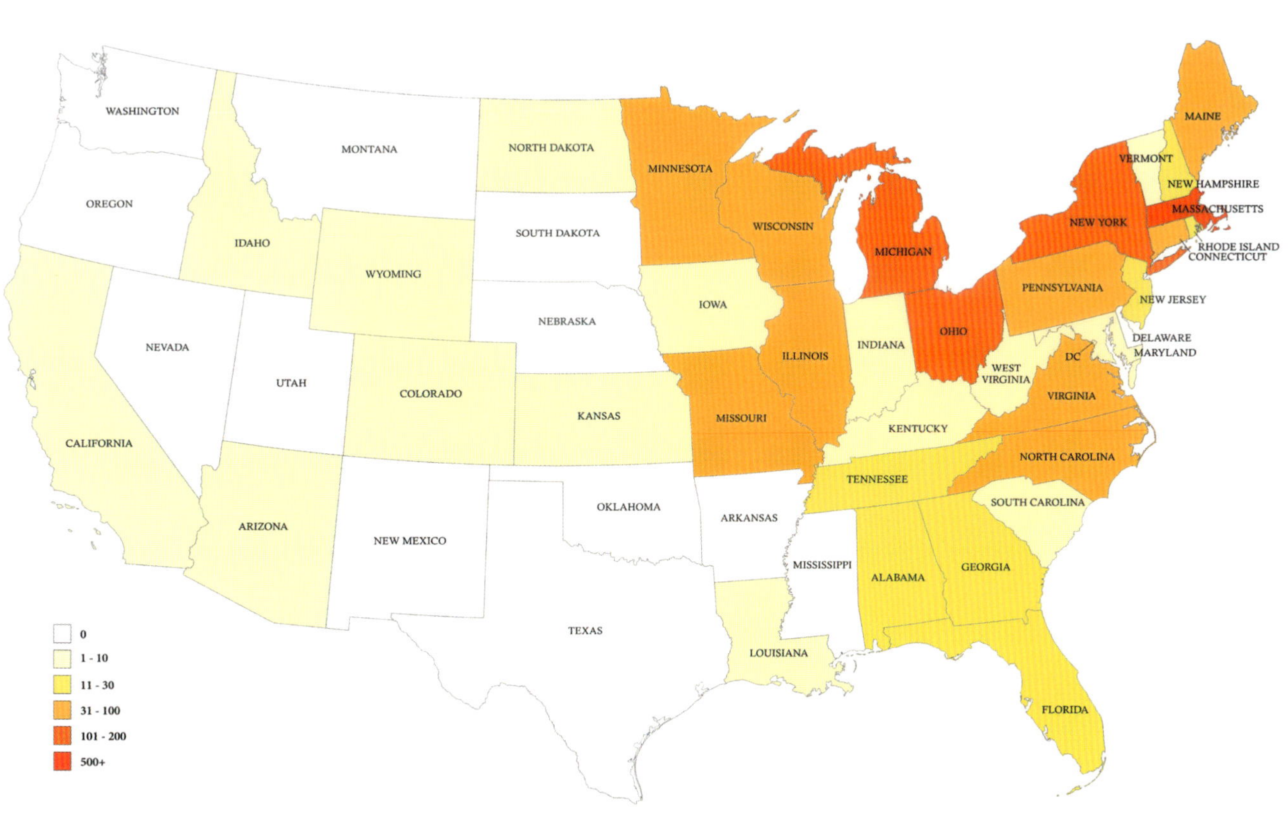

APPENDIX 3

Published Writings of Warren H. Manning

"The Best Hardy Herbaceous Plants and Their Cultivation." *Transactions of the Massachusetts Horticultural Society for the Year 1882, Part I,* 44–49. Boston: For the Society, 1882. (Paper delivered January 28, 1882.)

"The Best List of Old and New Herbaceous Perennials for General Cultivation; Also, Notes on Rare Herbaceous Plants Difficult to Cultivate, and on Improvement in Our Native Herbaceous Perennials." *Transactions of the Massachusetts Horticultural Society for the Year 1883, Part I,* 62–66. Boston: For the Society, 1883. (Paper delivered February 10, 1883.)

"Our Native Shrubs." *The Ladies' Floral Cabinet* 13 (February 1884): 40–41.

"Improvement of Home Grounds." *The Ladies' Floral Cabinet* 13 (May 1884): 151–53.

"Our Native Lilies." *The Ladies' Floral Cabinet* 13 (August 1884): 246–47.

"Weeds." *The Ladies' Floral Cabinet* 13 (October 1884): 312–14.

"Rocks and Rockeries." *The Ladies' Floral Cabinet* 14 (February 1885): 36–37.

"Our Native Climbers." *The Ladies' Floral Cabinet* 15 (January 1886): 8–9.

"Variety in Foliage." *The Ladies' Floral Cabinet* 15 (February 1886): 32–34.

"Winter Weeds." *Vick's Illustrated Magazine* 9 (February 1886): 43–46.

"Hardy Perennials for Beds." *Vick's Illustrated Magazine* 9 (March 1886): 77.

"A Winter Walk." *The Ladies' Floral Cabinet* 15 (March 1886): 68–69.

"Native Orchids." *The Ladies' Floral Cabinet* 15 (April 1886): 86–87.

"Evergreens for Small Places." *The Ladies' Floral Cabinet* 15 (June 1886): 141–43.

"Cambridge Botanic Garden." *The Ladies' Floral Cabinet* 15 (July 1886): 167–68.

"Native Plants in Gardens." *The Ladies' Floral Cabinet* 15 (July 1886): 179.

"The Wild-Garden." (Signed "X.Y.Z.") *Vick's Illustrated Magazine* 9 (July 1886): 200–201.

"Tree and Shrub Sports." *Vick's Illustrated Magazine* 9 (August 1886): 237–38.

"Street Trees." *Vick's Illustrated Magazine* 9 (November 1886): 329–31.

"Hardy Deciduous Shrubs." *Vick's Illustrated Magazine* 9 (December 1886): 363–64.

"The Old-Fashioned Garden." *The American Garden* 8 (March 1887): 79–80.

"The Sumacs." *Vick's Illustrated Magazine* 10 (April 1887): 101–3.

"Select Shrubs." *The American Garden* 8 (May 1887): 168.

"Front Yards." *Vick's Illustrated Magazine* 10 (June 1887): 170–72.

"Transplanting." *Vick's Illustrated Magazine* 10 (August 1887): 232–34.

"Unseasonable Flowers and Fruit." *Vick's Illustrated Magazine* 10 (October 1887): 301–2.

"Introduced Plants." *Vick's Illustrated Magazine* 10 (November 1887): 330–32.
"The Birches." *Vick's Illustrated Magazine* 11 (January 1888): 9–11.
"Weeping Forms of Trees." *Popular Gardening and Fruit Growing* 3 (June 1888): 207.
"School Yard Horticulture." *Popular Gardening* 4 (December 1888): 70.
"Along Fences and Walls." *The American Garden* 11 (August 1890): 502.
"*Desmodium and Lespedeza*." *The American Garden* 12 (July 1891): 440.
"Home Surroundings." *Gardening* 1 (October 1, 1892): 19–20.
"*Abelia Rupestris*." *Gardening* 1 (November 15, 1892): 74.
"Creeping Fig Vine." *Gardening* 1 (December 1, 1892): 89.
"*Ilex Crenata*." *Gardening* 1 (December 1, 1892): 90.
"The Purpose and Practice of Landscape Architecture." *Transactions of the Indiana Horticultural Society for the Year 1893,* 98–103. Indianapolis: Wm. B. Burford, 1894.
"Plants on the World's Fair Grounds: A Catalogue of Exhibitors and Hardy Plants at the Columbian Exposition, 1893; Together with a Critique of the Exhibitions, Technically Considered, of the Department of Horticulture — By Warren H. Manning." *Annals of Horticulture in North America for the Year 1893,* edited by Liberty Hyde Bailey, 136–63. New York: Orange Judd, 1894.
"Landscape Gardening." *Transactions of the Massachusetts Horticultural Society for the Year 1893, Part I,* 26–40. Boston: For the Society, 1893. (Paper delivered January 21, 1893.) Reprinted as a series in *The Canadian Horticulturist* as "Landscape Gardening I–IV" (January–April 1900).
"Home Surroundings: Choice of Locality." *Gardening* 1 (February 1, 1893): 147–48.
"The Proper Use of Formal Flower Beds." *Gardening* 1 (February 15, 1893): 163–64.
"Home Surroundings." *Gardening* 1 (May, 15 1893): 271–72.
"Books on Landscape Gardening." *Gardening* 1 (August 1, 1893): 361.
"Laying Out Home Grounds." *The Canadian Horticulturist* 16 (August 1893): 280–83.
"Rockeries." *The Canadian Horticulturist* 16 (October 1893): 357–58.
"Hardy Asters." *Gardening* 2 (October 15, 1893): 42.
"Planting about the Base of the House." *Gardening* 2 (November 1, 1893): 51–52.
"Popular Names of Plants." *Gardening* 2 (December 1, 1893): 92–93.
"Seaside Planting." *Gardening* 2 (April 15, 1894): 246–47.
"Recently Introduced Shrubs." *The Canadian Horticulturist* 17 (May 1894): 171.
"Planting a Bare Hill Top." *Gardening* 3 (November 15, 1894): 68.
"Notes on the Vegetation of the Reservations." *Report of the Board of Metropolitan Park Commissioners, January, 1895,* 69–81. Boston: Wright and Potter, 1895.
"Planting on a Sandy Hill." *Gardening* 3 (January 1, 1895): 120.
"Cost of Maintenance." *Gardening* 3 (August 1, 1895): 348.
"Shady Corners." *Gardening* 3 (July 15, 1895): 322.
A Handbook for Planning and Planting Small Home Grounds. North Billerica, Mass., 1897.
"Park Design and Park Planting." *First Report of the Park and Outdoor Art Association,* 50–55, 68–77. Louisville, Ky.: APOAA, 1897.
The Making of an Herbarium. Coauthored with Walter Deane. Southampton, N.Y.: Library Art Annex, June 1897.
"Designing Amusement Resorts." *Street Railway Journal* 13 (September 1897): 534–37.
"The Establishment of Public Parks." *American Gardening* 18 (October 1897): 694.
"In the Pine Barrens." *The Pinehurst Outlook* 1 (December 10, 1897): 7.
"Golden Gate Park." *Park and Cemetery* 8 (May 1898): 57.
"Landscape Phase of the University of California Plan." *The American Architect and Building News* 61 (July 16, 1898): 20–22.
"*Matricaria Discoidea* in Eastern Massachusetts." *Rhodora* 1 (January 1899): 18.
A Handbook for Planning and Planting Small Home Grounds. Menomonie, Wisc.: Stout Manual Training School, 1899.
"Report on Minneapolis Parks." *Seventeenth Annual Report of the Board of Park Commissioners of the City of Minneapolis, 1899,* 51–64. Minneapolis: Harrison & Smith Co., 1900.
Directions for Surveying and Arranging Home and School Grounds. Boston: Rockwell and Churchill Press, 1900.
"Landscape Gardening – I." *The Canadian Horticulturist* 23 (January 1900): 12–14.
"Landscape Gardening – II." *The Canadian Horticulturist* 23 (February 1900): 50–52.
"Arrangement of Home Grounds." *The Canadian Horticulturist* 23 (February 1900): 81–82.
"Landscape Gardening – III." *The Canadian Horticulturist* 23 (March 1900): 91–94.
"Landscape Gardening – IV." *The Canadian Horticulturist* 23 (April 1900): 150–152.
"Practical Aesthetics." *The Minnesota Horticulturist* 28 (September 1900): 339–41.

"Forestry in Massachusetts." *Forestry and Irrigation* 8 (February 1902): 80–83.

"The Influence of American Expositions on the Out-Door Arts." *Transactions of the Massachusetts Horticultural Society for the Year 1902, Part I,* 73–81. Boston: For the Society, 1902. (Paper delivered March 8, 1902.)

"How to Make a Garden – The Lawn." *Country Life in America* 1 (March 1902): 173.

"How to Make a Formal Garden at a Moderate Cost." *Country Life in America* 3 (March 1903): 186–89.

"How to Make a Formal Garden at a Moderate Cost." *How to Make a Flower Garden: A Manual of Practical Information and Suggestions,* edited by Liberty Hyde Bailey, 239–58. New York: Doubleday, Page & Company, 1903.

Suggestions for Beautifying Home, Village and Roadway. Boston: Youth's Companion, 1904.

"The History of Village Improvement in the United States." *The Craftsman* 5 (February 1904): 423–32.

"Rock Gardens." *New Cyclopedia of American Horticulture,* edited by Liberty Hyde Bailey, 5:1539–41. New York: Doubleday, Page & Company, 1906.

"Wild Garden." *New Cyclopedia of American Horticulture,* edited by Liberty Hyde Bailey, 6:1976–78. New York: Doubleday, Page & Company, 1906.

"Outdoor Art." *Park and Cemetery and Landscape Gardening: Special Civic Improvement Supplement* 15 (February 1906): 478–80.

"Jamestown Exposition." *Transactions of the American Society of Landscape Architects,* edited by Harold A. Caparn, James Sturgis Pray, and Downing Vaux (1906; rev. 1910), 83–87. Harrisburg, Pa.: J. Horace McFarland Co., 1912.

A Handbook for Planning and Planting Home Grounds. North Billerica, Mass.: Talbot Mills, 1907.

"Civic Horticulture and Civic Improvement." *Park and Cemetery and Landscape Gardening* 17 (October 1907): 197–99.

Report to Accompany a Plan for the University of Virginia, Charlottesville, Va. October 8, 1908.

A Report to Accompany Study for a System of Reservations for Ithaca, N.Y. January 3, 1908.

"The Framing of Home Pictures." *Country Life in America* 14 (May 1908): 52–53.

"Bringing in the Offscape." *Country Life in America* 14 (July 1908): 290–91.

"The Two Kinds of Bog Gardens." *Country Life in America* 14 (August 1908): 379–80.

"For General State Survey." *The Bostonian Magazine* 2 (November 1909).

The Improvements of Madison, N.J.: Report of Warren H. Manning to the Highway, Park, and Playground Committee of the Madison Civic Association. Madison, N.J., 1909.

"Conservation of Land Resources." *The Bostonian Magazine* 1 (December 1909).

"For General Survey of Commonwealth." *The Bostonian Magazine* 3 (January 1910).

"Villages for Workingmen and Workingmen's Homes." *Proceedings of the Second National Conference on City Planning,* 99–103. Cambridge, Mass.: The University Press, 1910.

"Villages and Homes for Working Men." *Western Architect* 16 (August 1910): 85.

Bangor City Plan: The Burned District. Bangor: The Civic Improvement Committee, 1911.

"Unique Little Gardens." *Country Life in America* 19 (April 15, 1911): 443–45.

"The Field of Landscape Design." *Landscape Architecture Quarterly* 2 (April 1912): 108–10.

A Step towards Solving the Industrial Housing Problem. American City Pamphlet Series, no. 131. New York: Civic Press, 1913.

"Some Data on Botanical Gardens." *Landscape Architecture* 3 (January 1913).

"The Billerica Town Plan." *Landscape Architecture* 3 (April 1913): 108–18.

Thomas Jefferson as an Architect and a Designer of Landscapes. Coauthored with William Alexander Lambeth. Boston: Houghton Mifflin, 1913.

"Beauty as a Resort Asset." *Northward-Ho!* 9 (September 6, 1913): 17–19.

"*Berberis Thunbergii* Naturalized in New Hampshire." *Rhodora* 15 (December 1913): 225–26.

"Discussion: Garden Cities." *Proceedings of the Third National Conference on Housing, Cincinnati, December 3–5, 1913.* Cambridge, Mass.: The University Press, 1913.

"Town Sites on Government Reclamation Projects." *Landscape Architecture* 4 (April 1914): 117–23.

"A Step towards Solving the Industrial Housing Problem." *The American City* 12 (April 1915): 321–25.

"The Art of Making Landscape Gardens." *The Standard Cyclopedia of Horticulture,* edited by Liberty Hyde Bailey, 1783. New York: Macmillan, 1915.

"Roadside Planting." *Billerica – The North Shore Edition* 4 (July 1915): 3–4.

"Evergreens." *Billerica – The North Shore Edition* 4 (August 1915): 3.

"Standardizing Scientific Name Abbreviations and the Common Names of Plants." *Landscape Architecture Quarterly* 6 (October 1915): 32–36.

"Wild Flower Preserves." *Billerica – The North Shore Edition* 4 (November 1915), 3.
"Horticultural Sports." *Billerica – The North Shore Edition* 4 (January 1916): 8–9.
"Our National Flower." *Billerica – The North Shore Edition* 4 (February 1916): 3–4.
"The Fugitive Literature of the Landscape Art." *Billerica – The North Shore Edition* 4 (March 1916): 4–15.
"National Parks, Monuments, and Forests." *Landscape Architecture Quarterly* 3 (April 1916): 106–9.
"Park Systems and Recreation Grounds." *Proceedings of the Eighth National Conference on City Planning, Cleveland, June 5–7, 1916,* 242–49.
"The National Importance of the Hudson–Mohawk Thoroughfare, and Objects in Its Landscape." *Journal of the American Institute of Architects* 5 (April 1917): 161–69.
"Planning the Cantonments: The Work of the American Society of Landscape Architects in Their Design." *The American City* 18 (April 1918): 331–36.
"A Simple Home-Ground on a Small Wooded Hillside." *The Small Place: Its Landscape Architecture,* edited by Elsa Rehmann, 63–73. New York: G. P. Putnam's Sons, 1918.
"A Description of Estates on the Community Lands about the Mayfield Country Club as Allotted by Frank C. Newcomer, Cleveland, Ohio." North Billerica, Mass.: Warren H. Manning Offices, 1918.
Warren H. Manning's City Plan of Birmingham. Birmingham, Ala.: Published by subscription, 1919.
"A National Plan Study Brief." Special supplement to *Landscape Architecture* 13 (July 1923).
Goodyear Heights. Akron, Ohio: George L. Curtis Printing Co., 1923.
"A National Park System." *Parks and Recreation* 7 (January–February 1924).
"Constructive and Cooperative Recreation." *Proceedings of the National Conference on Outdoor Recreation,* 68th Congress, 1st session, May 1924. Senate doc. no. 151.
"Exotic Trees for Forest Plantations." *American Forests and Forest Life* 33 (September 1927): 535, 568.
"Church Grounds." *The National Plant, Flower and Fruit Guild Magazine* 16 (September 1927): 10–12.
"Agassiz Park of Calumet, Michigan, Built by Community Effort." *Parks and Recreation* 11 (November–December 1927): 85–90.
"Minnesota." *The Minnesota Horticulturist* 56 (February 1928).
Regional Highways. Massachusetts Federation of Planning Boards, Bulletin no. 23. December 1928.
"Some Major Considerations in the Planning of Regional Highways for New England." *The American City,* November 1928.
"Street Widths in Some Cities of More Than 150,000 Population in the United States." *The American City,* April 1929.
"Michigan as a Field for Large-Scale State Planning." *American Landscape Architect* 1 (October 1929): 40.
"An Easterner Looks at Michigan." *The Magazine of Michigan* 1 (September 1929).
"Travelways of Beauty." *Landscape Architecture* 20 (July 1930): 323–26.
"Arbor Day." American Civic Association, Outdoor Art Department, leaflet no. 5 (1905), 1–8.
"National Planning Notes." *The Planners' Journal* 1 (July–August, 1935).
"Giving Land for Parks Is Contagious." *American Civic Annual, 1929,* 207. Harrisburg, Pa.: American Civic Association, 1929.

Notes

ABBREVIATIONS

MCL Warren H. Manning Collection, Center for Lowell History, University of Massachusetts Lowell

MPI Warren H. Manning Papers, MS 218, Special Collections Department, Iowa State University Library

WHM autobiography Warren H. Manning, "The Autobiography of Warren H. Manning" (1937), MCL, electronic transcript with original pagination prepared by LALH

WHM client list Warren H. Manning client list, MCL, re-sorted and converted to PDF by LALH; project numbers in the text and notes refer to this list

THE CAREER OF WARREN H. MANNING

1. At various times Manning also employed Charles F. Gillette, John Noyes, Bryant Fleming, Wilbur D. Cooke Jr., Arthur K. Harrison, Arthur L. Norton, Herbert Flint, Clarence C. Coombs, Marjorie Sewell Cautley, Helen Bullard, Richard K. Webel, and others who made substantial contributions to the field. For a complete list of employees, see appendix 1.
2. See Carl Steinitz, Paul Parker, and Lawrie Jordan, "Hand-Drawn Overlays: Their History and Progressive Uses," *Landscape Architecture* 66 (September 1976): 444–55. See also WHM, "The Billerica Town Plan," *Landscape Architecture* 3 (April 1913): 108–18.
3. See William Alexander Lambeth and Warren H. Manning, *Thomas Jefferson as an Architect and a Designer of Landscapes* (Boston: Houghton Mifflin, 1913), 104.
4. For more on Manning and wild gardens, see Robin Karson, "Warren H. Manning: Pragmatist in the Wild Garden," in *Nature and Ideology: Natural Garden Design in the Twentieth Century,* ed. Joachim Wolschke-Bulmahn, Dumbarton Oaks Colloquium on the History of Landscape Architecture (Washington, D.C.: Dumbarton Oaks Research Library and Collection, 1997), 113–30. At his ancestral home, the Manse, Manning maintained two bog gardens, which he described in horticultural detail. See WHM, "The Two Kinds of Bog Gardens," *Country Life in America* 14 (August 1908): 379–80.
5. WHM autobiography, 239–40. Integral to his concept was the idea that these large wild gardens would be at some distance, up to one hundred miles, from urban offices; busy executives would be able to access "these more distinctive wild land estates" by personal air travel, which Manning believed was fast becoming universally available.
6. Ibid., 156.
7. Ibid., 227.
8. Ibid., 18, 6.
9. "For me, a great thunder storm is the most spectacular evidence of the Infinite Power in Nature. Sunsets, too, and sunrises are so wonderful that it is always amazing to me that so many people regard so casually the miracle of changing cloud and sky colors and forms. There are cer-

tain sunsets which stand out in my mind as major events." WHM autobiography, 15–16.

10. Manning recorded a garden for G. W. Norris of Woburn, Mass. (project no. 1), and an estate for Robert J. Kimball of West Randolph, Vt. (project no. 3). WHM client list. Biographical information for this essay was drawn from several sources, primarily "Warren Henry Manning," in *The National Cyclopedia of American Biography* (New York: James T. White & Co., 1947); WHM autobiography; and "Jacob Warren Manning," in *American Series of Popular Biographies, Massachusetts Edition* (Boston: Graves & Steinbarger, 1901), 817–20.
11. Manning was among the contributors to a publication resulting from the effort. See L. L. Dame and F. S. Collins, *The Flora of Middlesex County, Massachusetts* (Malden, Mass.: Middlesex Institute, 1888).
12. WHM to Frederick Law Olmsted (FLO), November 7, 1887, copy in MCL.
13. WHM diary, February 28, 1888, May 16, 1888, and June 13, 1888, MCL.
14. Ibid., November 7, 1888.
15. "In the office of Mr. Olmsted, I was associated with his son, John C. Olmsted, Frederick Law Olmsted, Jr., Henry S. Codman, Charles Eliot and other aids [*sic*] who have since made their place in important professional activities. This association gave me an unrivalled opportunity to gain a far-reaching knowledge of the highest ideals and the best practice developments of landscape in its broadest phases. A member of the firm for whom I had the highest admiration was John C. Olmsted, with whom I traveled on many projects. He was quiet, thoughtful, and most efficient in gaining a full knowledge of all planning projects, and in seeing that they were well planned, recorded, and issued." WHM autobiography, 39.
16. Lance M. Neckar believes that Manning's first exposure to Eliot's methods occurred in 1893, when he was assigned to work with Gordon Taylor, the firm's topographer, to make sketch maps of the vegetation of the Boston Metropolitan Park System. See Lance M. Neckar, "Developing Landscape Architecture for the Twentieth Century: The Career of Warren H. Manning," *Landscape Journal* 8 (Fall 1989): 81.
17. Manning recorded the planting plan for the Massachusetts Building at the World's Columbian Exposition as a private job (project no. 21). He maintained a modest practice of his own throughout his years with the Olmsted firm.
18. WHM to Henrietta Manning, November 1893, MCL.
19. FLO Jr. to John Charles Olmsted (JCO), February 6, 1895. Olmsted Papers, Library of Congress (LC). In the same letter, Olmsted Jr. notes, "You know better than I Father's opinion of brilliant, variegated shrubs and trees."
20. FLO Jr. to JCO and Charles Eliot, May 25, 1895, and FLO Jr. to JCO, February 6, 1895, LC.
21. During Olmsted Jr.'s years at Biltmore, his father—regretful at not having a more developed knowledge of plants himself—aggressively pushed him to further his horticultural education. See Susan L. Klaus, *A Modern Arcadia: Frederick Law Olmsted Jr. and the Plan for Forest Hills Gardens* (Amherst: University of Massachusetts Press in association with Library of American Landscape History, 2002), 17–29.
22. Manning and O. C. Simonds discussed a joint practice in Chicago in 1893, but nothing came of the idea. WHM to Henrietta Manning, December 2, 1893, MCL. The Mannings had a child, Harold Warren, in 1895, whose birth may been a factor in Manning's decision to launch his own practice. They had lost their first infant, Harold Olmsted Manning, within a day of his birth five years earlier.
23. A ★ denotes sites covered in the project essays in this volume.
24. "Today I went out to the Manse—Mr. Manning's old family place—for lunch. We went thru his large library which he has put at my disposal, and over his place. He has several hundred acres of wood and hill and water and farm that are very lovely." Fletcher Steele to Mary Steele, August 1, 1909, Fletcher Steele Collection, Rochester Historical Society (RHS). On Manning's practice of requiring employees to work on the Manse grounds, see WHM autobiography, 48; and Egbert Hans, "The Life and Works of Warren H. Manning from His Incompleted Autobiography," undated, 134A–135, MCL.
25. See especially Manning's exchanges with J. H. Whittemore in 1895, Whittemore family papers, Naugatuck, Conn. Manning would later adopt this protocol, too, encouraging the men and women practitioners in his office to take clients when they struck out on their own.
26. A number of the Draper, Tufts, McCormick, Mather, and Whittemore projects are discussed elsewhere in this volume. Frank H. Peavey commissioned the Olmsted firm to design a country estate, Highcroft, on a high bluff above Lake Minnetonka, west of Minneapolis; Manning took over the job in 1896. He developed an extensive of design of formal gardens, lawns, and agricultural fields, emphasizing views to the lake. Manning also received jobs from many of Peavey's business associates, which, in turn, brought him into contact with other civic leaders, including Charles M. Loring, who was key to Manning's gaining work on the park system, to which he added

considerably. Through the same connections, Manning secured work on the Minnikahda Club and the Layfayette Club, and another forty-five commissions for private estates in the Twin Cities. Between 1902 and 1908, Manning was also hired to plan extensions to the University of Minnesota. For more on this constellation of projects, see Lance M. Neckar, "Warren H. Manning and His Minnesota Clients: Developing a National Practice in a Landscape of Resources, 1898–1919," in *Midwestern Landscape Architecture,* ed. William H. Tishler (Urbana: University of Illinois Press in cooperation with Library of American Landscape History, 2000), 142–58.

27. Charles Eliot died on March 25, 1897, and so never participated. J. C. Olmsted was active in the organization, however.
28. WHM autobiography, 122.
29. McFarland admired Manning's work; in an 1899 article titled "An American Garden" in the popular magazine *Outlook,* he praised a quarry garden that the landscape architect had designed for the shipping magnate Clement C. Griscom, in Haverford, Pennsylvania. See J. Horace McFarland, "An American Garden: Dolobran near Philadelphia," *Outlook,* October 7, 1899, 328–29. See also, by the same author, "Dolobran—A Wild-Gardening Estate," *Country Life in America* 4 (September 1903): 339.
30. Charles Mulford Robinson, "The Remaking of Our Cities: A Summing Up of the Movement for Making Cities Beautiful While They Become Busy and Big—A Chain of Great Civic Improvements Which Mark a New Era of Urban Development," *The World's Work* 12 (October 1906): 8046; Frank A. Waugh, *The Landscape Beautiful* (New York: Orange Judd, 1910), 207.
31. Before the partnership ended Manning Brothers also completed important jobs in Grand Rapids and Menomonie, Wis., Merion, Pa., Marquette, Mich., and St. Paul.
32. For these recruits, Manning looked in particular to the new programs of landscape architecture established at Harvard University, Massachusetts Agricultural College, and Cornell University.
33. Steele's letters to his parents provide a detailed account of his responsibilities in Manning's office. "Mr. Manning said 'I have decided to make you my private traveling secretary. It will be your duty to get a good working knowledge of every job I am working on. Then to accompany me on all my trips, see what is being done, make all my engagements for me and see that I keep them. Meet all my clients so that you can represent me when it is impossible for me to be present, study the ground with me so you can carry out my plans in the office when you get back. Make all my travelling arrangements, and finish a great many projects that I have only time to start. . . . You will work all day, get on trains at midnight, where I shall keep you up giving me reports, perhaps getting to your destination at three in the morning when you go to a hotel for a snatch of sleep before you are off for work at 6 or seven o'clock." Fletcher Steele to Mary Steele, July 23, 1909. All letters quoted in this note are from the Fletcher Steele Collection, RHS.

    August 1, 1909: Steele had been dispatched to Great Hill, the Galen Stone estate on Buzzards Bay, to supervise work on the ground. "I will have to work like a slave, driving stakes, climbing trees for the view, taking notes, meantime getting information on all the trees and shrubs and plants, writing letters, constantly ready to go to Carolina or Timbucktoo."

    September 10, 1909: "To be sure I am carrying out the details of his big ideas—a few of them—-now, but I am given a big leeway for my own conceptions to wriggle in, and I almost feel as tho' I were doing some big work myself."

    October 5, 1910: Steele wrote about "appalling" pressure of new work and described a "new experiment" in which he would be the connecting link between Manning's "sanctum sanctorum" and the drafting department. But he was soon dispatched to work on-site on new projects.

    February 10, 1911: Steele wrote of his dismay at Manning's need for instantaneous results and his own need to work through details. "A great many things are done slap-dash, anyhow, details are neglected, and the office is in a turmoil. . . . [A]s far as faults go, [Manning's] most marked failing . . . is the very one for which he criticizes me . . . 'You bring everything to me half done.' "
34. Manning held Taylor in particularly high regard. "Few, if any, men in the fine arts profession have accomplished so much in advancing their special interest in a practical and artistic way as has A. D. Taylor." WHM autobiography, 244.
35. Fletcher Steele to John Steele, February 10, 1911, RHS.
36. The letter continues, "He will start into details of direction of what he wants done on that point, get only well started & be called to the telephone. On leaving the phone he will immediately start to dictate a letter; halfway thru the letter he tries to recall some detail of the plan he is describing & go[es] out to the drafting room to see it. There he gets interested in how it is working out & will spend a few minutes working that out, when someone butts in to ask him a question & he turns his entire attention in another direction. Before he has explained half of what he wants in that case, he is called into see a

client, with whom he rushes out to get lunch, & is not seen again that day. Meanwhile everyone goes as far as they can, which often is not very far, & the next morning he comes in astonished that all the details which he had in his mind but has never mentioned, have not been attended to." Fletcher Steele to John Steele, February 10, 1911, RHS.

37. Matthew Medeiros, LALH research associate, computed Manning's office earnings for each of the years of his practice, based on office records in the MCL.
38. For more on Gwinn estate, see Robin Karson, *The Muses of Gwinn: Art and Nature in a Garden by Warren H. Manning, Charles A. Platt, and Ellen Biddle Shipman* (Sagaponack, N.Y.: Sagapress/Abrams in association Library of American Landscape History, 1995). The estate is also the subject of a chapter in Karson, *A Genius for Place: American Landscapes of the Country Place Era* (Amherst: University of Massachusetts Press in association with Library of American Landscape History, 2007), 61–88.
39. WHM, "Villages and Homes for Working Men," *Western Architect* 16 (August 1910): 85.
40. Peabody was also Charles Eliot's uncle.
41. Lambeth and Manning, *Thomas Jefferson as an Architect and a Designer of Landscapes,* 104.
42. A series of letters from Steele to his parents from late 1909 through 1910 chronicle work on the project, a large country estate for Egbert G. Leigh Jr., listed as no. 721. No plans for this job have come to light, but significant aspects of the design survive intact. The property is in private hands.
43. Fletcher Steele, "An Emergency Report for Bangor, Maine," *Landscape Architecture* 11 (October 1911): 1–15.
44. For excerpts from Steele's letters, see the essay on Great Hill in this volume.
45. Manning also collaborated with Chapman & Frazer in Kennebunkport, Maine, on a summer residence for George Herbert Walker, now the George H. W. Bush compound.
46. WHM, "The Nature Garden," undated typescript, MCL.
47. This work occurred in 1929. Ellen Shipman also redesigned the formal gardens at Gwinn estate, Tranquillity Farm, and Halfred Farms in Chagrin Falls, Ohio, whose 1920 plan was by Manning.
48. WHM, "The Art of Making Landscape Gardens," in *The Standard Cyclopedia of Horticulture,* ed. Liberty Hyde Bailey (New York: Macmillan, 1916), 1786.
49. Ibid.
50. The proposition catalyzed Steele's resignation from the firm. "It is Mr. Mgs dearest hope that the boy will enter his father's profession & in time take his father's place. At present it appears that the boy is interested in other things, but until he has tried every inducement, Mr. Mg will not lose the idea. This will not be for many years. And if he finally succeeds, it will continue to be, as it now is, a one man office & and second rate one at that for Harold has none of his father's constructive ability. . . . It would be out of the question for me to continue there under such circumstances." Fletcher Steele to John Steele, January 27, 1912, RHS.
51. George Manning, interview by Jane Roy Brown, December 2, 2005, LALH.
52. Three successive editions of the magazine were published. The second of these, the (Chicago) North Shore Edition, was underwritten by Harriet and Cyrus McCormick with Manning as "director" and Stephen F. Hamblin as editor. Contributors included Wilhelm Miller, O. C. Simonds, W. C. Egan, E. O. Orpet (superintendent of Walden), Charles Mulford Robinson, Ralph Rodney Root, and W. M. S. French (director of the Chicago Art Institute), among others. The third and final edition of *Billerica* was devoted to national planning issues.
53. Manning's practice of hiring women landscape practitioners was highly unusual for the day. Over the course of his career, Manning had several women designers, the best known of whom was Marjorie Sewell Cautley.
54. Robert Moses to Ross Kellogg, August 28, 1923, and Kellogg to Moses, September 5, 1923, Enfield Falls Reservation Commission Collection, The History Center, Ithaca, N.Y.
55. WHM, "Planning the Cantonments: The Work of the American Society of Landscape Architects in Their Design," *The American City* 18 (April 1918): 331–36.
56. Arnold R. Alanen and Lynn Bjorkman, "Early Twentieth-Century National Planning in the United States: The Vision of Warren H. Manning," in *Proceedings of the 1999 ASLA Annual Meeting,* comp. D. L. Scheu (Washington, D.C.: American Society of Landscape Architects, 1999), 44–45.
57. A copy of the "National Plan," 1919, is held in MPI.
58. Manning also designed Jemison's 550-acre private estate, Spring Lake Farm, outside Birmingham.
59. The Eldredge photographs in MCL, identified as "Company Photographs," provide an invaluable source of visual information about Manning's built work.
60. Overlay maps associated with this report are held in MCL.
61. An unsolicited letter from Manning to A. Lawrence Lowell, president of Harvard, written in March 1932, was typical. It reprises many of the interests and preoc-

cupations of Manning's career, among the most urgent of which was his cultural legitimacy. "I have a traditional interest in the University," Manning wrote, "as my ancestor William Manning was sent by the Cambridge church to England to bring over the Rev. Urian Oakes as a pastor. He was later President." Manning goes on to propose a consulting relationship with Harvard, involving his "personal aid to whoever is directly responsible for design, construction and upkeep [of the campus] and . . . its surroundings, its inlooks and its outlooks." The letter concludes with a cursory review of the unrealized potential and problems of Harvard's campus, focusing primarily on plantings, all with an eye to putting "Harvard in the forefront among universities." WHM to A. Lawrence Lowell, March 4, 1932, MCL.

62. Dan Kiley, telephone interview by author, April 8, 1988; and Dan Kiley, "Step Lightly on This Earth," *Inland Architect* 27 (March–April 1983): 58–65.
63. "May we not look forward to anti-gravity belts on which we may push buttons that will permit us to float up from the ground, out of the window [or] from roof tops and pass in any direction we may wish to go." WHM autobiography, 150–51.
64. George Manning interview.
65. The Warren H. Manning Papers at Iowa State University contain material related to Manning's work on the National Plan, speeches, articles, reports, client lists, drawings and plans from more than fifty of Manning's projects, glass lantern slides, and photographs.
66. "Warren H. Manning, Landscape Designer: A Tribute to a Pioneer in a New Profession," *Landscape Architecture* 28 (April 1938): 148–49.
67. J. Horace McFarland to Egbert Hans, July 19, 1939, MCL.
68. A. D. Taylor to Harold Manning, February 5, 1938, MCL.
69. Fletcher Steele to Harold Manning, March 9, 1938, MCL.
70. WHM autobiography, 227.

BIRMINGHAM DISTRICT PLAN

Birmingham, Ala.

Project no. 1057

1. "Notes and Events," *National Municipal Review* 4 (July 1915): 497 (quotation); "The Birmingham District Plan: Report of Warren H. Manning to the City Commission," December 1916, Birmingham Historical Society (a copy of the original in MPI); *Warren H. Manning's City Plan of Birmingham* (Birmingham, Ala.: Published by subscription, 1919).
2. *Warren H. Manning's City Plan of Birmingham,* 4.
3. Ibid., 31, 42.
4. WHM autobiography, 114.
5. During this time Manning also created several designs for Robert Jemison Jr.'s new "homeplace," Spring Lake Farms, in the Huffman section of Birmingham. See Philip A. Morris and Marjorie Longenecker White, eds., *Designs on Birmingham: A Landscape History of a Southern City and Its Suburbs* (Birmingham, Ala.: Birmingham Historical Society, 1989), 25–26.

MOUNTAIN BROOK ESTATES

Mountain Brook, Ala.

Project no. 1538

1. Egbert Hans, "The Naturalistic Development of Mountain Brook Estates," *American Landscape Architect* 2 (January 1930): 10–18. The final version of Manning's "General Plan" for Mountain Brook, dated March 11, 1929, is held by the Department of Archives and Manuscripts, Birmingham Public Library, in the Robert Jemison Jr. Papers.
2. Planning team: WHM to Robert Jemison Jr., August 6, 1928, Jemison Papers. The names of other professionals who worked on the planning for Mountain Brook appear in letters, financial reports, and other records in the Jemison Papers, including daily reports by Carl Lutender. See also the booklet *Mountain Brook Country Club* and correspondence among the professional consultants during design and construction, in the same collection.
3. The promotional brochure "Mountain Brook Estates" (Jemison Papers) describes how, in the grand tradition of country estates, the style of each house would fit the topography. Accordingly, the Jemison firm designed a distinctive model home for each section of the development: a Mount Vernon replica for the Mountain Brook section; an all-electric home for Canterbury Road; an English baronial home for Dell Road; and a German stone house for the Southwood Road area. See Julius Linn Jr., Katherine Tipton, and Marjorie White, eds., *The Jemison Magazine: Birmingham and Mountain Brook, 1926–1930* (Birmingham, Ala.: Birmingham Historical Society, 2012).

WARREN TOWN PLAN

Warren, Ariz.

Project no. 670

1. Miners and investors from Michigan and Minnesota formed the Calumet & Arizona Mining Company in 1901. They bought claims in the area known as the War-

ren District, named after the early prospector George Warren. Lynn Bjorkman, "Warren, Arizona: 'The City Beautiful' and 'An Ideal City in the West,'" *Mining History Journal* (Mining History Association, Sedalia, Colo.) 6 (1999): 52–62.

2. The *Bisbee Daily Review* published many articles on the progress of the Warren town site. The town's radial layout and broad boulevards prompted comparisons to the design of Washington, D.C. Undated articles from *Bisbee Daily Review,* Bisbee Mining and Historical Museum, Bisbee, Ariz.
3. An article by Huger Elliott in the *Architectural Review* and Manning's autobiography describe the central park as the dominant feature of the design, as the park forms an axis with the gap in the southern end of the valley. Manning notes the "visual terminus" of the mountains beyond; Elliott refers to the aqueduct as a "suitable city gate." WHM autobiography, 121; Huger Elliott, "An Ideal City in the West," *Architectural Review* 15 (September 1908): 137–42, quotation on 141.
4. WHM autobiography, 121; Elliot, "An Ideal City in the West," 138. Manning notes that company representatives Van Dyke, Hoveland, and Smith requested Spanish Colonial and Pueblo architecture and the use of these specific desert plants. Elliott describes the use of plant materials in the park for an effect of aerial perspective, with darker green plants at the lower end paling to gray-green foliage at the top of the park. He notes the beauty of the local flora, and the plan to have hedging, "greenswards," and accents using the native plants (141). The irrigation system is described in Bob Ring and Al Ring, "Warren, Arizona—The City Beautiful" (paper presented at the Arizona History Convention, Pinetop, Ariz., April 2001), 6, available online at www.ringbrothers history.com.
5. Manning's 1911 commission to design the lower half of Vista Park (project no. 911) was completed in July of that year. Woodward Architectural Group, "Warren: The City Beautiful, Vol. 1: Historic Building Survey and Historical Overview of the Warren Townsite, Bisbee, Arizona" (prepared for City of Bisbee, Planning and Community Development, September 1993), 30.
6. Ibid., 31–32. Phelps Dodge incorporated new ideas in community planning in the Third Addition: houses were built in groups to keep construction costs down, and prospective residents could apply for an affordable loan and choose from standardized designs; custom designs were subject to approval.
7. Ibid., 30.

ALFRED A. POPE ESTATE (HILL-STEAD)
Farmington, Conn.
Project no. 128

1. *Farmington Valley (Conn.) Herald & Journal,* August 27, 1898, quoted in "Hill-Stead Museum: Historic Landscape Report," prepared by Allyson Hayward, Landscape Historian (Reed Hilderbrand Associates Inc. Landscape Architecture, July 2002), 11, Hill-Stead Museum Archives, Farmington, Conn. (HSMA).
2. Theodate Pope's diary entry of February 13, 1889, discusses the Cleveland-area farm she and her father had been thinking of building. Several diary entries in 1889–90 note Theodate drawing "plans for the farm house." By 1898 the project has shifted to Farmington, and several letters paint a picture of Theodate leading this project and her father offering advice while traveling in Europe. Alfred Pope to Theodate Pope, letters 535, 540, 546; and Theodate Pope to William Rutherford Mead at McKim, Mead & White, letter 2193, HSMA.
3. Henry James, "New England: An Autumn Impression," in *The American Scene* (New York: Horizon Press, 1967), 45; originally published as "New England: An Autumn Impression – II," *North American Review* 180 (May 1905): 641–60.
4. There is extensive correspondence in the Hill-Stead Museum Archives, copied from originals in the McKim, Mead & White papers at the New-York Historical Society, between Theodate Pope and Egerton Swartwout.
5. Alfred Pope to Theodate Pope, September 11, 1898, letter 540, HSMA.
6. Hayward, "Hill-Stead Museum," 19.
7. Hill-Stead Museum Archives contains a set of ten professional-quality 8x10 photographs of the wild garden, but there is no record of the photographer's name or the date.
8. Pope collaborated with Farrand at the Westover School in Middlebury in 1912, and again in 1919. Paula Dietz, "The Sunken Garden at Hill-Stead," *Hartford Monthly,* May 1989, 54–59. Because it was commissioned under Theodate's married name, Farrand's plan likely was created between 1916 and 1920; Hayward, "Hill-Stead Museum," 19.

JOHN H. WHITTEMORE ESTATE (TRANQUILLITY FARM)
Middlebury, Conn.
Project no. 119

1. I am indebted to Dr. and Mrs. Scott Peterson, Thyrza

Whittemore, C. Michael Jacobi, and Robert L. Rafford for sharing information about the history of the property.

2. These included Middlebury School and Common (1896), Naugatuck High School (1900), Naugatuck Rail Station (1907), Westover School (1909), Naugatuck Savings Bank (1910), and Naugatuck Riverbank Improvement (1913). Manning also listed the two Whittemore children, Harris and Gertrude, as clients; Harris's job is dated 1898 and Gertrude's 1927.
3. J. H. Whittemore to Charles Eliot, July 11, 1893. This and all letters quoted are in the Whittemore family papers, Naugatuck, Conn.
4. Other buildings dating from the first phase of development include the farmer's cottage where Whittemore and his wife stayed during construction (also designed by McKim, Mead & White), a creamery, a barn, and a large carriage house north of the house.
5. John C. Olmsted, for example, seems to have advised on grade changes in the "long garden." J. C. Olmsted to J. H. Whittemore, August 28, 1895.
6. J. H. Whittemore to WHM, September 2, 1896. Theodate Pope also commissioned Manning for landscape work at Hill-Stead in 1896 and 1898.
7. Local residents estimate that the estate at its largest comprised nine hundred acres. Whittemore also acquired land across Lake Quassapaug to protect his view.
8. For example: "Am afraid you are going into more comprehensive plans than I intended. I have already expended so much for landscape work and have the grading and road-making so far advanced on the lake side of the main road that I do not care to make any addition or expensive changes on those tracts." J. H. Whittemore to WHM, September 19, 1896.
9. WHM, "Tranquillity Farm, Planting Instructions," September 24, 1896, Whittemore family papers.
10. This sequence of development is based on information in "John Howard Whittemore, A Memorial," privately printed brochure, n.d., Whittemore family papers. Manning wrote a section of the text.
11. Gertrude Whittemore commissioned Ellen Shipman to redesign the plantings in the formal gardens in the early 1920s.
12. The collection included hundreds of museum-quality works; the best known was Whistler's *Symphony in White, No. 1: The White Girl,* acquired the same year that Manning took charge of the landscape design and now in the National Gallery of Art. For more on the collection, see Ann Y. Smith, *Hidden in Plain Sight: The Whittemore Collection and the French Impressionists* (Waterbury, Conn.: Garnet Hill Publishing Company and Mattatuck Historical Society, 2009).
13. Manning listed one new owner, Charles H. Upson, as a client in 1930.
14. For more on the disposition of the house, see Liz Halloran, "Whittemores, Historic Trust Debate Future of Cottage," *Waterbury (Conn.) Republican,* December 9, 1984.
15. The National Register of Historic Places nomination form for Tranquillity Farm, prepared by Alison Gilchrist, 1982 (ref. no. 91002056), chronicles Whittemore's interest in forestry as well as agriculture. Profits from the sale of wood and farm produce (primarily chickens, eggs, and dairy products) helped support the farm operation.

ATHENS CITY PLAN

Athens, Ga.

Project no. 1428

1. "Athenians Will Attend Cornelia Meeting Aug. 22," *Athens (Ga.) Banner-Herald,* August 14, 1923; "Famous Landscape Gardener Speaker Here Monday P.M." *Athens Banner-Herald,* August 28, 1923.
2. "Famous Landscape Gardener Speaker Here Monday P.M."
3. "A Botanical Garden," *Athens Banner-Herald,* June 1, 1924.
4. Chas. E. Martin, "Beautiful Flowers and Natural Drainage of Athens Make City Distinctive One Says Manning," *Athens Banner-Herald,* August 24, 1924.
5. "City Plans Are Completed; On Display." *Athens Banner-Herald,* August 8, 1926. It is unclear whether any efforts were made to pursue this idea.
6. Warren H. Manning Offices, Inc., "A City Plan Study for Athens, Georgia," July 19, 1925, 6, Hargrett Rare Book and Manuscript Library, University of Georgia Libraries.
7. Ibid., 4, 9.
8. Ibid., 6.
9. Ibid., 4.
10. "A Legacy in Green," *Athens Banner-Herald,* June 10, 2005, http://onlineathens.com.

JEPTHA H. WADE ESTATE (MILL POND PLANTATION)

Thomasville, Ga.

Project no. 602

1. "Third Handsomest Place in the Entire South Is House of J. H. Wade, at Thomasville, Georgia," *Atlanta Constitution,* April 23, 1905.

2. "Hubbell & Benes" in *The Encyclopedia of Cleveland History,* ed. David D. Van Tassel and John J. Grabowski (Bloomington: Indiana University Press in association with Case Western Reserve University and the Western Reserve Historical Society, 1996); "Third Handsomest Place."
3. National Register of Historic Places nomination form, Millpond Plantation, prepared by Martha F. Norwood, 1976 (ref. no. 76000651).
4. "Survey of Mill Pond Plantation, Estate of J. H. Wade, Esq., Thomas County, Thomasville, Ga., October 12, 1904, no. 602-20," MPI.
5. Albert G. Way, *Conserving Southern Longleaf: Herbert Stoddard and the Rise of Ecological Land Management* (Athens: University of Georgia Press, 2011), 52–54, 93–95.
6. "Plan of Open Court, Estate of J. H. Wade," October 24, 1905, no. 602-22, MPI.
7. "Plan for Arrangement and Planting, Estate of J. H. Wade," September 21, 1904, no. 602-10, MPI.
8. Ibid.
9. Lorraine Meeks Cooney and Hattie Rainwater, eds., *Garden History of Georgia, 1733–1933* (Atlanta: Peachtree Garden Club, 1933), 401; "Plan for Arrangement and Planting."
10. National Register of Historic Places nomination form; Cooney and Rainwater, *Garden History of Georgia,* 401–3.

STANLEY FIELD AND ALBERT A. SPRAGUE II ESTATES

Lake Bluff, Ill.

Project no. 898

1. These were the Finley Barrell estate (no. 919) in Lake Forest and the Henry S. Bunting estate (no. 959), in Lake Bluff. WHM client list.
2. Sprague's wife, Frances, was Stanley Field's cousin. Susan S. Benjamin, Julie McKeon, and A. J. Chalom, "Village of Lake Bluff, Illinois: A Summary and Historic Resource Survey of the Estate Areas" (Lake Bluff, Ill.: Historic Preservation Committee, 2008; prepared by Benjamin Historic Certifications), 28. Sprague also served on the boards of prominent Chicago institutions, including the Field Museum of Natural History (built by Marshall Field & Company). Stanley Field oversaw the museum's construction. "Stanley Field, 89, Chicago Leader; Philanthropist, Member of Mercantile Family, Dies," *New York Times,* October 29, 1964.
3. D. H. Burnham & Company had designed several buildings for Marshall Field & Company. When Daniel H. Burnham, the firm's founding principal, died in 1912, William Peirce Anderson succeeded him on the Field estate. Kim Coventry, Daniel Meyer, and Arthur H. Miller, *Classic Country Estates of Lake Forest: Architecture and Landscape Design, 1856–1940* (New York: Norton, 2003), 199–200.
4. An early Manning drawing for the Field estate, "Preliminary Study for Arrangement, No. 898-41," is dated August 4, 1911 (MPI). Notes on archival photographs indicate that H. L. Flint of Manning's office was on the site from May through November 1913; series 5, box 50, folder 5, MPI. For unknown reasons, extant plans and photographs of Field's estate far outnumber those of Sprague's.
5. Coventry, Meyer, and Miller, *Classic Country Estates of Lake Forest,* 199.
6. An early drawing suggests that Manning may have determined the building's location himself or with the architect: "Plan Showing Location of Residence as Determined by Mr. Manning, Dec. 3, 1911 and as Staked on the Ground Dec. 5, 1911," January 18, 1912, no. 898-66, MPI.
7. Coventry, Meyer, and Miller, *Classic Country Estates of Lake Forest,* 200; notes on photograph by H. L. Flint (Manning associate), September 1913, series 5, box 101, folder 70, MPI.
8. Coventry, Meyer, and Miller, *Classic Country Estates of Lake Forest,* 199–200.
9. Julie McKeon, site survey, job nos. 898-1 and 898-2, Warren H. Manning Research Project, LALH.
10. Ibid.

FINLEY BARRELL ESTATE

Lake Forest, Ill.

Project no. 919

1. See Kim Coventry, Daniel Meyer, and Arthur H. Miller, *Classic Country Estates of Lake Forest: Architecture and Landscape Design, 1856–1940* (New York: Norton, 2003), 164–69.
2. Nichols later replanted the Barrells' formal garden, according to an undated photo postcard from the Rose Standish Nichols postcard collection, Nichols House Museum, Boston.
3. See M. H. Baillie Scott, *Houses and Gardens: Arts and Crafts Interiors* (1906; repr., Woodbridge, Suffolk: Antique Collectors' Club, 1995).
4. The tall pines along the ravine may remain from a previous 1860s development; an inset for Lake Forest on an 1861 Lake County, Illinois, map shows a house here, for the Shumways. The view to the ravine from the porch of

the Barrell house resembles the north vista at Wyldwood, the Lake Forest estate Manning designed for Clyde Carr.

5. Samuel Howe, "The Home of Mr. Finley Barrell, Lake Forest, Ill.," in *American Country Houses of To-day* (New York: Architectural Book Publishing Company, 1915), 227–29.

LAKE FOREST UNIVERSITY (LAKE FOREST COLLEGE)

Lake Forest, Ill.

Project no. 183

1. Michael H. Ebner, *Creating Chicago's North Shore: A Suburban History* (Chicago: University of Chicago Press, 1988), 243–46; Arthur H. Miller, "Hotchkiss, Almerin," in *Shaping the American Landscape: New Profiles from the Pioneers of American Landscape Design Project,* ed. Charles A. Birnbaum and Stephanie S. Foell (Charlottesville: University of Virginia Press, 2009), 144–46.
2. Franz Schulze, Rosemary Cowler, and Arthur H. Miller, *30 Miles North: A History of Lake Forest College, Its Town, and Its City of Chicago* (Lake Forest, Ill.: The College, 2000), 16–17; Kim Coventry, Daniel Meyer, and Arthur H. Miller, *Classic Country Estates of Lake Forest: Architecture and Landscape Design, 1856–1940* (New York: Norton, 2003), 36–43; Arthur H. Miller, "Overviews: The Campus Planned," in *Lake Forest College: A Guide to the Campus,* ed. Christopher Reed and Arthur H. Miller (Lake Forest, Ill.: The College, 2007), 13–14.
3. Schulze, Cowler, and Miller, *30 Miles North,* 53–61.
4. WHM, "Lake Forest University, Lake Forest, Ill. / Report on the Plan of Grounds and on the Location of Buildings, accompanying a Study dated June 1, 1897," Archives and Special Collections, Lake Forest College.
5. College trustee Charles Dyer Norton, who chaired the 1909 Plan of Chicago, may have guided the choice of architects. Norton's wife, Katherine McKim, was a niece of the influential Beaux-Arts architect Charles McKim, of the renowned New York City firm McKim, Mead & White. Benjamin Wistar Morris, trained at the École des Beaux-Arts in Paris, was the first to envision a plan for a development around a performance space on a Rockefeller midtown property, later Rockefeller Center. See Daniel Okrent, *Great Fortune: The Epic of Rockefeller Center* (New York: Viking Penguin, 2003), 24.
6. Miller, "Overviews: The Campus Planned," 18. Francis Willard Puckey had worked in the Shepley, Rutan & Coolidge office in Boston, and he married Charles Rutan's daughter. He also had worked with Charles Coolidge on the University of Chicago campus.
7. Benjamin Goluboff, "The Campus as a Natural Site," in Reed and Miller, *Lake Forest College: A Guide to the Campus,* 68–74.

CYRUS H. MCCORMICK II ESTATE (WALDEN)

Lake Forest, Ill.

Project no. 107

1. Cyrus H. McCormick II was the son of Cyrus Hall McCormick, the developer of the horse-drawn agricultural reaper that revolutionized grain farming on the midwestern prairies. Cyrus II became president of McCormick Harvesting Machine Company, which merged with several other companies in 1902 to become the International Harvester Company. In addition to documentation in MCL and MPI, archival records related to Walden are held by the Wisconsin Historical Society in Madison, which maintains the McCormick company and family archives, and by Archives and Special Collections, Lake Forest College Library.
2. In his "History of Walden," Manning recalls Cyrus McCormick's explaining that in their "search for a home site" the family had lived in Highland Park for two years at the Price estate. "As there were woodlands here I was able to do some chopping, but as most of our friends were at Lake Forest, and as there came to be an opportunity to secure a shore frontage lot which we had been looking for, we decided to go there." See WHM, "History of Walden, Estate of Cyrus H. McCormick, Lake Forest, Illinois," typescript, 1933, 2, Archives and Special Collections, Lake Forest College Library. Highland Park was laid out by Horace W. S. Cleveland and William M. R. French in 1869. Blair Lodge, designed in 1881 by the Chicago architect William Le Baron Jenney, was the former estate of railroad magnate John Insley Blair.
3. WHM, "History of Walden," 3–7.
4. In the plant index in Manning's "History of Walden," he classified the plants by three types of steep bank conditions: the lake bluff facing east, the north (sunny) side of the ravine, and the south (shaded) side. His notations record the common and botanical names of each plant, the location of its planting, the source, quantity, season and year, and its condition in 1933.
5. According to Manning, the main hall of the house included "a unique closet equipped with axes, saws, red and white strips for marking trees, with stakes and twine in cones for laying down Walden's ways." WHM, "History of Walden," 13. The description of the evergreen vista is from Louisa Yeomans King, introduction to Har-

riet Hammond McCormick, *Landscape Art, Past and Present* (New York: Charles Scribner's Sons, 1923), xix.

6. In a 1936 letter Manning recalled collecting stones at Walden Pond: "At a later period I went with Mr. [Minot] Pratt to select a carload of flat boulders from the Thoreau region for a step stone walk at Walden. This walk was from the Ravello to the road loop. I think they have been moved to another location." The stones may have been used for the path Harriet McCormick designed in 1916. WHM to F. A. Steuert, May 26, 1936, box 3, folder 32, MPI.
7. Although Manning advised on the siting of the house, he had little, if anything, to do with the formal gardens later designed on that property.
8. WHM to F A Steuert, May 26, 1936.
9. "Mr. McCormick's knowledge that Thoreau and his friend Minot Pratt had introduced over fifty new plants into the Concord woods to enrich the flora, led him to accept a like introduction of many new trees, shrubs, and herbs on the Walden ravines and shore bluffs and bottom lands, in upland woods and about the edges of lawns and fields." WHM autobiography, 63. See also "Walden as an Arboretum Unit," in "History of Walden," 44–45.
10. Warren H. Manning Offices, Inc., "Walden, estate of Cyrus H. McCormick Esq., Lake Forest, Illinois, Generic Study of Woody Plants," 1925, revised with Roy O. Walker, 1928, Wisconsin Historical Society.
11. King, introduction to *Landscape Art,* xx.
12. The original plantings of the formal flower garden were altered by Louise Shelton in 1915 and then revised again in 1921 by Helen Bullard, who was working for Manning's office. A completely new version of the garden, designed by Ralph Griswold in 1931, also met with Manning's approval. See Robin Karson, *A Genius for Place: American Landscapes of the Country Place Era* (Amherst: University of Massachusetts Press in association with Library of American Landscape History, 2007), 35–36.
13. WHM, "History of Walden," 47–48.
14. Ibid., 48.

BANGOR CITY PLAN: THE BURNED DISTRICT

Bangor, Maine

Project nos. 866 and 900

1. WHM to Everett F. Rich, September 9, 1910, and Rich to WHM, September 10, 1910, both in "The office files of Warren H. Manning bought by the Bangor Public Library in 1938 from his estate," Bangor Public Library (BPL). Rich, the treasurer of Bangor Savings Bank, served as secretary of the library board.
2. WHM to Professor F. W. Chandler, Massachusetts Institute of Technology, September 16, 1910, BPL. Manning solicited Chandler's opinion on an "outline" (draft) of his report before submitting a final version to the library trustees. WHM, "Outline of Report on Bangor Public Library Site, and Its Relation to a Civic Centre," September 16, 1910; "Report on a Site for a Public Library on Harlow Street, Bangor, Maine," November 5, 1910; "Bangor City Plan: The Burned District," May 22, 1911; BPL.
3. WHM, "Outline of Report on Bangor Public Library Site," 2–3.
4. WHM, "Report on a Site for a Public Library on Harlow Street," 3; Arthur L. Norton (Manning associate) to WHM, November 8, 1910, BPL. The detail the trustees did not like was the road behind the library building, which Manning modified according to Chandler's suggestions.
5. WHM, "Outline of Report on Bangor Library Site," 3. Manning cut this detail from his final report, but in a subsequent article in *Landscape Architecture,* Fletcher Steele noted that among the plan's benefits, "the cost of hauling will be much reduced." Fletcher Steele, "An Emergency Report for Bangor, Maine," *Landscape Architecture* 2 (October 1911): 15.
6. WHM, "Report on a Site for a Public Library on Harlow Street," 3; Wayne E. Reilly, "Danger of Fire Haunted City of Bangor in 1910," *Bangor Daily News,* January 1, 2011.
7. F. W. Chandler to WHM, September 30, 1910, and WHM to Everett F. Rich, November 5, 1910, BPL.
8. Deborah Thompson, *Bangor, Maine, 1769–1914: An Architectural History* (Orono: University of Maine Press, 1988), 502.
9. Ibid.
10. Steele, "An Emergency Report for Bangor, Maine," 6, 13–14.
11. Ibid., 9, 12.
12. Ibid., 13–14.

IRA M. COBE ESTATE

Northport, Maine

Project no. 913

1. "The Pleasing Future of Hillside Farm," *Waldo County Herald,* September 12, 1912; "Work on Magnificent Summer Estate at Northport, Begun," unidentified newspaper, August 1, [1912], clipping file, Bayside Historical Preservation Society, Northport, Maine (BHPS).
2. WHM, "Map of Property/No. 913-17," December 16,

1911, and J. V. Monahan, Superintendent's expense report (Manning office form), week ending September 28, 1912, collection of Gerald and Dorothy Reid. WHM, "Map of Property, Survey of Existing Conditions," December 16, 1911, no. 913-74, Reid collection; and photographs by A. D. Taylor (Manning office), May 24 and June 25, 1912, series 5, box 101, folder 1, no. 70, Roads and Finished Drive, MPI. Between 1909 and 1911 Manning's office listed three estate projects in Camden, approximately ten miles from Northport. WHM client list.

3. "Pleasing Future of Hillside Farm." Initially, the Cobes chose another Chicago architectural firm, Spencer & Powers, to design the residence, but for unknown reasons this design was not executed. "An Interesting Description of a Beautiful Summer Residence to Be Built at Northport by Ira M. Cobe of Chicago," *Waldo County Herald,* April 8, 1909; "[word missing] Build Fine Cottage," February 11, 1909, unidentified newspaper, clipping file, Belfast Historical Society and Museum, Belfast, Maine (BHSM).
4. "Big Northport Mansion for Millionaire Cobe," unidentified newspaper, May 24, [1913], clipping file, BHSM.
5. In addition to photographs held by the Reids, the collection of the Maine Historical Preservation Society includes a number of photographs and postcards showing the estate, though most are undated.
6. Stephen Hamblin (Manning office), "Garden Book – Various Instructions re: Plants," looseleaf notebook organized by year, 1913–1927, Reid collection.
7. Property deeds beginning Book 402, p. 335 (Cobe estate to Pingree), Waldo County Registry of Deeds, Belfast, Maine.

ALBERT H. CHATFIELD ESTATE

Rockport, Maine

Project no. 297

1. With his cousin and business partner, Harry Fowler Woods, Albert H. Chatfield headed Chatfield & Woods, a supplier of paper products, rope, and twine founded by their respective fathers in Cincinnati. Margo Stever, *Looking East: William Howard Taft and the 1905 Mission to Asia—The Photographs of Harry Fowler Woods,* www.ohiohistory.org/taft. Maine deeds do not record the size of the initial Rockport property purchases, but secondary sources variously report 120 and 100 acres. Chatfield eventually accumulated about 250 acres, according to his great-grandson Frederick H. Chatfield Jr.
2. The towns separated in 1891. Mary Sullivan, "Camden–Rockport's First 200 Years," *Camden–Rockport Bicentennial Commemorative Book* (Camden, Maine: The Camden Herald Publishing Co., 1969), 5. The WHM client list incorrectly records the project location as Camden.
3. Manning's first extant letter to A. H. Chatfield suggests that they had already discussed the estate. WHM to Albert H. Chatfield, October 19, 1900; WHM to Chatfield, November 5 and 7, 1900, and December 22, 1900; and summary note by Elizabeth Chatfield Gilmore. Unless otherwise noted, all correspondence is from the collection of Elizabeth Chatfield Gilmore.
4. WHM to Chatfield, December 22, 1900, and summary note by Elizabeth Chatfield Gilmore. Manning mentioned the prospective golf clubhouse and its proximity to the course in the letter, but because the club built a new course and clubhouse on Beauchamp Point in 1901, the site in Manning's letter was likely near Ogier Hill, northeast of the Lily Pond, where the first, rudimentary golf course was laid out.
5. No sources have been located to account for the ten-year hiatus between site planning and landscape construction. (Manning's client list indicates that the project resumed in 1912, but correspondence in the collection of Elizabeth Chatfield Gilmore supports that it was 1911.) Correspondence also suggests that Manning was more personally involved in the initial design phase. Manning office records show that eighty-two plans of the Chatfield estate were available after the practice closed, and that the Chatfields paid the office to mail them. Frederick H. Chatfield Jr. has a few of these in his possession.
6. WHM to Chatfield, October 19, 1900.
7. Handwritten note on back of undated photograph of the Barrett farmhouse, and early twentieth-century photographs of the house, collection of Frederick H. Chatfield Jr.
8. WHM to Chatfield, October 29, 1900. A 1911 Manning sketch plan shows walks linking the rear terrace to a rectangular garden off the northeast corner. "Suggestion for Stepping Stone Walks" (sketch plan), February 8, 1911, no. 297-46-1. Undated photographs in the collection of Frederick H. Chatfield Jr. verify that a rectangular rose and perennial garden, enclosed by high hedges, was built there.
9. WHM to Chatfield, November 2, 1900.
10. WHM to Chatfield, October 19, 1900. Manning apparently intended to treat both the field near the Gilbert house and the one behind the Chatfields' as wild gardens.
11. Ibid. The intention of keeping goats was to emulate the grazed look of the neighboring Henry estate on Beauchamps Point, which Helen Chatfield admired. Note on

back of photograph of sheep grazing near shoreline, n.d., photograph 11-47/7, side 2, MPI.

12. WHM to Chatfield, December 5, 1900. Manning also proposed that the Chatfields engage Harrison to prepare an herbarium of existing flora on the estate. Harrison worked for Manning from 1898 to 1899 and went on to teach landscape architecture at Massachusetts Agricultural College, now University of Massachusetts Amherst.
13. WHM to Chatfield, February 26, 1902.
14. "Plan for Planting in the Wild," January 26, 1911, no. 297-45-3; and WHM to Chatfield, February 7, 1911. Frederick H. Chatfield Jr. estimates that twenty-four acres are associated with Aldermere Farm on this plan; the remainder, surrounding Kentmoor and the stable, looks approximately equal to that. The plan suggests that the areas close to the house were graded and planted with typical garden species of the period, as described in earlier letters. "Suggestion for Stepping Stone Walks," no. 297-46-1.
15. "Plan for Planting in the Wild," no. 297-45-3; WHM to Chatfield, February 7, 1911, and February 9, 1911 (planting notes). A. D. Taylor designed the bathhouse landscape. Expenditures report, A. D. Taylor to Chatfield, October 19–December 21, 1912; February 15, 1913.
16. Taylor photographed the property, but these images have not been found. A. D. Taylor to Helen H. Chatfield, December 7, 1912. The last extant letter from Taylor to either Chatfield is dated February 21, 1913. By then the estate work was complete, although Taylor was also working on the Megunticook Golf Club as a Manning associate. Expenditures report, Taylor to A. H. Chatfield, October 19–December 21, 1912; February 15, 1913.
17. JoAnn Hottois, "Albert Davis Taylor: His Impact on 20th Century American Landscape Architecture Combined with a Bibliographic Compilation to Serve as a Resource to Encourage Future Research on A. D. Taylor," vol. 1 (master's thesis, Ohio State University, 1991), 34, 64n23, citing WHM to A. H. Chatfield, March 15, 1914, Albert D. Taylor Collection (MSS 171), Ohio Historical Society, Columbus.

MEGUNTICOOK GOLF COURSE

Rockport, Maine

Project no. 980

1. A. D. Taylor (on Manning letterhead) to Albert H. Chatfield, "Survey at golf club," expense report, October 19–December 21, 1912; and Taylor to Chatfield, February 15, 1913; both in collection of Elizabeth Chatfield Gilmore.
2. Theresa Mattor and Lucie Teegarden, *Designing the Maine Landscape* (n.p.: Down East Books and the Maine Olmsted Alliance for Parks & Landscapes, 2009), 115.
3. WHM client list. Several of the Camden projects on this client list were actually located in Rockport. Megunticook Golf Club, *Advantages of Situation: A Guide to Camden, Maine,* real estate booklet, c. 1904, 39; undated reprint edition, c. 1915, 81, Camden Public Library, Camden, Maine.
4. Golf course designer Alexander Findlay expanded this early six-hole course to nine holes in 1899. Mary Saltonstall (editor of an unpublished club history), e-mail to author, July 5, 2013. WHM to Chatfield, December 22, 1900, collection of Elizabeth Chatfield Gilmore.
5. Mattor and Teegarden, *Designing the Maine Landscape,* 115–16, 209n25; National Register of Historic Places nomination form, Megunticook Golf Club, prepared by Elizabeth Igleheart and Kirk Mohney, 1993 (ref. no. 93000636). Brigham also designed the Chatfields' summer residence. WHM to Chatfield, October 19, 1900, collection of Elizabeth Chatfield Gilmore.
6. Information on the Chatfield land donation was provided by Frederick H. Chatfield Jr. Property maps: "Fales Survey Map," c. 1768, and "First Division of Camden," c. 1770, collection of Camden–Rockport Historical Society, Camden Public Library.
7. JoAnn Hottois, "Albert Davis Taylor: His Impact on 20th Century American Landscape Architecture Combined with a Bibliographic Compilation to Serve as a Resource to Encourage Future Research on A. D. Taylor," vol. 1 (master's thesis, Ohio State University, 1991), 34, 64n23, citing WHM to A. H. Chatfield, March 15, 1914, Albert D. Taylor Collection (MSS 171), Ohio Historical Society, Columbus. On Taylor's topographic survey, see note 1.
8. "Compiled from survey by W. H. Manning with additional information by Albert D. Taylor, Landscape Architect, Cleveland-Boston" (plan), March 24, 1916, no. 44-7.

MASSACHUSETTS AGRICULTURAL COLLEGE (UNIVERSITY OF MASSACHUSETTS)

Amherst, Mass.

Project no. 752

1. WHM, "Report upon a Plan for the Massachusetts Agricultural College," June 24, 1911, 1, Special Collections and University Archives, University of Massachusetts Amherst (UM).
2. WHM client list.
3. Frank A. Waugh, "Development of the Grounds of the Massachusetts Agricultural College" (unpublished report, 1920), 9, UM; WHM autobiography, 244.

4. "Estate of the Mass. Agricultural College, Amherst. 1870," available at www.library.umass.edu/spcoll/archives/map_mac-1870.jpg.
5. Laura Wood Roper, *F.L.O.: A Biography of Frederick Law Olmsted* (Baltimore: Johns Hopkins University Press, 1983), 309–10.
6. Ibid.
7. Waugh, "Development of the Grounds," 3–4; Frederick Law Olmsted, *A Few Things to Be Thought of before Proceeding to Plan Buildings for the National Agricultural Colleges* (New York: The American News Co., 1866).
8. Waugh, "Development of the Grounds," 6–7.
9. Waugh, "Commission on Buildings and Grounds Meeting Minutes," May 19, 1908, UM; Waugh, "Development of the Grounds," 8–9.
10. WHM autobiography, 147; WHM, "President Butterfield's Letter to W. H. Manning dated June 11, 1908 – A Summary," n.d., UM.
11. Waugh, "Commission on Buildings and Grounds Meeting Minutes."
12. WHM, "Report upon a Plan," 2–5.
13. WHM autobiography, 147.
14. WHM, "Report upon a Plan," 2–7.
15. The buildings are French Hall and Fernald Hall. Waugh, "Development of the Grounds," 11.
16. WHM, "Study for Relocation of Infirmary," Massachusetts Agricultural College, December 20, 1913, UM.
17. University of Massachusetts Campus Planning Department, "Campus Physical Master Plan Update," 2007, 5–7. This document and the master plan mentioned in the next note are available at http://scholarworks.umass.edu/cp_masterplans.
18. UMass Amherst Campus Planning, Wilson Architects, Ayers Saint Gross Architects and Planners, "UMass Amherst Campus Master Plan," 2012.

CLEMENT S. HOUGHTON ESTATE
Chestnut Hill, Mass.
Project no. 579

1. Despite the coincidence of their surnames, no genealogical evidence links C. S. Houghton to A. A and A. B. Houghton, whose estate in South Dartmouth, Massachusetts, Manning also designed. (A separate essay appears in this book.) C. S. Houghton was the son of William Stevens Houghton from Boxborough, Massachusetts. By another coincidence, both Houghton families chose Chapman & Frazer and Warren Manning to design and develop their properties.
2. Judith Leet, "The Houghton Garden," in *The Gardens of Chestnut Hill* (Brookline, Mass.: Chestnut Hill Association, 1992), 8.
3. Chestnut Hill Garden Club, "Houghton Garden in the Webster Conservation Area, Chestnut Hill, Massachusetts" (Newton, Mass.: Chestnut Hill Garden Club, rev. May 1997), 4–5.
4. See Robin Karson, "Warren H. Manning: Pragmatist in the Wild Garden," in *Nature and Ideology: Natural Garden Design in the Twentieth Century,* ed. Joachim Wolschke-Bulmahn (Washington, D.C.: Dumbarton Oaks Research Library and Collection, 1997), 115. Although the Houghtons' wild garden resembles others Manning designed for private estates, research has not yet determined Manning's role, if any, in designing this one. WHM, "The Nature Garden," undated typescript, 1–3, MCL.
5. The shrub species were probably planted to complement the existing lowland forest plants. To bring out "the beauty of existing conditions" at the heart of the wild garden concept, Manning typically removed some existing plants and complemented the remaining trees and shrubs with flowering natives such as rhododendron, dogwood, and redbud. WHM, "The Nature Garden," 3.
6. Alison Bassett, "Houghton Garden Narrative, Prepared for Newton Planning Department Files," unpublished typescript, January 21, 2007, 1 (courtesy Alison Bassett); Chestnut Hill Garden Club, "Houghton Garden in the Webster Conservation Area," 4–5. In 1934 Martha Houghton became a founding member of the American Rock Garden Society.
7. Leslie Perrin Wilson, "Celebrating the Landscape Photography of Herbert Wendell Gleason," www.concordma.com/magazine/autumn02. A retired Congregational minister, Herbert Wendell Gleason returned to his native New England in 1899, where he photographed the iconic landscapes of Concord, Massachusetts, that Henry David Thoreau had described in his writings—a ritual he continued to perform for thirty-eight years until his death.
8. Leet, "The Houghton Garden," 7.
9. During the time when Martha Houghton sought to import plants from abroad, Steele vouched for her in a letter to the U.S. Department of Agriculture's quarantine officer for foreign plants. Fletcher Steele to R. S. Beattie, Pathologist in Charge, Foreign Plant Quarantine, U.S. Department of Agriculture, March 19, 1924, MCL.
10. Bassett, "Houghton Garden Narrative," 1–2.
11. Quoted in Chestnut Hill Garden Club, "Houghton Garden in the Webster Conservation Area," 5.

12. Leet, "The Houghton Garden," 10.
13. Bassett, "Houghton Garden Narrative," 1; Chestnut Hill Garden Club, "Houghton Garden in the Webster Conservation Area," 4–5.
14. "Houghton Garden Narrative," 1. The sources of funding for the 1999 rehabilitation were the Massachusetts Preservation Fund, Massachusetts Department of Environmental Management, the Chestnut Hill Garden Club, and Newton's Community Preservation Act.
15. After Manning died, in 1938, his son and office manager, W. Harold Manning, wrote to the firm's clients, offering to return copies of the drawings and plans for their properties for a modest copying and postage fee. The Manning firm's undated ledger for these transactions records that Houghton eventually paid $15, which suggests that at least some of the plans were returned to them at a later date. Manning office ledger, MCL.
16. Leet, "The Houghton Garden," 5–8.
17. Michele Hanss, Chestnut Hill Garden Club volunteer researcher, conversation with Jane Roy Brown, Newton, Mass., November 2011, LALH.

BANCROFT PARK
Hopedale, Mass.
Project no. 286

1. WHM client list.
2. John Garner, *The Model Company Town: Urban Design through Private Enterprise in Nineteenth-Century New England* (New York: Oxford University Press, 1992), 181.
3. For an overview of the garden city movement see Peter Hall, *Cities of Tomorrow: An Intellectual History of Urban Planning and Design since 1880,* 4th ed. (Oxford: Wiley-Blackwell, 2014), chap. 4.
4. Garner, *The Model Company Town.* The initial stage of construction at Bancroft Park is visible in Bert Poole Co.'s *Hopedale, Mass.,* 1899, available at http://old-maps.com.
5. Garner, *The Model Company Town.*
6. The layout of roads, alleyways, garages and houses is visible in Worcester County's *Map of Part of the Town of Hopedale,* 1898 (available at www.hope1842.com), as well as in the Sanborn Insurance Company map of Hopedale, 1920 (available in the Sanborn Maps collection at www.loc.gov). The archives of the American Textile History Museum in Worcester, Mass., include photographs of Bancroft Park in 1903.
7. Edward K. Spann, *Hopedale: From Commune to Company Town* (Columbus: Ohio State University Press, 1992), 172.
8. Garner, *The Model Company Town,* 161.

FRANK DUTCHER ESTATE (OAKLEDGE)
Hopedale, Mass.
Project no. 11

1. Lucy Lawliss, Caroline Loughlin, and Lauren Meier, eds., *The Master List of Design Projects of the Olmsted Firm, 1857–1979* (Washington, D.C.: National Association for Olmsted Parks and National Park Service, 2008), job nos. 01205 and 10150; *Fourth Annual Report of the School Committee of the Town of Hopedale, Massachusetts* (1889), 5, collection of Bancroft Memorial Library, Hopedale, Mass.; WHM client list.
2. Edward K. Spann, *Hopedale: From Commune to Company Town, 1840–1920* (Columbus: Ohio State University Press, 1992), 24, 132–34.
3. WHM autobiography, 107.
4. Ibid., 109.

GENERAL DRAPER HIGH SCHOOL
Hopedale, Mass.
Project no. 1549

1. General Draper High School was Manning's last project in Hopedale, where he had worked on over two dozen commissions. WHM autobiography, 108; WHM client list.
2. John Garner, *The Model Company Town: Urban Design through Private Enterprise in Nineteenth-Century New England* (New York: Oxford University Press, 1992), 141; Edward K. Spann, *Hopedale: From Commune to Company Town* (Columbus: Ohio State University Press, 1992), 185.
3. *Forty-Second Annual Report of the School Committee of the Town of Hopedale, Massachusetts,* 1927, collection of Bancroft Memorial Library, Hopedale, Mass.
4. Garner, *The Model Company Town,* 141.
5. WHM autobiography, 109.
6. The rear playing fields are visible in 1927 illustrations by J. C. Halden in the *Forty-Second Annual Report;* O. H. Bailey & Co.'s *View of Hopedale, Massachusetts* from 1888 (available at www.hope1842.com) shows a woodland along the east perimeter of the property.
7. Rachael Day, "History of the Hopedale Schools," 1954, collection of Bancroft Memorial Library, transcript available at www.hope1842.com.

HOPEDALE PARKLANDS
Hopedale, Mass.
Project no. 67

1. *First Annual Report of the Park Commissioners of the Town of Hopedale,* 1899, 44–45, collection of Bancroft Memorial Library, Hopedale, Mass. (BML).

2. WHM client list.
3. *First Annual Report of the Park Commissioners.*
4. Edward K. Spann, *Hopedale: From Commune to Company Town, 1840–1920* (Columbus: Ohio State University Press, 1992), 171–72.
5. *First Annual Report of the Park Commissioners.*
6. *Hopedale Parks Commission Report,* 1913, and *Second Annual Report of the Park Commissioners,* 1900, BML.
7. *Second Annual Report of the Park Commissioners.*
8. "A Capsule History of the Hopedale Park Commission," 2004, compiled by Richard Espanet from Parks Commission reports, available at www.hopedale-ma.gov; John Garner, *The Model Company Town: Urban Design through Private Enterprise in Nineteenth-Century New England* (New York: Oxford University Press, 1992), 245.
9. Espanet, "Capsule History of the Hopedale Park Commission," lists the disputed parcel as the Town Park, but the *Second Annual Report of the Park Commissioners* specifies that the parcel was west of Dutcher Street or along the pond.
10. Garner, *The Model Company Town,* 190.
11. Espanet, "Capsule History of the Hopedale Park Commission."
12. WHM, archival photos, c. 1903, MPI. Buildings are visible in the map *Upton Town, Hopedale Town,* in L. J. Richards, *Worcester County Atlas,* 1898, available at www.historicmapworks.com.
13. Over the next two years, the chestnut blight killed twelve thousand American chestnut trees in the Parklands, and the town planted scotch, red, and white pine as replacements. See Espanet, "Capsule History of the Hopedale Park Commission"; WHM autobiography, 108.
14. Gordon Hopper, "The Grafton & Upton Railroad," www.hope1842.com; "Hopedale Reconnaissance Report" (June 2007), prepared for the Massachusetts Heritage Landscape Inventory Program (available at www.mass.gov/eea), mentions the abandonment of the streetcars and the railroad; bus service is noted in Espanet, "Hopedale Parks History."
15. Espanet, "Hopedale Parks History."

GALEN L. STONE ESTATE (GREAT HILL)

Marion, Mass.

Project no. 812

1. Egbert Hans, ASLA, "A Seashore Summer Estate," *American Landscape Architect* 3 (October 1930): 26–29. Manning's office recorded Stone for two projects, both private estates in Marion: no. 254, 1899–1900; and no. 812, 1909–1911 (WHM client list). The first project, however, may have been the Stones' Brookline residence.
2. Fletcher Steele to Mary Steele, August 1, [1909], Fletcher Steele Papers, Rochester Historical Society, Rochester, N.Y. (RHS)
3. Hans, "A Seashore Summer Estate"; Steele to Mary Steele, August 1, [1909].
4. Steele to Mary Steele, September 4, 1909, RHS.
5. The rhododendron and azalea vistas appear on the only surviving Manning plan out of ninety-five created for the project (see illustration); this plan also shows the Azalea Vista meeting the southeast end of the Rhododendron Vista at an approximate 30-degree angle. Today they converge at an angle of approximately 85 degrees.
6. Hans, "A Seashore Summer Estate."
7. Galen L. Stone II, interview by author, July 14, 2010.
8. Ibid.; and Catherine Stone, interview by author, June 1, 2009.
9. Steele wrote that the senior Stone planned "extensive pleasure drives for the public," adding that "like other great landed men of the country, [Stone realized that] if they keep all the best park sites for themselves, the state will forcibly take it away from them." Steele to Mary Steele, August 1, [1909].

BILLERICA GARDEN SUBURB

North Billerica, Mass.

Project no. 1029

1. Manning writes in his autobiography that he was associated with the project until 1918 (101). He may have limited his direct involvement because he had many clients among the business leaders in Billerica and wanted to avoid the appearance of a conflict of interest.
2. When plans for the garden suburb were under way, Comey was on the board of the Massachusetts Housing Cooperative, a state agency that helped to promote affordable housing by strategically advising developers. See Margaret Crawford, *Building the Workingman's Paradise: The Design of American Company Towns* (London: Verso, 1995), 76; and *Annual Report of the Homestead Commission* (Boston: Wright & Potter, 1919), 8.
3. Arthur C. Comey, "Billerica Garden Suburb," *Landscape Architecture* 4 (July 1914): 147.
4. Patricia Henry, "North Billerica Garden Suburb: Affordable Housing for Workers in 1914" (master's thesis, University of Rhode Island, 2004), 32–41.
5. Ibid., 21–44.
6. American Planning Association, Massachusetts and Rhode Island chapters, "Massachusetts Suburb Named National Planning Landmark," *New England Planning,* March 2005, 1.

MANNING MANSE
North Billerica, Mass.
Project no. 319

1. *The Manning Manse Messenger* no. 1 (June 1925): 3.
2. William Henry Manning, *The Genealogical and Biographical History of the Manning Families of New England and Descendants* (Salem, Mass.: The Salem Press Co., 1902), 31, 121; Henry Allen Hazen, *History of Billerica, Massachusetts* (Boston: A. Williams & Co., 1882), 27.
3. Hazen, *History of Billerica,* 213; Manning, *Genealogical and Biographical History,* 64.
4. Hazen, *History of Billerica,* 275.
5. Lucinda Manning's will directed that the trustees rent the property and use the income to further religious education in the area. Manning, *Genealogical and Biographical History,* 65.
6. Ibid., 71–72; National Register of Historic Places nomination form, Manning Manse, prepared by Wendy Frontiero with Richard D. Manning, 1982 (ref. no. 82001912).
7. The kitchen garden and the evergreens are visible in Manning's photos of the Manse from April 1900 in the Manning Family Association Collection, University of Massachusetts Lowell (MFAC); WHM, with pictures by Herbert E. Angell, "The Framing of Home Pictures," *Country Life in America* 14 (May 1908): 52–53.
8. Myra Manning Koenig, "The Story of Manning Manse," MFAC. William Henry Manning also was using the name Manning Manse by 1902, when he published his history of the family.
9. Manning, *Genealogical and Biographical History,* 76–77.
10. WHM autobiography, 54.
11. WHM, "Manning Manse, North Billerica Mass, Juniper Cottage," January 1, 1907, MPI. These plantings are visible in photos taken by Manning around 1907, MFAC.
12. WHM, "The Framing of Home Pictures," 52–53.
13. Manning, *Genealogical and Biographical History,* 66.
14. WHM to Nettie Manning, April 7, 1914, and June 30, 1915, MCL.
15. Warren H. Manning Offices, Inc., Corporate Income and Profits Tax Return for Calendar Year 1918, June 11, 1919, MCL; WHM autobiography, 2.
16. WHM autobiography, 48; Egbert Hans also mentions this practice in "The Life and Works of Warren H. Manning from His Incompleted Autobiography," undated, 134A–135, MCL.
17. Egbert Hans, "Manning Manse: An Old Homestead at North Billerica, Massachusetts," *House Beautiful,* July 1921, 26–29, 66.
18. National Register nomination form. Photos taken in June 1930 show the addition in process; MFAC.
19. WHM to Nettie Manning, June 20, 1920, MCL; WHM autobiography, 56.
20. George Manning, interview by Jane Roy Brown, Topsham, Maine, December 2, 2005, LALH.
21. National Register nomination form; George Manning interview.
22. Remaining Manning-era trees, including several white pines over two feet in diameter, were located and photographed by the author during a visit to the Manse on June 16, 2013. Manning wrote an article about the unusual horticultural opportunities found in this bog and a swamp elsewhere on the property: "The Two Kinds of Bog Gardens," *Country Life in America* 14 (August 1908): 379–80.

ARTHUR A. HOUGHTON AND ALANSON B. HOUGHTON ESTATES
South Dartmouth, Mass.
Project no. 856

1. Dyer Davis and Daniel Gross, *The Generations of Corning: The Life and Times of a Global Corporation* (New York: Oxford University Press, 2001), 2–4. Amory Houghton Sr., the founder of Corning Glass, originally came from Cambridge, Mass., and while his descendents settled in upstate New York, where the glassworks was located, they retained their Massachusetts ties by establishing summer homes in Dartmouth.
2. *American Architect's Directory* (New York: R. R. Bowker, 1931), 180; WHM client list; Judith W. Rosbe, *Maritime Marion, Massachusetts* (Charleston, S.C.: Arcadia Publishing, 2002), 117.
3. WHM, "The Field of Landscape Design," *Landscape Architecture Quarterly* 2 (April 1912): 108.
4. "St. Aidan's Chapel History," www.staidanschapel.org/history.htm.
5. George James, "Arthur Houghton Jr., 83, Dies; Led Steuben Glass," *New York Times,* April 4, 1990.
6. "Flower Planting Plan for the White Garden for Mrs. Arthur A. Houghton, South Dartmouth, Massachusetts" (drawing), Office of Ellen Shipman Landscape Architect, New York, N.Y., February 1937, courtesy Johanna Hood.
7. "The Meadows: Estate of Arthur A. Houghton, South Dartmouth, Mass.," *Country Homes Magazine,* October–November 1918, 8–14.
8. Bristol Country Registry of Deeds, New Bedford, Mass., Book 1836, p. 407.
9. Mrs. Johanna Hood, interviews by author, Dartmouth, Mass., January–March 2012.

FULLER BROOK PARK

Wellesley, Mass.

Project no. 262

1. Town of Wellesley Natural Resources Commission, "Fuller Brook Park Preservation Master Plan" (2009), 9–10, available at www.wellesleyma.gov ("Preservation Master Plan").
2. WHM client list; WHM autobiography, 46.
3. The proposed land acquisitions were between Cottage Street and Abbot Road, and the area recommended for altering the streambed's course and elevation was between Cottage and Smith Streets. Designs for the bridges and culverts were for crossings at Grove Street, Forest Street, and Abbot Road. In 2010 Wellesley planning officials discovered a set of Manning's engineering drawings among the town's records, but his written recommendations do not survive. Archives, Wellesley (Mass.) Department of Planning.
4. "Preservation Master Plan," 16.
5. Ibid., 20, 10, 17. The 1920 expansion was between Cottage Street and Dover Road.
6. Ibid., 18–20, 8, 20–22.
7. WHM autobiography, 55.

AGASSIZ PARK

Calumet, Mich.

Project no. 1168

1. Office of Warren H. Manning, "Warren H. Manning's Michigan Undertakings," typewritten manuscript prepared for Prof. H. O. Whittemore, University of Michigan, 1930s, Warren H. Manning Collection, Bentley Historical Library, University of Michigan, Ann Arbor; Arnold R. Alanen and Lynn Bjorkman, "Plats, Parks, Playgrounds, and Plants: Warren H. Manning's Landscape Designs for the Mining Districts of Michigan's Upper Peninsula, 1899–1932," *IA: The Journal of the Society for Industrial Archeology* 24 (November 1998): 49–58.
2. Arthur W. Thurner, *Calumet Copper and People: History of a Michigan Mining Community, 1864–1970* (Calumet, Mich.: privately printed, 1974), 79; James MacNaughton to WHM, March 1, 1919, WHM to MacNaughton, March 5, 1919, and WHM to Paul Bartlett, June 1, 1921, all in the C&H Collections, Michigan Technological University Archives and Copper Country Historical Collections, Van Pelt and Opie Library, Michigan Technological University, Houghton, Mich. (C&H Collections).
3. Thurner, *Calumet Copper and People,* 45–46, 78; *Calumet News,* June 14, 1916; *Calumet, Hecla & Red Jacket, Mich., 1881,* bird's-eye lithograph by Henry Wellge, published by J. J. Stover, Madison, Wis., and 1893 photograph of baseball field, both in the C&H Collections.
4. WHM, "Agassiz Park of Calumet, Michigan, Built by Community Effort," *Parks & Recreation* 11 (November–December 1927): 3–5; Alanen and Bjorkman, "Plats, Parks, Playgrounds, and Plants," 55; MacNaughton to WHM, March 1, 1919; WHM to G. R. Agassiz, March 15, 1920; WHM, "Agassiz Park at Calumet," typewritten manuscript, March 1920; the last three items are in the C&H Collections.
5. WHM, "Agassiz Park at Calumet."
6. Ibid.
7. *Calumet News,* June 1 and 2, 1922; *Daily Mining Gazette* (Houghton, Mich.), September 27, 1923; WHM, "A Community Day at Agassiz Park," typewritten manuscript, March 1920, C&H Collections; WHM to H. E. Bullard, June 3, 1922, MacNaughton to WHM, September 18, 1923, and WHM to MacNaughton, November 22, 1923, C&H Collections.
8. MacNaughton to WHM, September 18, 1923, and December 22, 1932, C&H Collections; Holly Smith-Middleton, "Agassiz Park," in *Remnants of Corporate Paternalism: Company Housing and Landscapes at Calumet, Michigan,* ed. Arnold R. Alanen and Katie Franks (Omaha, Neb.: Midwest Field Area Office, National Park Service, 1997), 71–72; Alanen and Bjorkman, "Plats, Parks, Playgrounds, and Plants," 57–58.

GWINN MODEL TOWN

Gwinn, Mich.

Project no. 715

1. William G. Mather, "Some Observations on the Principle of Benefit Funds and Their Place in the Lake Superior Mining Industry," *Proceedings of the Lake Superior Mining Institute* 5 (1898): 12; W. H. Moulton, "The Sociological Side of the Mining Industry," *Proceedings of the Lake Superior Mining Institute* 14 (1909): 84, 88–96; Harlan Hatcher, *A Century of Iron and Men* (New York: Bobbs-Merrill, 1950), 244–49; *Iron Ore* (Ishpeming, Mich.), September 29, 1928, 3.
2. Cleveland-Cliffs Iron Company, *Annual Report, 1906* (Cleveland: The Company, 1906), n.p.; WHM to Nettie P. Manning, March 31 and April 2, 1907, MCL.
3. WHM, "Villages and Homes for Working Men," *Western Architect* 16 (August 1910): 85; Arnold R. Alanen and Lynn Bjorkman, "Plats, Parks, Playgrounds, and Plants: Warren H. Manning's Landscape Designs for the Mining Districts of Michigan's Upper Peninsula," *IA: The Journal*

of the Society for Industrial Archeology 24 (November 1998): 44–45.

4. Elsie E. Walker, "In the Heart of the Upper Peninsula, Model Town Is Soon to Be Ready for Population by Wholesale," *Detroit Free Press,* March 15, 1908; WHM, "Villages and Homes for Working Men," 85.
5. Walker, "In the Heart of the Upper Peninsula"; National Register of Historic Places nomination form, Gwinn Model Town Historic District, prepared by Arnold R. Alanen and Barbara Wyatt, 1999 (ref. no. 00000286).
6. Walker, "In the Heart of the Upper Peninsula"; Alanen and Bjorkman, "Plats, Parks, Playgrounds, and Plants," 47, 49; WHM, "Villages and Homes for Working Men," 85; Moulton, "Sociological Side of the Mining Industry," 86–87; Cleveland-Cliffs Iron Co., "Contract for Deed of Lot at Gwinn, Michigan," 1908, copy in Cleveland-Cliffs Iron Company Records, Central Upper Peninsula and Northern Michigan University Archives, Northern Michigan University, Marquette, Mich.; manuscript schedules for Marquette County, Mich., 1910 U.S. Census.
7. Arnold R. Alanen, "Gwinn: A Model Town 'Without Equal,'" *Michigan History,* November–December 1994, 35; Alanen and Bjorkman, "Plats, Parks, Playgrounds, and Plants," 49.
8. National Register nomination form; Jane Roy Brown, "Preservation Case Study: Gwinn, Michigan," *VIEW* no. 6 (2006), available at http://lalh.org/magazine.

WILLIAM G. MATHER ESTATE (CLIFFS COTTAGE)

Ishpeming, Mich.

Project no. 269

1. WHM autobiography, 68.
2. Beginning in 1906 his work Cliffs Cottage would overlap with the design of Mather's main estate, Gwinn, near Cleveland. The drip fountain originally proposed for the Gwinn estate, for example, was implemented at Cliffs Cottage.
3. Charlton's buildings at Gwinn include the store, bank, hotel, superintendent's house, high school, and town hall (fire hall). Steven C. Brisson, "D. Fred Charlton's Architectural Practice and Design in the Upper Peninsula of Michigan, 1887–1918" (master's thesis, Cooperstown Graduate Program, SUNY–Oneonta, 1992), 172.
4. "Supplementary Estimate to accompany Cliffs Cottage Jasper Street piers and fence, E & A #201," MSS-036/Gwinn Area/Cliffs Cottage, and "The Cleveland-Cliffs Iron Company, Mining Department, Statement of Charges to E & A 252, Improving Grounds at Various Mines and Locations for Season of 1912, Estimated by Warren H. Manning and Work Supervised by Mr. Cotter," MSS-036/Gwinn Area/Various Mines (includes itemizations for "Cliffs Cottage (Planting)" and "Cliffs Cottage Woods"), Cleveland-Cliffs Iron Company Records, Central Upper Peninsula and Northern Michigan University Archives, Northern Michigan University, Marquette, Mich. (CCI Records).
5. WHM autobiography, 79.
6. 1906 photograph, album of contact prints from glass plate negatives of CCI facilities, Cliffs Natural Resources Offices, Ishpeming, Mich.
7. "Ishpeming Improvement, Marquette Location, Traced by Warren H. Manning . . . Aug. 1911, No. 637-19," CCI Records.
8. The trellis can be glimpsed in a 1918 photograph reproduced in "Mr. Mather's Cottage and Grove," *Cliffs News,* 1975.
9. WHM autobiography, 70.
10. "Statement of Charges to E & A 252, . . . 1912"; "Mr. Mather's Cottage and Grove."

MACKINAC ISLAND STATE PARK

Mackinac Island, Mich.

Project no. 1028

1. Morgan H. Wright and Warren H. Manning, "Mackinac Island, Michigan, State Park & Private Claims" (1913), Mackinac Island State Park Commission, Mackinac State Historic Parks Library, Mackinaw City, Mich. (MSHPL); Mackinac Island State Park Commission, Minutes of Meetings (MISPC minutes), August 23, 1913, MSHPL.
2. WHM, "Mackinac Island, Michigan, State Park & Private Claims, Topography–Vegetation," MISPC, December 11, 1914, no. 1028-20, MSHPL; and WHM, "Mackinac Island, Michigan, State Park & Private Claims: A Plan for Its Future Development," April 18, 1914, surveyed and mapped under the direction of the MISPC, no. 1028-26, MSHPL.
3. MISPC minutes, July 12, 1915. It is still leased to Grand Hotel for the same purpose.
4. MISPC minutes, April 15, 1914. In 1938 Manning's son, Harold, sent the park commission an unpublished article by Manning about Mackinac Island, including pencil and pen-and-ink illustrations. The manuscript has been lost, but the drawings survive, including details of the 1780 Stone Quarters.
5. WHM autobiography, 144–45.
6. The project number for the Woolson Memorial is 1125.

Mather created a trust fund for the care of the monument, and the draft agreement was entered into the commission minutes. This includes a detailed description of the how the site should be maintained, with information clearly provided by Manning's office. MISPC minutes, June 8, 1916.

7. MISPC minutes, August 23, 1916.

MICHILIMACKINAC STATE PARK

Mackinaw City, Mich.

Project no. 1072

1. Mackinac Island State Park Commission, Minutes of Meetings (MISPC minutes), February 4, 1914, Mackinac State Historic Parks Library, Mackinaw City, Mich. (MSHPL).
2. MISPC minutes, July 10, 1915; WHM autobiography, 144.
3. Frank A. Kenyon, Mackinac Island State Park Commission Superintendent's Report, October 31, 1918, MSHPL.
4. Lynn L. M. Evans, "Picnics and Palisades: A Centennial History of Michilimackinac State Park," *Mackinac History* no. 4 (Mackinac Island, Mich.: Mackinac Island State Park Commission, 2009).

JOHN GATES WILLIAMS ESTATE

Ladue, Mo.

Project no. 1429

1. Manning recorded a total of thirty-three projects in St. Louis between 1898 and 1926. On his client list he entered the John Gates Williams estate in 1924, but the first drawing dates from the previous year. WHM client list; MS 218, Series 2, Drawings, Project 1429: John Gates Williams, St. Louis, Missouri, MPI; Esley Hamilton, "Warren Manning in St. Louis: An Introduction," *Society of Architectural Historians Missouri Valley Chapter Newsletter* 9 (Summer 2003), available at www.stlouis architecture.org.
2. The original acreage, Williams's profession, and other details were provided by his granddaughter Mary Randolph Ballinger, the estate's present owner, in a telephone interview with the author, July 17, 2014.
3. On a map sketched after meeting with his clients in September 1924, Manning indicated the house constructed so far, the unbuilt portion, and a barn at the bottom of the meadow. WHM, "Sketch Map for an arrangement of grounds and planting as determined in conference of Sep. 24 with Mr. and Mrs. Gates Williams at St. Louis," no. 1429-15x001, box 6, MPI. A plan drafted in October (no. 1429-5; see illustration) more clearly depicts these. The architecture firm is named in Hamilton, "Warren Manning in St. Louis." Principals James P. Jamieson and George W. Spearl (or Spoerl), had formerly worked at Cope & Stewardson in Philadelphia.
4. WHM, plan no. 1429-15x001.
5. Ballinger interview; WHM, plans 1429-15x001, 1429-5. Ballinger said elms lined the entrance drive; Manning's September 1924 sketch study mentions "existing elms"; and the October 1924 plan showed the drive allée. Photographs taken by Arthur Eldredge in the late 1920s suggest that Manning used plantings to shape a cleared property. Photograph nos. 121–12, 12115, 12117–18, MCL.
6. According to Mary Randolph Ballinger, the swimming pool was reputedly the first in St. Louis.
7. Ballinger interview.
8. Ibid.

LEONARD TUFTS ESTATE

Center Harbor, N.H.

Project no. 915

1. On the Olmsted, Olmsted & Eliot plans for the Pinehurst project Manning's titles are listed as both "supervisor of planting" and "landscape architect-in-charge."
2. Olmsted, Olmsted & Eliot to J. W. Tufts, February 3, 1896, Olmsted Associates Papers, Manuscript Division, Library of Congress.
3. Richard S. Tufts, "Warren H. Manning," unpublished manuscript, 1, Tufts Archives, Given Memorial Library, Pinehurst, N.C.
4. WHM autobiography, 97; WHM, "Pinehurst, N. C. (May 6) to Meredith, N. H. (May 18) by Auto, with Mr. Leonard Tufts, Dr. W. W. Marr, and 'Uncle' Charley Cotton," unpublished illustrated diary, Tufts Archives. The Tufts property encompassed parts of both Center Harbor and Meredith; in correspondence, Leonard Tufts referred to the locale as Meredith, likely because the train depot and post office for both towns were located there. Keewaydin, the Native American word for "northwest wind," referred to the property and the house.
5. Belknap County Registry of Deeds: Book 106, p. 286 (May 17, 1901); Book 113, p. 131 (June 30, 1904); Book 114, p. 395 (September 10, 1904); Book 120, p. 207 (April 13, 1907); Book 126, p. 25 (June 17, 1909); Book 133, p. 547 (April 10, 1912); Book 138, p. 348 (December 26, 1913).
6. Richard S. Tufts to Mrs. Gladys S. Bickford, undated, collection of the Centre Harbor Historical Society. Pinehurst

was built on a sand-filled pine barren, and Tufts reasoned that the higher-quality pasturage found in New Hampshire would enable the calves to develop sturdier skeletons.

7. Ibid.
8. WHM, "Estate of Leonard Tufts, Esq. Center Harbor, N. H., Boundary and Topographical Survey," February 1912, Belknap County Registry of Deeds, Plan Book 0003, p. 0210; Plan Book 0005, p. 0334.
9. Why Keewaydin was sold is unknown, but Tufts and his wife, Gertrude (who had died in 1940), had for many years been year-round residents of Pinehurst, N.C.

AMBROSE SWASEY PLOT, EXETER CEMETERY

Exeter, N.H.

Project no. 1081

1. The Exeter Cemetery was established in 1843 by four individuals, including Henry Flagg French, father of the sculptor Daniel Chester French. At the time, Exeter's four other burial grounds had filled to capacity and were experiencing vandalism and neglect. In 1888 the cemetery covered more than thirty acres; the "new portion" added sixteen acres, bring the total size to today's forty-six acres. The cemetery is located on the northern shore of the Little River, between Linden Street and the railroad. Charles Henry Bell, *History of the Town of Exeter, New Hampshire* (Boston: J. E. Farwell & Co., 1888), 410–11.
2. "Ambrose Swasey, Telescope Maker" (obituary), *New York Times,* June 16, 1937.
3. Ambrose Swasey to Dr. S. H. Dana, April 1, 1915, and WHM to Mr. Ambrose Swasey, April 1, 1915, Exeter Cemetery Association (ECA).
4. WHM, "Plan for Development," Exeter Cemetery, Exeter, N.H., July 12, 1915, ECA.
5. WHM to Mr. Ambrose Swasey, July 12, 1915, ECA.
6. WHM, "Suggestions for Rules and Regulations, Exeter Cemetery, Exeter, New Hampshire," August 1915, ECA.
7. Secretary of the Exeter Cemetery Association Trustees to Mr. Ambrose Swasey, 1916, ECA.
8. WHM, "Exeter Cemetery, Exeter, N. H., Preliminary Estimate to Accompany Plan Number 1081-21-B," August 1, 1916, ECA.
9. WHM, "Exeter Cemetery, Exeter, N. H., Plan to Accompany Proposed Lots for Ambrose Swasey, Esq.," July 23, 1917, ECA.
10. WHM to Ambrose Swasey, August 28, 1916, ECA; WHM autobiography, 177. In 1916 Bacon created the Swasey Pavilion, located at the intersection of Water and Front Streets in the center of Exeter, and may have designed the Swasey monument in Exeter Cemetery.

WILTON LLOYD-SMITH ESTATE (KENJOCKETY)

Huntington, N.Y.

Project no. 1417

1. Although Manning had numerous previous commissions both on Long Island's "Gold Coast" and in Southampton, he obtained this project through connections related to his work at Walden, the Chicago estate of Marjorie Lloyd-Smith's cousin, Cyrus McCormick II. Manning had been working at Walden for almost twenty years when he was contacted by the Lloyd-Smiths.
2. I am indebted to Jenny Lawrence for personal interviews and for creating a family memoir, "The Lloyd-Smith Women," which includes transcribed interviews and oral histories (conducted with her sister).
3. Mary Lou H. Brooks, "An Intimate View of the Kenjockety Bindery," *The Chautauquan* 72 (November 8, 1913): 200.
4. Manning's initial site report, February 18, 1924, Wilton Lloyd-Smith Residence, series 3, box 43, Bertram Grosvenor Goodhue Architectural Drawings and Papers, 1882–1980, Avery Architectural and Fine Arts Library, Columbia University (Goodhue Collection).
5. Ibid.
6. Goodhue's plans for the house were approved by the Lloyd-Smiths three days before he died on April 23, 1924. Arthur Fleming was a Southern California real estate investor and philanthropist. As president of the board of trustees of the California Institute of Technology, he gave land to the school and hired Goodhue to design a campus plan and key buildings.
7. Wilton Lloyd-Smith to WHM, November 26, 1924, Goodhue Collection.
8. WHM to Wilton Lloyd-Smith, February 18, 1924, Goodhue Collection.
9. WHM to John Knox, December 9, 1925, Goodhue Collection.
10. WHM, site visit report, March 8, 1927, Goodhue Collection.
11. WHM to "CL" (Carl Lutender), August 25, 1924; WHM to R. O. Walker, July 30, 1924, Goodhue Collection.
12. WHM to Wilton Lloyd-Smith, August 25, 1924, Goodhue Collection.
13. WHM to Wilton Lloyd-Smith, July 22, 1924, Goodhue Collection.
14. WHM to Mrs. Lloyd-Smith, November 8, 1929, Goodhue Collection.
15. WHM to Wilton Lloyd-Smith, September 11, 1925, Goodhue Collection.

16. Paula Rice graciously provided a detailed narrative of her efforts on the property; Dennis Flynn, MLA, supplied a copy of his 1995 site plan.

CAYUGA HEIGHTS
Ithaca, N.Y.
Project no. 682

1. Carol U. Sisler, *Enterprising Families, Ithaca, New York: Their Houses and Businesses* (Ithaca, N.Y.: DeWitt Historical Society of Tompkins County, 2002), 105–22. Although Sisler gives a thorough account of Newman and Blood's development of Cayuga Heights over time, she does not mention Manning's involvement. In Manning's autobiography Newman's first name is given as Isidore (112).
2. Local architects represented in Cayuga Heights include Arts and Crafts pioneer Gustav Stickley, of Syracuse, N.Y. See Ray Stubblebine, *Stickley's Craftsman Homes: Plans, Drawings, Photographs* (Layton, Utah: Gibbs Smith, 2006), 99, 286.
3. Sisler, *Enterprising Families,* 106, 112.
4. WHM client list; roll no. 6, Cayuga Heights, MPI.

CORNELL UNIVERSITY CAMPUS
Ithaca, N.Y.
Project no. 762

1. Liberty Hyde Bailey, "Landscape Gardening," *The Register: Cornell University* (Ithaca, N.Y.: Cornell University, 1893–1894), 94. See also "A Student's Problem in Landscape Gardening," *American Gardening* 14 (June 1893): 346–48.
2. Harold A. Caparn, James Sturgis Pray, and Downing Vaux, eds., *Transactions of the American Society of Landscape Architects from Its Inception in 1899 to the End of 1908* (Harrisburg, Pa.: J. H. McFarland Co., Mt. Pleasant Press, 1909).
3. This unofficial program had been overseen by Bailey and produced several notable landscape architects, including Fleming (1898–1901), Joseph Blair (1892–1896), Charles G. French (1887–1891), Frank Waugh (1898 graduate), David Williston (1896–1898), and Phelps Wyman (1893–1897).
4. *The Register: Cornell University* (1903–4), 307–8.
5. *The Register* for 1905–6 and 1906–7 lists Manning and Fleming each as a "Lecturer in Outdoor Art," and the Outdoor Art curriculum during this period identified them as "co-instructors." In the *Register* for 1908, Fleming is listed as an assistant professor in Rural Art, the program's new name. A. D. Taylor (then a graduate student and later a Manning employee) was an instructor, and Manning was no longer listed as faculty. Whether this change was due to Manning's increasing professional workload, a suggestion by the college administration, or to other reasons is not known. *The Register* (1907–8), 341.
6. A master plan for the university had been advocated some thirty years earlier by Cornell's first president, Andrew D. White, but was never completed. See K. C. Parsons, *The Cornell Campus: A History of Its Planning and Development* (Ithaca, N.Y.: Cornell University Press, 1968), 209.
7. It is unclear how much of later development followed the plan(s), although Parsons notes that of the recommendations, "many were incorporated in later campus plans and development." Ibid., 210.
8. Ibid., 243.
9. Ibid., 211.

ENFIELD GLEN STATE PARK (ROBERT H. TREMAN STATE PARK)
Ithaca, N.Y.
Project no. 1140

1. Catherine Faust, "Chronology of E. B. Green," and Lisa Brown, "The Architecture of E. B. Green: A Vanishing Urban Legacy," in *E. B. Green: Buffalo's Architect,* ed. Gerald C. Mead Jr., exh. cat., Burchfield Penney Art Center (Buffalo, N.Y.: Buffalo State College Foundation, 1997).
2. Ralph S. Hosmer, *The Cornell Plantations: A History* (Ithaca, N.Y.: The Cayuga Press, 1947), 196–97.
3. "Famous Enfield Glen Gift to State for Public Park," *Ithaca Journal-News,* May 15, 1920.
4. Elaine Treman, interview, May 15, 1950, Robert H. Treman Collection, The History Center, Ithaca, N.Y. (THC).
5. See WHM to the Finger Lakes Regional Park Commission, August 20, 1923, and September 3, 1923, in *Report of the Finger Lakes Regional Park Commission* (1923–24).
6. WHM to R. H. Treman, February 26, 1925, THC.

FINGER LAKES STATE PARKS
Finger Lakes Region, N.Y.
Project no. 1155

1. For an account of Manning's initial association with Treman, see the essay on the Robert H. Treman and Charles E. Treman estates. Enfield Falls Reservation (later Enfield Glen State Park) was renamed Robert H. Treman State Park in 1938, following his death, to honor Treman's donation and his legacy of conservation.

2. The mill and miller's home are now listed on the National Register of Historic Places. The area surrounding the mill, once the town of Enfield, is also the site of ongoing archaeological investigation.
3. The Enfield Falls Reservation Commission, chaired by Treman and in operation from 1920 to 1924, was the entity responsible for the park's development. For an overview of Manning's work for the commission, see the essay on Enfield Glen State Park in this volume.
4. Robert Moses to Ross Kellogg, August 21, 1923, EFRCC (V-6-4-5.1), The History Center, Ithaca, N.Y. (THC). Manning had already conducted some regional recreational studies for the City of Ithaca as early as 1907 (see the essay on Ithaca Improvement Plan in this volume). To testify to his surveying method, Manning forwarded to Commissioner MacDonald a letter from Leonard Tufts recounting a similar survey he had made of Pinehurst and Moore County, N.C., twelve to fifteen years earlier. WHM to Alexander MacDonald, undated, Finger Lakes State Parks Commission Papers, 1926–1977 (V-10-3-2 A, B, & C), THC.
5. WHM to Robert Moses, June 23, 1923, EFRCC (V-6-4-5.1), THC. The figure of 150 miles refers to the total linear measure of the lakes, as if laid end to end. Out of a total of eleven Finger Lakes, only seven fall within the ten-county region under the commission's purview.
6. Finger Lakes State Parks Commission Minute Book, vol. 1, 1924–1930, New York State Parks Finger Lakes Regional Office, Trumansburg, N.Y.
7. Moses to Kellogg, August 21, 1923, Moses to Kellogg, August 28, 1923, and Kellogg to Moses, September 5, 1923, EFRCC (V-6-4-5.1), THC.

ITHACA IMPROVEMENT PLAN

Ithaca, N.Y.

Project no. 685

1. For an account of Manning's initial association with Treman, see the essay on the Robert H. Treman and Charles E. Treman estates in this volume.
2. "Cascadilla Creek Banks to Be Bowers of Beauty," *Ithaca Journal,* May 1, 1913.
3. Carol U. Sisler, *Enterprising Families, Ithaca, New York: Their Houses and Businesses* (Ithaca, N.Y.: DeWitt Historical Society of Tompkins County, 2002), 23; for Manning's recommendation see "Cascadilla Creek Banks to Be Bowers of Beauty."
4. Manning's unpublished autobiography and surviving plans indicate that Treman had a prominent seat on Ithaca's Creek, Drainage, and Park Commission, which allowed him to begin regional park studies. This may also explain Manning's later involvement in Ithaca creek projects. WHM autobiography, 244.
5. These include plan 685-14-17, 1907 (see illustration) and plan 685-14, "A Study Showing the Relation of A Proposed Ithaca Road and Reservation System to the Glen Region of Cayuga and Seneca Lakes with Suggested Reservations and Road Extensions," December 30, 1907, MPI.
6. See the essay on Finger Lakes State Parks in this volume.
7. "Site plan, Dewitt Park Showing the Location of Trees, Walks, and Drives," October 5, 1906, no. 685-5, and "Planting Plan, West Buffalo Street," February 5, 1908, no. 685-17, MPI.
8. WHM autobiography, 111–21; "Cascadilla Creek Banks to Be Bowers of Beauty."

STEWART PARK

Ithaca, N.Y.

Project no. 1370

1. City of Ithaca, "Stewart Park," www.ci.ithaca.ny.us.
2. WHM client list; WHM autobiography, 112.
3. City of Ithaca, "Stewart Park."

ROBERT H. TREMAN AND CHARLES E. TREMAN ESTATES

Ithaca, N.Y.

Project no. 279

1. Carol U. Sisler, *Enterprising Families, Ithaca, New York: Their Houses and Businesses* (Ithaca, N.Y.: Dewitt Historical Society of Tompkins County, 2002), 19.
2. National Register of Historic Places nomination form, East Hill Historic District, prepared by Andrea Lazarski, 1979 (ref. no. 86001652).
3. "Landscape Artist Completes Plans," *Ithaca Daily News,* July 19, 1901.
4. Gibb finished the design unaided, however, as the firm disbanded mid-construction.
5. Sisler, *Enterprising Families,* 20.
6. WHM autobiography, 111. E. B. Green had studied and taught architecture at Cornell and had worked for three years in the Ithaca office of William Henry Miller. He had worked with Manning on private estate commissions in Buffalo.
7. "Landscape Artist Completes Plans."
8. Ibid.; *Ithaca Daily News,* November 2, 1901. Though Manning initially suggested putting out sheep to graze, as Olmsted had done at Central Park, it appears that

sheep were never involved in maintaining the Treman estates. Several years later, for his client Henry S. Sherman (project no. 1115, dated 1915) in Lyndhurst, Ohio, Manning also proposed residential grounds with "formal and informal gardens, sheep pasture and wild gardens." See WHM, "A description of estates on the community lands about the Mayfield Country Club as allotted by Frank C. Newcomer, Cleveland, Ohio" (1918), MCL, 9.

9. The Charles Treman residence served briefly as a fraternity house until it was destroyed by fire in 1944. Sisler, *Enterprising Families,* 29. The house was replaced with another Tudor structure, Von Cramm Hall. The Robert Treman house still stands, now housing Cornell University's George McT. Kahin Center for Advanced Research on Southeast Asia. The Van Cleef residence now serves as a Cornell-owned housing cooperative.
10. See Danny Perlstein, "Parking on Manning's Legacy," *Landscape Architecture* 94 (October 2004): 226–28; and Susan Hines, "The Rest of the Redbuds Story," *Landscape Architecture* 95 (November 2005): 16–18. The public protests were noteworthy for their highly publicized methods, including building a platform fifty feet off the ground in a pignut hickory tree and a rally resulting in over fifty arrests, including that of former Ithaca mayor Ben Nichols. As a result of the public outcry, the university began offering free public transit passes to new students. The parking area, designed by the Ithaca-based landscape architecture firm Trowbridge & Wolf, included bio-swales (planted drainage swales) to reduce its environmental impact and a winding walkway to echo the historic carriage path. See Trowbridge & Wolf Landscape Architects, "West Campus Residential Initiative DEIS," May 2002, available at www.cityofithaca.org/DocumentCenter/View/232.

GREENSBORO NORMAL AND INDUSTRIAL COLLEGE (UNIVERSITY OF NORTH CAROLINA AT GREENSBORO)

Greensboro, N.C.
Project no. 357

1. Manning employee list; Manning mentions placing "Miss Dees in charge of the office Jan. 1st [1900]" in a letter to Henrietta Pratt Manning, December 28, 1899, Manning Family Association Collection, Center for Lowell History, University of Massachusetts Lowell. Except where noted, other information is drawn from the finding aid for Warren Henry Manning Drawings, 1902–1920, Martha Blakeney Hodges Special Collections and University Archives, University of North Carolina at Greensboro (UNCG); and Hermann Trojanowski, "Spartan Stories: Campus Drawings of Warren Henry Manning" (blog post), January 21, 2013, uncghistory.blogspot.com.
2. WHM, "Grading Plan," May 29, 1902, UNCG.
3. UA104 Photographic Prints Collection, UNCG, photographs dated 1905, 1907, and 1907, http://libcdm1.uncg.edu/cdm; "Timeline of UNCG History: 1908," http://library.uncg.edu/info/depts/scua/exhibits/timeline/pages.
4. WHM, "General Plan," January 1909, and UA104 Photographic Prints Collection.
5. Although the Arts and Crafts Village was never built, surviving drawings and Steele's letters indicate that the Manning firm submitted preliminary designs for the proposed buildings. Fletcher Steele to Mary Steele, February 10, 1910, Fletcher Steele Papers, Rochester Historical Society, Rochester, N.Y.; WHM, "Sketch Plan and Elevations of Woodworking Building, Woodworking Building, Sketch Plan and Elevations of Metalworking Building, Sketch Plan and Elevations of Pottery Building, An Interior of Pottery Building, Weaving Building for Arts & Crafts Village," n.d., UNCG.
6. WHM, "Study for Location of McIver Statue," January 20, 1912, UNCG; UA104 Photographic Prints Collection, c. 1912.
7. WHM, "Report on the future development of the North Carolina State Normal School, at Greensboro, North Carolina," December 22, 1917, UNCG.
8. WHM, "Sketches for Concrete Seats," November 20, 1919, and "Sketch for Proposed Road Arrangement," March 30, 1920, UNCG.
9. UA104 Photographic Prints Collection, c. 1920, 1924, 1925; "Timeline of UNCG History: 1908"; UNCG Biology Department, "History of Peabody Park," http://peabodypark.uncg.edu.
10. UNCG Biology Department, "History of Peabody Park."

PINEHURST VILLAGE

Pinehurst, N.C.
Project no. 45

1. J. C. Olmsted, Reports of Visits, June 20, 1895, July 3, 1895, and September 1895, Olmsted Associates Papers, Manuscript Division, Library of Congress (OAP). According to James Walker Tufts's grandson Richard S. Tufts, the original land purchase on July 9, 1895, included 598 acres and was followed by five additional purchases, made by the end of 1896, totaling approximately 6,000

acres. Richard S. Tufts, "Warren H. Manning," unpublished manuscript, 3, Tufts Archives, Given Memorial Library, Pinehurst, NC (Tufts Archives).

2. Richard S. Tufts, *James Walker Tufts, Founder of Pinehurst* (Pinehurst: Pinehurst Publishing Company, 1978).
3. WHM autobiography, 94; Richard J. Moss, *Eden in the Pines: A History of Pinehurst Village* (Southern Pines, N.C.: Pinehurst Publishing Company, 2005), 20–21.
4. WHM autobiography, 94.
5. "Pinehurst Hotels and Cottages," brochure printed before 1902, Tufts Archives.
6. Rassie Wicker to Richard Tufts, July 4, 1966, Tufts Archives.
7. Olmsted, Olmsted & Eliot to J. W. Tufts, February 3, 1896, OAP.
8. WHM autobiography, 94; Olmsted, Olmsted & Eliot to J. W. Tufts, September 7, 1895, OAP. The suggestion of a nursery is included in a letter from the Olmsted, Olmsted & Eliot firm.
9. On the new house lots, see the National Historic Landmark nomination form for Pinehurst, prepared by Davyd Foard Hood and Laura A. W. Phillips, 1996 (ref. no. 73001361), copy in Tufts Archives. In 1905 the Tufts family began selling the house lots to private owners, fostering a large expansion of housing beyond the original limits of the village. On the ring road, see Richard S. Tufts, "Warren H. Manning," 3. The road was eventually completed sixty years later.
10. Leonard Tufts to WHM, July 13, 1920, Tufts Archives.
11. "A New Golf Resort in North Carolina," *Pinehurst Outlook,* February 1, 1920, 13, Tufts Archives.
12. Ibid.; Warren H. Manning Offices, Inc., "Knollwood, N. C., Study for development of Knollwood showing its relation to Pinehurst & Southern Pines," October 20, 1920, MPI.
13. Aymar Embury II also designed several buildings in Pinehurst around the same time.
14. Leonard Tufts to WHM, July 2, 1919, Tufts Archives.
15. WHM to Leonard Tufts, July 7, 1919, Tufts Archives.
16. WHM to Leonard Tufts, April 29, 1921, Tufts Archives.
17. Olmsted, Olmsted & Eliot to J. W. Tufts, October 8, 1895, OAP.
18. WHM autobiography, 100.
19. Tufts, "Warren H. Manning," 1.
20. Manning and Leonard Tufts correspondence, 1919–1929, Tufts Archives.
21. WHM autobiography, 99.
22. Ibid.

GLENDALE PARK

Akron, Ohio

Project no. 1583

1. At this time, Glendale Cemetery was one of the most impressive designed landscapes in Ohio. Laid out in 1839, the cemetery was modeled after Mount Auburn Cemetery in Cambridge, Mass. The 88-acre cemetery, in the Picturesque style, eventually expanded to cover 150 acres and included elaborate mausoleums in eclectic architectural styles, one of which would provide the final resting place for Frank Seiberling in 1955.
2. Meeting minutes, January 8, 1929, Akron Garden Club Collection, Archival Services, University Libraries, University of Akron. The plan and report have not been found.
3. Annual Report (1931), Akron Garden Club Collection.

GOODYEAR HEIGHTS

Akron, Ohio

Project no. 960

1. National Register of Historic Places nomination form, Hall Park Allotment Historic District, prepared by Carol Poh Miller, 2002 (ref. no. 02001274).
2. WHM, "A Step towards Solving the Industrial Housing Problem," American City Pamphlet Series, no. 131 (New York: Civic Press, 1913).
3. *The Wingfoot Clan* (Goodyear Heights, Ohio), February 2, 1918, 7.

FRANK A. SEIBERLING ESTATE (STAN HYWET)

Akron, Ohio

Project no. 908

1. WHM to F. A. Seiberling, June 23, 1911, Stan Hywet Hall and Gardens Archives, Akron, Ohio. All correspondence and documents cited are from the archives. For more on the development of the house and landscape of Stan Hywet, see Robin Karson, *A Genius for Place: American Landscapes of the Country Place Era* (Amherst: University of Massachusetts Press in association with Library of American Landscape History, 2007).
2. The house design was primarily the work of Charles S. Schneider, who resigned from George B. Post & Sons in 1912 to establish his own Cleveland-based firm. Schneider's architecture borrowed liberally from Compton Wynyates, a widely imitated sixteenth-century Tudor house in Warwickshire, as well as Ockwells Manor in Berkshire and Haddon Hall in Derbyshire.

3. WHM to F. A. Seiberling, June 23, 1911.
4. Charles S. Schneider to F. A. Seiberling, February 28, 1916; WHM to N. L. Palmer, March 7, 1916.
5. According to his business circular, Otsuka's approach emphasized the use of local "naturally fitted rocks and trees"; clients were to furnish their own laborers. T. R. Otsuka, "Terms and Conditions," memorandum on construction of Japanese Garden, n.d.
6. WHM, "List of Plants for Panels in English Garden," March 30, 1915.
7. Warren H. Manning Offices, Inc., "Memoranda of Recommendations and Suggestions of Visit of April 20, 1928."
8. WHM to F. A. Seiberling, July 20, 1917.
9. Judith B. Tankard, *The Gardens of Ellen Biddle Shipman* (Sagaponack, N.Y.: Sagapress/Abrams in association with Library of American Landscape History, 1996), 118.
10. Child, Hornbeck Associates, Inc. (Cambridge, Mass.), "Historic Preservation of Landscape and Gardens, c. 1911–16, 1928, for Stan Hywet Hall Foundation, Inc.," May 1984. The English Garden was restored in 1991–92, under the direction of John Franklin Miller. Irene Seiberling Harrison, the 102-year-old daughter of Frank and Gertrude, attended the opening. A restoration plan for Stan Hywet's approach road and ornamental apple orchard, commissioned from Douglas P. Reed in 1995, has been completed. Additional restorations to both the house and the landscape have continued through the years.

HENRY G. DALTON ESTATE (EDGEWATER)

Cleveland, Ohio

Project no. 1039

1. See Robin Karson, *The Muses of Gwinn: Art and Nature in a Garden Designed by Warren H. Manning, Charles A. Platt, and Ellen Biddle Shipman* (Sagaponack, N.Y.: Sagapress/Abrams in association with Library of American Landscape History, 1996).
2. "Henry George Dalton," in *The Encyclopedia of Cleveland History,* ed. David D. Van Tassel and John J. Grabowski, online edition, http://ech.case.edu; WHM client list.
3. Co-creators list for Edgewater Gardens (slide), SIRIS (Smithsonian Institution Research Information System), Archives of American Gardens. (SIRIS contains additional Edgewater data under the general keyword "Warren Manning.")
4. J. B. Davis & Son Civil Engineers, "H. G. Dalton Map Showing Surface Locations at Residence," Map 678, September 1, 1934, folder 486-A (revisions 5/17/1935 and 6/3/1939), courtesy Peter and Victoria Broer. The gardens are not named on the map.
5. Note on back of photograph of the pergola by A. G. Eldridge, July 1928, Warren H. Manning Offices, MCL.
6. Helen Thackery, "A Garden That Runs to Meet the Lake—Sand Beach Transformed into Green Lawn," *Your Garden: A Magazine for the Nature Lovers in the Territory of the Western Reserve,* February 1929, 9.
7. WHM, "Memoranda of Visit of August 9th in conference with Mr. and Mrs. H. G. Dalton, their Superintendent and Gardener, representatives of Mr. Garfield's office, Mr. Charles Irish, Mr. Egbert Hans (my associate), and myself," August 13, 1929, MCL.
8. Victoria Broer, interview by Mary Hoerner, June 2, 2012.

WILLIAM G. MATHER ESTATE (GWINN)

Cleveland, Ohio

Project no. 771

1. WHM to Mather, September 20, 1906, Project Records (Series 1), Charles Adams Platt Architectural Records and Papers, Avery Architectural and Fine Arts Library, Columbia University (Platt Records). The design history of Gwinn is the subject of my book *The Muses of Gwinn: Art and Nature in a Garden Designed by Warren H. Manning, Charles A. Platt, and Ellen Biddle Shipman* (Sagaponack, N.Y.: Sagapress/Abrams in association with Library of American Landscape History, 1995). Gwinn is also the subject of a chapter in *A Genius for Place: American Landscapes of the Country Place Era* (Amherst: University of Massachusetts Press in association with Library of American Landscape History, 2007). By 1906 Manning had worked for Mather's iron-ore company in several Michigan towns, including Gwinn, Ishpeming, Munising, Negaunee, and Marquette. This work spanned city and town planning, real estate subdivisions, industrial grounds, parks, and home grounds.
2. Mather was drawn to Platt's work through recent magazine articles. He may also have heard about the architect from his friend Charles Lang Freer, who would later commission Platt to design the Freer Gallery of Art in Washington, D.C. Platt's design approach influenced many of Manning's colleagues and, to a limited degree, Manning himself. See Keith N. Morgan, *Shaping an American Landscape: The Art and Architecture of Charles A. Platt* (Hanover, N.H.: University Press of New England, 1995), *The Muses of Gwinn,* and *A Genius for Place.*
3. In 1914 Ellen Shipman was hired to suggest enrichments to Frost's uninspired arrangements, which had devolved

into rows of red geraniums, but she and Jacques did not get along. She returned in 1935, at the request of Elizabeth Ring Mather (whom William married in 1929), and substantially revised the planting scheme in this area, adding ornamental cherry trees to surround a central pool, vines on the loggia and teahouse, and a broad range of herbaceous plants in shades of pale pink and apricot. Shipman's design specialty was flower gardens. She was frequently commissioned in this role on Manning's recommendation.

4. WHM to Mather, November 4, 1908, Platt Records.
5. Mather to WHM, September 15, 1909, Platt Records.
6. J. Horace McFarland, "An American Garden: Dolobran near Philadelphia," *Outlook,* October 7, 1899, 326–33.
7. For more on Eldredge, see Pamela Hartford, "Arthur G. Eldredge: Poet behind the Lens," *VIEW* no. 10 (2010), 24–27, available at http://lalh.org/magazine.
8. The first mention of Manning's attempt to persuade Mather to turn Gwinn into a public reservation appears in 1932. Mather wrote, "Perhaps we are selfish, and perhaps, further, we cannot afford any more to be selfish in this respect. . . . The next time you come out we will have a talk in regard to the matter." Five years later, Mather was still reluctant to commit to the idea, yet he wrote, "Your opinion on all these matters—dreams though some of them may be, yet we should all have dreams—are always welcome with me." Mather to WHM, December 6, 1932, and June 2, 1937, Platt Records.

HARRY B. STEWART ESTATE
Hartville, Ohio
Project no. 1579

1. F. A. Seiberling to WHM, September 27, 1928, Seiberling Papers (MSS 347), Ohio Historical Society, Columbus.
2. These drawings are now held in the Quail Hollow Garden Archive, Quail Hollow State Park, Hartville, Ohio (QHGA).
3. Catherine Seiberling Stewart oral history, conducted by Viola R. Beltz (1983), transcription. The elm trees were lost to Dutch Elm disease.
4. Warren Manning offices to Mr. H. B. Stewart, "Estimate of Cost of Plant Material for Estate of Mr. H. B. Stewart, Akron, Ohio," October 29, 1928, QHGA.
5. Egbert Hans to Mrs. H. B. Stewart, October 3, 1930, QHGA. Stewart bordered her "picking garden" with vegetables. See Meeting minutes, August 12, 1930, Akron Garden Club Collection, Archival Services, University Libraries, University of Akron.
6. WHM to Mrs. Stewart and Mrs. Seiberling, November 14, 1928. In correspondence related to the home grounds, Manning described Hans "presenting Mrs. Stewart's thoughts with reference to the rock garden." WHM to Mr. H. B. Stewart, October 29, 1928, QHGA.
7. WHM to H. B. Stewart, n.d., QHGA.
8. Manning office timesheets, MCL.
9. See Mackenzie Greer, "The Rock Garden of Quail Hollow," *VIEW* no. 8 (2008), 22–23, available at http://lalh.org/magazine.

JEPTHA H. WADE ESTATE (VALLEY RIDGE FARM)
Hunting Valley, Ohio
Project no. 712

1. *Guide to the Microfilm Edition of the Jeptha Homer Wade Family Papers, 1771–1957, from the holdings of the Western Reserve Historical Society, Cleveland, Ohio* (Woodbridge, Conn.: Scholarly Resources Inc., 2005), vii; "Wade, Jeptha Homer II," in *The Encyclopedia of Cleveland History,* ed. David D. Van Tassel and John J. Grabowski, online edition, http://ech.case.edu; Cleveland Museum of Art, "History and Mission," www.clevelandart.org.
2. Diana Tittle and Mark Gottlieb, *Hunting Valley: A History* (Cleveland: Hunting Valley Historical Society, 1999), 29, 80–82, 92–93. Wade served as vice president of Cleveland-Cliffs Iron Co. in 1891, following the merger of Iron Cliffs Co. with Samuel Mather's Cleveland Iron Mining Co., of which his grandfather, J. H. Wade, was a director. William G. Mather, Samuel's son, worked with J. H. Wade II and others to complete the merger after both the elder Wade and Samuel Mather died in 1890. Terry S. Reynolds and Virginia P. Dawson, *Iron Will: Cleveland-Cliffs and the Mining of Iron Ore, 1847–2006* (Detroit: Wayne State University Press, 2011), 80–82.
3. WHM, "Map Showing Vistas Cut and Reopened of Estate of J. H. Wade," December 1920, no. 712-91, Case Western Reserve University Farm, Hunting Valley, Ohio; and "Plan of Existing Plantings on the Estate of J. H. Wade," March 9, 1910, no. 712-87, MPI.
4. WHM, "Plan of Existing Plantings."
5. Ibid.; Tittle and Gottlieb, *Hunting Valley,* 81–82.
6. Tittle and Gottlieb, *Hunting Valley,* 130; "University Farm: History—Valley Ridge Farm," http://students.case.edu/farm/facilities/valleyridge.html.
7. Transfer Document, Case Western Reserve University Archives.
8. Estimate by the author, who is the Case Western Reserve University Farm horticulturist.
9. WHM autobiography, 70. Manning acknowledged that

goutweed (*Aegopodium podograria*) could become a rapacious pest in some places where he had introduced it, as in Ishpeming, Michigan, where the ground cover had "taken possession of a large woodland area, driven out most of the native plants, [and] made six to eight inch mats of dark-green summer foliage."

HENRY S. SHERMAN ESTATE

Lyndhurst, Ohio

Project no. 1115

1. "Ex-Judge Charles T. Sherman, the Eldest Brother of General and Secretary Sherman, Dies at Cleveland," *New York Times,* January 2, 1879; John D. Clough, *To Act as a Unit: The Story of the Cleveland Clinic* (Cleveland: Cleveland Clinic Press, 2004), 66. Sherman was related to the principal founder of the Cleveland Clinic, George Crile, through marriage; his wife, Edith McBride, was the sister of Crile's wife, Grace.
2. National Register of Historic Places nomination form, Elizabeth B. and Dudley S. Blossom Estate Service Compound, prepared by Betsy H. Bradley, 2003 (ref. no. 04000059).
3. The project is listed as Mayfield Community Lands Subdivision, no. 1090, WHM client list. Sherman's lot was number 28.
4. WHM, *A Description of Estates on the Community Lands about the Mayfield Country Club as Allotted by Frank C. Newcomer, Cleveland, Ohio* (North Billerica, Mass.: Warren H. Manning Offices, 1918), 7 (quotation), 19, 24; Roger Mezger and Jesse Tinsley, "TRW Donates HQ to Cleveland Clinic," *Cleveland Plain Dealer,* December 10, 2002.
5. National Register of Historic Places nomination form. By 2003 a shopping center occupied the site of the Blossom estate.
6. Aerial photos of Cuyahoga County, 1951, Cleveland Public Library Digital Gallery, http://cplorg.cdmhost.com.
7. WHM, *A Description of Estates,* 19.
8. *Beautiful Homes of Cleveland 1917* (Cleveland: The Cleveland Topics Company, 1917), 128.
9. National Register of Historic Places nomination form. It is likely that most of the features of the Sherman estate were demolished between 1980, when TRW acquired the property, and 1985.
10. Mattie Edwards Hewitt Collection [photographs] (P-96), folder 11, Ohio Historical Society, Columbus. The nine photographs, all showing exterior views, are undated. Harrison retired in the mid-1940s, suggesting that the photographs were likely taken before that time.
11. Mezger and Tinsley, "TRW Donates HQ to Cleveland Clinic."
12. In 1986 the American Society of Landscape Architects honored Sasaki with a Merit Award for its work on the site. "Yield to the Trees" and "Merit Awards," *Landscape Architecture* 77 (November–December 1987): 74–75, 84.
13. In addition to the Hewitt photographs, a photo in the archives of the Cleveland Clinic shows Mrs. Henry S. Sherman and her daughter Betty under the pergola at the west entry to the walled garden at Betty's coming-out party, June 1934. Cleveland Clinic Foundation Archives, Beachwood, Ohio.
14. Clough, *To Act as a Unit,* 143; Mezger and Tinsley, "TRW Donates HQ to Cleveland Clinic."

MILL CREEK PARK

Youngstown, Ohio

Project no. 1318

1. WHM to Hugh Imlay, September 7, 1920, Mill Creek Park correspondence records, 1891–1936, Mahoning Valley Historical Society archives, Youngstown, Ohio (Correspondence Records, MVHS).
2. Bridgett M. Williams, *The Legacy of Mill Creek Park: The Biography of Volney Rogers* (Youngstown, Ohio: Youngstown Lithographing Company, 1992), 37. Rogers became legal counsel to the American Civic Association in the late 1880s; the organization's goals included "the preservation and development of landscape and the advancement of outdoor art." Moved to preserve the creek's dramatic gorge, Rogers conceived the idea of Mill Creek Park and wrote the state enabling legislation to create it. Williams, *The Legacy of Mill Creek Park,* 37; John C. Melnick, *The Green Cathedral* (Youngstown, Ohio: Youngstown Lithographing Company, 1976), 33.
3. Volney Rogers, *A Partial Description of Mill Creek Park, Youngstown, Ohio* (Youngstown, Ohio: Privately published, 1904), 27.
4. Eliot and Cleveland, hired separately by the park commissioners, apparently made their respective design contributions during the same period, 1891–1897. Eliot designed West Cohasset Drive, High Drive, and Valley Drive, while Cleveland designed most of the other drives and trail locations in the earliest sections of the park. Following the retirement of Cleveland in 1895 and the death of Eliot in 1897, Volney Rogers played a large role in the design of vistas, bridges, trails, and roadways. Mill Creek Park, minutes of the park commission, February 2, 1891, and June 25, 1892, and various historical drawings and plans, Mill Creek MetroParks archives

(MCMP), Canfield, Ohio; Correspondence Records, MVHS.

5. WHM to Imlay, September 7, 1920. Previously, Imlay had worked under Manning's direction at the estates of A. A. Sprague II and Stanley Field in Lake Bluff, Illinois, begun in 1911.
6. The staff also drafted planting plans for four specific sites: the Falls Avenue entrance with its statue of Volney Rogers (1920); the Park Office (1922); the Edith Kaufman Quarry Garden, north of Lake Newport and along Glenwood Avenue next to an upscale 1920s neighborhood that bordered earlier parkland (1929); and a rock garden in memory of Mary Baldwin on the east side of the Lake Newport dam (1932). In his letters, Manning also suggested plants for the quarry rock faces in the Bear's Den, for the Big Cut, and for roughs in the golf course. He mentioned perennials, shrubs, and trees to be moved to create the edge of Lake Newport and its surroundings within the proposed Lake Newport development area. He also submitted plant lists and general categories of plantings for other sites. MCMP.
7. MCMP; Correspondence Records, MVHS, 1920–1930.
8. WHM to park commissioner Walter C. Stitt, August 29, 1922, Correspondence Records, MVHS; map of cross-park roadway and expansion south, submitted to Youngstown Planning Commission December 21, 1923.
9. WHM to Imlay, January 26, 1927, Correspondence Records, MVHS.
10. WHM to Imlay, January 25, 1924, and August 18, 1926, Correspondence Records, MVHS.
11. WHM to Imlay, January 26, 1927, Correspondence Records, MVHS.
12. Correspondence Records, MVHS.

TOD HOMESTEAD CEMETERY

Youngstown, Ohio

Project no. 833

1. The Tods grew wealthy from coal and limestone deposits on their land and from iron furnaces near the homestead in Brier Hill during the post–Civil War industrial boom in the Mahoning Valley, which became the nation's second-largest steel-making region. Tod Family, in "Builders of Youngstown" files, Mill Creek Park archives, Youngstown, Ohio.
2. *Youngstown Telegram,* November 20, 1908.
3. Minutes of the Tod Homestead Cemetery board of trustees, January 1909–January 1922 (October 1911–September 1916 missing), Tod Homestead Cemetery archives (THCA). The recording secretary initially mistyped O. C. Simonds's name as C. S. Simonds, but the correct name appears later in the minutes.
4. In December 1909 the commissioners approved $1,000 plus expenses for Manning's initial commission. Between 1910 and 1913 Manning received $1,888.43 for his services. Minutes of the Tod Homestead Cemetery Board of Trustees, 1909, THCA.
5. A cemetery ledger notes annual payments to nurseries for trees, shrubs, and bulbs from 1911 to 1917, when Manning was laying out the cemetery. Cemetery ledger, 1911–1919, THCA.
6. Manning likely recommended Schweinfurth to Volney Rogers for work in Mill Creek Park, as the park paid Schweinfurth for design work in the same month that the cemetery board hired Manning. Mahoning Valley Historical Society archives, Youngstown, Ohio (MVHS).
7. The cemetery also contains markers and entry stone walls with piers (c. 1931), relics of the Youngstown Federation of Women's Clubs' initiative to commemorate American war dead along a memorial route called the "Road of Remembrance." The Mahoning County Committee engaged Manning to survey the ninety-eight miles between Kingsville and East Liverpool. Donald J. Lynn, "Report of the Road of Remembrance Committee," carbon copy, n.d., MVHS. This project appears on the WHM client list: no. 1622 (1929). The route (now Rte. 193) ran from Lake Erie at North Kingsville Village to Route 422 in Youngstown and was dedicated by the state legislature in June 1930. Carl E. Feather, "Route 193—The Road of Remembrance," *Ashtabula (Ohio) Star Beacon,* May 21, 2009.

BELLEVUE PARK

Harrisburg, Pa.

Project no. 798

1. McFarland was also the founder and first president of the American Civic Association. Manning seems to have offered minimal advice on his property, which was the site of significant trial gardens for many types of plants, particularly roses. For more on Breeze Hill, see J. Horace McFarland, *Memoirs of a Rose Man: Tales from Breeze Hill* (Emmaus, Pa.: Rodale, 1949).
2. I am indebted to Michael Barton and his students at Pennsylvania State University for their research on Bellevue Park and assistance with Harrisburg research generally. For more on the subdivision, see Jeannine Turgeon and Michael Barton, eds., *Bellevue Park: The First 100 Years: An Anniversary History by Its Residents* (Bloomington, Ill.: Xlibris, 2009). According to Dan Deibler, Manning's

on-site representative for the project was W. G. Wallbeck. Deibler, "Developing Bellevue Park: The Early Years, 1907–1945," in Turgeon and Barton, *Bellevue Park,* 17.

3. These include water, sewer, electrical, telephone, and gas lines as well as a fire alarm system.
4. The text of the promotional brochure is included in Turgeon and Barton, *Bellevue Park,* 23–31.
5. The Bellevue Park Association, chartered in 1914, came to assume responsibility for enforcing adherence to deed restrictions, which also stipulated setbacks, height limits, and other design regulations.
6. The Arts and Crafts building was moved to a lot in Bellevue Park in 1923 to serve as a community center.

HARRISBURG PARKS
Harrisburg, Pa.
Project no. 322

1. WHM autobiography, 122. When the commission came to the firm in 1901, Manning was in practice with his brother Woodward, and the firm was known as Manning Brothers. The partnership was dissolved in 1904, when Manning resumed his solo practice. The beautification initiative was first proposed by Mira Lloyd Dock, an activist and forester.
2. This information is drawn from Manning's "Report on a Park System for Harrisburg, Pennsylvania," September 16, 1901, MCL. The parkway was to wind along the Paxtang Creek Valley, around Wetzel's Swamp, and double back along the river. Not all sections of the parkway system were realized.
3. Manning presented his park plan to the Civic Club in October 1901. His lecture notes include references to park systems in other American cities. See "Address before Civic Club Harrisburg Pa.," September 16, 1901, MCL.
4. See "Old State Capitol columns at Harrisburg Bridge entrance, detail about column base" (plan), 1903, no. 322–44, MPI. In 1913 concrete steps and sidewalk were constructed along the downtown river frontage to solve continuing problems with erosion.
5. J. Horace McFarland, *The Awakening of Harrisburg: Some Account of the Improvement Movement Begun in 1902; with the Progress of the Work to the End of 1906* (Philadelphia: National Municipal League, 1907).
6. Photographs commissioned by Manning from Arthur G. Eldredge suggest that many parkways continued to retain their original rural appearance even two decades later. The 1927–28 Eldredge collection is now in the University of Massachusetts Lowell archive.
7. Manning also advised the city to add amenities to amuse park visitors. These would eventually include tennis courts, picnic pavilions, a nine-hole golf course, and a four-story observation tower. Manning's direct design involvement in these improvements is unlikely.
8. Reservoir Park still provides visitors with long views and reliable breezes. It is home to many civic festivities and the site of the National Civil War Museum.
9. WHM, "Report on a Park System,"
10. At its largest in 1913, Wildwood Park covered 666 acres. A zoo opened there in 1929, and in the 1930s the WPA built several new facilities and bridle trails. Maintenance declined during the postwar years, and by the 1960s the park was derelict. In 1964 Harrisburg Area Community College was deeded 157 acres to develop a campus, and in 1976, I-81 was built on park land taken by the federal government, reducing the site to 229 acres. Although much reduced in size and severely compromised by traffic noise, Wildwood Park still offers a haven to nature seekers and many species of birds and plants.
11. Manning's records list twenty-nine design projects in Harrisburg. In 1925 plans were advanced to create a park on wetlands Manning had identified as a future park site in his 1901 report. Here, as at Wildwood Park, a lake would provide a centerpiece for the layout, though on a much smaller scale. During the 1930s formal gardens (not of Manning's design) were added to the perimeter, and Italian Lake Park, as the neighborhood is known, soon became a desirable place to live. It remains so today.
12. Charles Mulford Robinson, "The Remaking of Our Cities: A Summing Up of the Movement for Making Cities Beautiful While They Become Busy and Big," *The World's Work* 12 (October 1906): 8046–47. Robinson added that Harrisburg "took steps to make itself worthier and 'the Harrisburg Plan' wrote itself large in municipal history" (8047).
13. The loop follows the riverbank walk, tracing the path of the old Cameron and Paxton parkways, cutting through Reservoir Park and the old Wildwood Park, turning south toward Italian Lake Park, and back to the Susquehanna.

CLEMENT A. GRISCOM ESTATE (DOLOBRAN)
Haverford, Pa.
Project no. 42

1. Frederick W. Barclay served as Manning's assistant on the project. In several articles Barclay is referred to as a graduate of Massachusetts Agricultural College; according to various college publications, however, he was enrolled during the late 1890s but withdrew before graduating.

2. George E. Thomas, Jeffrey A. Cohen, and Michael J. Lewis, *Frank Furness: The Complete Works,* rev. ed. (New York: Princeton Architectural Press, 1996). A descendent of one of the original Quaker families granted land by William Penn, Griscom named his estate "Dolobran" after the Lloyd ancestral homestead in Wales. The Welsh translates to "meadow bird."
3. Samuel F. Hotchkin, *Rural Pennsylvania in the Vicinity of Philadelphia* (Philadelphia: George Jacobs, 1897), 142.
4. A. H. Mueller, Philadelphia, Pa., 1896 map; J. L. Smith, Philadelphia, Pa., 1900 map, Lower Merion Historical Society, Bala Cynwyd, Pa.
5. J. Horace McFarland, "An American Garden: Dolobran near Philadelphia," *Outlook,* October 7, 1899, 330; Hotchkin, *Rural Pennsylvania,* 142.
6. J. Horace McFarland, "Dolobran—A Wild Gardening Estate," *Country Life in America* 4 (September 1903): 342; Frederick W. Barclay, "*Pellaea Artopurpurea* in Cultivation," *The Fern Bulletin,* January 1897, 25.
7. Wilhelm Miller, "Wild Gardening for Minnesota," *Minnesota Horticulturist* 43 (June 1915): 245; Kathy O'Loughlin, "Half an Acre, Not Including the Grounds," *Main Line Times,* September 8, 2001.

WILCOX PARK

Westerly, R.I.

Project no. 245

1. The Babcock family presence in Rhode Island dates to the 1640s, when James Badcock (Babcock) came to Portsmouth, R.I., from England and in 1662 settled in Westerly. Rowse Babcock was a seventh-generation descendent of James Babcock. Rowse owned a woolen mill in Westerly and served as president of the Phenix Bank. He married Mary Townsend, and the property that would become Wilcox Park was part of the couple's estate; it likely became available for reuse after Mary's death in 1898. A. Emerson Babcock, *Isaiah Babcock, Sr., and His Descendants* (New York: Eaton & Mains, 1903), 88, 89, 145.
2. National Register of Historic Places nomination form, Wilcox Park Historic District, prepared by D. W. Chase, 1973 (ref. no 73000011). Stephen Wilcox, a Westerly native, partnered with George Babcock in the 1860s to invent the water tube steam boiler, patenting a version in 1867 and founding Babcock & Wilcox in 1881. See www.invent.org. The library building was completed in 1894.
3. WHM to the Board of Trustees of the Westerly Memorial & Library Association, March 30, 1899, collection of the Memorial & Library Association of Westerly, R.I. (MLAW). As president of the Memorial & Library Association, Charles Perry represented the trustees in communication with Manning. In 1903 he hired Manning to design the landscape at his Margin Street residence in Westerly, where Manning placed a fish pond, stone pergola, and gardens with specimen trees. William Richard Cutter, ed., *New England Families, Genealogical and Memorial,* vol. 4 (New York: Lewis Historical Publishing Company, 1914), 1698–99; Charles Perry obituary, *New York Times,* August 23, 1929; Rhode Island Historical Preservation & Heritage Commission, *Historic Landscapes of Rhode Island* (Providence: Historical Preservation & Heritage Commission, 2001), 123.
4. The species noted by Manning were likely growing on the Rowse Babcock estate property, although Manning did not specifically state this in his report.
5. WHM to the Board of Trustees, March 30, 1899.
6. WHM to Arthur Harrison (Manning employee), September 13, 1899, MLAW.
7. WHM to the Board of Trustees, March 30, 1899.
8. In 1899 the wood-frame houses were removed, and in 1902 the brick house was replaced by a new building housing the Westerly High School.
9. Manning's correspondence with Perry and the trustees during the summer of 1899 suggests that he and his associates located sources of plant material and obtained quotes, and that the paths were laid out and the entrance was constructed. Correspondence between the parties stopped (or is missing) until September of 1903. When it resumed, the correspondence focused on planting only.
10. Arthur Harrison to WHM, September 14, 1899, MLAW.
11. "Planting List, Westerly Library, Westerly, R.I.," September 23, 1899, MLAW.
12. See William H. Jordy, *Buildings of Rhode Island* (New York: Oxford University Press, 2004), 411. Construction of the new entrance likely took place around the time of the removal of the Westerly High School (1939).
13. Rhode Island Historical Preservation & Heritage Commission, *Historic Landscapes of Rhode Island,* 123.
14. Memorial & Library Association of Westerly, *In the Park: 100 Years in Wilcox Park* (Westerly: Memorial & Library Association, 1998), introduction.
15. In 2004 the National Register listing was updated from "locally significant" to "nationally significant" based on Manning's work.
16. Rhode Island Historical Preservation & Heritage Commission, *Historic Landscapes of Rhode Island,* 123.

FAIRYLAND ESTATES

Chattanooga, Tenn.

Project no. 1439

1. "Crest Lodge: A Club Residence in Fairyland," Lookout Mountain Fairyland Club brochure, 1926, 8.
2. William M. Lesley commissioned Manning to design a landscape for his private residence. See WHM client list.
3. Although there is some uncertainty over who originally conceived of miniature golf, Garnet Carter is credited as the first to develop it as a franchise. He patented a prefabricated version of the game under the name Tom Thumb Golf, and by 1930 he had sold 6,000 golf course kits. See National Register of Historic Places nomination form, Lookout Mountain Fairyland Club, prepared by Kenneth H. Thomas Jr., 1990 (ref. no. 90000991); and Tim Hollis, *See Rock City: The History of Rock City Gardens* (Charleston, S.C.: The History Press, 2009), 20–22.
4. Hollis, *See Rock City,* 16–17; National Register nomination form; "Fairyland Tavern Finished in April," November 25, 1924, Clipping Files, Chattanooga Public Library.
5. "Hiking Lookout: Chronological History," www.hikelookout.org. Johnson Pike is now part of Tennessee State Rte. 58.
6. Many of the hillsides were added to the Chickamauga & Chattanooga National Military Park, and codeveloper Garnet Carter had reserved some of the most stunning rock formations for his own property, the future Rock City Gardens.
7. WHM autobiography, 166; National Register nomination form; "Club History," www.lookoutmountaingolfclub.com.
8. William F. Hull, *Images of America: Lookout Mountain* (Charleston, S.C.: Arcadia Publishing, 2009), 96; Hollis, *See Rock City,* 16–17; "Fairyland Tavern Finished in April."
9. WHM, "Study for Development of Fairyland Estates: 1439-16-92," January 1925 (see illustration); National Register nomination form. Manning also mentions the project's expansion in "A Few Subdivisions Planned by This Office during the Past Few Years," November 25, 1925, MCL.
10. This description of the early road network is based on U.S. Geological Survey maps for Chattanooga, Tenn., 105-SE, and Fort Oglethorpe, Ga.–Tenn., 106-NE, 7.5 Minute Series (Washington D.C.: USGS, 1936).
11. WHM client list.
12. "Hiking Lookout: Chronological History." These camps are visible on U.S. Geological Survey maps for Chattanooga, Tenn., 105-SE, and Fort Oglethorpe, Ga.–Tenn., 106-NE.
13. Hollis, *See Rock City,* 16–17; National Register nomination form.

UNIVERSITY OF VIRGINIA

Charlottesville, Va.

Project no. 760

1. WHM autobiography, 139. Manning also expressed his admiration of Jefferson in *Thomas Jefferson as an Architect and a Designer of Landscapes,* a book he coauthored with William Alexander Lambeth (Boston: Houghton Mifflin, 1913). Plate 22 of the book is Manning's "Plan of Existing Conditions" at the university.
2. "Board of Visitors Minutes," June 15, 1908, 356, and November 5, 1908, 369, University of Virginia Archives, Special Collection Library, University of Virginia (UVA). Over the course of his term as consulting landscape architect, Manning would produce eighty-five plans or drawings for the project.
3. WHM, "Report to Accompany a Plan for the University of Virginia, Charlottesville, Va.," 2, UVA.
4. Later, in 1910, the board consulted Manning on the design and placement of an entry gate at this approach. Manning recommended Henry Bacon, architect of the Lincoln Memorial, for the commission. See WHM, "Report to Accompany a Plan," 2; "Board of Visitors Minutes," May 6, 1910, 266.
5. WHM, "Report to Accompany a Plan," 3–5.
6. Ibid., 5.
7. Ibid., 6; WHM autobiography, 142.
8. WHM, "Report to Accompany a Plan," 6–7.
9. Ibid., 8–9.
10. "A Statement of Accomplishment and of Recent Growth," *University of Virginia Record* 3 (April 1910): 17.
11. WHM autobiography, 142 (Manning incorrectly gives Bacon's first name as Lester); WHM, "Business Accounts 1905–1917," MCL.
12. "Board of Visitors Minutes," October 17, 1922, 369.
13. "From Village to Grounds: Architecture after Jefferson at the University of Virginia," online exhibit, University of Virginia Library, www.library.virginia.edu/exhibitions.

JAMESTOWN EXPOSITION

Norfolk, Va.

Project no. 597

1. At the time, Manning was practicing with his brother J. Woodward Manning as Manning Brothers, although

they dissolved the partnership at the close of that year. WHM, "Jamestown Exposition," paper delivered at the ASLA meeting of December 11, 1906, revised February 11, 1910, in Harold A. Caparn, James Sturgis Pray, and Downing Vaux, eds., *Transactions of the American Society of Landscape Architects, from Its Inception in 1899 to the End of 1908* (Harrisburg, Pa.: J. Horace McFarland Co., 1912), 83–87; WHM to Henrietta Manning, October 3, 1904, MCL.

2. The Hampton project (no. 321) was the Hampton Agricultural and Normal Institute, 1901–1902 (WHM client list). Mike Gregory, *Expo Legacies: Names, Numbers, Facts and Figures* (Bloomington, Ind.: AuthorHouse, 2009), 161.
3. WHM, "Jamestown Exposition," 84. Among the earlier projects that Manning and Peabody & Stearns worked on in common, though not necessarily at the same time, were the World's Columbian Exposition in Chicago (1892–93) and the Groton School in eastern Massachusetts (Manning in 1896; Peabody & Stearns in 1899). WHM client list; Annie Robinson, "The Architecture of Peabody & Stearns," www.peabodyandstearns.com.
4. Robert W. Rydell, *All the World's a Fair: Visions of Empire at American International Expositions, 1876–1916* (Chicago: University of Chicago Press, 1987), 162–78.
5. Mike McKinley, "The Cruise of the Great White Fleet," *All Hands,* April 1987, 4–15, available at www.history.navy.mil.
6. "What Does Jamestown Mean?," introduction, in *Myth and Memory: An Exhibition at the Library of Virginia,* www.lva.virginia.gov/exhibits.
7. WHM, "The Influence of American Expositions on the Out-Door Arts" (paper delivered March 8, 1902), *Transactions of the Massachusetts Horticultural Society for the Year 1902, Part I* (Boston: For the Society, 1902), 74.
8. "Why the Jamestown Exposition Was a Dismal Failure," *New York Times*, December 1, 1907; Brian de Ruiter, "Jamestown Ter-Centennial Exposition of 1907," *Encyclopedia Virginia,* www.encyclopediavirginia.org.
9. "Why the Jamestown Exposition Was a Dismal Failure"; Anna Maxwell, letter to the editor, *New York Times,* April 28, 1907.
10. WHM, "Jamestown Exposition," 83–87.
11. Ibid., 83–84.
12. Ibid., 85–88. Manning describes the survey map and town plan, but only an undated plan of the exposition grounds and a bird's-eye drawing of the completed (or perhaps envisioned) site, also undated, are known to exist now. They are in the digital image collection, MPI.
13. Photographs, MPI.
14. WHM, "Jamestown Exposition," 88; undated site plan and photographs, Jamestown Exposition, MPI.
15. WHM, "Jamestown Exposition," 87–88.
16. WHM, "Civic Horticulture and Civic Improvement," *Park and Cemetery and Landscape Gardening* (Chicago) 17 (October 1907): 197–99.
17. "Historic Homes Still Stand on Naval Station Norfolk," *The Flagship* (online publication), Norfolk Naval Base, May 3, 2007, www.norfolknavyflagship.com; "Jamestown Exposition Site, Norfolk City, Virginia," National Register of Historic Places, National Park Service, www.nps.gov/history/nr/feature/Jamestown.

MILWAUKEE PARKS

Milwaukee, Wis.

Project no. 46

1. *First Annual Report of the Park Commissioners of the City of Milwaukee* (Milwaukee, Wis.: Ed. Keogh, Printer, 1892), 8, 21–26. Criteria for park land selection specified that sites contain native forest trees and topographical features that could be transformed into park attractions. The only boulevard constructed was Newberry, linking Lake Park and Riverside Park.
2. Ibid., 18, pertaining to West Park.
3. The commissioners agreed to pay the Olmsted firm $12.50 per acre. *Second Annual Report of the Park Commissioners* (Milwaukee: Ed. Keogh, Printer, 1893), 17.
4. *Eleventh Annual Report of the Park Commissioners* (Milwaukee: Ed. Keogh, Printer, 1902), 10.
5. Mitchell Park Conservatory was constructed in 1898–99. *Eighth Annual Report of the Park Commissioners* (Milwaukee: Ed. Keogh, Printer, 1899), 8, 19. *Ninth Annual Report of the Park Commissioners* (Milwaukee: Wehake, DelaHunt & Smith Co. Printers, 1900), 6.
6. To create the water mirror, workers excavated 9,000 cubic yards of topsoil and 28,000 yards of subsoil. The city used the subsoil to build the roadway into the park from Twentieth Avenue and stockpiled the topsoil for later use in flower beds and lawns. To build the boating lake in Mitchell Park, workers preserved a sixty-year-old elm tree growing on the site of a proposed island by raising the 75-ton tree to an elevation ten feet higher than its original position. *Twelfth Annual Report of the Park Commissioners of the City of Milwaukee* (Milwaukee: Ed. Keogh, Printer, 1903), 11; *Fourteenth Annual Report of the Park Commissioners of the City of Milwaukee* (Milwaukee: Cannon Printing, 1905), 5–7.
7. *Thirteenth Annual Report of the Park Commissioners* (Milwaukee: Ed. Keogh, Printer, 1904), 5.

8. Ibid. Although there is no documentation that Manning worked on Humboldt Park, a purple beech tree, uncommon in southeastern Wisconsin but a signature in many Manning projects, suggests he advised on the abundant tree plantings there.
9. Manning office ledger, June 15, 1901–January 20, 1905, MCL.
10. *Thirteenth Annual Report of the Park Commissioners,* 21. Ferry & Clas received partial payment for plans and specifications for the Lake Park pavilion. The firm also designed the bridge over the ravine northeast of the pavilion; *Fifteenth Annual Report of the Park Commissioners* (Milwaukee: Meisenheimer Printing Co., 1906), 23. Several other bridges in Lake Park had been designed and built previously by Oscar Sanne; *Second Annual Report of the Park Commissioners,* 22, 24; *Third Annual Report of the Park Commissioners,* 12.
11. *Thirteenth Annual Report of the Park Commissioners,* 6. Carpenter was hired on in November 1903 for a two-year term beginning February 1, 1904. Before he was hired, a separate foreman managed each park.
12. In 1937 the County Park Commission took over the management of all the city parks. Milwaukee County Park Commission, single-page document indicating the change in governance, n.d., copy in the author's possession.
13. The extent of Manning's work in Washington Park is unclear, other than completing a topographical survey of new land added to the park and a plan for improvements to that parcel submitted to the park commissioners during the Manning Brothers practice.
14. The lake at Washington Park is in poor condition, and the site's rolling topography increases security problems. Whitney Gould, "Faded Glory," *Milwaukee Journal Sentinel,* September 8, 2003.
15. Manning had also proposed entrance gates and walls around Kosciuszko Park, but it is unclear whether these were ever built. The *Fourteenth Annual Report of the Park Commissioners* is ambiguous: "Plans for the new addition were completed, and as much work, in accordance with these plans, was done as our funds would admit" (8).

About the Contributors

Arnold R. Alanen, Honorary ASLA, is a landscape historian and professor emeritus in the Department of Landscape Architecture, University of Wisconsin–Madison.

Lynn Bjorkman is a historic preservation planner based in Madison, Wisconsin; she has also served as a community planner for the National Park Service at Keweenaw National Historical Park in Calumet, Michigan.

Christopher Bond is the farm horticulturist and Farm Food Program coordinator as well as an instructor at Case Western Reserve University Farm in Cleveland, Ohio.

Steve Brisson is deputy director of Mackinac State Historic Parks, Mackinac Island, Michigan.

Jacob Brown works in urban public project administration in Chicago.

Jane Roy Brown, the former director of educational outreach at LALH, lives in western Massachusetts and is a writer and editor for the New England Wild Flower Society.

Margaret Carpenter, a landscape historian, managed the reconstructed Beatrix Farrand sunken garden at Hill-Stead Museum and has been active in reconstructing the gardens at the Morrill Homestead in central Vermont.

Staci L. Catron is director of the Cherokee Garden Library at the Atlanta History Center and specializes in American landscape history and historic preservation.

William Grundmann is associate professor emeritus, Department of Landscape Architecture, College of Design, at Iowa State University.

Pamela Hartford is an independent landscape historian and preservation consultant living in Salem, Massachusetts.

Mary Hoerner has documented over sixty historic landscapes throughout Ohio.

Robin Karson, a landscape historian, is the founder and executive director of the Library of American Landscape History in Amherst, Massachusetts.

Daniel Krall, ASLA, is associate professor in the Department of Landscape Architecture at Cornell University.

Martha Lyon, ASLA, is managing principal of Martha Lyon Landscape Architecture, LLC, a planning, design, and preservation firm in Northampton, Massachusetts.

Matthew Medeiros is a communications specialist at the University of Massachusetts Amherst and former coordinator of the Warren H. Manning Research Project.

Arthur H. Miller, retired archivist and librarian for special collections at Lake Forest College, writes and lectures about the history of Lake Forest, Illinois.

James O'Day, ASLA, is a historical landscape architect and writer based in Washington, D.C.

Christopher Patzke, a graduate of University of Virginia, is a landscape historian and landscape architect practicing in Massachusetts.

Joan Randall is a landscape historian retired from the Ohio Historic Preservation Office in Columbus.

Terri Rochon, a graduate of the Radcliffe Seminars in Landscape Design History, lives in San Diego.

Rebecca Rogers is an architecture and landscape historian whose recent research is concentrated on northeastern Ohio.

Maureen S. Thompson is adjunct faculty at Montgomery County Community College in Pennsylvania.

Gloria Schreiber is a horticulturist and landscape historian currently restoring the Manning garden of H. B. Stewart Sr. at Quail Hollow State Park and has a lilac nursery in Hartville, Ohio.

Marjorie Longenecker White, longtime director of the Birmingham (Alabama) Historical Society, is the local authority on the work of Warren H. Manning in Birmingham.

Kevan Williams is a designer and journalist from Athens, Georgia, whose work has appeared in *Landscape Architecture, Parks & Recreation Magazine,* and *Flagpole Magazine.*

Index

Page numbers in *italics* refer to illustrations.